From Empire to Orient

FOR SEAN AND EAMONN

FROM EMPIRE TO ORIENT

Travellers to the Middle East 1830-1926

Geoffrey P. Nash

I.B. TAURIS

LONDON · NEW YORK

Published in 2005 by I.B. Tauris & Co Ltd
6 Salem Road, London W2 4BU
175 Fifth Avenue, New York NY 10010
www.ibtauris.com

In the United States of America and Canada distributed by Palgrave
Macmillan a division of St. Martin's Press
175 Fifth Avenue, New York NY 10010

ISBN 1 85043 767 X
EAN 978 1 85043 767 3

A full CIP record for this book is available from the British Library
A full CIP record for this book is available from the Library of Congress

Library of Congress catalog card: available

Printed and bound in Great Britain by TJ International Ltd, Padstow,
Cornwall
Camera-ready copy edited and supplied by the author

Contents

Acknowledgements

The germ of the idea on which this book is based came to me at a British Council conference on travel writing held at Warwick University in December 1997.

Although the idea was entirely my own, I wish to thank Susan Bassnett who led a conference which in some ways was a breakthrough for the study of travel writing in the UK.

The idea's gestation period has seemed a very long one, but I must thank the University of Sunderland for bearing with me and allowing me a sabbatical in 2002.

To Peter Durrans I owe a debt for his careful induction of me into some of the mysteries of British imperial historiography, and to Peter Clark for deepening my knowledge of Marmaduke Pickthall.

I would also like to acknowledge the use of the following libraries and the help given me by their staff: the Literary and Philosophical Library, Newcastle; the Robinson Library, University of Newcastle; the University of Durham Library; and the London School of African and Oriental Studies Library.

Once, during the occupation of Iraq, a certain British officer asked: 'Is the *azan* I hear being called now from the minaret harmful to British policy?' When he was told that it was harmless, he said: 'Then let him call for prayers as much as he wants.'

Introduction

While travel writing has recently become a vogue discipline, the Middle East, not a specially favoured destination for contemporary travellers, is now an area of anxiety for westerners because of its supposed links with terrorism. What, therefore, is to be expected from a study about travellers to the Middle East of over a hundred years ago? Nostalgia perhaps, or antiquarianism, or merely another exercise in academic formalism? Popular interest in the mysteries of the desert or the exotic qualities of oriental societies clearly no longer coheres around images from the Bible or the *Arabian Nights*, as it did in the nineteenth century. While these cultural artefacts may have been absorbed in the Disney production line, they have for a long time been in retreat before the onset of film, video and electronic games in which simulations of modern warfare and stereotypes of Arab enemies more usually predominate. Nineteenth-century travellers like Richard Burton, Charles Doughty and Wilfred Thesiger might be known to the general reader as upper-class Englishmen who quitted civilisation in search of adventure, inspiration, or sheer escape from the industrial world. On the other hand, 'Lawrence of Arabia', to those who have seen David Lean's now more than forty-year old film, is a figure whose popular myth conjures heroism, danger and past colonial power. But even the few who are acquainted with the controversies surrounding Edward Said's *Orientalism* and the studies of Middle East travellers that revise his theory in feminist or other directions, might well agree with Said himself that the topoi of travellers to the deserts of pre-modern Arabia is an overworked seam that little repays revisiting.

This study does not set out directly to contest such preconceptions. Rather, its aim is, among other things, to present a timely reconsideration of some key British travellers to the Middle East. In the process, hopefully fresh perspectives will inform and partly dispel old stereotypes. One example is the notion that most Victorian and Edwardian travellers to the Middle East were either British spies or misfits disguised in native dress.[1] Probably the most obvious example of a professed imperialist travelling with strategic concerns uppermost in his mind was George Nathaniel, latter Lord, Curzon. Dedicated to the pursuance of a successful political career, this future Viceroy of India was hardly a social misfit. Of all the travellers mentioned below he made the least concession to native dress but moved about Asia as an unabashed aristocrat whose intention was to make his Britishness apparent to all he encountered. As for spying, he approached decaying eastern fortifications with the same directness as he checked evidence of British commerce in local bazaars. On the other hand, William Gifford Palgrave, perhaps the best known traveller-as-spy-in-native-disguise, was a complex individual for whom identity was not fixed and who changed his own more than once in the course of his life and travels. Palgrave's journeys were a means to the discovery of larger truths than mere political information. Of the travellers who consciously identified with the eastern peoples whom they encountered, the Tory gentleman and anti-imperialist, Wilfrid Scawen Blunt, and Cambridge Orientalist, Edward Granville Browne, were the most vociferous in announcing their newly found friends to the European world on their return. Their careers support one of the key areas of innovation in understanding Middle-Eastern travel that this study seeks to illuminate. Instead of reinforcing cultural stereotypes and re-entrenching notions of European supremacy, Blunt and Browne's espousals of Egyptian and Iranian nationalism cut across established orthodoxies concerning the East in the period leading up to the First World War.

In fronting the notion that travellers carry their stereotypes with them and return with them largely undisturbed, this study aims to open up the proposition that cross-cultural encounter did in certain instances result in enhanced understanding of the target eastern cultures. In these cases, travellers brought back new vocabularies, influenced by if not directly acquired in the East. 'In various ways [...] the world beyond Europe was seen to offer possibilities of self-knowledge and growth.'[2] One of the clearest aspects of this positive engagement to emerge from my study will be the extent to which appreciative, sometimes self-transforming, estimations of Muslim culture and of Islam itself were carried back by some western travellers from eastern lands. Even figures like Curzon and Mark Sykes, who never lost their patrician sense of the need for British governance over the East, and who admired the oriental scene for its picturesque qualities, professed admiration for aspects of Muslim culture, however statically and conservatively construed. True, the element of escape, or in Curzon's trope, retracing the steps of our ancestors, may have motivated such constructions. As Philip Darby phrases it: 'There are qualities missing in European civilization, perhaps lost on the march forward, which could be found in the tropics, the desert and [...] the islands. Thus the political theme of Europe regenerating a lifeless Asia had its literary and artistic counterpoint in the thought that the less sophisticated world overseas might be able to rejuvenate a greying Europe.'[3] Superficially, this might take the form of importing eastern fads and fashions; but at a deeper level it required negotiating one of Christendom's oldest taboos: that of the demonic duplicity of the Muslim religion. Some, like Palgrave while traversing the heartland of strict Arab Islam, wore Christian bigotry as a protective if hidden armour, or claimed as much on returning home, the better to occlude the fascination with which the feared belief-system had in reality engaged their inner selves. Others felt the manifest strength of Muslim belief a potent influence in their personal struggles with unbelief. So powerful was this engagement that in a few notable cases

(Burton and Palgrave being obvious examples) stories circulated of their having made profession of Islam.

Besides elucidating the motivation of personal search behind travellers to the region, the focus of this study of travel writing on the Middle East is the public scope of its reports and narratives, and the manner in which these fed into debates about the politics of imperial expansion. 'One of the truisms of the scholarship on travel to, and travel writing on, the Middle East is that both were indices to Western and especially British political and military superiority.'[4] The Islamic world, as Edward Said argued, was the 'Orient' most immediately contiguous to the West. The period chosen, 1830-1926, is, roughly speaking, Europe's late imperial century. Its inception coincides with the culmination of the Greek revolt and the deepening crisis of the Ottoman empire first addressed by the traveller, radical M.P. and Turcophile, David Urquhart, in *Spirit of the East* (1838).[5] The terminal point is marked by the throwing of the Sunni Islamic world into confusion by the fall of the caliphate (1924), the direct result of the final collapse of the Ottoman empire and its temporary substitution by Britain's informal imperialism in the Middle East, described as regards its Arab theatre in T.E. Lawrence's *Seven Pillars of Wisdom* (1926). It was in this Orient that Britain's strategic involvement with India collided with France's imperial ambitions and Russia's southward expansion. By around 1830 Britain began to establish the policy of backing the Ottoman empire as a bulwark against the expansion of both these powers, while for the most part refraining from international entanglements herself. Then occupation of Egypt in 1882 registered a change of policy. Executed for reasons to do both with Egypt's foreign debt and her strategic position en route to India, this action embroiled Britain in further territorial expansion. Once the key to Britain's eastern policy, the Ottoman empire towards the end of that century began to be looked upon as incorrigibly corrupt and a liability. Progressively, the old alliance with Turkey was discarded. But as Urquhart the political adventurer and Palgrave the political explorer both agreed, Turkey was the key to the Islamic revival. In the Disraelian scheme of things she was Great Britain's natural ally.

Through most of the nineteenth century Afghanistan and Persia were also considered crucial because they bordered India. In both countries Britain vied with Russia for influence and control. Nevertheless, at the beginning of the twentieth century, both Turkey and Persia were sacrificed to Edward Grey's 'paranoiac' fear of Germany. Few, however, could have imagined at the inception of the First World War what would be its result for European imperial rivalries in the East. In 1918 the configuration of Great Power interests that had sustained the 'Eastern Question' through most of the nineteenth century came to a precipitate end. Having spent the major part of the last hundred years trying to defend the Ottoman empire against Russia and to a lesser extent France, suddenly the British had supplanted all the other powers east of Suez. 'In a matter of months a vast Middle Eastern *imperium* had fallen into their laps'. Though the early twenties did see a resurgence of

Russia in its new Bolshevik form and a revived nationalist Turkey, according to John Darwin, by 1926 'the risk of Great Power rivalry in the Middle East had all but vanished'.[6]

Britain and Europe's relations with the Islamic world were a crucial and persistent challenge for foreign policy within the hundred years covered by this study. The period begins with the issue of the reform of the Ottoman empire, and the question as to what would be the future for that empire's Islamic underpinning should reform take root along western lines. In *England and the Middle East, The Destruction of the Ottoman Empire*, Elie Kedourie clearly formulated an opposition between 'The Urquhart School of Orientalists' (Blunt's phrase) and mainstream imperialist thinking of the Victorian Age.[7] The present study is concerned with elaborating this fissure. Central to its argument is the proposition that pro-Islamic, partly anti-imperialist positions were developed by some British figures during the period in question. The key issue for both imperialists and pro-Islamic travellers and writers alike was could – and would – the Islamic world reform, and if so, by what agency – by its own genius; in conjunction with Europe; or under Europe's tutelage? The first area of contention is the likely success or failure in Ottoman Turkey of the western-inspired reform programme known as the Tanzimat. The British occupation of Egypt raised the principle of reform again. For a British imperialist like   Lord Cromer, consul-general and de facto ruler of Egypt between 1883 and 1907, effective change and modernisation could best be brought to Egypt by permanent British occupation. Reform, or a lack of it, also held vital implications for a stagnant Persia caught between British and Russia's mutual contest in the Great Game. Then, in the first decade of the twentieth century, debates surrounding the viability of programmes of change thrown up by the Turkish and Persian revolutions manifested once again the divide between government and radical supporters of eastern causes. The argument over Britain's instigation of the Arab revolt and opposition to Ottoman Turkey during the First World War then caused a bitter split between these dissidents themselves according to their pro-Arab or pro-Turk sympathies.

In the pro-Islamic camp, writers as various as Urquhart, Palgrave and Blunt espoused at one and the same time 'authentic' indigenous traditions, as well as forces for change, both of which they saw as centred on Islam. The importation of western ways into the East was on the whole anathema to both imperialist travellers and those sympathetic to eastern self-determination. But while the imperialists saw the need for reform, they gave it little constructive backing, believing that the Turkish empire or Persia would remain entrenched in their conservative backwardness. The pro-Islamic writers and travellers, however, searched for indigenous currents of development and self-renewal. Their dissent turned on the degree to which the European presence was deemed a help or hindrance to what they deemed as the progressive forces within the Islamic countries. Where this presence was obtrusive, that is for all practical purposes acquisitive and appropriating in intent, the friends of

Islamic reform demanded its withdrawal and branded it predatory. Where Britain's help was not forthcoming, and Muslim nations appeared threatened by the reactionary power of Russia (and equally, by obscurantist forces from within), they raised voices against British hypocrisy and betrayal of the cause of progress and freedom. Appeals were made to Britain's imperial mission to safeguard and protect the weaker nations and it was claimed the interests of those nations marched in tandem with Britain's own. Broadly the same liberal discourse that had been applied to the oppressed nationalities of Europe was extended to the Islamic nations of the East.

In addition, positive images of Islamic societies were enunciated that implicitly argued their capacity to engage with the modern world in a creative manner. Such positive projections may be said to connect the writings of each of the sympathisers with the Orient. For David Urquhart, any project that sought to engraft or superimpose western categories on an eastern nation with cultural specificities of its own represented in itself an act of aggression. When it came to the progression of Egypt from 'oriental despotism' to enlightened modern state, Blunt's polarisation from Cromer over the agency of imperialism in Egypt engaged the possibilities of an alternative, reformed and revived Islamist discourse, a notion which Browne later extended and applied to the Persian constitutional and the Young Turk revolutions. Viewed by Curzon and his disciples as an effete and unstable player within Britain's imperial strategy in the East, Persia was a cause passionately espoused by Browne as a nation ready for and entitled to its independence and autonomy. For his part, the Turcophile novelist and traveller, Marmaduke Pickthall, after starting out from a position of support for British imperial rule in India and Egypt, came to reverse his belief in Britain's benevolent intentions toward the East because of her failure to support the Young Turks and the lead a reformed Turkey might give to the Muslim world.

In theoretical terms, scrutiny of the debates outlined above requires further revision of some of the main tenets of Edward Said's *Orientalism* in order to allow for the possibilities of opposition to and contestation of the established discourses of imperialism and Orientalism. This is not to argue, however, that Said's work is no longer valid in a great deal it has to say about representations of the East made by, amongst others, western travellers and imperial administrators on the scene. Indeed, since *Orientalism* was published in 1978, a great deal of discussion and debate has centred on its central thesis, the existence of a coherent (some have argued monolithic) western discourse on the Orient. Rejected by some, the concept of Orientalism has been refined and reformulated by others.[8] Still further work has been awaited on the part played by Islam in Orientalist discourse. Said's deconstruction of the politically motivated denigration of Islamic faith and culture by the likes of Cromer, Balfour and Curzon must remain central to any discussion of Victorian imperialism. Yet the official Orientalist discourse was not as dominant as Said suggested. Rana Kabbani and Ali Behdad have written on the predisposition of an establishment renegade like Wilfrid Scawen Blunt

toward eastern culture and political freedom.[9]   Awareness of the extent of
Blunt's political and spiritual identification with the trend towards Muslim
modernism has for sometime been restricted to specialists in the field of
Oriental Studies.[10] The appearance of this work will hopefully contribute to
new perspectives on Blunt that place him within the frame of colonial and
postcolonial discourse and at the same time situate him in the continuing
debate about the West's relations with the Islamic world.

Blunt – who only receives passing mention in Said's work – is an
obvious figure in the development of a new perspective on Orientalism and
Islam in the age of imperialism. But other equally important figures have
been misinterpreted, neglected, or forgotten, and their writings and activities
might be used to demonstrate a tolerant, even radically favourable disposition
toward Islam during a period when the East appeared increasingly vulnerable
to western encroachment. From the 1830s to the late 1850s, David Urquhart
established himself as a foundation figure for discourse(s) that developed
later in the nineteenth century arguing for Muslim practice to be the basis of
reform in the East. Again, Urquhart's role in the promotion of Ottoman
Turkey as a fit and in some ways superior partner to Christian Europe has
long been known about by historians but is rarely rehearsed today. Yet
Urquhart began a Turcophile trend that continued well into the twentieth
century, and from this devolved a narrative of western betrayal of eastern
'awakenings' that fanned out into the discourse of European supporters of
other oriental/Islamic causes. Arguably this narrative, which attempted to re-
set the record straight vis-à-vis Turkish 'atrocities' against Balkan and
Armenian Christians by laying a fair (and perhaps sometimes rather more
than fair) share of blame on the eastern/Balkan Christians themselves, as well
as their western European allies, has been eclipsed by the anti-Islamic narratives of our own time. So deeply was pro-Turkism ingested by one British
gentleman, the novelist and traveller Marmaduke Pickthall, that he went a
step beyond Blunt and Urquhart and converted to Islam. Where Blunt had
favoured the Arabs, Pickthall saw the Turks as the agency best suited for the
piloting of modernist Islam within the twentieth century Muslim world. His
virulent support for the Young Turk programme curiously foregrounded its
potential as a force of revolutionary Islamic modernism rather than a secular
nationalism later to be subsumed in Attaturkism.

Confirmation that Orientalism was not a monolithic and stable discourse emerges then from investigating the pro-Muslim writings and agita-
tions of figures like Urquhart, Blunt and Pickthall. In addition, new readings
of well-established contributors to Orientalist discourse can also yield less
rigid interpretations. The reputation of the half-Jewish, quondam Jesuit
traveller to Arabia, William Gifford Palgrave, is that of a bitterly anti-Islamic
polemicist. But this is founded on readings of his canonical travelogue, *A
Narrative of a Year's Journey to Central and Eastern Arabia*, alone. Palgrave's later sojourns as British consul in Trebizond and Abkhazia helped
him formulate an expertise in new developments in Ottoman Islam and its

peripheries that he articulated in much more sympathetic terms in essays for *MacMillan's* and *Fraser's* magazines in the late 1860s and early 1870s. Even arch-imperialist establishment figures like Curzon and Mark Sykes allowed Muslim structures, albeit conservative ones patronizingly construed, to impact in their travel writings of the period 1893-1915. Curzon proposed a dichotomy in his travel philosophy between a political and an aesthetic Orientalism, the latter shaping his representations of Muslim societies in terms of past glories and present decay. Sykes likewise wished to preserve authentic Muslim expression within the diverse racial constituents of the Ottoman empire -before the outbreak of hostilities in 1914 impressed upon him the fatality of the Ottoman project. Perhaps the most learned and effective exponent of an eastern cause in the latter days of imperialism was the Cambridge Orientalist, Edward Granville Browne. Browne's propagandist endeavours on behalf of the first Iranian revolution of 1905-1911 have been expounded by the Iranian scholars, Mansour Bonakdarian and Abbas Amanat.[11] His ambivalent contribution to academic Orientalism and his polemical argument with expounders of the Saidean type of Orientalism, such as Curzon and the London *Times* foreign affairs journalists of the early 1900s, evidence to the existence of diverse, sometimes contradictory discourses within Orientalism.

Overall, then, by re-phrasing and re-positing the different writings of British travellers and imperialists on the Middle East within the hundred years between the end of the Greek revolt and the final eclipse of the Ottoman empire by Attaturk, it is possible to observe more complexity in British writing on Islam and the East than the mainly hostile corpus proposed by Said. One of the beneficial effects of so doing should be to demonstrate that pro-Islamic western voices did exist which were able to challenge the negative and chauvinistic pronouncements of those who denigrated Islam as part of their project to rule over the East. This book aims to present these voices alongside those of the opposing imperialist camp. Chapter 1 outlines the process of European penetration into the East, and also traces the hopes and programmes for Islamic reform within the period. The parameters of the debate are set. Fifty years ago, A.J.P. Taylor counted Urquhart, Blunt and Browne high among his list of 'troublemakers' – those dissenters who in successive epochs argued vociferously against British foreign policy. By anathematising their country's overseas manoeuvres and choice of allies each of them embellished a narrative of betrayal. Programmes of eastern reformers and their links with British travellers are also discussed.

Chapter 2 raises the issue of Britain's patronage over the Turkish empire. This begins in what we might with hindsight call the foundational pro-oriental project of David Urquhart, who in attacking Palmerston's foreign policy probably gave the lead for several generations of British anti–imperialist voices. In addition, it was Urquhart who first opened up a space by which it was possible to argue for the uniqueness, and in some respects superiority, of eastern institutions and peoples. He became a very effective propagandist for the Ottoman empire, proclaiming its strength and value as a model of eastern 'authenticity'. Another pioneer traveller, this time to Arabia, Palgrave began as a Jesuit in the pay of Napoleon III; his later encounter with rank–and–file Turks led to a volte–face in his assessment of Islam that has mostly passed unremarked. Now he wrote of the scope of Islamic renewal in articles like the 'Mahometan Revival', and argued for the exigency and appropriacy of Muslims' filiation to Britain's empire in the East.

Chapter 3 is concerned in the main with the debate over imperialism in Egypt conducted between Wilfrid Scawen Blunt and Lord Cromer. It is argued that the British occupation transformed Blunt's patriarchal Oriental-ism into an anti–imperialist position that expounded the politics of an Islamic revival already heralded in his *Future of Islam*. Cromer's *Modern Egypt* in turn contests and endeavours to marginalise Blunt's *Secret History of the British Occupation of Egypt*. In the name of an official historical narrative constructed around Foreign Office and diplomatic sources, Cromer aimed at promoting an apologetic for his own bureaucratic mastery of empire. Blunt may have lost the play for Egyptian independence in 1882, but his propa-ganda on behalf of an oppressed nation of the East fuelled later campaigns, such as the agitation against Grey's policies. It is suggested that it might be better to remember Blunt for this anti-imperialist radicalism than for his anachronistic 'discovery' and promotion of the desert Arabs. (The link with Lawrence and the Arab Bureau is discussed in chapter six.)

Between 1887 and 1894, George Nathaniel Curzon made five eastern journeys including two that took him around the world. Chapter 4 examines their underlying purpose: to establish for their author an acknowledged expertise on his subject – Asia/the Orient – so furthering a political career that would later promote imperial dominance over large areas of the East. Curzon tacitly distinguishes between his aesthetic enjoyment of oriental travel and his political assessment of the weaknesses of Islamic peoples that made them fit subjects for aggrandisement by Britain's imperial competitors. His travel writings, speeches, and other desiderata on the Orient, as well as his practical influence as patron, impacted on the writings and field activities of Tory imperialists like the political officers in the Arabian Gulf, Percy Cox and A.T. Wilson. The 'Curzon version', especially in its delineation of 'the Persian character', is also observed in the writings of Valentine Chirol, director of the foreign desk at *The Times* in the early 1900s.

Edward Granville Browne's neglected masterpiece of travel writing, *A Year Amongst The Persians* (1893), laid the foundations for his passionate espousal of nationalist politics, which is examined in chapter 5. This culmi-nated in his writings on behalf of the Persian revolution of 1905-11. The spiritual quest that had drawn Browne to Persia in the first place led him to encounter there all the streams of Persian religious expression. Informed of their existence by reading the French diplomat/traveller and supporter of the Aryan myth, Arthur de Gobineau, he found in the Babi movement, with its claims of fulfilling the prophecy of the Mahdi, the channel of renewal that he believed Persia was waiting for. Then, disillusioned by later Babi schisms, Browne switched his hopes for Persian renewal to the political arena. His defence of the Persian revolution is weighed against his professional Orientalism and the imperialist writing of David Fraser, the *Times* reporter in Persia.

Blunt's legacy for sponsorship of the nation of Islam, crystallised over the question of the caliphate, is revisited in chapter 6. Marmaduke Pickthall's choice of Turkey as the vanguard for a revolutionised Islam disqualified him from the role of British agent behind the lines in the Great War. Instead during that conflict he continued his agitation in favour of the Young Turk revolution. In contrast, Mark Sykes, like Pickthall a one time Turcophile and traveller in the Ottoman empire, switched to supporting its partition and became instrumental in shifting British support to the Arabs. The writings of British travellers and imperialists on the politics of Islam appear to achieve closure (tragedy repeated as farce?) in T.E. Lawrence's self–referential deployment of the twin motifs of betrayal and national patronage in *Seven Pillars*. Finally, issues raised in this study that I consider remain embedded within the East-West encounter of today are reviewed in the 'envoi'.

1

Britain, Islam and Empire: some dissenting voices

The best chance for the East is, that the nations of Europe should destroy each other.
W.S. Blunt, *Gordon at Khartoum*, p. 353

The purpose of the present chapter is to set the parameters of this study. It will be necessary to give an historical sketch of the impact changes in the world, most notably the emergence of an expansive and belligerent Europe, presented to the Islamic East during the period under review. This will in turn raise the issue of the West's imperialism and the character of, at least in the British context, its engagement with Muslim countries.

Nineteenth-century history topics such as 'the Eastern Question' or 'the Scramble for Africa' reflect the standard historiography on this area of study.[1] The Eastern Question was generally formulated on the premise that the last bastion of oriental power – the Ottoman empire – was decrepit, incapable of reforming itself, and near to death. Europe's Christian powers were sucked into the resulting vacuum, and the ramifications of Turkish collapse were invariably considered from the point of view of Europe. How 'the East' felt about the Eastern Question was discussed, if at all, by specialists in Oriental languages. Muslim nations and peoples who might have had an interest in the Ottoman empire's continuance as the last powerful standard bearer of Islam were not prioritised by historians of imperialism. Even less space was devoted to the possibility that there might have existed contacts across the East-West divide which developed along the lines of mutual interests and sympathies. Even when the East began to 'write back' in form of academic contestation of the West's representation of the East and eastern peoples, such contacts, made for the most part by travellers across cultures, were barely discussed (and here Said's *Orientalism* comes to mind).

After foregrounding some of the salient issues raised by British imperialism in the Middle East then, an inventory will be made of the most important individuals in this category of traveller. Preliminary outlines of their contacts with the East, and the debates they engaged in with the foremost imperialists of the time, will be given. For the purposes of this book,

the focus will be on British travellers to the Middle East, who brought back
with them ideas and suggested programmes of action concerned with specific
Muslim countries and peoples. The last section will attempt to tie these in
with the currents of change within Muslim societies, personified by
outstanding eastern thinkers and reformers many of whom had direct contact
with the British travellers.

Europe devours the Islamic Near East

> But those people will never begin to advance ... until they enjoy the rights of man;
> and these they will never obtain except by means of European conquest.
> Winwood Reade, quoted in V.G. Kiernan, *The Lords of Human Kind*, p. 23.

The hundred years between 1830 and 1926 more or less cover the high tide of
European imperialism as far as the Near East is concerned. An overview of
the impact of this imperialism on Islamic lands would begin with a recession
of Ottoman power that reached its final stage at the end of the Great War, and
conclude with the break up of the empire. According to Kedourie, in the
1830s a policy toward the Ottoman empire began to take shape.[2] The Greek
war of independence had drawn Britain into momentary hostilities with
Turkey (1827-28). However, immediately afterwards she adopted a hands-off
doctrine as far as French and – pre-eminently – Russian encroachments on
Ottoman domains were concerned.

At the same time as sustaining the empire's territorial integrity, Britain
aimed to bring pressure on the Sultan to instigate meaningful reforms. During
the so-called Tanzimat (re-organisation) period of 1839-76, a royal decree of
1839 pledged reform of the administration, the system of tax farming, and
military conscription. A further decree of 1856 re-affirmed these principles
and guaranteed the equality of all the Sultan's subjects, regardless of race or
religion. 'The decrees [...] sought to break down the religious and cultural
autonomy of the *millets* [or separate religious communities] and to create the
notion of a common Ottomanism, which would in theory replace the religious
ordering of society in which Muslims were dominant.'[3] Such a metamor-
phosis would fundamentally upset the balance not only of Turkey, but also of
the entire Muslim world. Europe would have succeeded in eroding from
within the Muslim character of the last great Islamic empire. The Tanzimat
reforms might be said to have further breached the empire's stability from
within and augmented the damage already inflicted by the secession of
Greece (after revolts of 1821 and 1831) and, from the early nineteenth
century, the effective autonomy of Serbia (eventually declared independent in
1878). The religious millets were not absorbed into a common Ottoman
identity but becoming increasingly secularised 'operated to foster nationalist
and separatist tendencies among many of the religious communities rather
than to diminish separatism'.[4]

The reforms upset the balance between Muslims and Christians, although this could not have remained unaltered given the continuing receptivity of the Christians to many of the technological and ideological innovations of their co-religionists in western Europe. A wake-up call and presage of what was to come could be seen in the events of 1860 in Syria and Mount Lebanon. Already favoured by Ibrahim Pasha during the occupation of Syria in the 1840s, the Christians had outgrown their previous equilibrium with their Muslim neighbours, encouraged by European consuls who favoured one or other Christian community.[5] France was the traditional protector of the Maronites, rivalled by Britain's sponsorship of the Druze and Russia's patronage of the Greek Orthodox. According to William Cleveland, there were consequences of the Maronites' special treatment:

> Encouraged by the promises of equality contained in the Otttoman decress of 1839 and 1856, Maronites and other Christians expanded their commercial activities, entered into lucrative relationships with European representatives, founded new educational institutions, and generally asserted themselves in a manner that the Druze and Sunnis saw as overstepping the bounds of was permitted to minority subjects in a Muslim state. The smouldering Muslim resentment over this change in the accepted social and political order erupted into a brutal civil war. It began in 1860 with Druze attacks on Christian villages in Mount Lebanon and soon spilled over into the quarters of Damascus, where several thousand Christian were massacred and European consulates were burned.[6]

Intervention by Europe resulted in the creation of autonomous administrative status for Mount Lebanon, confirming France's status as the protector of the Maronites. The Crimean War had been fought only a few years earlier (1854-56) to forestall Russian demands on the Porte that had begun with her self-declared mission of protecting all the Ottoman empire's Christians. The leverage that such a pretext gave a European Christian power, already bolstered by the capitulations, progressively chipped away at Ottoman integrity, emboldening the subject Christian nations to redouble their efforts to achieve independence. 'The great crises of the Eastern Question arose mainly from the European efforts to prevent the Ottomans from enforcing their authority'.[7] The 'Eastern Crisis' of 1875-78 saw Bosnians, Bulgarians, Serbs and Montenegrins up in arms; Turkey was drawn into direct confrontation with Russia, and Britain sent her fleet through the Dardanelles. The Russo-Turkish War of 1877-78 resulted in severe Turkish losses and the threat of Russia taking Istanbul. At the Congress of Berlin (1878), Bulgarian gains were emasculated but the Ottoman empire still lost territory. Austria took charge of Bosnia Herzegovina, and Serbia, Montenegro and Rumania were given formal independence, and Britain gained control of Cyprus. In spite of Russia's failure to sustain her victories in the form of a Greater Bulgaria,

> she had won, though with difficulty, a great military victory over the Turks: its effects could not be wished out of existence. [...] Much of the achievement of the Russian armies and Russian diplomacy were therefore permanent.[8]

Two years before the Congress of Berlin, Turkey and Egypt both declared
themselves bankrupt. Their finances had been for some time imploding under
the weight of debts, frequently raised at exorbitantly high rates of interest on
the European bourses. In Turkey's case, the greater proportion of these funds
were soaked up by the costs of re-organising her armed forces undertaken
against the background of the European military threat.[9] In Egypt costs had
accrued from schemes to copy the European infrastructure by the building of
railways, the re-planning of Cairo, and the construction of the Suez canal
(opened in 1869). The Khedive Ismail's extravagant projects might have been
the cause of his country's predicament, but E.J. Hobsbawm sees bankruptcy
as leading to a common outcome for both Egypt and Turkey. 'It mobilized
those militant consortia of foreign bondholders or governments acting for
their investors, which were to turn nominally independent governments into
virtual or actual protectorates and colonies of the European powers – as in
Egypt and Turkey after 1876.'[10] British attitudes towards the Ottoman empire
changed definitively after that date.

> Thereafter, British policy aimed at sedation rather than conversion, and expansive
> plans for co-operation gave way to the calculated and admirably economical 'lan-
> guage of menace'.[11]

But it was Britain's unilateral occupation of Egypt in 1882, launched to put
down the Urabi revolution and secure Egypt's debt for foreign bondholders,
that constituted a watershed in imperial aggrandisement, as well as holding
important implications for attitudes towards empire within Britain.

As the new century opened, among the significant Islamic nations only
Turkey, Afghanistan and Persia were left as nominally independent states
owing to their designated roles as buffers between the Russian and British
empires. The main concern of imperial strategists like Lord Curzon was that
Russia's expansion into Central Asia, absorbing Bukhara, Khiva, and Kokand
by 1873, carving out a huge empire in predominantly Muslim lands, should
proceed no further. In Aden and the Arabian Gulf Britain had herself been
gaining mastery, bringing the Arab sheikhdoms under her control by getting
them to sign treaties pledging in return for her protection not to deal with any
other foreign power. Curzon's benchmark was that neither Russia nor any
other power should gain a foothold in the Gulf.

In the case of Persia, national self-determination appeared increasingly
more precarious. Squeezed between the imperial ambitions of the two great
European imperial powers of the East, Persia was to all intents and purposes a
medieval state. Her Seistan province bordered on northern India, and the
Russian Trans-Caspian railway ran within a hundred miles of Persia's own
northern border. Enmeshed on account of her feckless rulers in a net of
foreign loans and foreign monopolies exercised over her revenues, trade and
economic life, a decrepit Persia moved from one crisis to another while
revolutionary change was building.

A coalition of Shi'ih clergy, nationalists and radicals influenced by the social democratic ideas infiltrating from neighbouring Russian Azerbaijan, lead a people disenchanted by their rulers' abject failings to demand constitutional government, which the Shah granted in December 1905. 'It was the combination of inefficiency, extravagance, and lack of patriotic feeling with tyranny which proved insupportable; and a constitutional form of Government was sought not so much for its own sake as for the urgent necessity of creating a more honest, efficient, and patriotic Government than the existing one.'[12] This rationale for change could almost equally have been applied to Turkey at the same period.

When in July 1908 Young Turk officers in Macedonia rallied to the demand of the re-instatement of the 1876 constitution, they were successful because the Ottoman empire could no longer endure the more than thirty years stagnation brought about by Sultan Abdul Hamid's autocratic rule. In both Persia and Turkey, the name of Britain was popularly acclaimed as synonymous with progress and reform and because many believed that Britain had no self-serving interests or desire for territorial acquisition in either country. Would she come to the aid of what some at home were calling the 'eastern awakening'?

The interface of Great Britain with Islamic countries during this period of high imperialism (1880-1914) was not of course an isolated occurrence. Other European nations also impacted on the Islamic world, from France in western Africa, and with Italy in Mediterranean North Africa, to the Dutch who were consolidating their hold over Indonesia and the Dutch East Indies. France's involvement in Algeria had started in 1830, and continued to intensify accompanied by her annexation of Tunisia (1881) and expansion into Morocco (1902-12). Supplanted in Tunisia and defeated by Abyssinia (1898), Italy succeeded in seizing Tripoli from the Ottomans in 1908. Britain, which had clashed with France at Fashoda in Sudan in 1898, and was shadowing Russian intentions in Persia and the Gulf, eventually realised the importance of coming to an understanding with her two great imperial rivals.

The Anglo-French agreement of 1904 meant that France finally gave her consent to Britain's occupation of Egypt, while as a quid pro quo, Britain recognised France's interests in Morocco. 'What [...] could be more natural than to barter British support in Morocco for French support in Egypt?'[13]

The Anglo-Russian convention that followed in 1907 appeared to some a less satisfactory arrangement. On the face of it, both powers were doing no more than guaranteeing Persia's territorial integrity while recognising each other's de facto interests in the northern and southern parts of the country. In practice, Russia interpreted the agreement as giving her carte blanche to de-stabilise the Persian revolution, a feat she eventually accomplished in the face of effectual British acquiescence, when Russian forces ended Persian parliamentary government in late 1911.[14]

At the same time, Britain established a hold 'on the south-eastern sphere of influence allocated to her by the [...] Convention, and on the coastal area of the neutral zone, where British troops were stationed.'[15] Britain's liberal credentials (she was after all ruled by a Liberal Government from 1905-16) were as little manifest in her policy towards Turkey as they had been in Persia.[16] In spite of her past friendship with Ottoman rulers and her popularity in the early days of the Young Turk revolution, British foreign policy had been set down by the Conservative Foreign Secretary Lord Lansdowne and followed up by the Liberal Sir Edward Grey. Britain was pledged to the Triple Entente with France and Russia. But these two countries were no friends of Turkey, who, perceiving how the ground stood, gravitated towards Germany, Britain's chief European enemy. Critics of Britain's policy toward Turkey even argued that Britain had already entered into negotiation with her allies as to who would get what when the Ottoman empire was partitioned.

After hostilities had started, Turkey made a belated entry largely at the behest of her proactive War Minister Enver Pasha. Turkish troops acquitted themselves creditably during the Gallipoli (1915) and Mesopotamian campaigns (1916-17), but after the defeat of 1918, the Turks were left fighting for survival in their Anatolian heartlands. The Treaty of Sevres (1920) would have partitioned these between the French and Italians, and ceded further territory to Greece and an independent Armenia. The resurgence of Turkey in the Greco-Turkish War (1920-22) under the nationalists led by the hero of Gallipoli, Kemal Attaturk, resulted in the recapture of land lost to the Greeks. But the nationalists formally ended the six-hundred-year-old Ottoman dynasty and abolished the Islamic caliphate.

The dissolution of the Ottoman empire left Muslims without a distinctly Islamic state in a world controlled by the expansionist European powers.[17] Ataturk and Reza Shah ensured Turkey and Iran each achieved national coherence under a 'strong ruler' in the 1920s. But it remained to be seen how effective ideas of nationalism imported from the West would be in satisfying the longings of the diverse Muslim populations of the Near East in the years to follow. Britain, which in the event had gained most from her former ally, emerged after the Treaty of Versailles (1919) as the dominant power in the Middle East, with mandates over former Ottoman Arab territories now cobbled together as Transjordan, Iraq and Palestine, while France held the mandate for a reduced Syria.

Two of Britain's protégés in the Arabian peninsula competed for the privilege of being the foremost independent Arab state in the region. Sultan of Najd Abdul Aziz Ibn Saud, who had remained neutral during the war, swallowed up the former Sherif of Mecca's Hashemite Kingdom of Hijaz in 1926. Upheavals in Egypt (1919) Syria (1925) and Palestine (1920) were signs that the old Ottoman Arab domains were less than happy with their fate under the colonial powers. Fatefully, the Balfour declaration (1917) and the establishment of a Zionist foothold within Palestine opened the way for the ignominy of non-Muslim control over the holy city of Jerusalem.

Imperialist and Anti-imperialist alignments

According to the foremost historians of imperialism of today the 'distinguishing feature of imperialism' was that

> it involves an incursion, or an attempted incursion, into the sovereignty of another state. Whether the impulse is resisted or welcomed or whether it produces costs and benefits are important but separate questions. What matters for purposes of definition is that one power has the will, and, if it is to succeed, the capacity to shape the affairs of another by imposing upon it. The relations established by imperialism are therefore based on inequality and not upon mutual compromises of the kind which characterise states of interdependence.[18]

Historians have been engaged for some time in debate over the existence of 'formal' and 'informal' stages of empire. John Darwin explains:

> Imperialism may be defined as the sustained effort to assimilate a country or region to the political, economic or cultural system of another power. 'Formal' imperialism aimed to achieve this object by the explicit transfer of sovereignty and, usually, the imposition of direct administrative control. Its 'informal' counterpart relied upon the links created by trade, investment or diplomacy, often supplemented by unequal treaties and periodic armed intervention, to draw new regions into the world-system of an imperial power.[19]

One approach has sought to divide nineteenth- and early twentieth-century imperialism into distinct phases. Demarcations have stressed the 'informal' empire of the early and mid eras of the Victorian age as compared with greater focus on 'formal' empire in its last stage. According to Paul Kennedy, 'the decades between Waterloo and Disraeli's Crystal Palace Speech can never be called anti-imperialistic'. The difference, as far as Britain was concerned, was that 'late nineteenth century imperialism [...] was increasingly an imperialism of fear [...] and a growing "siege mentality".' This phase was conducted as 'a struggle for survival'.[20]

Robert Young argues: 'British imperialism could be said to have been officially inaugurated with the government's decision to bombard Alexandria, and occupy and invade Egypt [...] Increasingly it also implied a policy of pursuing national prestige through conquest and territorial expansion abroad.'[21] D.K. Fieldhouse suggests the high imperialism of the period after the Congress of Berlin (1878) was mainly directed by Germany's entry into the imperial carve up.[22] Certainly, as the nineteenth century drew to a close, Britain's policy calculations came to be dictated less by her eastern possessions than by her mounting paranoia over German power in Europe.

Specific British involvement in Islamic lands remained largely undifferentiated from the larger issue of imperialist expansion into non-European areas of the world. British policy towards exerting pressure on Muslim countries can be said to have developed in line with the same imposition upon non-Muslim lands, with perhaps a tendency toward indirect rather than direct imposition of her will. Peter Sluglett's summary of British activity in the Middle East up to the end of the First World War establishes this as largely an exercise in 'informal' imperialism:

> in addition to the annexation of Aden and the arrangements with the rulers of the smaller Persian Gulf sheikhdoms [...], Britain established unequal treaties with the rulers of Afghanistan, Bahrain, Iran, and Kuwait (and rather late with Qatar), invaded and occupied Egypt, established an Anglo-Egyptian 'Condominium' over the Sudan, took control of Cyprus, and entered into friendly relations with the ruler of Najd. At the same time, Britain began to dominate the trade of the eastern Mediterranean, and to join in the scramble for railway concessions in the Ottoman empire.[23]

With India, Britain possessed many millions of Muslim subjects. The traditional policy of supporting Turkey against dismemberment was linked to the hold of India, and voices like the explorer W.G. Palgrave's counselled care on their account when it came to British relations with Muslim peoples. The so-called 'Eastern Question' stimulated reactions that ran to bitter divisions, as could be seen in Gladstone and Disraeli's clash over the Bulgarian 'atrocities' (1876).

When within a few years Britain became involved in the Egyptian crisis of 1881-82, 'only a handful of men tried to present the Egyptian case': this curiously uncontested occupation constituted the great debate that never got underway.[24] In the clear field opened by absence of substantive opposition 'it remained only to make the occupation palatable to parliament and the public. This was achieved by emphasizing the national interest rather than by referring to specific business and financial concerns, and by stressing the spurious danger to the Canal and to the freedom of the seas, the duty of defending British lives and property, and the need to uphold Christianity in the face of militant Islam.'[25] But a generation later a shift in contemporary political culture saw the case of Egypt return to contribute significantly to emerging theorisations of imperialism.[26]

Attitudes to British expansion during this stage of imperialism were by no means uniform. Imperialist sympathisers, of varying degrees of intensity, could be found both among Liberals and Conservatives. These included Prime Ministers Salisbury, Rosebery, Balfour, and Asquith, and ministers Charles Dilke, Joseph Chamberlain, Edward Grey, and Lord Haldane. Colonial administrators of the stamp of Lords Cromer, Curzon and Milner became in some respects ideologues of British imperialism. However, other political leaders such as Gladstone, Campbell-Bannerman and Sir William Harcourt were sceptical about empire. What Blunt termed 'the non-conformist conscience of the old-fashioned Liberals of England' was still alive and opposed to empire on principle.[27] Even some Conservatives, amongst whom Blunt himself could be counted, were opponents of the new imperialism from the 1880s onwards.

After Egypt, the next time the East became a strident topic of political division in Britain again was during Edward Grey's period as Foreign Secretary. A chorus of dissent raised against Grey's foreign policy emanated largely from radical circles, preponderantly Liberal with some Labour, but joined on occasion – such as over Persia – by Conservative imperialists like Lord Curzon, dismayed by the Government's appeasement of Russia.[28] Essentially, the radicals' liberal politics anathematised an alliance of constitutional England with despotic Russia that meant the abandonment of "'the old Liberal policy of supporting struggling nationalities" for "a series of deals between expanding Empires".'[29] Grey's critics discerned a unifying factor behind 'apparently unrelated' episodes of imperial aggrandisement – Persia, Morocco, the Congo, Tripoli. That factor was 'a dread, an obsessive fear of Germany'.[30] But coming from the largely Christian non-conformist wing of the Liberal party that had supported Gladstone's Midlothian campaign against Disraeli's pro-Turk policy, the radicals' position on Muslim states was equivocal. While they initially welcomed the Young Turk revolution, their Christian principals soon led them, in the form of the Balkan Committee, to support the Balkan Christians against the formers' Pan-Islamist policies, for 'they had long desired the expulsion of the Turk from Europe'.[31]

However, a tiny group, representing an all-party mix, stuck to Turkey. The Anglo-Ottoman society was founded in January 1914 and included among its supporters the former British ambassador to the Porte, Sir Louis Mallet, the independent-minded Conservative M.P. Aubrey Herbert, the veteran socialist friend of Latin America, R.B. Cunningham-Graham, and Professor E.G. Browne of Cambridge. An active official in the society was Marmaduke Pickthall, novelist and regular writer of Turcophile articles in the radical New Age journal. Links between the embattled Muslim nations and their western friends were expressed in the committees and groups aiming to maintain pressure on the government's foreign policy. Browne was also a member of the extra-parliamentary Persia Committee, which he effectively ran together with the Liberal M.P. H.F.B. Lynch. The Committee's activities included a monster public meeting held at the Albert Hall in January 1912, as well as the prominent publicising of the Persian issue by Browne in the press. The Egypt Committee, sponsored by Wilfrid Scawen Blunt and administered by several Irish nationalists, was another pressure group that briefly published its own journal, Egypt, between 1911 and 1913. These pressure groups had available to them a developed if minority discourse that nevertheless represented an alternative response to British imperialism in the Middle East.

Eastern dissidence as a career: the ideas and personalities

Comparing the second volume of the diaries of Wilfrid Scawen Blunt (1840-1922) with the first published a year earlier, E.M. Forster wrote in 1920:

> there is added a tragic unity that was lacking before, for all the entries, so various and so dispersed, gradually flow together like little rills until they form the deathly torrent of the Great War. That war, according to Blunt's interpretation, is essentially Oriental. Germany is indeed the chief villain, but the chief victim is not Belgium but Islam. In the slow agonizing prelude the Germans and French intrigue in Morocco, Cromer rivets English rule upon Egypt, Italy attacks Tripoli, England and Russia apportion Persia, the Balkan Confederacy nearly captures Constantinople: and Turkey, obliged to choose between two gangs of robbers, chooses the Teutonic. Then is the grim perversion of Calvary accomplished, and the followers of Christ, who have developed economic imperialism and scientific warfare, spoil the followers of Mohammed, who have developed neither and were hoping to live the lives of their fathers. Blunt would not have dreaded a purely European conflict, because it would only have shattered the industrial civilization that he disliked and avoided, and that, in his opinion, brings no happiness to men. His detachment is amazing. He dreaded a war because it must involve Asia and Africa, and complete the enslavement of the conservative Oriental nations, whom he loved and who loved him.[32]

Perhaps it is not surprising that the celebrated author of a canonical novel famed for its criticism of the British empire in the East should have leant a ready ear to the doyen of anti-imperialist writers on the Orient. Admitting Blunt to be something of a non pareille, Forster sympathises especially with his quixotic reading of the recent past. To make the Islamic world, not gallant little Belgium, the chief casualty of the First World War barely two years after its closure would have been perverse to a British readership of the time. To ourselves, positioned as we are told in the midst of a 'clash of civilizations' in which the West and Islam are notionally at loggerheads, Blunt's logic might not seem so far-fetched. In fact, his shifting of the axis of political geography eastward was not entirely without precedent in the nineteenth century. For most in the political establishment Britain's possession of India as the jewel in the crown of her empire meant the East was not without its priorities, though few would have occluded Europe in order to valorise the Orient to the extent Blunt had done.

The sympathy for Islam and the Islamic nations pioneered by the Scottish traveller, David Urquhart (1805-77), created notionally at least what Blunt called the 'Urquhart School of Orientalists', which the Middle-East specialist Elie Kedourie characterised as standing in opposition to the establishment view of the 'Eastern Question'.[33] Urquhart and Blunt's names feature prominently in a list made fifty years ago by the British historian, A.J.P. Taylor. In a series of talks Taylor distinguished as 'troublemakers' those dissenters who, in some way or other, epoch by epoch, argued vociferously against British foreign policy.[34] One other name on Taylor's list, Cambridge University Lecturer in Persian, later Professor of Arabic, Edward Granville Browne (1862-1926), was a friend and associate of Blunt's. To these must be added traveller, novelist contemporary of D.H. Lawrence and E.M. Forster, translator of the Qur'an and convert to Islam, Marmaduke Pickthall (1875-1936). Each one of these figures possessed diplomatic connections, many with the East. As a young man Urquhart was briefly first secretary at the British embassy in Istanbul. Blunt also spent ten years in total in the diplomatic service as a young man, while Browne tutored a generation of aspiring diplomats in oriental languages at Cambridge. Pickthall was an exception in that his application to the Levant consular service was turned down, but, were it not for his pro-Turk politics, he might well have gone to Arabia in place of T.E. Lawrence.

Each of these contributed incrementally to a narrative with respect to Britain's dealings with Muslim peoples that in part represented a significant breach within the British educated class's attitude toward the Islamic Middle East. They also engaged in a specifically English activity of berating the homeland for dereliction of duty with respect to smaller or weaker nations they deemed it Britain's part to sponsor and protect. By anathematising his country's overseas manoeuvres and, as he thought, appeasement of reactionary Russia, between the mid-1830s and late 1850s, Urquhart embellished a narrative of betrayal and probably gave the lead for several generations of British anti-imperialist voices. Blunt's strident condemnation of Britain's occupation of Egypt in 1882 was in the same vein, as was E.G. Browne's very public exposure of his country's sacrifice of the constitutional movement in Persia (1905-11), and Marmaduke Pickthall's arraignment of British cold-shouldering of the Young Turk revolution (1908-14).

As a contrast, pro-imperialist travellers and writers' texts might be juxtaposed alongside the above, so setting up a debate over political aspects of Orientalism that have largely been overlooked. Urquhart's successors engaged with the imperialist/ Orientalist discourse of Lords Cromer (1841-1917) and Curzon (1859-1925), his epigones, Percy Cox (1864-1937) and A.T. Wilson (1884-1940), and, during the first decade of the new century, the anti-Islamic reports of Times correspondents in Turkey and Persia, Philip Graves, Valentine Chirol, and David Fraser. The travellers might be divided into three categories according to how they connected their travels in the Orient with the positioning of their native land. All three groups agreed in a broad sense that Britain's power of protection should be exerted over peoples/nations/religious groupings – even an entire empire – of the East. Travellers like Urquhart and W. Gifford Palgrave, who journeyed or resided there in the earlier half of the century (from the early 1830s to the end of the 1860s), believed Britain and her empire ideally represented a disinterested but benevolent patron to the Muslim world. They aimed at persuading British leaders and public opinion that their country's moral responsibility – and practical interests – demanded that Britain should engage the Ottoman empire

in a mutual rapport that would, among other things, result in her protection
and patronage of millions of Muslims.

The second group, from the 1880s up to the Great War, consisting of
Blunt and his collaborators, defined patronage in a more specialised sense,
arguing in effect that Britain should sponsor specific eastern nations – Egypt,
Persia, Turkey – by guaranteeing their self-determination and enabling their
reforms. The third group, active during virtually the same period as Blunt and
his friends, identified with and articulated the ideas of the age of high
imperialism. Western rule benefited inferior or degraded races – among
whom they counted most of the peoples of the East – and must be imposed on
them with or without their consent. The Edwardian proconsuls Lords Cromer
and Curzon were among the outstanding articulators of this view which
gained its disciples particularly among servants of empire and conservative
journalists and, in Curzon's case at least, was strengthened and confirmed by
his travels among oriental peoples. For the last group Britain's political,
diplomatic and economic activities resulted in no betrayal of these peoples
per se – only a potential weakening of the British empire in allowing its
competitors to encroach upon and aggrandise territories contiguous to its
imperial domains in the East.

But for the would-be patrons and sponsors there were many occasions
to denounce Britain's bad faith toward Muslim nations and peoples. The
occupation of Egypt became the pivot of imperial and anti-imperialist
argumentation as epitomised by the debate between Lord Cromer and Wilfrid
Scawen Blunt. What happened there had ramifications for other Islamic
centres, such as Tunisia, Morocco, and Tripoli at the opening of the new
century. The diplomatic consequences of British intervention in Persia were
too fearful to contemplate, but the prospect that Russia would intervene
(especially after 1907) exercised the fears of an imperialist like Lord Curzon
and the Liberal E.G. Browne, albeit from polar perspectives. On the Persia
question, Curzonian Tory imperialists, pro-Balkan Christian Liberals, and
pro-Persian Liberals like Browne joined together to attack Grey's pusillanimous appeasement of Russia. When the European war finally did break out in
the late summer of 1914, there were hopes that Turkey would remain neutral.
Her entry on the side of the Central European Powers in the late autumn
extended the conflict to the Middle East, and British policy quickly came
round to the premise of partitioning the Ottoman domains. In Cairo and
London, plans were laid for inciting the revolt of Arab lands against Istanbul,
and Pickthall's former pro-Ottoman ally now adviser on Middle East policy
to the British government, Mark Sykes, provided much of the theoretical
aliment that fed the British-sponsored Arab risings beginning in 1916.

The political underpinning of the eastern dissidents' behaviour was
never defined in clear party terms. Beginning with David Urquhart's campaigns over three decades, from the 1830s to the late 1850s, and continuing
through the later activism of Blunt, Browne and Pickthall, sympathetic
propaganda in favour of Islamic culture or on behalf of eastern nationalisms

invariably cut across contemporary socio-political currents. Robert Young's categorisation of anti-colonial discourse according to humanitarian, liberal or Marxist divisions cannot fully explain the orientations of the figures I am discussing.[35] Urquhart's campaigns and written discourse, for example, intersect with the radical currents of his age, specifically playing off radical concerns with the secret diplomacy of governments and a more widespread Russophobia.[36] Urquhart also took a more than superficial interest in economics, arguing for the liberalisation of Turkish markets at the same time as he eulogised the pre-industrial methods of commerce still adopted by indigenous Ottoman traders. His belief in the capacity of free trade to break down monopolies and aggrandisement by large states might have classified him as a Cobdenite were it not for the polar stances he and Cobden took on Turkey and Russia. Nevertheless, Urquhart's alignment with the radicals of his day was always dubious, muddied as it was by his Tory leanings with respect to questions of reform at home, and his idiosyncratic insistence on the applicability of natural law to social and international relations. (He claimed to descry formulations of this same natural law in the Islamic shariʿa and Catholic canon law; there is indeed a similar pursuit of correspondences in Urquhart's thinking to that ascribed by Foucault to pre-seventeenth century discourse.)* For Marx, Urquhart remained the idiosyncratic highland gentleman of European education with a quixotic affinity for Turkey.[37]

It was within the context of early nineteenth century Ottoman reverses that David Urquhart emerged as a puissant Russophobe publicist, promoting Turkey as a unique polity well capable of withstanding predatory European states if British diplomacy would but stand up to Russia. In the 1830s and early 40s, the Muhammad Ali crisis threatened the very existence of the Ottoman sultanate, and Britain, France and Russia vied with one another for influence in the Near East. It was during this period that Urquhart's influence as a polemicist and expert on eastern affairs reached its apogee. He denounced Russian perfidy in the Portfolio, a periodical of his own devising, formed Committees for the Investigation of Diplomatic Documents (or foreign affairs committees) with a membership derived in many instances from Chartist ranks, and made attacks on Palmerston. Later on Urquhart's voice was voluble in opposition to the Government's prosecution of the Crimean War (1854-56) in the Liberal press, making him once again (briefly) a notable if idiosyncratic figure on the radical fringe.

A key practitioner of early Victorian British writing on the East, by his cross-cultural dressing and mastery of Turkish, he was for a period absorbed within an oriental culture, gaining acceptance within it as a privileged westerner who, having assimilated its norms, might be trusted to mediate its interests to his own compatriots. In this way Urquhart achieved the dual gratification of obtaining recognition from both Europeans and orientals. At the same time, his writings articulate an emergent discourse of free trade

---

*   See chapter 2

liberalism alongside ambivalence toward industrial society and celebration of archaic values of patriarchy and medieval commercialism. These concerns figure in his commentary on the efficacy of trading practices and political and social governance within the Ottoman empire in his best known work of travel, Spirit of the East (1838). Urquhart's first trumpet blast in favour of British protection of Turkey, Turkey and Its Resources (1833), argued both for the superiority of Turkey's system of indirect taxation through munici-palities and the establishment of a free trade arrangement that would see Britain's finished industrial goods imported into Turkey in exchange for raw materials. This work also called for British diplomatic support for Turkey.

Overall, the reciprocity argued for by the authenticity and durability of Turkey's institutional framework, the moral cause of Britain's diplomatic support, and the advantages to both of closer economic ties, fed unwittingly later into the imperialism of free trade. Urquhart invested in reversing the terms of western cultural chauvinism vis-à-vis the East at the same time as promoting British provenance over the Ottoman empire and with it the very westernisation he so vociferously attacked. With the formation of the Liberal Party Urquhart's brand of radicalism appeared antiquated. It also took a generation or more before the campaigns he instigated with regard to the evils of government policy in the East were re-embodied in a new cause. Neverthe-less, his campaigns of the 1830s up to the aftermath of the Crimean War continued to reverberate for those who would valorise the culture and politics of the East over the imperialism of the West. While the project of bolstering Ottoman Turkey lost its relevance to British statesmen by the close of the Victorian age, Urquhart's 'heirs' continued to argue for Britain's practical and moral support of Muslim nations by appealing to morality and reciprocal self-interest.

The new generation of agitators against government policy in the East would be led by a Tory squire whose indictment of an expanding British empire was built upon travels made to Asia Minor, North Africa, and India. Blunt's politics are no easier to fix than Urquhart's. Born into the Tory country gentry he never cut his ties with High Society. During his 'political phase' in the mid-1880s he intrigued with both Liberals and Tories, flirted with Randolph Churchill's Fourth Party, and even canvassed joining the Irish Nationalists while on some issues, particularly economic ones, he sympa-thised with H.M. Hyndman's Marxist Social Democratic Federation. Blunt's attacks on imperialism and his support for indigenous nationalisms would seem to align him with the radical wing of the Liberal Party, and, notionally at least, it was on this basis that he carried on a dialogue with Gladstone during the Egyptian crisis, and campaigned for Irish Home Rule.

His attitude towards the politics of Islam started out from a vaguely humanitarian advocacy of Muslim autonomy under the protection of the British empire, swinging round to a fully fledged and belligerent anti-imperialism as a result of personally experiencing the crushing of the Egyptian national movement in 1882. Thereafter he would readily employ the discourse of a crusader for justice in the humanitarian mould (as in his pamphlet 'Atrocities of British Justice Under British Rule in Egypt' (1906)), and in his diaries on occasion adopt an Islamic rhetoric against the unbelieving European infidel. Blunt began his career in the East alongside his wife, Lady Anne, discovering the Bedouin culture of the Arabian peninsula. Adopting the role of patriarchal explorer, he proffered his masculine imprimatur as editor of Lady Anne's Pilgrimage to Nejd (1881), going on to establish himself as an authority on Bedouin ethnography to colonial-style organisations like the Royal Geographical Society. These beginnings would seem to situate him within an Orientalist domain. Just as Urquhart had celebrated the authenticity of Ottoman cultural and social practice, Blunt became the advocate of an ideal Bedouin shepherd kingdom of the desert in which rule was maintained by generosity (the outlay of gifts), there was little crime, and political rebels were judiciously forgiven. But he went a step further than Urquhart in arguing for this model to be installed throughout the domains of the Ottoman empire including Syria and Iraq.[38]

Barely a few years after the journey to Najd, Blunt visited Jeddah and Cairo where he conducted discussions with Muslim ulama and came to the conclusion that the caliphate should be returned from Istanbul to Arabia. This became the central idea of The Future of Islam (1882). Blunt's approach to Arab and Islamic issues began henceforth to embody apparent inconsistencies. On the one hand promoting the Najdian model of Arab shepherd kings, he was 'striking a blow for the principle of aristocracy'.[39] But his immersion in the practical politics of the Egyptian revolution of 1882 found him embracing a movement with a popular head, the fellah army leader Colonel Urabi. Blunt's support for the Egyptian national movement was underwritten by a strong personal attraction to a progressive form of Islam embodied in the ideas of the Islamic reformer and future Egyptian Grand Mufti, Muhammad Abduh. Blunt fell quite naturally into a sponsoring mode engaging the Urabist forces with the claim that he could mediate their cause with the British government of W.E. Gladstone.

As matters turned out, in exhorting the Egyptian parliament and military to unite against a potential European intervention Blunt may have done the national movement more harm than good. His subsequent account of the revolution, Secret History of the English Occupation of Egypt (1907), presents a teleological narrative that promotes the superior Islamic and national awakening of Egypt over the perfidious employment of Britain's military might in the interests of European bondholders. The text is especially marked by its incorporation of Muslim foreboding over the intrusion of the European Christian enemy into the Islamic domain (dar al-islam).

Undoubtedly a fascination for Islam helped crystallise the anti-imperialist leaning that had already surfaced in Blunt's mind during a visit to India in 1879. At a critical moment – he was specific in designating the Congress of Berlin of 1878 as the turning point – Britain had begun to reverse its support for the Muslim world by withdrawing its support for the Ottoman

empire. This helped instigate the descent of European imperialism upon the
Muslim lands of North Africa.[40] In the process what respect Muslims might
have entertained toward Britain was turned to bitterness. Britain's action over
Egypt represented a betrayal of the programme of co-operation between a
revived Islam and the British empire that Blunt had set out in The Future of
Islam. 'What little faith he had had in England's good intentions vanished;
now he clearly saw British Imperialism as his real enemy and the enemy of
Islam.'[41]

Now Blunt engaged in a war of attrition with the British imperialist
establishment. He wrote letters to newspapers, political pamphlets, and
contributed to the pro-nationalist journal he helped form, Egypt. Although his
personal commitment to Islam as a spiritual creed may have been a casualty
of his late Victorian agnosticism, he continued to fight for the political causes
of Muslim peoples and nations up to the First World War when he retired
from engagement in active political discourse. His disagreements with the
political establishment entered the public record with the publication of
Secret History followed by Cromer's disdainful riposte in Modern Egypt
(1908), and the second volume of Blunt's 'Egyptian memoirs' Gordon at
Khartoum (1911). In 1910, in an address read out for him to the Egyptian
National Congress in Paris, Blunt declared himself 'an Egyptian nationalist,
an extremist even if you will'.[42] An idiosyncratic rebel who up until his
Egyptian embroilment wrote 'simultaneously [...] about and against both
Oriental and orientalist cultures', Blunt ended up inscribing a counter-
Orientalist discourse at the heart of Europe's power.[43]

Blunt's projects to nurture liberal and progressive strains within the
Islamic world set an example for Edward Granville Browne to follow.
Browne's upper middle-class manufacturing background locates him more
easily than the others within a specific political tradition: that of a nineteenth
century Liberalism that sought to bring principles of constitutional government to every small nation that desired them. It was through study of a
movement of dissent in mid-nineteenth century Persia that emerged around
the charismatic figure of Ali Muhammad who took the title of 'the Bab', that
the young Cambridge academic cut his teeth as an Orientalist. This popular
religious revolt threatened the authority of both the Qajar state and highest-
ranking Shi'ih mujtahids. Browne travelled east in 1887-88 taking with him a
latent need to identify with an eastern nation, and a strong desire to encounter
the essentialist Aryan Persia he had read about in the writings of French
diplomat, traveller and Orientalist, Arthur Comte de Gobineau. He also went
in search of living witnesses to the Babi revolution and packed, or picked up
along the way, a strong prejudice against the Qajar monarchy that had
instigated the massacre of Babis of 1852. His narrative A Year Amongst the
Persians (1893) evokes the ambience of extravagant religious speculation, ex-
tremism and intolerance, as well as heroism, out of which the Babi
manifestation was born. Browne eventually worked through an extended
early commitment to Babism to become an authority on Islamic Persia and

the most prominent British propagandist for Iranian nationalism in the opening decades of the twentieth century.

Pointing out the similarity of Browne's campaign for Persia and Blunt's for Egypt, Mansour Bonakdarian has presented the former as an Orientalist who articulated and opened up a space for Iranians themselves to articulate a discourse of 'Persia for the Persians'.[44] Browne carefully gave voice to a Persian awakening, aware that it might upset British susceptibilities imbricated in an imperialism that feared nationalist stirrings in Ireland and India. As a professional Orientalist, he was also well attuned to the presence in imperialist narratives of an Orientalism that sought to disable Islamic nationalisms by representing Muslim peoples as weak and corrupt. Partly to offset these, Browne developed a Persian national narrative of his own. In this he challenged popular imperialist encapsulations of 'the Persian character' which typically built on the cowardly apolitical figure of Hajji Baba, the eponymous anti-hero of James Morier's early nineteenth century novel.[45] In The Persian Revolution, 1905-1909 (1910), Browne insisted on the self-sacrificing potentialities of a people that had already produced the type of heroism displayed by the much-persecuted Babis, and otherwise promoted the virtues of a nation that had 'reached years of discretion and need[ed] no tutor'.[46]

Having failed in his campaign to effect a change in Britain's policy toward Iran, Browne like Blunt (with whose ideas he was closely acquainted) apprehended the political and military dangers accumulating against nominally independent Muslim states such as Persia and Turkey. In the face of expansive European aggression he argued for a defensive co-operation among Muslim peoples, be they Turks, Persians, Egyptians or Indians, and argued in this context for a Pan-Islamic movement. In The Persian Revolution, Browne also introduced the name and ideas, albeit in a modified form to suit the sensibilities of his British readers, of the influential Pan-Islamist thinker and agitator, Jamal al-Din al-Afghani (1838/39-1891). Thus, in his public lectures, letters to the press, pamphlets and books, Browne did his utmost to defend the Muslim East by a discourse that aimed to persuade by awakening his compatriot's liberal conscience. He consciously mitigated the more extreme elements among the Persian revolutionaries and played down their secular and clerical divide, displaying keen tactical awareness.

But in the event, despite all of his efforts, the success of Browne's mission was conditioned by the factors of the period, chief amongst them the Anglo-Russian convention of 1907 against which he argued so bitterly. When the effects of the agreement began to be realised and blatant Russian interference threatened the revolution in which he so passionately believed, he returned repeatedly to invoke 'England's responsibility' and called upon her to act. His consistent championing of progressive movements within the East, particularly his formation of alliances with Persian nationalists and radicals like the social democrat, Hassan Taqizadeh, present Browne as a western liberal stretching his hands out towards a nascent oriental liberalism. The fragility of this project, exposed by the realpolitik of Britain's adhesion to the European pre-World War One system of alliances, exemplifies the doomed nature of all such enterprises between the Islamic world and the West in the early twentieth century.[47]

Browne's own alienation from the Liberal England that had helped form him in turn alienated the establishment against which he inveighed. Although he was protected by his Cambridge position, his attacks on the government led to him being snubbed in the affair of public honours.[48] Browne came to espouse an almost cynical contempt for European involvement in the affairs of eastern nations. Yet there are ironies in the manner in which his legacy has panned out. An ardent democrat and despiser of the Persian monarchy, at least in its Qajar form, Browne's Persian national narrative leant significant impetus to the later dynastic nationalism of the pro-western Pahlavis. With the help of European Orientalists they incorporated Aryan myth and the glorification of pre-Islamic Iranian dynasties into their ideology.[49] Then again, in his championing of the Iranian Pan-Islamic figure al-Afghani, Browne might be said to have aligned himself with the kind of anti-western, anti-imperialist, clerical-radical alliance that swept away the Pahlavi dictatorship in 1979.

'He is the only contemporary English novelist who understands the nearer East'; such was E.M. Forster's verdict on Marmaduke Pickthall.[50] But there was little in the novels and reviews Pickthall published in the first decade of the twentieth century to suggest his emergence as one of the most persistent and doctrinaire of Turcophile propagandists from 1912 onwards. What Egypt was to Blunt, and Persia for Browne, Turkey under the Young Turks became for him. In Marmaduke Pickthall's case, his active promulgation of Islamic modernism in Turkey led to a different conclusion than Blunt and Browne's adoption of eastern causes. The most conservative of the pro-Islamic voices, Pickthall paradoxically is at the same time the most radical, his insistence that he was a loyal supporter of the British empire making his place in the cabal of anti-imperialists an equivocal one. Pickthall romanticised Disraeli, making the Tory leader the originator of a creed of empire in which British imperial provenance nurtured and looked over the empire's Muslims at the same time as it sustained Ottoman Turkey. This allowed him space to excoriate the 'Gladstonian' Liberal/radical betrayal of both the old Ottomans and the Young Turks. But this party feeling was ultimately spurious: Pickthall knew that since Salisbury the Conservatives had adopted the same policy towards the Eastern Question as the Liberals. His argument was with the new imperialism of narrow European aggrandisement. In spite of his doctrinaire support of Cromer in Egypt against the nationalist cause there, Pickthall's claim to be a traditional patriotic Tory was belied by his ever-deepening immersion in Islamic culture. That process eventually cut him away from his own nation's politics even as it led him to create for himself the more innovative subject position of a British Muslim.

The adherence to Turkey is perhaps all the more surprising given that before his sojourn in Istanbul in the spring and early summer of 1913, Pickthall was a seasoned traveller in greater Syria (bilad al-sham) and Egypt. The Turkish characters in his novels up till then had mostly been representatives of the wily and devious ruling elite of the Ottoman Arab principalities, while the author's affinities seemed to be invested in his ordinary Arab Muslim characters. But Pickthall was not to be counted among the small but influential group of British colonial Arabists who hatched up the Arab revolt in Cairo in the first years of the Great War. No less than them a believer in the British empire, Pickthall had other plans for his nation's patronage in the Near East.

He had inherited several key Urquhartian tenets – whether directly absorbed from their originator is unclear. The first was that Turkey could progress on the strength of her own resources if allowed to do so unhindered by Europe. The Turks were the racial aristocracy of Islam, apparently innately favoured for their qualities of organisation and tolerance to rule the other Muslim and non-Muslim races of their empire. This was the positive part of Urquhart's message. As he went along Pickthall also re-formulated Urquhart's old suspicions toward Russia and the British ruling elite. ('Diplomacy' is a term of obloquy in Pickthall's articles and frequent cryptic reference is made to 'our unknown rulers'.) Given that he got on well with the colonial class in Egypt such dissident attitudes might have seemed surprising, until it is recalled that in his youthful travels in Syria he displayed a penchant for donning the native garb, attracting local Arab companions, and generally slighting the expatriate community.

What is apparent from his articles in the New Age is that Pickthall had absorbed a pro-Turkish narrative that accounted for western European enmity towards Turkey by a combination of factors. Duplicitous European diplomacy in which Russia was the chief villain; perversion of European public opinion by the anti-Islamic prejudices pedalled by eastern Christians; and the betrayal of the auld alliance with Turkey by the British political establishment, were the main causes behind the anti-Turk tendency.[51]

The modern reader of Pickthall's articles cannot fail to register the inherent dualism of his discourse, in spite of their author's disclaimers over the unremitting support he afforded Young Turk ideology and practice. More challenging, however, is his proposition that dismantling the Ottoman empire was neither in Britain's interest nor the Islamic umma's, and in fact could only conduce to the greater disorder of the world. From the nineteenth century Ottoman experience he pointed out that Muslims were rarely happy when under Christian rule or when Christians appeared to receive favoured treatment within the empire. It was therefore essential that a Muslim polity such as the Turkish empire be supported and sustained. This was the reason why Pickthall could not give his blessing to schemes for breaking up the Ottoman dominion and parcelling out its parts into smaller Muslim nations under European sponsorship. When it came to receiving the advances of modern civilisation, Arabs were no replacement for the Turks. Central to Pickthall's argument was the role of Turkey as the conduit of progress and development to the Islamic world. Along with it went the warning that by quenching that light the western powers were fanning the fires of fanaticism and storing up problems for the future.

Islamic Reformers and British Travellers

> Profit from the example of the Ottoman Empire. Iran, faced with the onslaught of European conquest, is not in the least different [...] The essential point is that the surging power of Europe has rendered impossible the survival of barbarian states. Henceforth all governments in the world will have to be ordered like those of Europe, or to be subjugated and conquered by European power.
> Malkum Khan on Persian reform, quoted in Hamid Algar, *Mirza Malkum Khan*, p. 70.

The decline of Ottoman power began to manifest itself in the middle of the eighteenth century, and to be confirmed by military defeats and the loss of the Crimea to Russia towards that century's close.[52] These reverses impressed on Muslim rulers and elites a political dilemma they could scarcely avoid: 'how to introduce into the body politic those changes in institutions and political morality which, in the modern world, were the sources of strength.'[53] Posed under duress by Europe's spreading power and its technological and economic superiority, the proposition was arguably of a different order to a Muslim polity than to a non-Muslim one. Islam's very *raison d'être* was the establishment of God's rule within an historical community ruled by God's law, the *shari'a*. From the inception of the Islamic community (*umma*) up to the Mongol invasions and destruction of the Abbassid Caliphate in 1258, the 'Muslim could look upon a world in which the essence and the existence of Islam more nearly converged. The religious reality in which his faith taught him to believe, and the historical reality by which he saw himself surrounded, seemed in reasonable equilibrium.'[54]

If the Muslim world recovered post-1258, no little credit was due to the emergence of the Ottoman empire; yet the assurance of Islam triumphant was now on the wane – 'the Muslim world seemed to have lost the capacity to order its life effectively; Muslim society was losing its once firm, proud grip on the world.'[55] By the late eighteenth century, the rise of the puritanical Wahhabi movement in Arabia, and its attempt to return the *umma* to its pristine purity by smashing the accretions that had perverted it, sign-posted the need of internal reform. At the same historical moment, an exuberant (the adjective is Smith's) rejuvenated Europe emerged to press home that same issue from without. Eventually the question of reform in the Muslim *umma* would hang fire between indigenous recognition of its necessity and its extraneous imposition. The would-be reformer had to occupy an exposed space in the interstices between the conservatism of his fellow Muslims and the arrogant aggression of Europeans whose political model he sought to emulate.

According to S.H. Nasr three positions emerged from 'the Western conquest of Islam'. First, the Mahdist tendency that drew the inference from Islamic decline of 'the imminent appearance of the Mahdi and the final eschatological events leading to the end of the world'. Second, 'puritanical or "fundamentalist" tendencies' arguing that Muslims had 'ceased to follow Islam properly and should return to the practice of their religion in its pure form and with full vigor so as to defeat the non-Islamic forces.' Third, the 'modern reformist' contending that 'the Islamic message had to be changed, modified, adapted or reformed to suit modern conditions and to be able so to adapt itself to the modern world as to be able to overcome Western domination.'[56]

Twentieth-century western commentators formulated the conditions of possibility of a Muslim response to the modern world in a variety of ways, but generally they have been more interested in Nasr's modern reformism or what we might simply call Islamic modernism. In his series of lectures *Modern Trends in Islam*, H.A.R. Gibb posited the existence of an abstract entity he termed 'the Muslim mind' which he set up against western thought. The problem for the Muslim mind was aligning the 'pure thought' of western ways of thinking with a medieval belief in a 'mechanical process' of amassing the 'known' the 'given' and 'the eternal'. These consisted 'at least [in] a fixed sum of knowledge, most of which was in the possession of some persons or other.' The 'Muslim mind', prone to gain knowledge 'by an amassing of what already existed or, at most, by deductive reasoning from accepted axioms', must encounter enormous difficulty in order to address the thought processes that had constructed the modern world.[57] Edward Said argued later that such dichotomising proceeded in a domain of 'abstractions' and 'metaphysical speculations', and eventuated in Gibb's 'hostility to modernizing currents in Islam and his stubborn commitment to Islamic orthodoxy'.[58]

From a generation earlier than Gibb, Arnold Toynbee and Kenneth Kirkwood conceived of another dichotomy, this time with respect to specific historical Muslim responses to the West. For them, such responses could be categorised within two groups – the 'Zealots' and the 'Herodians'. The former included the eighteenth century Wahhabis, the nineteenth century Mahdiyyah of Sudan, and the Sanusiyyah of Libya. They espoused a violent, primarily negative and reactionary modus operandi that entailed returning to the desert and falling back on the practice of their forefathers. On the other hand, the 'Herodians', as their name suggests, were an elite cadre who from within the court adopt an absorptive approach and operated reforms dictated from above which the authors implicitly valorise as rational and pragmatic. (The biblical nomenclature once more suggests the authors' western perspective.) Historically the 'Herodians' are represented by the Ottoman sultans and reforming politicians of the Tanzimat. They clearly fulfil the role of Muslim modernists and it is clear that Toynbee and Kirkwood, in contradistinction to Gibb, seemed to have no problems with this orientation.[59]

Two specialised studies of Islamic modernism, first published in the 1960s, analyse the tendency within Arab and Turkish thought. They are Albert Hourani's, *Arabic Thought in the Liberal Age, 1789-1939*, and Serif Mardin's *The Genesis of Young Ottoman Thought*. Both Hourani and Mardin articulate their subject through the lives and thought of specific influential individuals. Hourani begins with the Egyptian and Tunisian reformers of the third quarter of the nineteenth century, Rifa'a al-Tahtawi and Khayr al-Din, before proceeding to a discussion of Jamal al-Din al-Afghani and Muhammad Abduh. Mardin's account of the 'Young Ottoman' movement includes the important Turkish writers and publicists, Namik Kemal and Ziya Pasha. Hourani's study emphasises the trend he is discussing as basically a response to the impact of the West upon Islamic societies. He sees the main problem of al-Tahtawi and Khayr al-Din as being 'how to become part of the modern world while remaining Muslims [...] they had to defend modern civilisation in traditional Islamic terms.'[60]

For example, as a Tunisian minister during the high Tanzimat period of the 1860s and very briefly as Ottoman Grand Vizir, Khayr al-Din's attempts at instituting reforms in administration, finance and education lead him to conclude: 'in the present age the only way of strengthening the Muslim States was by borrowing ideas and institutions from Europe, and to convince ortho-dox Muslims that to do so was not contrary to the *Shari'a*, but in harmony with its spirit.'[61] Both Khayr al-Din and al-Tahtawi were among the early Muslim recipients of some form of European education or training; the latter was sent to Paris for this purpose by Muhammad Ali in 1826 and stayed there five years.[62] Hourani emphasises how they had no sense of Europe as a political danger. Their generally positive image of Europe was acquired in 'a happy interlude of history, when the religious tension between Islam and Christendom was being relaxed and had not yet been replaced by the new political tension of east and west.'[63]

This state of affairs is reflected in the writings of Namik Kemal, who brought back from a sojourn in Europe admiration for the system of law he observed in England, and for the political thought of France from where he absorbed the idea of progress, which he proceeded to apply to his own country.[64] By the 1870s, however, the whole project of reform had become more complex. Kemal's advocacy of Ottoman modernisation had been schooled by the corrupt 'suave Europeanised statesmen of the Tanzimat', and also by a national pride wounded and insulted by European invasiveness. The Young Ottomans, Mardin observes, were once represented 'as the inheritors of a Western-oriented tradition' but in reality had 'more complex intellectual antecedents'. In Kemal's case these factors would help move him toward both a nationalist and Pan-Islamic positioning partially in response to the growth of Russian sponsored Pan-Slavism.[65]

If the Tanzimat period had been about Muslim 'internal decline, how to explain and how to arrest it', with Europe as political teacher and ally, the period 1875-82 gave a new turn to the relationship between Europe and the Near East. Modernists and reformers would need to face not only the issue of Muslim decay but the new problem, 'that of survival: how could the Muslim countries resist the new danger from outside?'[66] In addition to – or more likely as a result of – the threat against the Islamic *umma* from without, reaction from within froze the institution of reforms the modernists deemed essential if Islam was to survive. The turning point was the fall of the Grand Vizier, creator of the Ottoman constitution of 1876, and most conspicuous of modernists, Midhat Pasha, and the re-instatement of absolutist power by his persecutor, Sultan Abdul Hamid.

The most important Muslim figure reacting to the encroachment of Europe on Muslim domains during the last quarter of the century was Jamal al-Din al-Afghani. An Iranian who posed as an Afghan, Jamal al-Din travelled the *umma* endeavouring to awaken it to the danger of European imperialism and to activate it into a radical response. Behind certain of the key events of the period between the tail end of the Tanzimat and the start of the constitutional revolution in Persia, Jamal al-Din is often said to have had a hand. A lay figure, he attracted the jealousy of the *ulama* during his first brief visit to Istanbul in 1869. There followed a seven-year period in Cairo which brought him a number of ardent disciples, and where his ideas helped crystallize the Egyptian national movement that was to emerge a few years later around Urabi. From Egypt al-Afghani moved on to India and later Paris, where he entered into dialogue with Renan on the matter of religion, science and rationality, and had some contact with the Mahdi in Sudan through students he had known in Egypt.[67] His last years were spent in Iran and Turkey, and represented futile efforts on his part to enlist Shah Nasir al-Din and Sultan Abdul Hamid in his schemes for Islamic unity and political revival. Jamal al-Din is also credited with having influenced the tobacco protest in Iran in 1890-91, and posthumously, the revolution that broke out in that country at the end of 1905.

A disciple of al-Afghani's from his time in Egypt was a young Islamic doctor who eventually reached the rank of Grand Mufti. Initially sceptical about Urabi, Muhammad Abduh took part in the national movement of 1881-82, and was exiled for his pains. Later he joined Jamal al-Din in Paris from where the two brought out the periodical *al-Urwa al-Wuthqa* which agitated against imperialism and urged the Muslims to establish unity among themselves. Subsequently, Abduh moved away from al-Afghani's brand of political agitation becoming a reformer who emphasised the need for Islamic thought to be brought into line with the modern era, a project he backed up by trying to initiate reform of the religious educational system in Egypt.[68]

According to Gibb, '[Islamic] modernism itself is largely a product of European influences'.[69] The positions of both al-Afghani and Abduh, if this assessment is correct, were essentially reactive. If they drew their resources

mainly from Islam (though in al-Afghani's case, this is suspect), the terms
under which they attempted to initiate their reforms were not of the Muslim
world's making.[70] One figure who understood this disparity and who was
prepared to go much further than any of the reformers mentioned above in
respect of accepting the modern world on western terms was the Armenian
Iranian, Malkum Khan. If al-Afghani's rationalism on occasion bordered 'the
limits of man's freedom within the Islamic scheme of things',[71] the only
constraints Malkum Khan was prepared to acknowledge were the inhibitions
of his preponderantly Iranian audience: 'for tactical purposes his proposals
were usually presented under an Islamic guise', a guise which was 'often
extremely thin'.[72]

The son of an Armenian Christian who had nominally converted to
Islam, Malkum Khan derived from his father 'a belief in the tactical
desirability of the use of Islam for the promotion of westernizing reform'. At
the age of ten he travelled to Paris where his studies convinced him of the
easy applicability of a 'comprehensive westernization'.[73] Malkum spent a
decade in Istanbul (1862-71) at the height of the Tanzimat reforms, and these
encouraged him to address to Iran the message that she could do no better
than to profit from Turkey's example and embrace the ways of Europe. Like
al-Afghani, Malkum attempted to draw royalty into his schemes of reform,
and his influence on Shah Nasir al-Din, though not without its up and downs,
was longer lasting than, if ultimately equally as abortive as al-Afghani's.
During a life spent for the greater part away from Iran he managed to hold
diplomatic office in the service of that country despite his involvement in
scandal and his publication (from London) of the periodical *Qanun*, in which
constitutional ideas that may have had some bearing on the Persian constitutional revolution were promoted.

So much for the most prominent, though not the only, figures in the
reform movement in the Islamic world of the latter half of the nineteenth
century. Whatever the significance of their impact in the East – and this
remains a matter of conjecture and debate[74] – not only has much attention
been paid them by western scholars, but crucially for this study, they also
helped form the views on Islam of some of the western travellers and Orientalists under discussion. However, before proceeding to a review of contacts
between these two groups, some remarks about two other eastern figures
connected with the reform of Islam would be useful. These are Ali
Muhammad of Shiraz, known as the Bab, and Husayn Ali of Nur, called
Baha'ullah, founders of the Persian Babi and Bahai movements respectively.

In his *Modern Movements Among Moslems*, the missionary S.G. Wilson
assigned both to the Mahdist category, arguing that, even if he favoured an
elevation in the condition of women, the Bab was no social reformer. If
'politically the Bab proposed no reforms', his movement 'shook and
shattered the power of the Shiah Mujtahids [and] helped awaken modern
Persia to bring about independence of thought.'[75] The Bab was executed in
1850; his followers subsequently dividing according to whether they gave

their loyalty to his designated successor, Subh al-Azal (and were called Azali Babis) or his half-brother, Baha'ullah (and were called Bahais). Just as the Bab had done, Baha'ullah advanced strong millenarian claims, but distanced the Bahais from the kind of militant opposition to the Qajar rulers demonstrated by the Babis. Modernist elements are, however, to be found in Bahai thought of the period according to Juan R. Cole. Baha'ullah and his son, Abdul Baha, displayed democratic sympathies which by nineteenth-century Middle East standards were liberal and even dissident. Cole points out that in their enforced exile from Iran, the Bahai leaders' paths crossed with those of other Middle East reformers: Malkum Khan in Baghdad in the early 1860s, and Young Ottomans exiled alongside Bahais in Akka in Syria in the 1870s. There even existed ambivalent connections between the Bahai leaders and Jamal al-Din al-Afghani.[76]

Foremost among these for having direct contact with Muslim reformers was Wilfrid Scawen Blunt. He knew personally and was on terms of some intimacy with Jamal al-Din al-Afghani who stayed for a while in Blunt's London house in 1885. He also encountered Malkum Khan in June 1880 during the latter's period as Persian Ambassador in London. But his closest link was with Muhammad Abduh, whom he had first met in Egypt in January 1881 and with whom he continued on terms of warm friendship until the latter's death in 1905. Blunt was also acquainted with Tanzimat statesmen like Khayr al-Din and Ahmed Vafik, both of whom he saw on his visit to Istanbul in the autumn of 1884, as well as Midhat Pasha with whom he had an audience in Damascus in 1878. Blunt's involvement with Islamic politics and connection with key Muslim political figures was serious enough to have been written about by oriental scholars such as Sylvia Haim, Albert Hourani, Nikki Keddie, and Hamid Algar. Haim was particularly interested in the intertextuality of Blunt's *Future of Islam* and the writings of the Arab nationalist al-Kawakibi. Hourani also found this text of interest for the manner in which it blended the ideas of al-Afghani, Abduh, and Blunt's own. 'The book [...] contains an exposition of the nature of the Islamic community and the way to reform it, and it is perhaps possible to accept this as a true report of what was thought at the time in Afghani's circle.'[77] For both Haim and Hourani, Blunt's treatment of the issue of the caliphate is forward looking and possibly influenced Arab thinking – a case of double transfer of ideas if correct.[78] Like Hourani, Keddie probed Blunt's dealings with Jamal al-Din over the matter of possible mediation between the British Government and the Mahdi. For his part, Algar analysed Blunt's report in *Secret History of the English Occupation of Egypt* for its elucidation of key aspects of Malkum Khan's ideas and personality.[79]

What is perhaps especially significant is the way in which Wilfrid and Lady Anne Blunts' journeys in Syria and central Arabia to the end of the 1870s formed the overture to Wilfrid's engagement with the politics of Islam. As travellers who set out, in Hourani's phrase, as 'European romantics', they 'perhaps' imbibed from their visit to the Rashidi capital Hayil and their experience of 'this flourishing Arab polity', the notion that 'in spite of the decay of the more advanced Islamic countries, Muslim society still contained in itself the seeds of its own revival.'[80] Hence Blunt's first main idea: the transference of the caliphate from the Turks to the Arabs, from Istanbul to Cairo or Mecca, and around it a dismissal of Turkish reformers like Midhat Pasha whom the Blunts considered besotted with European schemes of progress, with trams, canals and railways. Elie Kedourie afforded Blunt's ideas serious consideration, connecting them to an essay Blunt wrote in the *Fortnightly Review* of July 1880. Here Blunt accounted for the malignity of Ottoman rule by its contamination at birth with the evils of Byzantium, called for the dismemberment of the empire, and the application of the 'communal' principles of Hayil to Iraq and Syria, probably under European protection.[81] Blunt's ideas about the partition of the Ottoman empire and the reconstruction of its Arab Muslims lands along the pattern of the desert kingdom of Najd were easy to caricature. But Kedourie's point was that whereas such views 'would have been regarded before 1914, as ignorant and lunatic fantasies […] in 1919, they became the ground on which staid Civil Servants, and politicians in a hurry, built their plans.'[82] With hindsight it is possible, and for Kedourie in the early 1950s it was highly desirable, to give Blunt's ideas this spin: to connect them with the exploits of T.E. Lawrence and with the mandates of the post-1918 period.[83]

Equally, however, if the romantic archaism of Blunt's desert kingdom scheme were to be set against his Islamic modernism, it would be his advocacy of the anti-imperialism of Jamal-al-Din and affinity with the educational/rational reform project of Muhammad Abduh that was foregrounded. Certainly, Blunt endeavoured to widen his contact with Islamic elites in the 1880s, and this entailed not writing off the Ottoman empire as a lost cause, even though during the Hamidian period it bore all the hallmarks of such. In 1884 he went to Istanbul with the purpose of urging 'the Sultan to take a lead in reform. He must do so now, or he will lose his hold over Islam forever, but I do not expect to succeed; all is too rotten there for any solid building.'[84] Clearly, Blunt's views had changed after the *Fortnightly Review* article of 1880 and the diary entry of 1884. In the former he expounded ideas of self-determination for eastern nationalities that proved a useful *entre* in lobbying Gladstone (significantly, Gladstone had been interested in an independent Armenia, a cause that interested Blunt not in the least.)[85]

By 1884, Blunt had steeped himself in the ideas of al-Afghani and Abduh and was more concerned about the political and spiritual reform of the Islamic *umma*, less about national/ racial utopias. Blunt names the summer of 1880 as a turning point for this: he realised that his 'thought of freeing and reforming the East […] had begun at the wrong end […] I must first make myself thoroughly acquainted with [Muslims'] religious ideas.'[86] The trigger for this change had been his encounter with Malkum Khan who voluntarily related a spiritual autobiography in which he featured as the quondam head of 'a religion which was founded some years ago in Persia'.[87] This might well have suggested to Blunt the potent image of himself as a sponsor of religious reform in the East.[88]   Either way, he now hit upon the need for reform to come, if it was to come, not from above, imposed by a Europeanised ruling elite such as Midhat and the other Tanzimat reformers represented, but from within the law of the Qur'an and the *hadith*. This was where al-Afghani came in. He (or his ideas as refracted through Abduh and his other Egyptian disciples) convinced Blunt that 'if rightly interpreted and checked the one by the other, the law of Islam was capable of the most liberal developments and that hardly any beneficial change was in reality opposed to it.'[89]

It was this belief in a form of Islamic modernism that carried Blunt through the Egyptian crisis of 1881-82, and propelled him in the direction of converting to Islam. By the time he had lost his conviction that Islamic reform was possible, his anti-imperialism was so dyed in the wool that he could hardly have seen his way to relinquishing his support for eastern revolutions in Egypt, Turkey and Persia.[90]

In his espousal of eastern reform, Browne moved in the opposite direction to Blunt. Instead of beginning by privileging the political and the racial/nationalist cause, then moving on to the internal reform of religion, as Blunt did, Browne began with a movement whose millennial, messianic overtones predicated a total spiritual transformation of the Shi'ih branch of Islam. As a young man and traveller, Browne saw Persia partly through the eyes of Gobineau. It was Persia's location in the Aryan myth and the Frenchman's representation of the Christ-like Bab and his followers' heroic martyrdoms that moved him, rather than a pre-occupation with Islam per se. He played a pioneering role in introducing the history and doctrines of the Babis and Bahais to a western audience, (Browne met both claimant's to the mantle of the Bab, Subh al-Azal and Baha'ullah, on a trip to the Middle East in 1890). He was perhaps for a period as taken with their mission of Persian renewal as Blunt had been with Islamic modernism and Egypt.[91]

It would, however, be the political ideas of the Islamic reformers rather than the Babis' religious ones that eventually engaged the mature Cambridge professor. The names of both Jamal al-Din al-Afghani and Malkum Khan feature in his *Persian Revolution*, although it is obvious who Browne considered the greater figure. He met Jamal al-Din in 1891 in Malkum Khan's house in London. Typically, Browne is not reticent about his admiration of Jamal, but he is cryptic in his criticisms of Malkum. Although Keddie is not outright in her association of Browne with the Iranian revolutionary's oriental biographers, it seems he, along with them, as a result of dependence on limited sources, exaggerated al-Afghani's contacts with and influence on the 'government men and scholars in the countries he visited'.[92] Browne portrays al-Afghani as 'this remarkable man, who during a period of at least twenty years, probably influenced the course of events in the Muhammadan East more than any other of his contemporaries.' He was a figure to write whose biography would involve composing 'a history of the whole Eastern Question in recent times'. But Browne was aware the majority of his fellow

countrymen reading his account of al-Afghani would 'unhesitatingly put him
down as a singularly dangerous and unscrupulous intriguer, who was
prepared to go to any length to attain his ends.'[93] We wait for Browne's
confirmation or denial of this charge but none follows. His method is to
interpose long quotations from his sources within his commentary so as to
defer his own judgements. These, when they come, combine objective-
sounding phraseology with unqualified encomium:

> This remarkable man, […] a wandering scholar with no material resources save
> only an eloquent tongue and pen […] a sincere and passionate love of Islam, of
> which he acutely felt the present decadence, literally made kings tremble on their
> thrones […] he it was to whom the present Constitutional Movement in Persia in
> large measure owes its inception. He also did much to awaken the independent
> Muslim States to a sense of their imminent peril and the urgent need of combina-
> tion to withstand the constant aggressions of the great European Powers, and he
> might with justice be termed the founder of Pan-Islamism in the sense in which I
> have defined it.[94]

Browne's admiration for al-Afghani does not balk at his incitement to
violence – indeed his influence over the assassin of Nasir al-Din Shah is
clearly stated. As for Malkum Khan, Browne has little to say in direct assessment of his overall impact on politics, other than to quote from copies of his
periodical Qanun. Hints at his predilection for membership of secret societies
(which is evidenced by quotation from Blunt's account of his meeting with
Malkum) suggest Browne's scepticism, but then Jamal al-Din had not been
above involvement in such activities himself.[95]

The two Turcophiles, David Urquhart and Marmaduke Pickthall,
promoted their pro-Turk ideas in different historical moments, exerting in the
process an influence of extreme contrast. Urquhart established his reputation
as an authority on the Ottoman empire at a time when very little direct information was coming through to form home opinion. The crux of British policy
in the Middle East was 'whether the Ottoman Empire would reform or would
not reform'. The British ruling elite, from Urquhart's contemporary, Stratford
Canning, right up to Lord Salisbury, who was Blunt's, had little stomach for
the Ottoman empire. But they feared the consequences of its dismemberment
and so remained wedded to a policy based on an implicit contradiction, 'the
desire to reform [it] on European lines and the desire to preserve it'.[96]

In such an atmosphere, Urquhart established close links with Sultan
Mahmud II, whose reforms he broadly supported, and with some of his
ministers. He also funnelled his ideas back to Britain during his time as first
secretary to the Istanbul embassy, by winning over press correspondents at
home. In point of fact, Urquhart was an intriguer, whose political ideas sometimes appeared less important than the fact that it was he who propounded
them. Kedourie identified him as the founder of a trend, a 'deviation' from
'the high road of doctrine concerning the Ottoman Empire in the nineteenth
century'. Urquhart, he argued, originated a discourse on Ottoman reform that
broadly ran as follows:

The Ottoman Empire suffered from misgovernment, from disorder, from rebellions not because of an inherent fault in Easterners, but because of the interference and the intrigues of Europeans and the misguided attempts to copy European institutions and manners [...] [The] principles [of the Muslim religion] [...] contain the true essence of liberty and democracy; if they were followed, individual liberty and public order would be secure in Ottoman lands.[97]

Urquhart's writings do appear to lend credence to this view. The pedagogic import of his most influential piece of travel writing, Spirit of the East, was not so much to urge the necessity for reform. Rather it proposed the eastern mercantilist model as an alternative to early nineteenth century western industrial society, with its political dogmatism and harsh imposition of an economic law that disabled the poor and alienated the worker from his handiwork. Although he supported the reforms of Mahmud II, Urquhart wrote pessimistically of

seeing the best interests of my country sacrificed, and the conservative principles of the Turkish government and society undermined, less by foreign and hostile influence, than a fatal imitation of Western manners, prejudices, and principle.[98]

The corruption of the Ottoman government 'was largely due to Western interference in Eastern institutions'.[99] On the other hand, Urquhart consistently argued for the strength of Ottoman Turkey, claiming European interference, which had begun during the Greek War, had worked to weaken her. 'Turkey must be "constrained to make concessions" to diminish "the amount of future sacrifices", in other words, they "seek to disarm Turkey in the interest of her defence".' Concerning the diplomatic build up to the Crimean War, he declaimed: 'Turkey is not weaker than Russia, and but for the interference of Europe it would be Russia, not Turkey, that would at this moment not only be heard of as in danger, but that really would be so.'[100] In spite of Kedourie's criticisms, which were aimed at another audience at another time, Urquhart's dialogic discourse on Ottoman reform – probing and contesting the European system of diplomacy and its anti-Islamic bias – opened up a different perspective to standard renditions of the Eastern Question which have only recently resurfaced in the work of western historians. That is: to what extent was Turkey's predicament of her own making, and how far was it the creation of European diplomacy?[101]

Such a proposition would have been well understood by Marmaduke Pickthall, but in another context. Between his time and Urquhart's not only the failure of the Tanzimat but the years of ossification of Hamidian rule supervened. Pickthall's presumption of European interference in Turkish affairs was not that its modus operandi would corrupt Ottoman authenticity, but that it worked to sabotage Turkey's progress and reform. Pickthall became progressively a partisan of the Young Turks and their programme of reform. During his short three month visit of 1913 his best contacts were the reformers, Ali Haidar Bey, a son of Midhat Pasha, and the Foreign Minister in the Young Turk government, Prince Said Halim, a descendant of Muhammad Ali, the founder of modern Egypt.[102] He also made the acquaintance of other key figures in the Young Turk leadership, continuing to champion them even after the debacle of 1918.

Of all the pro-eastern voices Pickthall's is the least inhibited about European modernity and its impact on the Islamic world, at least in so far as political reforms are concerned. According to Peter Clark,

> The Ottoman Empire, in its extent and durability, was the most successful Islamic empire in history. Islam was the basis of the Turkish empire and Pickthall saw, as few other westerners saw, that the Young Turks were inspired by a reforming Islam that demanded education, social improvement and enhancement of the status of women.[103]

Although 'the public effect of Pickthall's wartime activities was total failure',[104] his embracing of Islam as a convinced modernist is a testimony of sorts to the colloquy of western sympathisers with Islam and the Islamic reformers. In India in the late 1920s and early 1930s, Pickthall was able to express his modernist interpretations of Islam in public lectures, and through the reviews and papers he published in the Indian Muslim journal, Islamic Culture.

The 'naturalness' of the engagement with Islam and the Muslim world so far as the westerners were concerned perhaps does not require emphasising. For them to enter the political fray both at home and in the East, debating political ideas, contesting authority, freely furthering the causes in which they believed, is surely what we might expect from a confident expansive culture such as the West's was in the period under scrutiny. This is exemplified in the sort of aristocratic pride that helped Blunt publish a work on the caliphate and draw up a manifesto for the Egyptian national cause as though these were almost unexceptional activities. On the oriental side the picture was different. Of the reformers discussed above, probably only Malkum Khan (and that for the reasons that set him apart from the other Muslims) demonstrated the panache and freedom from constraint that might normally be associated with the western travellers. For the others, as Hourani pointed out, issues such as the dissolution of the last protecting empire of Islam and the transfer of the caliphate were not matters to be concluded on in haste – or perhaps even considered at all.[105] Their position perhaps demanded a greater courage: to move beyond long accepted boundaries; to waken to the dangers facing their own culture and then start out on confronting them.

Conclusion

A ground plan has been laid for the remainder of this study that includes key figures in a century-long debate over Europe's relations with the Islamic East. The historical events and conditions that underpin this debate have also been outlined. In the chapters that follow, the main concern is with articulation of the specific issues cohering, at given moments, around the central questions so far raised. These questions – to do with the capacity of the East to reform itself, and the desirability or otherwise of European involvement in the development of Muslim societies – of course registered shifts in emphasis according to the circumstances of different epochs. However, to avoid too rigid a reliance on genealogies and periodisation, the approach adopted will be one that establishes the existence of discourses that, though they are flexible and manifest modification, also demonstrate consistent (if sometimes disjunctive) features.

In the next chapter we shall see how David Urquhart set out the parameters of a foundational discourse for those travellers and writers who wished to question the more established axioms of British disquisition on the East. Urquhart's writings register an inclination both to contest assumptions behind European politico-cultural superiority over the East, while at the same time contributing to these. His desire to defend Ottoman institutions from western tampering is on the other hand undermined by his invocation of a spreading British influence in the Ottoman empire in the form of trade and an embedded, proto-imperialist patronage. Urquhart's legacy to later travellers, sympathisers with eastern nations and Turcophiles, therefore represents a split between advocacy of eastern uniqueness and self-sufficiency, and proposals that inclined toward eastern dependence on Britain. Both these tendencies are comprehended in the writings of W.S. Blunt and T.E. Lawrence, and can be said to exist, to varying degrees, in those of most (though not all) of the other writers discussed in the subsequent chapters.

Associated with the issue of British patronage over the East is the deployment of the motif of her betrayal of that trust. In Urquhart, earlier Blunt, Browne and Pickthall, Britain is a liberal power for whom considerations of altruism and imperial interests should cause her to embrace the aspirations of reforming Islamic nations. Such a notion stands as a benchmark against which to set later recidivist backsliding, which Blunt's later writings, and those of Browne, account for in terms of the corrupting effects of imperialism upon the national character. Against these they maintained, respectively, traditional aristocratic and liberal standards of Britishness, nostrums that delivered them far from the national establishment of their time. It is, however, the Tory Pickthall, moving from a traditional loyalism to the edge of national apostasy and eventual conversion to Islam, who might be said to have accomplished the longest journey. Specifically, then, discourses that argued for the integrity and autonomy of non-European cultures and their resources, and questioned notions of Britishness and empire, conducted debates with, and even went so far as to contest, dominant, establishment orthodoxy centred on imperialism and Orientalism.

2

David Urquhart, W.G. Palgrave and the patronage of the East

David Urquhart has either been relegated to specialist monographs on the genealogy of English radicalism; discussed for his contribution to the construction of the Eastern Question; produced as an advocate of the institution of the Turkish bath, or simply forgotten.[1] Drawn to the East initially as a partisan of Greek independence, he very quickly transferred his allegiance and became a strong, almost fanatical, admirer of Ottoman Turkey.

I shall argue that Urquhart's career not only demonstrates a discursive instability within Orientalism; it also intersects with an emergent discourse of free trade liberalism as well as an ambivalence toward industrial society that celebrates the archaic values of patriarchy and medieval commercialism. Urquhart's sense of national identity does not appear to have been compromised by the bitter invective he levelled at his country's ministers. Nominally at least, he retained the Calvinism of his lowland Scots upbringing; but later in life he did approach the papacy in anything but a narrow sectarian spirit in aid of his scheme of promoting a universal morality based on canon law. The influence of Islam on him was powerful but not easily defined. Urquhart frequently applauds the tolerance of Islam in his writings, and developed a strong preference for Muslims over eastern Christians. What specifically concerns me here are the arguments Urquhart adduced for the patronage of Muslim nations by Britain, and the case he brought against successive British governments for betraying this trust. In addition, I shall examine the confidence he expressed in both the resource of the Islamic religion and the intent of Muslim peoples to survive the changes brought about in the world by western pre-eminence. In the process, Urquhart emerges as a political enthusiast and maverick, a powerful egoist, and founder of a sect or at the very least a school proclaiming a narrative of betrayal.

From Lord David to 'Daoud Bey'

The day will come when it will be wondered that I could have been doubted.
David Urquhart, letter to *The Morning Herald*, August 1854, quoted by Jenks,
'The Activities and Influence of David Urquhart', p. 321.

Born in 1805 the second son of the second wife of a Scottish Laird, Urquhart
has been variously described as a 'seer and prophet', excessively paranoid, a
'half-mad' meddler in politics who was guilty of 'insane vanity', and 'one of
the most critical observers on the state of the Ottoman Empire in the early
nineteenth century'.[2] Jeremy Bentham 'had a high opinion of his capacity',
and there was 'always about him a clear-cut hardness and secure superiority
which recall Bentham and his school'.[3] The Utilitarian philosopher had urged
Urquhart to travel in the East, and in 1827 he joined the Greek war of
independence, taking part in the defeat of a Turkish squadron in the bay of
Salona. After receiving a serious wound, he left Greek service in 1828. Later,
in his book, *Spirit of the East*, Urquhart would write of his initial partisanship
for the Greeks and hatred and aversion for the Turks. But he had been won
over by the 'personification of stoical firmness and of dignified resignation'
of the Turks in defeat, so far as to become nostalgic for Turkish power as
symbolised by the recession of their flag: 'now disappeared from the castles,
where I saw it so lately, reddened at once in anger and with shame'.[4] So
began a vocation perhaps all the more notable for its reversal of the Romantic
veneration of Greece, embracing instead Europe's time-honoured religious
bogeyman, who re-appears in nineteenth century stereotypes as the 'lustful'
and 'the terrible Turk'.[5]

The short period 1831-37 has been adjudged the most influential in
Urquhart's career. It was during this time that he became one of the most
prominent 'advocates of the advantage to Britain of a free and independent
Turkey'.[6] This coincided with a sudden manifestation of anti-Russian feeling,
which he was partially responsible for fanning.[7] Between 1831-32, Urquhart
acted as 'confidential agent' in Istanbul of Stratford Canning, the British
ambassador extraordinary.[8] During the following year he worked on a
memorandum on Anglo-Turkish commerce in which he argued knowl-
edgeably and persuasively for the establishment of free trade between the two
countries so as to, among other things, reduce Britain's trade imbalance with
Russia. *Turkey and Its Resources*, one of the rare works King William IV had
read to him from cover to cover, followed hard upon. Urquhart had found an
ally in the King, who agreed he should tour Turkey and Central Asia to report
upon their commercial and political condition.

By the time Urquhart got as far as Istanbul, war in the East seemed
imminent. The implications of the Treaty of Unkiar Skelessi gave Russia an
alarming level of control over Turkey; 'precisely when fear of Russia was
beginning to awaken British interest in the maintenance of Turkey [...]
[Urquhart's] ideas attracted attention which was keen, if not always

favourable.'[9] Finding his book had been translated into Turkish, and that his opinions on financial matters were sought after, Urquhart decided to remain at the Turkish capital.[10] There followed a period in which Urquhart, together with Ambassador Ponsonby, worked in the aim of persuading the government to adopt their pro-Turk policies. In his reports to the Foreign Office, Urquhart moved from the commercial to the political, becoming in the process increasingly more bellicose as far as Britain's relations with Russia were concerned.

In the summer of 1834 he toured the northern shores of the Black Sea, giving his support to the Circassians in their grievances against the Tsar. Palmerston recalled him before he could commit Britain too far, but his patience with the Scot led to Urquhart being offered the post of consul-general in Istanbul. This he refused believing his publicist's skills could be employed better back in London, where he brought out a pamphlet entitled *England, France, Russia and Turkey* in which he pronounced the imminent danger of Russia's occupation of the Straits. Finding that his ideas on Russia had gained currency in the London press, Urquhart expanded his propaganda by starting his own periodical.[11] The *Portfolio* published (with Foreign Office connivance) damning Russian despatches passed on by a Polish refugee, some of which were reprinted in the mainstream newspapers.

In 1836, Urquhart took up the post of secretary to the embassy at Istanbul. His sense of his own infallibility now came into play: together with Ponsonby he was responsible for setting up the 'Vixen' affair. (The 'Vixen' was a British schooner hired by Urquhart and his friends and sent to a Circassian port with the intention of breaking a Russian embargo. The intention was to trigger hostilities between Britain and Russia. Public opinion was indeed inflamed, but Palmerston and the Tsar refused to rise to the bait.) It was during this period that Richard Cobden wrote of Urquhart in his pamphlet *Russia*:

> One active mind has, during the last two years materially influenced the tone of several of the newspapers of the kingdom, in reference to the affairs of Russia and Turkey, and incessantly roused public opinion through every accessible channel of the periodical press against the former, and in favour of the latter nation [...] How far this indefatigable spirit has been successful in his design to diffuse a feeling of terror and a spirit of hatred towards Russia in the public mind, may be ascertained by any one who will take the trouble to sound the opinions of his next neighbour upon the subject, whom ten to one, he will find an alarmist about the subtlety of Pozzo di Borgo, the cruelty of the Czar and the barbarism of the Russians.[12]

In Istanbul, Urquhart had set up his own lines of contact with the Porte, eventually going so far as to leave the embassy and 'live like a Turk among the Turks', causing his close relationship with Ponsonby, who had now become jealous of Urquhart's influence, to break down.[13] Urquhart's first incarnation, that of diplomat to the Porte, had been replaced by that of confidant and advisor, an unofficial position of intimacy which, when added to Urquhart's break up with Ponsonby and the disarray this was causing in the Istanbul embassy, so alarmed Palmerston that he had Urquhart recalled home and – on the death of the King – his diplomatic papers cancelled. Urquhart's hero-worshipping biographer admits her subject's career as a diplomat was 'a conspicuous failure'.[14] Having succeeded in alienating the entire European community in Istanbul, Urquhart, not for the first time, had remained unshakeable in his self-belief and unabashed by the opinions of those around him. After the period 1831-37, Urquhart's public reputation in Britain suffered vicissitudes of adulation and ridicule; he built a network of disciples and sympathisers who valorised his personal fixity and self-conceit.

Britain and Islam: finding a modus vivendi

> If Mr.Urquhart were not a British subject, he would decidedly prefer being a Turk; if he was not a Presbyterian Calvinist, he would not belong to any other Religion than Islamism.
> Karl Marx, *The Eastern Question*, p. 35

In 'The Mohammedan Controversy', an essay originally published in the *Calcutta Review* of 1845, the eminent British Orientalist William Muir wrote: 'Mohammedanism is perhaps the only undisguised and formidable antagonist of Christianity [...] in Islam we have an active and powerful enemy; – a subtle usurper, who has climbed into the throne under pretence of legitimate succession, and seized upon the forces of the crown to supplant its authority.' Muir could scarcely conceal his pleasure that the age of Islamic domination was at an end. For most of twelve centuries, during which Christianity was the 'mortal foe' of Islam: 'the rapidity of its early conquests, and the iron grasp with which it [...] retained and extended them, the wonderful tenacity and permanent character of its creed – all combined to add strength to its claims and authority to its arguments.' Now the last expansionist Muslim power, Ottoman Turkey, had been checked. British dominion had extended to India. The evangelical revival had superseded the laxity of the eighteenth century when those at the helm had been 'men without faith'. Now British Protestantism was excellently placed to roll back the Islamic tide, beginning with India and Persia where missionary activity had already engaged the mullahs in disputation. Political hegemony and the missionary enterprise went hand in hand. And 'after the first feelings of irritation' subsided, conquest invested 'the conqueror's faith and opinion with the prestige of power and authority'.[15]

A decade and a half earlier, David Urquhart had conducted a remarkable conversation with an Ottoman Imam and his friends in the Albanian town of Scodra. Urquhart reported the dialogue within a customary didactic frame in *Spirit of the East*. Where his compatriot Muir warns about making any concession to Muslim beliefs, Urquhart treats the truth claims of the New Testament and Qur'an with blithe disinterest. His own Protestant faith had no images, crosses, adoration of the Virgin Mary, confession of sins, or prayers to saints. Therefore the 'true character of Christianity was not less hostile than Islamism to the Christianity which exists in the East'. In effect, there was no difference between Protestantism and Islam, but for the Qur'an, which added nothing new and was 'but a repetition of the Gospels'. Only the Muslim declaration of faith, and the claim of finality for its Prophet, necessary for the early distinctiveness and hence survival of Islam, separated the two religions. Why allow this to 'become a barrier between them [the Ottomans] and a nation who had every interest to support their independence, and to improve their condition'?[16] Urquhart's message, decoded by his Muslim listeners in studied silence, on the face of it reverses Muir's propagation of the old religious antagonism. The Muslims are proffered the hand of Britain's friendship – for Urquhart is under no illusion that his words are anything other than political in context. Eschewing the evangelical's crude triumphalism, Urquhart's speech is still no less a discourse of power than Muir's.

Putting aside the project of nineteenth century evangelism and its relationship with imperialism, Muir's discourse operates within the same terrain as Urquhart's vis-à-vis a growing British hegemony in the Muslim East. The difference lay in the dispensation rather than the provenance of this control. Urquhart and his followers believed power should be deployed in such a way as to create reciprocity (though not one of total equality) in preference to a wholesale European takeover of the Orient. Their approach towards Islam, it should be stressed, was one of genuine respect rather than policy alone. An empathetic Orientalism might be said to characterise their position in contradistinction to the religious Orientalism of Muir, and the imperialist Orientalism of the proconsuls of the later twentieth century, who argued the irreparable decline of the Islamic East out of the conviction of racial and cultural superiority.

On the question of Islamic reform, which meant how far the Tanzimat policies should go, and how successful they were likely to be, we can expect no direct answer from Urquhart. I shall try to show below how his ideas about Ottoman reform aided by British sponsorship were in part irreconcilable. These centred around his desire to see Turkey change only in accordance with its ancient principles, while at the same time he was instrumental in arguing for her opening up in the name of international free trade. It is important to bear in mind that Urquhart's formative experience of Turkey was in the 1830s, a period during which the Tanzimat experiments were first starting to take shape under the reforming sultan, Mahmud II. Urquhart's attachment to the Ottoman court during the stints he spent in Istanbul meant he gained first hand contact with the Sultan and his reforming minister, Reshid Pasha. Urquhart could (and later on did) claim to have had a significant influence over the early stages of what was to be the Anglo-Turkish trade agreement. Otherwise he seems to have been more engrossed in intriguing with Ponsonby, jealously watching for Russian influence at court, and interfering in ministerial appointments, than registering the new measures for change.[17] That is not to say that he was unaware of their impact. On his travels he frequently met disgruntled Ottoman officials who were only too ready to criticise effects of the military reforms such as the implementation of the new uniform, and the upsetting of the traditional balance between the Muslim and Christian *raya* populations. On these and other issues, such as the sending of Turkish students to western Europe and the importation of European fashions into Turkey, Urquhart was more than ready to express a view.

Later he would attack what he took to be direct European political inter-ference in the Ottoman province of Lebanon. Overall, however, he paid less attention to practical measures for reconstituting Ottoman society, and expended instead much greater effort in presenting to his English readership a variegated description of Turkey's unique qualities. What kind of advocate of the Ottoman Orient was Urquhart then? We will try to address this and some of the other issues raised in chapter 1 by an examination of his key writings on the East. It may be useful to observe the *pedagogic* and *performative* character of Urquhart's mediation of the East, terms that are apposite for one who combined the dominie's urge to set out, teach and instruct, the publi-cist's and political activist's roles of dissemination and agitation, and a rare traveller's gift for penetration of and assimilation to an alien culture.

The Grammar of The East

> Placed among a strange people, if you inquire, you must use language not applicable to their ideas; if you argue, you deal with your impressions, not theirs; but when you put yourself in a position similar to theirs, you can feel as they do, and that is the final result of useful investigation. Burke, in his essay on the 'Beautiful and Sublime,' mentions an ancient philosopher who, when he wished to understand the character of a man, used to imitate him in everything, endeavour to catch the tone of his voice, and even tried to look like him: never was a better rule laid down for a traveller.
> *Spirit of the East*, 1, p. 10.

In describing eastern culture to his English contemporaries, Urquhart's purpose always seems to have been to eschew closure, as well as to urge the westerner to discard his observational apparatus in order to learn instead the grammar of the East. 'It is with the manners of a people as with their language; no part can be correctly described, no passage accurately applied, unless the mind of the one, as the grammar of the other, has been laboriously studied, and is perfectly understood.'[18] Urquhart leans towards the views of twentieth century linguists when he argues that language determines and structures how a culture sees the world, and that the vision of different languages is always discrete, never precisely the same:

The man who sees the East for a day can sketch external objects by the words which exist in European language: but, to be able to convey thoughts, he must feel as they do, and describe those feelings in a language which is not theirs; and that is an overwhelming task. Language is the conventional representation of impressions: but where impressions are not identical, they cannot be conveyed by common sounds; and, therefore, where there is difference of impressions, there is no common language.[19]

The interface of western and eastern cultures had for too long been troubled by a mutual incongruity that on Europe's part amounted to an invariable misapprehension of oriental civility. It was inevitable that 'when a stranger enters a new country, he will be struck only with those points of manners which he does not comprehend; and the native having no difficulty in understanding himself, cannot comprehend the effect which he himself produces on the stranger.'[20] Urquhart's advice for the western traveller to imagine himself accoutred in the gorgeous raiment of the East while residing on luxurious divans is no mere indulging of Orientalist fantasy. The grammar of the East was not such as could be absorbed in an opium-induced trance or an onrush of eighteenth century sensibility. The Turkish *majlis* or reception room expressed the social manners and gradations that animated Muslim Ottoman society as a whole, and the blundering European entered it in complete ignorance of the ceremonial purposes constituting its spatial organisation.

The commonest mistake of the European was to define the oriental according to his own *weltenschau*; to impose alien concerns on to the target culture. Dual categories such as progressive/ backward, constitutional/ despotic, tolerant/fanatic were expressive of an occidental, not an oriental vocabulary. 'We consider "progress" synonymous with well-being, and stationariness expressive of barbarism [...] the eastern[er...] looks on that which is stationary as that which is excellent.' West to East, there was, for example, no exact transference of a term like 'feudalism' since the conditions of feudalism had been different in a country like Turkey to those of western Europe. The difficulties that stood in the way of 'a correct estimate of the East' resided 'solely in a European's preconceived opinions, that is in his deficiency in simple terms'.[21] Lack of awareness of such structural difference perpetuated the European practice of assimilating or appropriating the target culture to their own. As Andrew Wheatcroft puts it, 'Europeans considered the Ottomans backward and corrupt in exactly the measure that they did not measure up to the standards of Western civilization [...] But there is rarely any recognition in Western accounts of the empire that reform in the Ottoman lands might be equally incremental, and by slow stages, as at home.'[22]

Foucault's articulation of the relationship between power and knowledge may aid our understanding of the archaism that lies behind Urquhart's advocacy of the 'authenticity' of Ottoman Turkey, and, connected to this, his empathetic Orientalism. Urquhart approaches the contiguities of Foucault's respective interests at a number of points. Although he was never committed to an asylum, his enemies dismissed him as 'mad' (or twentieth century critics put it, 'paranoiac'). His oppositional stance to the 'totalitarian discourses' of imperialism and Orientalism situates Urquhart, *avant la lettre*, within the realm of genealogy or 'insurrection of knowledge' argued by Foucault. Urquhart perpetually sought a subject or subjects that could be shown to embody the moral law he believed was the key to all problems of a social or political nature, but passed from one to another having only elucidated the correspondence in a dispersed, fragmentary way. In addition, Urquhart's constant search for the 'true' meaning of language links him to an anti-enlightenment project which can be expressed as a straining after a pre-renaissance similitude in opposition to the eighteenth century's rationally conceived construction of an artificial system of signs. In Urquhart's discourse this pursuit is part of an archaism that rejects the 'new technologies of power' that Foucault figures growing up around the eighteenth century European state.

> Not only did the monarchies of the Classical period develop great state apparatuses, (the army, the police and fiscal administration), but above all there was established at this period what one might call a new 'economy' of power, that is to say procedures which allowed the effects of power to circulate in a manner at once continuous, uninterrupted, adapted and 'individualised' throughout the entire social body. These new techniques are both much more efficient and much less wasteful (less costly economically, less risky in their results, less open to loopholes and resistances) than the techniques previously employed which were based on a mixture of more or less forced tolerances (from recognised privileges to endemic criminality) and costly ostentation (spectacular and discontinuous interventions of power, the most violent form of which was the 'exemplary', because exceptional, punishment).[23]

Against this new system of power Urquhart sets up a preferred system of governance, which corresponds to Foucault's arbitrary medieval power, but which Urquhart valorises as despotism of the individual in opposition to the modern European tyranny of law. Whereas the former was arbitrary and spectacularly destructive, it brooked recovery, and at the same time, by virtue of its de-centred and diffuse operation, was enabling and tolerant of communal autonomy and industry. Urquhart's singularity – what exemplifies his attempts at asserting oriental difference against both progressive and reactionary European interventions – was his emplacement within his description of an oriental utopia of an indestructibility that appears to counter his iterated forebodings of dissolution. According to Urquhart the politics that underpinned the diverse communities of the Ottoman Balkans possessed all the resilience of embodied natural law:

> For fifty years, in Turkey, convulsion has followed convulsion as wave rolls after wave; and Europe, judging by its own cumbersomeness of machinery, and consequent difficulty of readjustment, has looked on each succeeding disaster as a prelude to the fall of the Ottoman empire. Turkey's political state may be compared to its climate: an unexpected hurricane in a moment wastes fields and forests, covers the heavens with blackness, and the sea with foam. Scarcely is the

devastation completed, when nature revives, the air is all mildness, and the
heavens are sunshine. All destructively, and as suddenly do political storms and
military gatherings overwhelm the provinces; and no sooner are they past, than
industry is busy preparing her toil, and security is scattering seed, or wreathing
flowers.[24]

Ottoman tyranny was random and unexpected, but it was the tyranny of one
man only. Recovery came because it escaped the universal 'systemic of
despotism' that in Europe functioned as the 'tyranny of the law' as embodied
in centralized power, the divisive operation of party politics, and oppressive
taxation. Western European nations were not moral entities but were constructed out of hegemonic forces that could not tolerate opposition because
this emerged out of principle rather than personality. Eastern revolts could be
quenched with very little bloodshed because they invariably issued from
individualised resistance, or the assemblage of forces around individual
authority. By the spreading influence of Europe such outbreaks were being
replaced by 'national opposition', challenging 'governments of opinion',
bringing in their wake 'deep-rooted and immovably fixed animosity and
strife, respecting the measures which this government of bayonets and gun-
powder ought to adopt.'[25]

Urquhart's dream for the East was that its amazing system of checks
and balances would continue to operate – indeed, he stressed frequently the
strength these gave Turkey in spite of the absence of anything approaching an
Ottoman patriotism, at least among the Christian *rayas*. The Porte had
favoured the local independence of the various religions and nationalities in
the empire. 'But in the East, as in Europe, there is a strong tendency to
nationalization by race and language. That tendency, fostered by the policy of
the Porte, may, in its reorganization, strengthen, instead of overthrowing, its
authority.' The wonder was 'that this mass should have held together, not that
it should be destitute of patriotism now. But though patriotism, in our sense
of the word, is wanting, local attachments, and the common bond of race,
religion, and language, supply its place. On these attachments local admini-
strations are grafted'.[26]

There wanted only reform of the abuses at the top, a spreading of the
good things on show at the base of the pyramid up to its apex, and Turkey
might be restored to its pristine health. Urquhart conceived of the extent of
the reformer's brief as: 'taking, in all things, the law as it is […] to restore, or
rather to fix, the currency – to separate the judiciary from the civil authority –
to reduce the pashas to their real functions of prefects of police; […] organize
the army – and there all reforms ought to cease.'[27] For the Ottomans – and
this was a crucial statement that would reverberate through later formulations
of counter-Orientalism – had merely allowed the old laws to fall into
abeyance, laws that had existed in the original Arab system – 'all prudent
reform in Turkey must reduce itself to a restoration of the ancient rule originally derived from, and lately revived in all its ancient purity in, Arabia
itself.'[28]

Urquhart's desire to preserve an 'authentic' Orient from western contamination, foregrounding its holistic coherence and arguing its superiority to western complexity and alienation, sets up an aporia when juxtaposed against his privileging of British intervention in the cause of the defence and preservation of Ottoman society.[29] The imprecation to enlist Britain's support is, necessarily, a dangerous task. The power that was the engine of modernization is called upon to bring its aid to a society threatened by 'the whirlwind of Western opinion that has swept Turkey, after devastating Greece'. Turkey was 'in a state of transition from its ancient municipal and "custom" basis to the new principles imported from Europe, of standing armies and custom-houses.'[30]

Urquhart's writings may be said to lay bare a recurrent split within Orientalism. His reversal of the usual Orientalist discourse upholding western civility and asserting eastern barbarism is in the cause of a way of life he himself had sampled and approved, and had every reason to wish maintained.

> That contrast of the mild, quiet, docile existence of the court and camp – that easy and elegant costume – those tasteful rooms and comfortable divans [...] what a relief, too, from European tedium, politics, theories, systems, argumentation, and learning![31]

The problem was: the Ottoman East was vulnerable to European ways on account of its malleability, what Urquhart terms its 'docility of mind' or 'spirit of imitativeness', which led to the Turks' 'imitation of those nations whose policy has been so injurious to them'. This imitation, which was outwardly most obvious in the matter of dress, was the more deadly because: 'Their imitation of Europe will be without knowledge or discrimination. That which we possess of value can only be obtained by years of labour [...] that which is valueless is easily adopted and mimicked, if not copied.' Sending young orientals to Europe 'denationalize[d]' them; they would return home 'depraved in morals, presumptuous in disposition, and intractable to the habits and customs of their compatriots. They will have lost their simplicity of mind: they will carry back the mental maladies of Europeans.'[32] In actuality, Bernard Lewis wrote, the reforms of the Tanzimat period accomplished just that:

> In the old order there had been an accepted set of social loyalties and obligations, to which most men had tried to conform. With the destruction of the old order this complex web of social relationships and loyalties was torn asunder, and in its place came a new set of imported and alien institutions, with little meaning for the new officialdom and none at all for the people whom they ruled. There had always been a gulf between the rulers and the ruled. It now became fantastically wide, as the progress of Westernization added to the differences of power and wealth those of education and outlook, home and furnishings, even food and dress.[33]

Urquhart knew the inevitable introduction of modernity must sap the *geist*, engendered across centuries, which held the Ottoman polity together: 'It is impossible that a people should adopt a double type of distinct customs, nor can they admit a new impression without disturbing and destroying the old;

and as custom is the regulator and symbol of thoughts, feelings, duties, nothing can be more dangerous to the constitution of a state, and the morality of a people, than a change of custom.'[34] Writing in 1852, Urquhart bemoaned changes in costume in the military as 'hideous and foreign' and saw the introduction of European-style salutes as inimical to Turkish notions of integrity, identity and difference. 'A change such as this once effected in the army, it will unquestionably spread to the nation, and hurry it on in that melancholy course which the English designate "free and easy," and the French applaud as *"manières sans gêne,"* which is no manners at all.'[35] Although he advocated restoration of native costumes in the army and 'sedulous preservation of social manners and etiquette' he knew the dangers the Ottoman empire was running. Setting aside the scheming of Russia, Urquhart continued to foresee the main danger for Turkey as 'Mussulman schism' – 'If the Turkish government has ceased to be Turks, how shall they exist?'[36]

Performing the East: the Traveller and Cross-Cultural Dressing

If, as the above suggests, Urquhart foregrounded dress as a key indicator of the political and cultural coherence of the Ottoman empire, it is probably not surprising that in his personal encounter with the East he advocated the benefits of cross-cultural dressing. Ironically, as far as his early diplomatic career was concerned, far from aiding Urquhart, this aspect of his behaviour acted as a sign of his transgression of diplomatic protocol. His biographer, with a perhaps unintended *drôlerie*, comments: 'The English Mission [in Istanbul] was singularly and collectively shocked at finding one of its official representatives adopting Turkish dress and Turkish habits, and eating Turkish food in the Turkish manner.'[37] Yet this, together with energy spent on trying to introduce the Turkish bath into Victorian England, might be comprehended in Urquhart's strange heresy that 'Eastern methods could be applied to Western people'.[38]

According to John Rodenbeck, westerner travellers in the East tended to wear native clothes for a variety of reasons, most of them connected with exigency. By the mid-nineteenth century, the spread of westernisation to many eastern towns and cities made the choice of eastern dress a garb of affectation. Before then, however, to do so was usually the effect of compulsion, a desire for comfort, or aesthetic preference.[39] Urquhart though does not merely assume that donning eastern clothes is advantageous to the traveller either in terms of comfort or ease of social intercourse. These factors he takes for granted. For him cross-cultural dressing was integral to his own performance of the East.

This is best observed in his travel books, especially, *Spirit of the East*, Urquhart's account of his journeys along the newly established boundary between Turkey and Greece. A considered exegesis of a set of experiences transposed into a form that goes beyond the routine travelogue, the writing takes on the character of personal testimony, even articulation of a new faith in which the teller maintains his emotions firmly within the iron bonds of an idiosyncratic rationality. The pedagogy, unlike in his political pamphlets, articles and books, is here absorbed within the context of a lived encounter. The expressed engagement with an eastern culture is performative and trans-formational at one and the same moment. As Hillis Miller puts it, 'a perfor-mative utterance makes something happen [...] brings something new into the world'. Urquhart's discourse constructs moments of revelation as though they are not the product of foreknowledge or speculation: 'Action or conduct precedes conviction and the knowledge (or conviction of knowledge) convic-tion brings, not the other way round. Performance precedes knowledge.'[40] Equally, the strain of the dominie runs through much of Urquhart's travel writing too, particularly in the later *Pillars of Hercules* (1850) and *Lebanon: A History and a Diary* (1860) where the pedagogic motive has almost entirely taken over.

As a reporter on the eastern scene, Urquhart's strictures are part of a discourse that privileges the expert who has made personal sacrifices in order to acquire knowledge about the Orient. Such an enterprise required 'long and assiduous application', sole engagement in that pursuit, 'energy and persever-ance', and the 'sacrifice of all [...] accustomed comforts, luxuries, and enjoy-ments'.[41] Initially, it was the urge to master the question of the struggle between the Ottoman empire, the Greeks and the Albanians that drove Urqu-hart. In time, the possession of expert knowledge entitled him to make pro-nouncements about how oriental travel was to be most profitably conducted. This can be seen over the issue of cross-cultural dressing, which Urquhart claimed was a sine qua non for the would-be traveller wishing both to under-stand the culture of the East, and to be in a position to do so in the first place.

> A European, possessing perfectly their language and their literature, having that character of mind which is fitted to gain influence over them, will yet remain, however he may be really respected, distant from their society; [...] let him change, however, his costume, and his position is immediately changed. But the costume alone is of little, if any use, until a man is capable of acting his part as those who wear it.[42]

Adoption of oriental costume represented both a rejection of the system of dragomans, which Urquhart held in contempt, and serving notice that one intended to circumvent the centuries of hostility and suspicion that had separated Christian Europe from Ottoman Turkey. The Turks had been at least in part to blame for the erection of barriers by their 'ignominious treatment' of European visitors marked by their alien dress and manners. This had the effect of nullifying any desire on the part of the westerners to inquire into the mind and institutions of Turkey and Islam. There was now 'scarcely an Englishman acquainted with the Turkish language', and the character of modern writing on Turkey was (a reference to Kinglake perhaps) 'too frivolous and childish even to merit censure'.[43]

The salutary effects of dressing as the natives did was first brought home to him, Urquhart claims, when he discarded his blue jacket for a brightly coloured dressing gown and started to go barefoot. In due course, his grasp of the subtleties of the semiology of eastern dress led him to counsel a friend who had adopted what he thought was authentic Turkish get-up, only to encounter ill treatment at every turn:

> 'You have shaved your beard and whiskers *not quite* to the line of your turban, so that a lock of hair has appeared close to your ear, which is the distinctive sign of Jews who shave their beards!' 'What a pity,' he said, 'that I did not hear this before, instead of after, my journey.' I thought that the pity was that a man should travel in a country before studying its manners, and reason on it before understanding its feelings.[44]

Doubtless Urquhart's performance of the East was as self-serving as any of the other western travellers in the ego-satisfaction derived from a mastery of oriental language and customs. However, in his case the adoption of eastern robes was not in order to facilitate a more convenient vantage point from which to 'report on' the Orient. Urquhart's report does not so much sum up oriental life for the Western audience, thereby asserting European mastery over it, as assert its difference. Burton's accounts of the East, according to Said, are suffused by 'a sense of assertion and domination over all the complexities of Oriental life'.[45] In contrast, from Urquhart's cross-dressing emerges a performance of Turkish language and manners that is openly assimilative, and gains him not only the authority to report on Turkish manners and customs to his compatriots, but also credence among the Turks to mediate European ambitions and intentions. Given his consistent pro-Turk positioning, it is hard to believe that Urquhart was engaged in the one-way penetration of oriental society that, arguably, sustained Lane's or Burton's representations of 'the Orient' to the West. His cross-dressing is transgressive in the sense that it shocked early Victorian diplomatic circles while at the same time it engaged the empathy of the Turkish aristocracy. That it was devoid of what Said calls 'the strategy of disguise' is, however, a significant divergence from the others. Instead of being a performance from the outside, it enacts an interior transformation the object of which is not to deceive, but to empathise, to learn.

Preserving the East by Trade

> Domestic industry is practised in the East. It was practised in ancient times in every portion of the globe. The opposite plan was the discovery of England; it has been, in her own estimation, her greatness. It has given her colossal riches as the gain of a few, and unparalleled misery as the gain of the rest.

Urquhart, *Free Press*, 1 December 1955, quoted in Robinson, *David Urquhart*, p. 76.

There is a discernable split between Urquhart's romantic Orientalism with its espousal of traditional cultural forms, and his desire to promote greater British involvement in Ottoman affairs; his wish to keep the Turkish empire undivided and untainted, at the same time as helping it receive the impetus for judicious reform. Urquhart's first trumpet blast on behalf of British influence in Turkey, *Turkey and Its Resources* (1833), proclaimed her municipal organisation and use of direct taxation with the assertion that these 'render a people indestructible'.[46] The Turkish system of direct taxation entailed the election of elders who were responsible for the management of communal debts and the collection of government and municipal taxes. The equal distribution of taxation united villagers because it made for equal burdens and mutuality in all things.

> They rejoiced in each other's prosperity, bewailed each other's misfortunes; they reproved the idle, lest he should be a charge to the rest; they watched the fugitive, lest his debts should be thrown on the community; they repressed the robber, not to suffer in his stead; and were happy when the submissive were not punished for the rebellious, and when the living had not to pay for the dead.[47]

This system of forced guardianship, which Urquhart believed resembled the voluntary associations of the Anglo-Saxons, was however the lot of the *rayas* or non-Muslim subjects of the sultan and in practice was restricted to the European domains of the empire. This autonomy encouraged communities like the Greeks and Armenians to maintain their language and customs in tact, so long as they were able to survive the random depredations inflicted on the rural peasantry by village *aghas*, local pashas, and the military.

Urquhart goes further in celebrating the Turkish genius per se, in the process re-writing traditional prejudices about Islam and Ottoman history. As a religion Islam taught no new dogmas and established no new revelation. It gave a code to the people and to the state a constitution, limiting sovereign power by making the executive subject to a law empowered by religious sanction and moral obligations.[48] In the hands of the Turk, instead of constituting a fanatical tyranny, the religion had proved tolerant of other faiths. Urquhart quotes an English traveller in 1669 who counted at Tournovo in Thessaly three mosques for eighteen churches – such tolerance was 'a most remarkable feature in Islamism'. Far from being the Greeks' oppressors, the Turks had 'twice restored to them their country, after overthrowing the Albanians', had continued to defend them against 'their historic enemy', and had allowed them financial autonomy and freedom in commerce.[49]

The Ottoman empire had stood for as long as it had because of the principle of non-interference in the local administration of the countries it ruled. Overall, 'a comparison with these principles, of those who have regulated the colonial policy of some other nations, might be instructive.'[50] Still, Urquhart openly acknowledges the absence of gratitude accorded the sultan by his Christian subjects. The *raya* had 'no conception of benefits flowing from these institutions, operating through the moral character impressed by them on the community.'[51] The paradox in Urquhart's assessment of the efficacy of Ottoman municipal organization was that he saw in it the bedrock of a holistic system that ensured the continuing existence of the Ottoman polity, rather than an aspect which – given the *raya*'s paucity of attachment to the Porte – could (as had already been displayed in the Morea) be easily detached from the empire.

He attributed the longevity and continuation of the system to a tolerance that was characteristic of Islam as a whole. While the corruption of the higher echelons of Ottoman government was plain to see, Urquhart adjudged the system capable of being cleared of the abuses of weak central government and local anarchy by judicious reform and – crucially – the stimulation of the Ottoman economy by reciprocal trade arrangements with Great Britain and the latter's stalwart diplomatic support. If the Ottoman domains are pictured as a vast trading area, the European parts, in particular, were beneficiaries of the same spirit of non-interference that animated the municipal organizations. Commerce, manufacturing, and agriculture were allowed to thrive when free from the perennial oppression of the pashas. The profits of the Ottoman peasant were his own so long as he could evade the robbery of the government agent. Thus the *raya* population always had hope, and there were no paupers in Turkey.

Everywhere he travelled in Roumelia, Urquhart could always find hospitality in a hut that boasted at the very least a carpet and cushion. The cottage industries Urquhart celebrated in European Turkey were, he afterwards claimed in *Spirit of the East*, enabled by the Ottoman conquest in the late Middle Ages, which had brought the arts of dyeing, printing, and weaving. In Amelakia in Thessaly, a joint stock company had been founded in the eighteenth century 'in which the interests of industry and capital were equally represented'. The town, which had received plaudits by French travellers, was, Urquhart claimed, only a model for a thousand other hamlets in the same region and indeed throughout the Ottoman empire. Urquhart believed the new Greece – which had incorporated the Morea but, after the London Protocol of 1830, lost most of Thessaly, had inherited a 'liberality of sentiment and opinion' as fruit of the Ottoman municipal system.[52] But Capodistrias's dictatorship, the revolt of Muhammad Ali, and Russia's continuing agitation, threatened the fabric of the way of life he so valued.

It was to the advantage of Britain that a free and independent Turkey should exist. An Anglo-Turkish trade agreement would provide transit to British goods, open up a rich market to British industrial products within Turkey, as well as countering Austria and Russia's policy of erecting protective tariffs. Urquhart extolled Ottoman freedom of commerce or unfettered right to trade which he associated with the same spirit that encouraged hospitality to strangers and the journey of pilgrimage: 'commerce renewed its sacred character, even when entirely distinct from religion'.[53] In Ottoman

realms he identified a straightforward commercial ethos that contrasted with
the complexities of European trade:

> The extreme simplicity of commerce, from the absence of legislation on the
> subject, is visible in the establishment of a merchant: no books save one of com-
> mon entry, are kept; no credits [...] are given; no bills discounted; no bonds, nor
> even receipts; the transactions are all for ready money; no fictitious capital is
> created; no risk, or loss from bankruptcy, to incur. A merchant, whose capital may
> exceed twenty thousand pounds, will, very possibly, be without a clerk; and a
> small box, which he places on his carpet, and leans his elbow on, encloses, at once,
> his bank and counting house.
>
>   The merchant who travels by caravan, has really few risks to encounter, and
> but trifling expenses. He lodges without expense, and in full security, in a Han; he
> is never alarmed by the dangers of fluctuations of price; he has nothing to fear
> from the ignorance or dishonesty of an agent or broker; he brings his goods, or his
> money, to be exchanged for the article he wants; sees, and examines it before he
> buys; he has not the precarious chance of realizing a large fortune, but has the
> certainty of reaping the reward of his industry. With very small capital specula-
> tions can be undertaken. A merchant can commence traffic without corporate
> rights or previous connection; intelligence, industry, perseverance, and frugality,
> are the qualifications he requires, and however small may be his profits, if his
> expenses are still smaller, he considers himself on the road to wealth.[54]

This passage evidences to Urquhart's strange blend of patriarchy and
archaism, utopian rationalism, and liberal free trade axioms. His eulogizing
of Ottoman local institutions and eastern commerce underscores the belief
that not only were things done differently in the East, they were done more
morally. This anti-western slant affixes to his Victorian free trade creed a
romantic Orientalism that is characteristic of his idiosyncratic brand of
radicalism. Europe's bankruptcies, like its implementation of indirect taxation, evidenced to the failure of moral principle Urquhart descried in the
West. 'No one would deny that the efficiency of a government would be
immensely increased; its character elevated; the resistance, opposition, and
discontent of the people prevented, and the penal code, losing half its cruelty,
would gain double efficacy, by not placing morality and law in opposition –
if the revenue were raised without legislative interference in commerce.'[55]

    Urquhart prided himself on the logic of his moral positions, but his
theories on Ottoman local government and commerce contained at least one
fatal flaw. On the one hand, the Ottoman system was praised for its resilience
and moral principle and contrasted with Europe's combination of class based
legislation and a commercial practice that left a peasantry like Spain's prey to
a corrupt centralised government and the injustice of indirect taxation.
Laudably, he took Turkey's European critics to task for failing to acknowledge in the system he described 'so eloquent a contradiction of our
preconceived notions of indiscriminate despotism and universal insecurity of
the East.'[56] The shortcomings of the Ottoman system were its imperfect
organization of production and antiquated communications and transport
facilities. Manufacturers and peasants were at the mercy of unscrupulous
village *aghas* and pashas, and, unsurprisingly, the local goods could not

compete in quality with Britain's. For her part, Britain could supply the necessities as well as the luxuries of the eastern populations, allowing them to direct their attention exclusively to agriculture and the furnishing of raw produce (such as silk in the Levant and cotton in Egypt). The gain to both parties was dressed up in all the moral earnestness of the free trade creed.

> It is, indeed, impossible not to regret that a gulf of separation should have so long divided East and West, and equally impossible not to indulge the hope and anticipation of a vastly extended traffic with the East, and of all the blessings which follow fast and welling in the wake of commerce.[57]

But the contradiction in Urquhart's argument resided in what free trade would mean for indigenous industry and crafts – the same in which he had found so much to praise. Urquhart may have been 'one of the first to perceive that a reduction in the prices of British goods would enhance the Turks' buying power, and thereby expand the Turkish markets for British manufactures.'[58] But if his plans for the replacement of finished eastern products by British ones were to be fully implemented, how could the traditional societies he so ardently embraced withstand the impact of being opened to the full consequences of the nineteenth century system of free trade? For King William IV and the northern manufacturers, as Bailey put it, there was great appeal in a policy that argued 'that Turkey was an almost limitless market which Britain might exploit to her advantage'. (Interestingly, other than his spreading of the message that 'the decadent Empire could be given new life', according to Bailey's rendition, Urquhart's influence on the Tanzimat is to be seen almost wholly in economic terms.)[59]

There can be no doubt that Urquhart genuinely believed close economic relations with the Ottoman empire would strengthen Turkey. Little twenty-first century hindsight is needed, however, to see the reduction of the Ottoman domains to the status of cash crop and raw material producers for the sophisticated European market. (When in 1849-51 Urquhart visited the Lebanon, he was told: 'Formerly, we sold our tobacco and silk and made our clothes. Now we buy everything but abbas [cloaks], and you no longer take our produce'. His reply was 'we never took' their goods and he blamed the Ottoman government for its greed in raising duties. Nevertheless, he reported the popular belief that 'England had cheated the Sultan. England is now a dark cloud overhanging the Lebanon, oppressing it with spinning-jennies, treaties, intrigues and bewilderment'.)[60] Between, on the one hand, Urquhart's promotion of the virtues of Ottoman municipal organization and domestic industry, and his belief in the benefits of unlimited British access to Ottoman markets, lies an un-vocalised aporia. Such an arrangement could only stoke the European influence over the Orient he so persistently condemned. But being Urquhart, he seems not to have noticed this.[61]

Intervention, Treachery and Betrayal

The power of England [...] does not reside in her bayonets [...] it resides in the
confidence which men have placed in her firmness and integrity [...] When she
proclaims herself the lover of peace at the expense of honour, when she asserts
herself the friend of the powerful and the ally of the aggressor, she ceases to have a
situation among mankind [...] because her character has sunk.
Urquhart, quoted in Robinson, *David Urquhart*, p. 62.

Urquhart continued to argue for Turkey's strength – especially her military
capability – up to and after the Crimean War. Besides his call for a restoration
of the ancient rule of oriental societies (which Kedourie believed was the
chief legacy of the 'School of Urquhart'), the second principle Urquhart
passed on to an anti-imperialist, counter-Orientalist tendency was the accusation of betrayal levelled against British foreign policy in the East. At the
subliminal level such a charge may compensate for the invocation of British
support in the first place. Even if (as we saw) Urquhart did not face up to this,
given the criticism he made of European interference of any kind in oriental
affairs, it was always logical that British involvement would yield results that
were less than ideal. His high point of influence had passed by the close of
the 1830s. But for the next two decades he continued to give voice to the
'well-worn theme of overseas intervention, imperialism and corruption'. The
formula, argues Miles Taylor, originated in the atmosphere of radical opposition to the Whig governments of the 1830s.[62] In one of his main anti-
governmental planks of the 1840s and 50s – the repudiation of secret
diplomacy – Urquhart was (like Blunt) at least partially guilty himself. When
the power and influence to indulge in this activity had been his – as during
his period as secretary to the Istanbul embassy – he was only too happy to be
involved in intrigue. Now he no longer held an official position, he switched
his address from government circles to public opinion, honing his message to
two elements – condemnation of British policy toward Turkey, and the indictment of Palmerston. He 'launched his campaign in 1838-39 with a blizzard of
pamphlets, books, and letters to editors on policy in the East.'[63] In a letter to
The Times Urquhart claimed the credit for the Anglo-Turkish trade agreement, which he had indeed helped to draft in its earlier stages. Where, in its
provision for higher import duties, it diverged from his original draft, he now
attacked it for 'the frustration of every object that had originally been contemplated'. At the same time, his free trade axioms made him a welcome
speaker to commercial groups all over the country. In Parliament, Stratford
Canning, Peel and Stanley backed his attacks on Palmerston. Urquhart was
now at the peak of his influence with the press and the radicals. But in the
'forties a new note appeared in the charges he made against Palmerston,
whom Urquhart now accused of treason, collusion with Russia, and being a
paid agent of the Czar.[64]

The Muhammad Ali crisis of 1840-41, in which Britain joined with
Russia, Austria and Prussia to sign the Four Powers convention against

France's support of the Egyptian pasha, gave evidence to Urquhart of Palmerston's treacherous collusion with Russia. The affair was to be the occasion of Urquhart's first political drubbing. He had been making contacts with some Chartists with the aim of convincing them that working people's ills stemmed entirely from their government's foreign policy. He began to form groups, known as foreign affairs committees or Committees for the Investigation of Diplomatic Documents. A delegation was sent to Paris in the autumn of 1840 to show popular support for the breached Anglo-French alliance. The event proved a fiasco as the French Government had eventually 'acquiesced in the great power settlement and Urquhart coldly abandoned the foreign policy committees, in some cases leaving paid missionaries stranded in distress.'[65] He now dug himself into a trench vis-à-vis British policy in the East. Acerbic assaults from his pen followed over the Opium Wars in China and the Afghan War, the latter prompting him to compare English activities in Asia with those of Genghis Khan.[66] Along with his Turcophile principles went an obsessive suspicion of Russia that made him 'a fanatical Russophobe propagandist of European significance'.[67] British foreign and military policy was as wrong when it developed a forward stance in India or Afghanistan as when it worked in tandem with Russia over Muhammad Ali. In each instance Britain was merely reacting to Russia: removing Indian princes and breaking treaties in India, drawing British forces into war to protect Afghanistan against a Persia goaded on by Russia, and joining with Russia against the French.

> The English Government at once displays the utmost anxiety to advance the designs of Russia, and the utmost abhorrence of whoever could be associated with Russia, overstepping all limits of law, right, constitutional check and prudence, first to confer on Russia the power and influence of her co-operation, and then to destroy those who in morbid fear she falsely assumes to be friends of Russia.[68]

These evils found their personification in Palmerston, who in 1840, in a letter to Prime Minister Lord Melbourne, Urquhart accused of High Treason. In 1843 he revived the *Portfolio* to pursue this line, but Urquhart was in an even better position to censure the Foreign Secretary when he entered parliament as member for Stafford in 1847. Here he continued to argue for Palmerston's impeachment, but got his ally Anstey to propose the motion in parliament the following year. In the event, the debate passed off like a damp squib. *The Times* dismissed the treason charge as 'too monstrous, too incredible, too unworthy to answer'. In fact, 'Urquhart's accusations were so absurd that they did little to injure Palmerston, even though some of them were repeated by no less a figure than Karl Marx.'[69] Urquhart's son noted:

> To Urquhart, Palmerston was the representative of the great Adversary, of that immoral principle in the affairs of nations which he identified with Russia; and he was prepared to prove that in spite of the appearances of hostility Palmerston's policy had always in the long run been to the advantage of Russia [...] [But] it is a long step from failure, and even injustice, to treason.[70]

In the early 1850s, events in the East drew Urquhart once more into the
public limelight. He toured the country addressing meetings and re-forming
the foreign policy committees. His message approached the issues surrounding the Crimean War in a characteristically idiosyncratic way. In the summer
of 1853, he published a book entitled, *The Progress of Russia in the West,
North and South*, in which he had predicted there would never be a conflict
between Britain and Russia. At the meetings he addressed he spoke of the
evil of secret diplomacy, and also made clear he regarded most European
republicans and nationalists (including Mazzini) as spies in the pay of Russia.
As for Britain's declaration of war against Russia in 1854, that was totally
spurious. He criticised British policy for preparing the way for a partition of
Turkey by secret diplomacy, and he regarded the Crimean War as a sham to
effect partition. The blundering war effort was condemned as predetermined
treachery, in effect, accusing not merely Palmerston, but the whole cabinet of
treason.

In spite of this extreme position, Urquhart's expertise in eastern affairs
was sought after, even as his conclusions were vigorously challenged in the
radical press. Still, he was able to ventilate his opinions uncontested in the
Free Press, the paper of the foreign policy committees that Urquhart started
in 1855. Indeed, his influence over the working class members of the foreign
affairs committees has remained a conundrum. During the Crimean War the
government was certainly deeply unpopular due to its shambolic handling of
the military campaign. But while Urquhart's demand for the impeachment of
ministers may have pleased radicals, his dismissal of the European exiles as
Russian stooges certainly had the opposite effect.

Arguing that Urquhart's most successful year was 1857-58, not 1854-55,
Miles Taylor states that part of his appeal at that moment resided in well-
worn theme of overseas intervention, imperialism and corruption. 'For once
[this] made perfect sense in the light of the English bombardment of the
Chinese port of Canton and in the aftermath of the Indian mutiny [...] Since
the Afghan war of 1842 he had been warning that the source of the decline of
the English polity lay in military conquest in the Indian sub-continent. In
1857-58, however, this was no longer the prophecy of an isolated radical.'[71]
According to Taylor, the cause of the eventual of eclipse of Urquhart's influence over the radicals, fitful and uneven as it had been after the 1830s, was
that a message that chimed in so well with the non-interventionism of the
Mid-Victorian period had by the 1860s been subsumed within the new
Liberal party. Urquhart's political relevance was effectively over by the end
of the 1850s, although the foreign policy committees continued, and Urquhart's supporters engaged in the Governor Eyre case of 1865 on the side of
the Jamaican negroes. Failing health saw Urquhart retire to continental
Europe for his last decade or so of life. His last crusade was to see him
embrace the idea that Roman Catholic canon law might help bring about 'a
single morality to individuals as nations'.[72]

Urquhart had spent the period 1849-51 in the Turkish empire, for the most part in Mount Lebanon. There he engaged in agitation against the Anglo-French arrangement whereby power was devolved to a Turkish governor and two deputies appointed from each of the warring Druze and Maronite communities. Uniting with a Turkish faction within the country, Urquhart tried to organise Druze and Maronites to support direct rule by the Turks. By encouraging the merchants of Beirut to present a petition to the Porte for a reduction in duties, Urquhart also alienated the Turks and had to leave the country under a cloud.[73] However, the journey through Lebanon represents more than a further instance of Urquhart's quixotic meddling in the cause of an arcane and discredited principle. The historical survey in *Lebanon: A History and A Diary* (1860) argues that the Druze and Maronites had originally been one people, and that they had maintained a *modus vivendi* in the Mountain under a neutral Muslim emir until the interference of the European Powers. Britain and France's meddling in their affairs began with Napoleon's invasion of Egypt in 1798. France subsequently gave tacit support to the invasion of Syria by Muhammad Ali's son Ibrahim (an action which Palmerston opposed). This rivalry brought about 'wars of extermination' in the Lebanon, with France supporting the Maronites and Britain the Druze. In addition, the country had to suffer the imposition of 'prohibitive duties on its own exports by the Turkish government in a Treaty forced on her by England'. At the root of the problem was Russia, whose policy it was to drive a wedge between Britain and France so as to use it as a pretext to 'descend on the Bosporus'.[74]

Lebanon is impressive not because of its further exposition of Urquhart's Russophobia; instead it presents a unique exposé of western political interference in the East and in so doing reverses his earlier idea of British patronage of Ottoman Turkey. The pedagogic note may be overt, but there is also – for Urquhart – a new satirical tone that, however impractical turning the clock back and freeing the Lebanon from European control might have been, still contests the moral pretensions of intervention in eastern affairs, and calls into question the benefits to its non-Muslim citizens of a carve-up of Ottoman domains by the European Powers.

The situation that most excited Urquhart's ire was the role being played in Lebanon by the British consuls in Beirut and Damascus – '"General Rose" and "General Wood" – the forms under which these were known'.[75] He was himself mistaken for some kind of representative of the British government, and on more than one occasion asked 'when will you come to take possession of this country?' Frequently it was necessary to disabuse his listeners of their wildly inaccurate assumptions. To a Christian audience in Tripoli his riposte was: 'What kind of subjects should we find in traitors?'[76] As for the Christian emir who acted as the deputy for the Maronites: 'I freed him at once from all embarrassment, by telling him that I was not only no agent of the English government, but that I deplored its measures and did what I could to oppose them.' For the Maronites in particular Urquhart could find little affinity,

except when he found the Christian emir's children spoke fluent Turkish and
were dressed 'exactly like the children of the Sultan'.[77] The irony was not lost
on him when he saw Christians wearing the garb of Muslims, when Muslims
were 'abandoning these things to become like Christians'. Of his first visit to
a Maronite monastery Urquhart writes: 'I found this one, politically and relig-
iously, a nullity'.[78] Later he discovered why the Christians of Tripoli had
treated him in such an inhospitable and sullen manner: they had taken him for
a Protestant. The Catholic Maronites had reason to be hostile towards this
sect of their fellow Christians. The Protestants were most frequently American missionaries who, aware their cause was hopeless among the Muslims,
directed their energies toward converting the native Christians, with the result
that in one locality they had been driven out. For Urquhart the Americans'
activities were further proof of the venal motives behind western meddling:
the missionaries needed to get flocks somehow in order to justify the remit-
tances from home that supported their pleasant lifestyle. Urquhart was convinced that the division of Lebanon and Syria along confessional lines
according to the sponsorship of Britain, France and Russia brought 'no
benefit to any', but rather encouraged Christian and Druze laziness and declining industry: 'they [the Druze] all represented their political condition as
improved, and their material state as deteriorated'. The Christians made
demands of reparation against the Turkish pashas where before they would
have 'submitted in silence'.[79] But he reserved his most acerbic sentence for
the pretension of his own country, making play with the notion of European
consular influence by reversing its application to the British empire:

> Ireland may any day be converted into a Lebanon, if you will, only get two
> politico-religious Consuls at Dublin, Limerick, or Cork, or at all three. What a
> precious life of it the Lord Lieutenant would have! Imagine the delightful Blue
> Books to be published at Berlin and Vienna [...]

> If the Turkish Government was fit to understand a joke, would it not announce to
> the French Government the necessity under which it was placed, of sending
> Consuls for the protection of its co-religionaries to Algiers; and to the English
> Government, the same necessity for the appointment of Consular Agents at
> Hyderabad and Delhi?[80]

To cap it all, Urquhart could quote a dispatch by Lord Stratford de Radcliffe
threatening Turkey with implied British pressure on the Muslims of India
unless the Porte yielded to certain demands of intervention in its internal
affairs.[81]

    The arraignment of Britain in *Lebanon* for interfering in what remained
an area of the East under Ottoman suzerainty should probably not be considered a point of departure or even a destination in Urquhart's thought. After
all, the 'well-worn theme of overseas intervention, imperialism and corruption' continued to be Urquhart's trademark from the moment he was severed
from Palmerston and the Whigs in 1837. In a sense, at the same time as
Urquhart launched on his salient statement of oriental authenticity in *Spirit of
the East*, he had already composed his narrative of England's betrayal of

eastern culture. In a key passage in that text he laid down the philosophical terms of his alienation from his own nation. Typically, at the heart of this formulation was embedded a moral crux: England had achieved 'an importance in Europe wholly disproportionate to her power, *in consequence of her national justice*' (italics my emphasis). It was her moral destiny to be the power that prevented aggression and maintained the peace, 'seeking herself for no accession of territory, she must endeavour to prevent such attempts on the part of others, and thus she becomes the champion of international right.' England's policy of ensuring no power was able to subject 'Europe to a single despotism' made her a disinterested force upholding the equilibrium, cured as she was from 'the rage of conquest'. But the seeds of the destruction of that position had been sown in the eighteenth century, under the kind of epistemic shift Foucault conceived of as bringing into being the new technologies of power embodied within the European state. Accordingly, Urquhart accuses the western governments of becoming daily 'more involved in regulations, subdivided into departments, and buried under details'. The resultant 'confusion of mind' leading to 'error in action' accompanied a 'gradual centralization of power' that 'paralysed the executive by excess of burden'. Local autonomy decreased, and with the breakdown of the organic links that held communities together nations 'ceased to act and feel as moral unities'. Then the old 'fanaticism of religious intolerance was transferred to politics' resulting in the nations rushing to bloody encounter over, Urquhart implies, mere cosmetic differences in their social systems.[82]

The very forces that fuelled her expansion were responsible for Britain's apostasy from her almost providential role as disinterested arbiter of power. But though this seemed to be an ineluctable process, Urquhart the pedagogue and moralist obfuscates the logic of his own argument by charging Russia with having suborned the British government. Everywhere he travelled in the East, Britain's role as protector seemed to be understood. The power of England, this led him to believe, was not located in its military force, 'but [in] the veneration with which her name is pronounced in the Atlas, on the glaciers of the Alps, on the heights of Pindus, and in the vales of the Caucasus, on the plains of Poland, and the steppes of Astrakhan.'[83] In Morocco he was told, 'we have God in Heaven, and only England on earth'.[84] Turks and Greeks continually impressed upon him: '*If we could but enlighten England*, we would be safe'.[85] England, the lone power for good in the dispensation of nations, had sold its soul to Russia's Satan; the whole Urquartian system thus reduces itself to a Manichean equation.

There is, however, one curious incident reported in *Spirit of the East* that closes the gap between Urquhart the anti-imperialist free trader, and the sort of quasi-messianic imperialism that we might encounter in Lord Cromer or Alfred Milner. This story in fact suggests – something we perhaps should not find surprising – that Urquhart was not without personal imperial longings himself. In the mountains bordering Albania and Greece, freshly briefed about a traveller who had been captured and mutilated by *klephti*

(Greek bandits), Urquhart is himself seized by a robber gang. Fully expecting to be sent back 'without nose, lips or ears', and especially fearing the one Albanian in the group who has a particularly threatening manner, the Briton faces down his captors by his cool mien of authority. Won over, the men beseech Urquhart to lead them against the Turks!

> I felt that a soldier of daring, and a man of energy, might have changed the face of the East, if philosopher enough to ascend to the sources of the distinct currents of opinion from the East and the West, then meeting and struggling on this arena. I was convinced, also, that the name of Englishman alone might instantaneously have given importance to such a gathering, and led to rally round it sections, interests, and races, which scarcely any other watchword would call together.[86]

Urquhart's meditations on the affair certainly articulate his always barely concealed self-conceit and messianic pretensions. In addition, they signpost a proto-imperialist discourse which, we might say, was always embedded in notions of British patronage over the Ottoman empire.

Patron or Successor? Britain, Turkey and Islam in the writing of W.G. Palgrave

> The sword of Islam, though rusted, has not yet lost its virtue
> Palgrave, *Essays on Eastern Questions*, p. 29.

Urquhart was not alone in arguing for the patronage of Muslim nations by Britain, nor in expressing conviction in both the resource of the Islamic religion and the intent of Muslim peoples to survive the changes brought about in the world by western pre-eminence. Another traveller switched his ideas on eastern affairs and came out in favour of the power and durability of Islam over the peoples of the East. There can have been few more *political* travellers during the nineteenth century than Gifford Palgrave. As a secret emissary of Napoleon III bent on spying out the hitherto uncharted territory of central and eastern Arabia he gained his reputation as an authority on the Arabs, especially the Wahhabis, whose territories in eastern Arabia he was among the first European travellers to penetrate. It is this area of his writing that has generated most interest up till now. Half-Jewish through his father, and conventionally Anglican by upbringing, Palgrave shocked his family by turning Jesuit while embarked upon his first career in the Indian army.[87] After returning from Arabia, he rejected Catholicism, but Blunt later learnt from Francis Palgrave that his brother had returned to the bosom of that church near the end of his life: 'he was anxious I should believe Gifford was never really, or ostensibly a Moslem'.[88] As this statement suggests, the question of Muslim influence on Palgrave was equivocal. In his writing the Arabian explorer was unclear about the extent of his connection with Islam during his journeys which were mostly conducted in disguise.

On the other hand, the pull of the East resulted in Palgrave's late identification with Shintoism, which Francis accounted for in terms of his brother's predilection for 'things often unknown and inexplicable to Western civilisation'.[89] Polemical and overtly antagonistic to Islam during his Jesuit period, later, as British consul in Soukhoum Kale in Russian Abkhazia and the Ottoman territory of Trebizond on the Black Sea, Palgrave's encounters with rank-and-file Turks resulted in a mostly unremarked volte-face.[90] Now he wrote of the scope of the force of Islam as a perennial code of belief rather than a political system. He argued for the appropriacy of Muslim filiation to Britain's empire in the East in the event of continued Ottoman decline: an adventitious policy that would later appeal to other Turcophiles when it became clear Britain would no longer support the territorial integrity of an apparently fatally beleaguered Ottoman state.

The greatest source of disappointment in Palgrave's life must have been the failure of his government to recognise and utilise his expertise in eastern affairs by appointing him to one of the consular positions he most craved: Istanbul or Cairo. In 1882, he wrote a long, opportunist letter to Gladstone, proffering his personal 'admiration and gratitude' for the Prime Minister's Levantine policy, and arguing for British action in Egypt independently of France by 'a detailed account of his experience and knowledge of Egypt since 1861'.[91] At the end of his life, he wrote from Montevideo:

> although Lord Salisbury or anyone else is quite indifferent to me: nor have I now any patron or well-wisher among the 'heads' that I know of, still there is at least a possibility of a better post and a less meagre salary; and while that is the case, one would not willingly throw up the game.[92]

Most probably Palgrave's hopes had been damaged irreparably by his connection with the Jesuits, and with France, Britain's traditional rival in the Levant. Obsequious as was the letter he wrote to Gladstone, the Grand Old Man's confidence in his correspondent's loyalty could hardly have been enhanced by his declaration that he had once plotted to replace the Khedive Ismail by another of Muhammad Ali's progeny, Prince Halim, as a vassal of the French in their take over of Syria. Palgrave's cosmopolitan leanings and fluid religious affiliations brought twists and turns in his political and religious allegiances. In the words of one commentator, his 'perception of his own national identity was flawed' and this may have helped turn him into the lone-seeker who attracted the unwelcome reputation of being a betrayer of his country.[93]

When it came to the issue of patronage of the East – which race had performed the most illustriously in history, which possessed the potential for revival and was the more worthy of nurture and respect – Palgrave's inconsistencies were perhaps commensurate with his own shifting ideas and predilections. The subject of, *A Narrative of a Year's Journey in Central and Eastern Arabia* (1865), is of course the Arabs. But as previous commentators on Palgrave like Tidrick have shown, there were favoured Arabs, and Arabs such as the *bedu* who were no better than that desert beast of burden the camel. For Palgrave the Jesuit, the matter of race predominated over that of religion, and where it came to articulating the role of Islam in the life and culture of the Arabs religion was precisely the value he desired to factor out. Palgrave knew there was no hope in converting the Arabs of the peninsula to Christianity, in spite of the hyperbole he had indulged in when in Syria about his own plans for mass conversation. The text in question excoriates the fanaticism of the Wahhabis, but praises the 'master mind' of Muhammad for his achievement of establishing his ascendancy over the entire peninsula, only to condemn:

> the deadening fatalism of his religious system, that narcotic of the human mind [that] stopped for ever the very progress to which he had himself half opened the way by his momentary fusion of Arabia into a common nation with a common aim.[94]

Such dichotomising of race and religion is apparent in Palgrave's accentuation of the laxity of Muslim belief in areas of Arabia outside the net of Wahhabi Najd. It is stretched to unlikely lengths in his assertion that the Omanis were set apart from 'the troublous Mahometan world, abolishing alike the pilgrimage of Mecca and the law of the Coran [...] at liberty to follow what form of government and of religion pleased them best.' When Palgrave argues that the Arabs are by nature 'endowed with a remarkable aptitude' for 'progress in practical and material science', it is to re-assert his point that this would be possible only 'when the Coran and Mecca shall have disappeared from Arabia'.[95] Although this message doubtless sprang from his Jesuit indoctrination, there is a clear contrast between it, and the articles he was writing for *Fraser's* and *Macmillan's* magazines barely five years after the composition of *Central and Eastern Arabia*.

The pieces that form the collection, *Essays on Eastern Questions* (1872), have several contexts worth situating, each of which should be seen as a further facet of Palgrave's urge to achieve recognition. The products of their author's protracted stays in the East as a representative of the British government, the essays seek to build on the eastern expertise of Palgrave the oriental traveller, at the same time as they represent an important point of departure. Like his Arabian travelogue they propose explanations of un-known, if less spectacularly unfamiliar terrains – the mainly non-Arab domains of Asiatic Turkey. However, this time there is a new framing. The generalised western perspective applied to *Central and Eastern Arabia* is replaced by a focus in which the culture and politics of these Turkish or Turkic societies is aligned with British imperial interests. If the earlier text concentrated on the isolated Arab heartlands' resource and potential *pour se civiliser*, the essays project an already established polity, in which an Islamic faith, far from being debilitating as it was in the Arabian context, becomes the approved central weave. Such a change in perspective is not to be explained merely in terms of difference of subject. To account for it we must look at the situation in which Palgrave found himself.

First of all, he needed to supplement his meagre consul's income, in order to marry and raise a family. To achieve this, his best bet was to utilise the profile won him by the publication of *Central and Eastern Arabia* and write for serious but well-read periodicals. But to whom, other than an immediate readership, should his report be addressed now that he had foresworn his priest's weeds? Whether or not he had ever personally entertained an anti-Islamic prejudice, this was no longer de rigueur. For a knowledgeable British diplomat functioning out of the Ottoman empire, this might even be considered otiose. As the imperial power in India Britain was a Muslim power of sorts. A decade after the Mutiny and the abolition of the East India Company, from a governmental point of view the British occupation of India was becoming more serious and regularised.

In 1866, one year after his publicised recantation of Catholicism, Palgrave presented to the British Association a paper entitled 'North and South Arabia'. Significantly, he concluded his observations 'on a political note, saying the Wahhabee country could never be of practical importance to the English nation, surrounded as it was by desert, but that Oman, a rich and beautiful region similar to the district of Bombay, would soon become important both politically and commercially.'[96] The linkage of Arabia with India was perhaps an afterthought, but it indicated a new direction, albeit one that ultimately proved futile for Palgrave's desired career orientation. His absorption in the task of explicating eastern, predominantly Islamic subjects within an imperial frame to an educated English readership became a prolonged exercise to identify himself with a stable sponsor in whose interests he might inscribe the kind of reports that would bring him acclaim, and which might be constructed out of a deep personal engagement right up to the time of his death. It was out of this context that the eastern essays were composed.

This is not to assume that the transformation of Palgrave's view of Islam and its prophet was entirely opportunistic. The new positive estimate given to Islam did indeed coincide with some astute political judgement preparatory to future substitution of British over Ottoman governance of Muslim peoples. But Palgrave shows he is under no illusions that brotherliness rather than mutual self-interest actuated current amity between Britain and Turkey. And in his concession of limitations to the scope of European pre-eminence vis-à-vis the *dar al-Islam*, we see the kind of personal predilections already noted as characteristic of Palgrave's own spirit of search. What is produced is in fact a discourse poised between an Orientalist prospecting for weakness and potential imperial expansion, and affirmation of the authenticity and strength of traditional Islamic structures.

These are weighed against the westernising agency of the Tanzimat and the class it had thrown up. Here Palgrave comes close to articulating the resurgence of a Muslim spirit as a reaction to western penetration of Ottoman society. ('The Westerly breeze that for some years past, sweeping over the

Bosphorus and the Aegean, is now awakening a yet stronger counterblast of Easterly antagonism.')[97] Urquhartian themes raise their heads again: the Ottoman army is praised for its strength and its incorporation of the perennial Muslim virtues. No alcohol is consumed here as it is by the westernised Effendi class: 'it is when enrolled in the ranks of the army that the Muslim thoroughly feels himself a Muslim, and acts accordingly.'[98] In contrast, Tanzimat reforms in the countryside impact on the strength of Muslim consciousness, weakening and abasing the old landowning class, as they nominally handed the land over to the peasants. But in reality the latter were saddled with crushing tax burdens. The two core classes of the Ottoman polity were alienated from the new measures: 'in their minds [...] the present Government, the whole Stambool Effendee clique, with their reforms, loans, French civilisation, centralisation, and novel taxes, are no better than traitors to the Empire and to Islam.' Although the Tanzimat had 'levelled in the dust the old aristocracy', the conservative spirit of peasant and noble lived on. The unsettling of the old balance between Muslim and *raya* elicited the former's foreboding: 'day by day they [the Christians] rise above us'.[99]

Palgrave's ideas on Islam had now undergone a remarkable turn about. Where the Jesuit had berated the fanaticism of the Wahhabi and predicted advancement for the Arab only after he had thrown off the yoke of Islam, the sympathetic consul shifted the blame for Muslim 'fanaticism' back upon the westerner. Outbreaks of violence and fanaticism, having national or political issues at their root, were 'nowise of a religious character'. These were frequently triggered by 'foreign usages ostentatiously paraded [such as displays of drunkenness or unveiling] in contravention to what the "natives" consider as conventional decorum or morality.'[100] The sickness of the Ottoman empire, Palgrave goes so far as to say, was not the fault of Islam, which showed 'very few symptoms of sickness, and none at all of decrepitude'. On the contrary, as encapsulated in the title he gave to an article he published in *Fraser's Magazine* in February 1872, there was taking place a 'Mahometan Revival'.

Strange to say, given the bias against it already noted in *Central and Eastern Arabia*, one of the sources of this renewal was the Wahhabi movement, which now emerges as a sort of Protestantism that 'both modified and purified the very system it condemns'.[101] Palgrave is able to descry a sea change in Islamic society as compared to between thirty and one hundred years ago. The features of this are succinctly outlined as: 1) a tendency to reaffirm an education based on Islam 2) a decline in the use of alcohol and improved observance of the Ramadan fast 3) a diminution in the number of Europeans employed in the military and public works departments 4) repair and new-building of 'mosques, colleges, schools and chapels' 5) increase in the number of pilgrims to Makkah, and 6) moves towards unity amongst Sunnis and Shi'a in face of the infidel. Such a combined alignment with respect to western intrusion indicated a dual response in which Muslims incorporated acceptance of European inventions but disdain for 'the woeful instability of modern European institutions'.[102] Coming as they do a mere four to five years before the politically-inspired reaction implemented by Abdul Hamid against the 1876 constitution, and the abortion of the Tanzimat project of more than forty years duration, Palgrave's observations represent a reading of the signs of the times which might be characterised, depending on one's point of view, as either prescient or perfunctory.

Britain had to recognise that Anglo-Turkish friendship was an alliance of convenience that meant she stood further off from the enemies of Islam rather than in close relationship of brotherhood with the Turks. Nevertheless, the policy had a positive effect in making British India a *dar al-iman*, or territory in which the faithful might safely dwell 'in toleration, in justice, and truth'.[103] Commonality also existed in the need for firm treatment of fanaticism (by the sword). In Turkey's case the Wahhabis were the threat, in Britain's the extremists of the Indian North-West frontier. Where it was politic to conciliate disaffected traditional elements, both British and Ottoman imperial rulers could demonstrate a cognate readiness to trim sails.

Palgrave's articulation of a Muslim response to European imperialism is contextualised according to a proposed British strategy of containment of the Islamic revival within its own imperial domains. This does not hinder him though from hinting at eventual British absorption of further Ottoman territory such as Egypt. However, it could be argued that his enthusiasm for Britain's imperial mission, intersected as it was by his own desperate desire for career advancement, and his past record as a Jesuit working in the pay of France, has a hollow centre. Other pieces in *Essays on Eastern Questions* toy with British anxieties at the spreading Russian empire in Central Asia, and prognosticate on a rejuvenation of those Ottoman territories contiguous to Russia while 'the Turkish Empire slowly withers, as wither it eventually must, to the West'.[104] But no Curzonian grand strategy emerges. This, if we accept Tidrick's picture of 'the disappointed patriot who went to his grave convinced of his final unity with God', should perhaps not surprise us. 'Were it not for his hatred of the Moslem religion', she continues, 'he might have found in Arabia [...] the ideal community of which he dreamed'.[105] Alternatively, another identity, half-Muslim, half-European, could be excavated from Palgrave's many layered personality, caught between East and West like the eponymous hero of his 1872 novel, *Herman Agha*:

> The sun was warm as well as bright, I drew back from the heat of its rays into the shade accorded by the acacia on my right hand, seated myself comfortably with my back against the upper chamber wall, lighted a small travelling pipe which I usually carried about me, and felt, – for one who had so lately been a European and a Christian, – very Mahometan, Oriental, and imaginative.[106]

Conclusion

In discussing Urquhart and Palgrave's unstable discourses on the East, I have specifically foregrounded intersections of religion and nationality, and characterised the shifting Orientalism on which such discourse was founded by the use of the epithets 'empathetic', 'romantic', and 'counter-Orientalist,' which could be juxtaposed alongside and sometimes placed in opposition to much less well-disposed Orientalisms, such as the evangelical strain of Muir, and the imperialist one of Cromer which I intend to discuss in the next chapter.

In both Urquhart and Palgrave's writings, I have uncovered dissatisfaction with western influences on the East, at the same time as they promoted British protection of Muslims out of which an imperialist emphasis could easily emerge. As far as Urquhart and Palgrave's advocacy of Ottoman Turkey is concerned, it is perhaps necessary merely to confirm how this marched in tandem with an important, if hardly as enthusiastic, British establishment pro-Ottoman policy. Both travel writers endeavoured to input into that orientation their own ideological redactions of Turkish and Islamic authenticity and superiority. But only in Urquhart's case, and that for a limited period in the 1830s, was a public impact of sorts achieved. Urquhart's rapid fall from favour and brief revival during and immediately after the Crimean War emphasises the peripheral nature of enterprises founded on the celebration and defence of specific eastern causes. Not only did he trail the path for later campaigns of a similar character, but he also inscribed in advance the bitterness and failure such projects seemed fated to encounter.

Travellers' advocacy of political positions might coincide with political moments favourable to the cause, but 'committed' stances were doomed when the public mood changed or political exigency dictated other policies. Palgrave's alignments appear retrospectively too evanescent and founded in personal introversion to have been taken seriously. For his part, Urquhart may have started a 'school' and set a precedent for future narratives of betrayal, but his reading of imperialism was set in an early nineteenth century mould. This had lost its meaning by the time (1877) Salisbury 'concluded that it was no longer practicable to defend British interests by sustaining the Ottoman empire. A bankrupt Turkey was incapable of insulating Anglo-Russian hostility. The time had come for a more direct defence "by some territorial rearrangement".'[107] Such an alteration in official thinking was arguably of greater substance than a temporary diversion in foreign policy. It made Palmerston's eastern policy and the mundane encroachments in India look positively anaemic. Urquhart did not live to see the mother of Britain's betrayals – her discarding of an eastern policy (excluding India and Afghanistan) of non-intervention by the invasion of a nation embarked on one of the earliest experiments in eastern national self-determination. Palgrave did, and cravenly backed the occupation of Egypt, but the desperation of his personal situation perhaps made this forgivable.

3

W.S. Blunt:
From Oriental Traveller to
anti-imperialist Agitator

Trust not for freedom from the Frank.
Lord Byron

Of the nineteenth century oriental travellers and writers on British imperialism in the East, with the exception of Richard Burton, Wilfrid Scawen Blunt has probably received the most attention from scholars of the last twenty years. In line with my remarks in chapter 1, I shall argue that as regards the formation of his later political thought, recent treatment of Blunt has frequently over-emphasised his desert journeys of the late 1870s and his promotion of the Arab Bedouin and Arab cultural nationalism.[1] This emphasis has been responsible for short-changing his absorption within the project of Islamic modernism as set out by Jamal al-Din al-Afghani and Muhammad Abduh. It has also distorted his interest in the wider Islamic cause, that is to say, his concern for other Islamic nations and peoples beside the Bedouin of the Arabian peninsular. (Egypt, Blunt's longest-standing anti-colonial cause, remained on the periphery if not completely outside the discourse of Arab nationalism almost up to the end of the period under review.)

As a result of his championing of an Arabian caliphate, Blunt undoubtedly gained for himself a pro-Arab and anti-Turk reputation; his views on the dissolution of the Ottoman empire crystallised in the 1880s into a conviction that Turkey would never reform with Abdul Hamid at the helm. Nevertheless, he blamed Europe for intensifying the Sultan's intransigence and Islamic reaction, and saw the only hope for Turkey to be the re-instatement of the constitution of 1876 – the policy, as it transpired, of the Young Turks. By the first decade of the twentieth century Blunt was in agreement with E.G. Browne on the need for a wider Islamic front to defend the *umma* against European imperialism. However, since it was first hand contact with the affairs of Egypt that helped forge Blunt's radical anti-imperialism, this chapter is primarily concerned with that country, and more particularly, the debate he conducted with Lord Cromer. This articulates much of Blunt's key

writings on the Muslim world, setting them, in the form of Cromer's imperialist discourse, against the 'official' Orientalism of the time.

Blunt's attraction to the East probably began at no precise moment. His
visit to Istanbul with Lady Anne Blunt in 1873 is cited as his first eastern
journey, but he had already visited that city briefly thirteen years earlier
during his youthful career in the diplomatic service when he had become
acquainted with the aristocrat and convert to Islam, Lord Stanley of Alderley.
Some biographers see the collapse of Blunt's own Catholic faith during his
years in the diplomatic service as crucial for the eventual identification he
showed for the East.[2] For Ali Behdad, Blunt must be included among those
British Orientalists 'from Sir Richard Burton to T.E. Lawrence [who] were
driven by a positivistic urge to find an "elsewhere" still unexplored by previous travelers, a place where a traveler could still become a pioneer, a heroic
adventurer, and have an "authentic" experience of otherness.'[3]

In Blunt's case, however, the initial urge to experience otherness eventuated in a lifelong acculturation, domestication even, of the East, as seen in
his wearing of Arab robes on his English estate as well as during his annual
residence at his Egyptian property, Shaykh Obayd. It is true that Blunt's
journeys of the 1870s, in Turkey (1873), Algeria (1874), and Egypt (1875-76)
set up in his mind his first big idea about the Islamic Near East: a contrast
between miserable and ill-governed rural peasantries on the one hand, and
independent and noble Arab tribes of the desert on the other.[4] The peasants
suffered under diverse rulers, one of who was the Ottoman Sultan, but the
colonial French and the Egyptian Khedive Ismail also shared in the blame. In
1877-79, he and his wife, Lady Anne, undertook 'two vast [...] journeys such
as no European had undertaken before that time' across the deserts of north
and central Arabia.[5] The second published account of their travels, *A Pilgrimage to Nejd* (1881), featured a eulogy of the Arabian style of government they
had found at Hayil, and confirmed their enthusiasm for the Arabs.

Significantly, when considering the later direction his politics took,
Blunt at this period had ideas of connecting the attractive 'other' with the
British empire: after their first visit to Hayil in 1879, he and his wife toyed
with the idea of returning the next season to enlist Ibn Rashid in an alliance
with Britain. While at this point he was 'still a believer, though with failing
faith, in the sincerity of British Imperial protection' it was on their visit to
India, following on the journey to Hayil, that the foundations for Blunt's anti-
imperialism were laid.[6] By the close of 1881, he had addressed the Royal
Geographical Society, published an article on the Euphrates Railway, edited
and published his wife's two travelogues, *Bedouin Tribes of the Euphrates*
(1879) and *A Pilgrimage to Nejd*, and received visitors to his newly established Arabian stud at his Sussex estate. His 'growing repute as a traveller'
appeared secure.[7] Perhaps his vanity was flattered enough for him to be
convinced of his role as an emerging Orientalist and force of influence on
colonial policy. Yet within a year, in spite of the publication of *The Future of
Islam* (1882), which still conceived of the Muslim world as potentially

connected to Britain's imperial matrix, Blunt's course had been radically altered. The locus of this re-alignment was Egypt, and the cause a polarising disagreement with his own government over that country's independence.

Cromer: the authority to speak for Egypt

Absent though he was from Egypt during the events of 1881-82, the figure who for Blunt (and many others) came to epitomise the entire enterprise of British imperialism in that country was Evelyn Baring, later Lord Cromer. Baring's background perfectly fitted him within the world of 'gentlemanly capitalism' that, it has been argued, moved Britain's empire in the nineteenth century.[8] But his most recent biographer Roger Owen emphasises how character as well as family connection (he was cousin to the in-coming Viceroy Lord North-brook) helped Baring get his first important appointment in India in 1872. This Indian experience in turn enabled Baring to secure a post in Egypt in 1877 as a civil servant who had been attracted by 'the offer of important work […] on a salary of £3,000 a year [which] seemed almost too good to be true.'[9] He acquitted himself so well as one of the four European commissioners to the Public Debt run up by the Khedive Ismail that he was appointed the English half of the dual Anglo-French controller-general-ship in 1879. In 1883, after a three-year spell back in India, and one year after the British occupation, Baring was back again, this time as consul-general, a position he turned into that of virtual ruler of Egypt.

Having begun his career in the Royal Artillery, Baring made the transition to imperial administrator in spite of a lack in his formal education. Probably his key transition, however, was from that of self-proclaimed radical Liberal during his earlier empire service in Corfu (1858-64), Malta (1864-67), and India (1872-76), to comfortable collaborator with the Conservative Lord Salisbury and, eventually, as Lord Cromer, Edwardian imperial proconsul. Nevertheless, as Owen points out, throughout his career there remained a consistency in Cromer's modus operandi:

> It seems unlikely that, even in his radical days, Baring was ever a real democrat in the sense of believing that the election of representatives was the best way of finding out where a people's interests lay. What was needed instead was some other method by which the weight and privilege of the upper classes should be balanced against the needs of those further down the social scale [….] [This] could be the work of a small, disinterested, and, above all, intelligent cadre of selfless administrators, which was the Whig ideal. Transferred outwards to the Empire, he saw this same ideal as the model for imperial government from the 1870s onward.[10]

According to Owen, two 'themes' marked Cromer's later career in Egypt: recognition of the need 'to have the "permanent interests" of Egypt at heart'; and a personal battle between himself and the shadow of the Khedive Ismail in which the latter represented 'the prince of all evil'.[11]   These factors,

alongside Cromer's unstinting confidence in his own prowess as the intelligent selfless administrator par excellence, were, as we will see, built into
Cromer's major public statement on his rule in Egypt, the two volume
Modern Egypt, in which he claimed for himself a unique authority to speak
for Egypt.

In 1883 Baring carried over to Egypt from his stint in India a genuine
concern for the over-taxed peasantry, and an understanding of the need to
keep in advance of local public opinion as expressed in the vernacular press.
He came intent on 'leading the Egyptian people from bankruptcy to solvency
and then onward to affluence, from Khedivial monstrosities to British justice,
and from Oriental methods veneered with a spurious European civilization
towards the true civilization of the West based on the principles of the
Christian moral code.'[12] But if India had seen Baring at his most radical, this
was, according to Owen, 'a position from which he was to spend the next ten
years in slow retreat'.[13] Crucially, as a proven administrator with a proclaimed sympathy for the ordinary people over whom he would govern, he
brought to Egypt a specifically disparaging estimation of Muslim laws and
institutions. In a 'Memorandum on the Central Asian question' of 1877,
Baring valorised the Russian empire above the Ottoman. 'Russia is in a backward condition but I cannot but think that so much as the Bible teaches a
purer and more humanitarian religion than the Koran, by so much does
Russian civilization bear with it a potentiality for progress ... superior to any
that is possible under the effete and decaying laws and institutions of Ma-
homedanism.' In 1879, he expressed himself less sanguine about the
possibilities of Islamic reform than the then Foreign Minister, Lord Salisbury.[14]

Baring's approach to Egypt, not unsurprisingly, prioritised European
(and most desirably British) control over her disorderly and despotically administered affairs. Indeed, control is the master-code behind Cromer's argument in Modern Egypt, a text constructed with the hindsight provided by
more than a decade of British occupation. Cromer's task is to make what
looked at the time to many like a policy of drift that ended unwittingly with
Britain's sole occupation of the Nile valley, into a harmonisation of the key
players' interests – Britain's, France's, the Khedive's and the fellahin's.
Urabi – the effective head of the Egyptian revolution – is excluded as the
villain of the piece. Cromer's discourse shows a sliding of Egyptian interests
into European, and more specifically British interests. Referring to the period
when he was first engaged in Egypt as one of the European commissioners of
the Public Debt, Cromer envisages a unity of interest between the Egyptian
peasants and the European bondholders. 'Both were interested in being
relieved from a system of government which was ruinous to the interests of
one class and in the highest degree oppressive to the other.'[15] This making of
common cause between the European moneylenders and the lowest strata of
Egyptian society which was being fleeced to pay them their interest, is
projected in the cause of the struggle against oriental despotism. 'It was not

attachment to the interests of the bondholders, but compassion for the down-trodden people of the Nile valley, that led him to give his life to Egypt.'[16] Sole responsibility for Egypt's woes is made to rest with Ismail, thereby highlighting Europe's mission to reform the corrupt system of oriental government. After Ismail was deposed in 1879, the two new Anglo-French controllers-general, de Blignières and Baring, acted behind the scenes 'to carry out the "delicate task" of "controlling, guiding and invigorating" without appearing to govern.'[17]   In his memoranda of the period, Baring adopted the same tone as he would in 1896, when he wrote the first draft of Modern Egypt. His 'language describing what he calls the "spirit of the Control system" is that of a member of a self-confident administrative elite [...] of Plato's Guardians [...]'[18] Within four years of his return to Egypt then, Baring had transformed his assessment of the conditions over which he presided. The temporary occupation he had envisaged in 1883, particularly after the Drummond-Woolf convention had failed to secure international agreement on Egypt's security, now had the makings of a long-term one. Baring had begun the process of establishing himself as the sole arbiter of that country's affairs, functioning as the enlightened bureaucrat whose authority derived from his superior knowledge and western culture, and his self-proclaimed custodian-ship of the interests of the Egyptian people.

Blunt: Egypt as a subject of political discourse

He was constitutionally unfitted to write contemporary history. His discretion is questionable. His judgement superficial: he records gossip as fact, and allows prejudice to colour his narration.
DNB, 'Blunt, Wilfrid Scawen'

Blunt, as we saw, visited Egypt for the first time in 1875-76 as a man of independent means with an interest in travel in the Middle East. A second extended stay in Egypt followed in 1880-81. Wishing to study Arabic and the culture and politics of Islam, he journeyed on to Jeddah and Syria. On his return to Egypt at the end of 1881, he found the Urabi revolution in full swing, and was quickly drawn in. Returning to London in the spring of the next year, he engaged in further agitation in its support, but after the defeat of the Egyptians at Tel al-Kabir in the September, and his active prosecution of the Egyptian leader's defence, Blunt was for several years persona non grata in Egypt. From 1887 to 1905, he took up annual winter residence at Shaykh Obayd, a property that he had purchased outside Cairo during his second visit in 1881.

According to Kathryn Tidrick, 'the great irony of Blunt's career was that when he finally saw political action it was on behalf of a man who was very far from being a "real Arabian".'[19] But Blunt's support for Urabi, the Egyptian colonel of peasant (*fellah*) origin who led the national movement, was not an oversight caused by his ignorance of race. As the long preamble to the *Secret History* reveals, Blunt had been filling himself in with respect to the Arab and Islamic scene prior to his involvement in the events of 1881-82. His collaboration with the Egyptian Islamic reformer, Shaykh Muhammad Abduh, and through him his conversance with the Iranian agitator and Muslim thinker, Jamal al-Din al-Afghani, resulted in the publication in 1882 of *The Future of Islam*, a piece of writing that credits Islam as a living reality with serious political implications for the British empire, rather than the moribund religion portrayed by the European Orientalists. It is significant that at the point at which he first engaged with the Egyptian national movement, Blunt was the advocate of a transfer of the caliphate from Ottoman Turkey to an Arab centre such as Mecca or Cairo, and that he believed the issue was serious enough for a representation to be made to Prime Minister Gladstone on its behalf. 'England [...] in dealing with Islam [should not ally herself] with what may be called the Crusading States of Europe'. Whether she liked it or not, 'Mohammedanism is not merely an opinion; a certain political organization is a condition of its existence, and a certain geographical latitude [...] it is a force which cannot remain neutral – which will be either a friend or a foe.'[20]

Employed in the diplomatic service for eleven years, and with connections by birth and marriage to the highest circles, Blunt began by using his knowledge and interest in Islamic affairs to endeavour to reconcile the nationalist forces and Great Britain's representatives in Egypt. He acted as go-between between the British Agency (his former associate in the diplomatic corps, Edward Malet, was consul-general) and leading Azhar clerics and liberal-constitutional politicians in the national movement. In spite of one modest success over a military issue the mediation was short-lived.

Blunt's enthusiasm for the Egyptians alienated the cautious Malet, upset by his publication of a manifesto of the nationalist cause in *The Times*. Blunt 'had appealed as it were over the head of the Foreign Office and his own to the Press'.[21] With the British controller of finance, Auckland Colvin, Blunt's own distaste for the political complexion of the behind-the-scenes manipulation of the Khedive, and the advice and information being sent to England (Colvin doubled as correspondent for the influential *Pall Mall Gazette* read by Gladstone) resulted in embittered separation. (Blunt's criticism of Colvin's methods obfuscates the fact that he was prepared to adopt similar tactics himself – indeed, the *Secret History* scarcely attempts to make a case against the secret diplomacy and old-boy network by which government – and foreign policy in particular – worked. Blunt always remained an unreconstructed advocate of aristocracy). The resulting polarisation (characteristically personalised by Blunt – Egypt 'had become a trial of strength between us') threw Blunt into the arms of the nationalists and turned him into the *enfant terrible* of Cairo and London society.[22]

Thereafter, Blunt competed with Malet and Colvin for the ear of London – especially that of the Press and Gladstone. When he realised the inequality of the competition (together Colvin and Malet had control over the telegraph as well as Foreign Office dispatches), Blunt returned to England to fight the nationalist corner there. His involvement with Egypt therefore developed specifically out of his interest in Islamic political discourse. On his arrival there in 1881 he was quicker and better prepared than most other Europeans to place the Urabi movement within the broader sweep of Islamic politics. Instead of dismissing it as an inconvenient and potentially dangerous army mutiny as would Cromer, Blunt was sympathetically disposed to the religious and political ideas that cohered around it. In committing himself to the Urabist cause, Blunt brought a discourse already settled on the ripeness of the Islamic (especially the Arabic-speaking) world for reformation and political renewal. Within a short period he had convinced the Egyptians of the usefulness of making a statement of their beliefs and objectives that could be presented in Europe. He also set about representing the case for Egypt's national self-determination to key figures in England, most notably Gladstone, with whom he had a long initially encouraging interview, and to whom he addressed lengthy letters on the situation in Egypt.

Two Narratives of Progress and Reform

1. From Liberalism to Imperialism

They assumed to teach the East the goodly ways of the West, and their pupils, they hoped, would be convinced of the excellence of these ways and be eager to learn and follow them.
Kedourie, *England and the Middle East*, p. 25.

Cromer's narrative in *Modern Egypt* is unified by a logocentrism that underwrites the imperial destiny of Great Britain – and of Lord Cromer. His method claims the virtues of authoritative history: his sources are the official diplomatic ones as present in the Foreign Office archive and related by the British figures who played a leading part in Egypt. The words 'accurate', 'accuracy', inaccuracy', and 'inaccuracies' occur in total seven times in the opening three pages, while 'administrative', 'administered', and 'administration' number together six entries from pages four to six. These terms foreground the kind of authority Cromer claims for himself in *Modern Egypt*. Within a discourse that marks professionalism and bureaucratic efficiency and control, the binary opposites are amateurism and the 'half-truths' that become 'fiction' and 'myths'. Blunt is slated for the second category; he is 'an enthusiast who dreamt dreams of an Arab Utopia', and is dismissed as having 'no political training of any value'.[23] According to Cromer, Blunt's fundamental mistake was to seek to unite the army, led by Urabi, with the constitutionalist politicians, thus making European intervention inevitable. This referred to the infamous episode of the telegrams Blunt sent from London to Cairo in the spring of 1882 imploring the religious, political and military

factions to declare their unity under the threat of European annexation. By
arguing that Blunt pushed the political logic of the national movement toward
confrontation with Britain and France, Cromer dismisses Blunt as a political
naive.[24] Blunt's statements, where they are quoted, are generally noted for
their partisanship and inaccuracy. But in the most extensive passage devoted
to him, Cromer rubbishes the 'overestimate' given to Blunt's influence over
Gladstone by reproducing an extract from a letter by Gladstone embedded
within a letter by Granville to Cromer himself. All three conspire to write off
Blunt for his misrepresentations and contraventions of establishment codes.
Gladstone's letter ends with the remark that what Blunt has written (coming
as it does though his close friend and Gladstone's private secretary, Eddie
Hamilton) 'is personal and *tutoyant*, not official'.[25] Cromer in his response
advises Granville not to correspond with Blunt as this, he implies, would
have the effect of lending official value to his statements. Blunt is thus placed
outside the bounds of authoritative discourse.

The discourse of *Modern Egypt* functions as a vindication of the confla-
tion of interests mentioned above: those of the British empire and those of the
Egyptian fellahin. The premise is that this symbiotic relationship could justify
the control Britain exercised over Egypt, and was worth that country's
relinquishment of anything but a long-term hope of national freedom. 'What
Egypt most of all required was order and good government. Perhaps, *longo
intervallo*, liberty would follow afterwards.'[26] Edward Said discussed how
Cromer's notion of imperial governance centres on 'subject races' and the
imposition of imperial rule on the understanding that 'subject races did not
have it in them to know what was good for them'. Cromer's characterisation
of 'the mind of the Oriental' is formed along a fault-line that fixes this as
illogical, untrained, given to deceit, lethargy and undirected loquacity – in
contradistinction to the logical, coherent, ordered Anglo-Saxon race.[27] Mired
in this narrow imperial terrain, Cromer dismissed the nationalists as 'unrepresentative' just as he condemned Urabi as a mutineer and his movement
unsupported by the majority of Egyptians.

In *Modern Egypt*, Cromer is presented with the task of, on the one hand,
explaining the hesitant progress of the British government towards eventual
occupation of Egypt, and on the other, demonstrating the irrefutable benefits
this outcome brought to the country. His justification for his work in Egypt
centres on 1) the corruption of the existing regime there, and 2) his rescuing
of the country – in particular the fellahin – from the worst abuses of this
arbitrary and disorderly power. As British commissioner of the Public Debt
between 1877 and 1879, Cromer claims the British government held the
interests of the European bondholders no closer to heart than those of the
fellahin. The force of such a statement redounds as much to his own credit as
it does to the detriment of the Khedive Ismail, who almost all European
commentators of the time held solely to blame for the fellahin's misery. 'The
British rulers of Egypt had every reason to encourage the belief of the
Egyptian people that Ismail was responsible for their miserable condition.'[28]

As Colvin put it in his history, *The Making of Modern Egypt*: 'The country was in the utmost misery; the indebtedness of the fellah was universal; there was no justice; no order, or system, in the collection of the land revenue and taxes. The finances were bankrupt, and the European creditor was in possession.'[29]

Cromer himself does not waste time blaming Europe for this state of affairs. Ismail had simply fallen in with the worst company, and his fate demonstrated the truism: 'the maximum amount of harm is probably done when an Oriental ruler is for the first time brought in contact with the European system of credit.' Given the ancient history of despotic rule in Egypt, the problem was how to reform this eastern society without 'shaking the props which had so far held [it] together'.[30] As a commissioner, Cromer had overseen a range of measures designed to further financial reform: they all required time to regulate and capable administrators to implement – but how could these reforms take root without addressing the present government apparatus i.e. the Khedive himself? Ismail was no better than the French kings of the *ancien régime*; the problem was how to 'place some check on [his] arbitrary power', his pretensions as a moderniser having translated into European-derived innovations that were 'least suitable to an Oriental community, and least worthy of being copied'.[31] What Egypt needed was the kind of professionalism and bureaucratic efficiency that Cromer and the Frenchman de Blignières had brought as commissioners and later controllers-general of finance. Authority rested on the shoulders of those who performed such functions, required as they were 'to pull the strings behind the scenes, but appear on the stage as little as possible'.[32]

The issue of reform in Egypt – accepting that this was indeed Cromer's prime motivation rather than a smokescreen to occlude the more basic matter of Britain's imperial strategy and Cromer's own instinct for power – was precisely what separated Cromer and Blunt. Both agreed that 'The East [...] is languishing for want of a Revolution'. For Cromer, 'orientals' were incapable of accomplishing anything more than palace intrigue or mutiny. The deposition of Ismail brought his replacement by his son Tawfiq – 'a young prince animated with the best of intentions'. But before the 'calm waters of peaceful progress could be reached', 'a serious collapse of the State machinery' presented itself in the form of the army 'mutiny' led by Urabi, a movement whose leading feature was that it combined vague national aspirations, which were incapable of realisation, with 'the time-honoured tactics of a mutinous praetorian guard'.[33]

Parliamentary government was out of the question – Britain had destroyed Egypt's nascent parliamentary institutions in the intervention of 1882, and as we have seen, Cromer held these in low esteem anyway, as applied to subject peoples. The only hope for reform was through Britain's control. Cromer's argument for the benevolent direction he believed he exercised over Egypt, and the authority that entitled him to speak for Egypt, were both self-referential, and take on providential overtones. He quotes Lord Dufferin, who the British Government sent to report on Egypt in the months immediately after the occupation, when it was still thought desirable to evacuate British forces. 'If [...] I had been commissioned to place affairs in Egypt on the footing of an Indian subject State, the outlook would have been different. The masterful hand of a Resident would have quickly bent everything to his will.' Cromer adds: 'many people were of opinion that the course indicated by Lord Dufferin was the best to adopt'. By freeing up interpretation of the term 'the representative of the British Government in Egypt', Cromer is able to read retrospectively his own accession to the throne of Egypt. This representative, 'would of necessity be more than an ordinary diplomatic agent', that is, of greater historical moment than Cromer's predecessor, the neurotic Malet, who, 'promoted' to the ambassadorship of Belgium, opens the way for Cromer's almost messianic advent as that 'masterful Resident' unwittingly foretold by Dufferin.[34]

2. The Renewal of Islam

If Cromer's discourse on Egypt bares many of the features of Orientalism, to what extent is it possible to speak of Blunt's, as an overt challenge to this, and therefore, in effect a form of counter-Orientalism? According to Elizabeth Longford, by 1877 'the East had begun to dominate Blunt's imagination. He suspected that Islam might fill the religious void.'[35] During his visit to India in 1879, he began to ask awkward questions about the providence of Britain's empire in the East. The *Secret History* also calls attention to his wife's descent from Lord Byron (she was his granddaughter) and posited the romantic notion 'that to champion the cause of Arabian liberty would be as worthy an endeavour as had been that for which Byron had died.'[36] The visit to Jeddah in 1881 took on the character of a pilgrimage. Blunt, in the words of Thomas Assad, 'saw that to be effective in his mission he had to work from within Islamic thought rather than as an outsider [...] to sit under the Ulema, or learned men.'[37] It is significant that Blunt's 'mission' entailed learning about Islam from the inside, at the same time as using this knowledge to set himself up as an authority on 'the regeneration of the East'.[38] This mixing of the roles of acolyte and authoritative interpreter in part defines Blunt's character and must be taken into consideration in any reading of his political crusades, as well as discussion of his putative counter-Orientalism.

What is of significance for this whole area is the synchronicity attached to Blunt's investigations. His ideas on Islam as expressed in the *Future of Islam*, says Hourani, feature 'the gist of what [he] learnt from [Muhammad] 'Abduh, and through him from Jamal al-Din [al-Afghani]' in addition to his own 'gloss on the thought of the Islamic reformers'.[39] Hourani believed, however, that the emphasis on the impending doom of the Ottoman sultanate and its replacement by an Arabian caliphate was twenty years ahead of Arab thinkers and 'more likely to occur to an European than to an Arab Muslim with a sense of responsibility for the safety and unity of *dar al-islam*.' Nevertheless, he did not doubt 'the strength of [Blunt's] feelings about Islam and the Muslims'.[40] Blunt's romantic attachment to the image of Arabia he and his wife had constructed from their visit to Najd undoubtedly coloured his ideas about an Arabian caliphate and brings an admixture of anachronism to his reformist discourse. But Blunt's association with al-Afghani and Abduh – figures to whom much print has been devoted as the fathers of Islamic modernism – brought a counter-balance that was certainly fortuitous, in the sense that his concern with the renewal of Islam coincided with the activism of these seminal figures in Islamic thought. As a result, a seriousness and weight is added to Blunt's discourse, and this in part delivers it from the anachronistic idealism of his earlier writings. At the same time, it may be considered credible as an exercise in a form of counter-Orientalism.

According to Nikki Keddie, al-Afghani's contribution to the formulation of an Islamic response to the impact of Europe implies recognition of the 'dual role of Western countries as menace and model'.[41] For his part, Blunt started out with the hope that the British empire might help further 'Eastern liberty' rather than 'the selfish purposes of English imperialism'.[42] *The Future of Islam* emphasises the need for British goodwill and understanding of the Islamic world and its path of renewal. On his second visit to Egypt in November 1880, Blunt found much improvement since his last one: Ismail had been deposed and he was sanguine about the 'protection and supervision' the Egyptian Government 'gets from England'.[43] It was only under the pressure of events as they unfolded that the balance turned in direction of Europe's menace to the East.

Blunt seems to have regarded reform in the Islamic world as a process that was or needed to be self-fuelled. In writing *The Future of Islam* he 'committed [himself] without reserve to the Cause of Islam as essentially "the Cause of Good" over an immense portion of the world, and to be encouraged, not repressed, by all who cared for the welfare of mankind'.[44] European influence ought not to be direct, indeed he disparaged Europeanisers like the Turkish reformer Midhat Pasha who he met in Syria dismissing his ideas as shallow and 'of that commonplace European kind which so often in the East do service for original thought and depth of conviction.' In Turkey and Egypt the Europeanisers of recent years 'had introduced their changes as it were by violence [...] with no serious attempt to reconcile them with the law of the Koran and the traditions.'[45] In contrast, Jamal al-Din al-Afghani – 'the true originator of the Liberal religious Reform movement among the Ulema of Cairo', demonstrated his originality in this, that he:

> sought to convert the religious intellect of the countries where he preached to the necessity of reconsidering the whole Islamic position, and, instead of clinging to the past, of making an onward intellectual movement in harmony with modern knowledge. His intimate acquaintance with the Koran and the traditions enabled him to show that, if rightly interpreted and checked the one by the other, the law of

> Islam was capable of the most liberal developments and that hardly any beneficial
> change was in reality opposed to it.[46]

From al-Afghani's ideas, as mediated by his disciple Muhammad Abduh, Blunt derived the impression that the Islamic world was on the move. In Abduh he found a wide and tolerant understanding of Islam in its relations with Judaism and Christianity.

> He would hear nothing of intolerance, nothing of bitterness between believers so
> near akin [...] and he believed the world to be progressing towards a state of social
> perfection where arms would be laid down and a universal brotherhood proclaimed
> between the nations and the creeds.

To his delight and astonishment, Blunt was won over by this presentation of Islam, 'based on [Islamic] texts and traditions', because these ideas 'were very close to my own'. Moreover, Abduh assured him they were also beginning to be shared by students throughout the Muslim world.[47]

Just as Keddie reads liberal and anti-western components into al-Afghani's thought, Blunt's understanding of the position of Islam in the modern world was to be affected by the march of European imperialism. At the same time as he was engaging with the Islamic reformers of Egypt, European penetration of North Africa had reached new levels with the French occupation of Tunisia. Going back to the Congress of Berlin in 1878, Blunt perceived retrospectively the implementation of an imperialist policy that gave France its prize, Austria the go-ahead in Bosnia, and eventuated in the carve up of Africa. 'Above all', this 'destroyed at a critical moment' Britain's standing in the Muslim world, reversing her policy of influencing Ottoman reforms and progressively 'embitter[ing] Moslem hearts against her'.[48] Blunt appreciated that the Islamic reformers were also in dialectical opposition to other trends within the Muslim world, which he associated with the Ottoman Sultan Abdul Hamid. Where al-Afghani and Abduh led the impetus to liberal reform, Abdul Hamid embodied the fanatical, reactionary forces. Blunt's positioning of himself alongside the Muslim liberals pitted him during this period against the Turkish element in the Islamic world. He also, as we have seen, favoured a liberal reform of Islamic thought from within rather than that imposed from outside by Europeanisers.

In 1881, the influence of al-Afghani in Egypt was still fresh, but Blunt may have been led to overemphasise the currency of his ideas within al-Azhar.[49] His own journeys in Arabia had at first disposed him towards the Arabs of the desert as the source of Islamic renewal, yet the brand of Arabian government that they espoused would have been considered anachronistic by the majority of Arabic speakers. Before January 1882, Blunt also leaned toward a British protection of Islamic modernism. But the occupation of Egypt that year would lead him into strident denunciation of European politics and culture that allied him with the Muslims – reconstructed and unreconstructed – and accounts for the deepening counter-Orientalist note in his discourse.

The Occupation and its Aftermath: 'Something like order restored' or 'A fictitious condition of anarchy and rebellion'?

> Did anyone really suppose that if we did not possess an Indian empire we should have interfered in Egypt?
> Kimberley, Secretary of State for India, quoted in Lowe, *The Reluctant Imperialists*, p.73

According to M.E. Yapp, 'The British occupation of Egypt in 1882 bears a misleading impression of inevitability and design. In fact, a study of the sequence of events shows that British action was unplanned and undesired.'[50] Why then did Blunt see in the events leading up to the occupation evidence of a conspiracy; and Cromer, looking back over a similar gap of more than twenty years, the fulfilment of a prophecy? To answer these questions it might be useful to imagine ourselves peering through the kind of doubled-ended telescope that used to feature on seaside promenades. Looked at through the end that magnifies close up, the occupation appears the result of a succession of British diplomatic blunders in part precipitated by Machiavellian French manoeuvres but with Britain providing the trump card. This narrative is more or less endorsed by both Cromer and Blunt. However, seen through the lens that makes near objects seem far off, ample scope exists for descrying patterns and design.

Having discredited Blunt's account of the English occupation, Cromer must have felt his narrative replete with the stamp of authenticity. The story is signposted by a 'prophecy':

> Egypt was to fall to Kinglake's Englishman [...] it was to fall to him, although some were opposed to his going there, others were indifferent as to whether he went or not, none much wished him to go, and, not only did he not want to go there himself, but he struggled strenuously and honestly not to be obliged to go.[51]

The prophecy was 'fulfilled' after the rout of the Egyptians at Tel al-Kabir and the capture of Cairo. The reader who gets this far in the narrative (p.331 of volume 1) is not only reminded of the prophecy for a third time, but is in a position to give his assent to the proposition. Cromer's grand narrative, passing through khedivial despotism, Urabi's treachery, Ottoman double-dealing, French obduracy and a British Liberal Government's honourable bumbling, arrives at its foreordained conclusion – British occupation. It was true that 'before resorting to extreme measures every possible endeavour should have been made to control' the 'Egyptian movement', but by the time British ships bombarded Alexandria, 'any hope of controlling [it], save by the exercise of material force, had well-nigh disappeared.' The capture of Alexandria stood for Egypt as a whole: 'something like order restored'.[52]

Cromer therefore seems to want his cake and eat it. Reforms might perhaps have been carried out without foreign occupation under the Khedive

Tawfiq with a watered-down Council of Notables, under European tutelage. The fly in the ointment was the army: it was Urabi's 'mutiny' that was disabling of the European facility to pull the strings behind the scenes. The moment power passed from European hands, the need to 'restore order' became paramount. As for Urabi, Cromer repeats the standard estimate of his character and crimes by drawing on the negative report of the very British stalwarts who had agitated for his defeat: Colvin, Malet, and the vice-consul, Sir Charles Cookson. Cromer concurs with the charges made at his trial – Urabi was guilty of rebellion and treason against the Khedive. His chief motivation in seizing power was the oriental's fear of intrigue against him. As for the notion that Urabi's rebellion had any support among the people, the slogan 'Egypt for the Egyptians' is contemptuously demolished. Once the foreigners and the Turko-Circassian aristocracy were eliminated, what did Egypt consist of but ignorant fellahin, a native Egyptian squirearchy, the Copts, and the Ulama of al-Azhar? These latter might have prospered for a while like Jacobins under an Urabi-led dictatorship, but this would have deprived Egypt of the fruits of western civilization.[53] Given that foreign occupation was (bashfully-'perhaps') inevitable, the Egyptians were fortunate it had not been left to the Turks, French or Italians to execute. Or was it not her destiny to be governed by Britain? (Cromer disingenuously never explicitly states this belief.) Even then, however, the Englishman had no sooner 'plant[ed] his foot firmly in the valley of the Nile [than...] he struggled to withdraw it.'[54] It needed the providential appearance of 'the man' (the masterful hand of a Resident) and the promptings of the infernal agency of the Mahdi in Sudan to place the prophecy on a sure foundation and justify the entire narrative.

Blunt also chooses a narrative schema for his history of the occupation, in addition to placing the reader in the thick of events as he offers a blow-by-blow account based on quotations from his diaries of the time. A retrospective, interpretative commentary contextualises the diary entries and supplies an overarching design to the narrative. In this way Blunt invites us to view the occupation and its aftermath through both ends of the telescope. In contrast to Cromer's authoritative imperial tones, Blunt develops a discourse that bares the mark of embitterment brought about by the apparent victory and ascendancy of the imperial project. His task is to present a counter-narrative – hitherto blocked by the achievement of British power in Egypt – that privileges the aims and record of the Urabi revolution and empowers it by the authority of Islamic and humanitarian codes. Where Cromer relies on official diplomatic sources, Blunt uses off-the-record information from well-placed friends (such as Gladstone's secretary Hamilton, and the ex-Viceroy of India, Lord Lytton) and powerful figures he meets socially (such as the Italian ambassador to the Congress of Berlin, and Lord Vivian, one of Cromer's predecessors in the European financial control of Egypt). His purpose is to project kudos for his revelations, and sometimes to reinforce a charge of high-up chicanery. A chance encounter with Dilke, Granville's number two at Foreign Affairs, convinces Blunt of his malign influence over the lethargic Foreign Secretary, and the evil intentions of the French Premier Gambetta, who Dilke is courting to sign an Anglo-French commercial treaty. Another tip leads him to declare that the Rothschild's were pushing for intervention in Egypt in the name of 'the money interests of all the Stock Exchanges of Europe'.[55] At the same time as he is courting Gladstone, Blunt boasts of friends with access to the Conservative opposition.

According to Peter Mansfield, Blunt 'greatly exaggerated his political influence and gravely misled the Egyptian nationalists in this respect.'[56] But the fact that he gets more than a passing mention in *Modern Egypt* (which, however, completely occludes his success in saving Urabi at his trial) indicates the anger Blunt's interventions caused the governing elite. In his diary entry for 27 February 1882 he reports that with the exception of Sir William Gregory, he is estranged from the English colony in Cairo. But he claims his and Gregory's letters to *The Times* have invested Urabi with a 'halo of romance' – this at a time of bitter anti-nationalist feeling in England owing to the Irish situation.[57] At the height of the intervention controversy in June, he wrote to a confidant in Cairo: 'people are very angry here with me, but I do not care, so long as Egypt gets her liberty'. Of the culmination of Blunt's battle with Malet and Colvin, and his estrangement from Gladstone, he makes the astonishing claim: 'England [...] had never looked so foolish [...] We had won our diplomatic victory against the Foreign Office too thoroughly', only to add: 'It was to be the turn now of England's fighting forces'.[58] At such points, we are tempted to concur with Cromer's charge about Blunt's political naivete.

However, Mansfield suggests that Blunt understood the Egyptian national movement better than Cromer. His presentation of Urabi as a genuine national leader and patriot, albeit a flawed military commander (with a trace of physical cowardice), goes a long way towards rescuing him from Cromer's oriental stooge. Blunt was in a position to quote from Urabi's memoirs, letters and conversations, and these belie the official propaganda about Urabi's fanaticism and atrocities, which Blunt convincingly dismisses as got up or staged by the Khedive's agents. Probably his major achievement in *Secret History* is to vindicate the comparative benevolence of the Egyptian nationalists, even if his own prescriptions appear impossibly high:

> My idea of a policy for the Egyptians [he writes to Hamilton] is, that they should act by a rule diametrically opposite to the common Oriental ones. I would have them tell the truth, even to their enemies – be more humane than European soldiers, more honest than their European creditors. So only can they effect that moral reformation their religious leaders have in view for them.[59]

But as the military might of Europe moved in, Blunt could only spell out the war agenda of imperialism:

> With the example of Tunis before Mohammedan eyes it was indeed impossible not to see what was being prepared for Egypt by the European powers, the creation of

a fictitious condition of anarchy and rebellion which should justify intervention for
the protection of the life and property of Europeans.[60]

(Later, Blunt argued that British intervention in Egypt had delivered a fateful
reversal to 'all Mohammedan lands [...] in their work of liberal enlighten-
ment, and thrown [this] back for a whole generation on lines of fanatical
reaction').[61]

The hero of his narrative is in fact Blunt himself. The *Secret History*
celebrates his discovery of the new hope of a reformed Islam, his sponsorship
of Egypt's national awakening before the strongest government in Europe,
and, though these efforts are ultimately destroyed by Manichean forces, his
rescue of liberty's prince (Urabi at his trial) from the twin evil powers (the
Khedive and the British). Where Cromer embeds his ego within a discourse
of professionalism and bureaucracy, Blunt projects his through a series of
personalised encounters revealing the nefariousness of imperial managers and
the unscrupulousness and treachery of politicians back in the metropolis.
Fired with a message of hope that he brings to the imperial aristocracy, the
hero comes, through a series of triumphs and vicissitudes, to the cruel
understanding that his society is corrupt and fit for the fire:

> We fail because we are no longer honest, no longer just, no longer gentlemen. Our
> Government is a mob [...] For a hundred years we did good in the world; for a hundred
> we shall have done evil, and then the world will hear of us no more.[62]

Imperialism rooted – Islam at bay

If the British invasion of Egypt represented a watershed for European
imperialism, it had a similar effect on Blunt's eastern 'career', separating this
into two phases. In the first, he had hoped Britain might sponsor and protect
Islamic reform; in the second, he saw Britain as its prime enemy. Nevertheless, even though it had been defeated in Egypt in 1882, in India the
following year Blunt still believed 'in the possibility of a liberal Mohammedan reformation' while pondering his own role in Muslim affairs.[63] Blunt's
support for the Egyptian revolution had put him 'in communication with
some of the liberal leaders of the Pan-Islamic movement' and proved a
passport to the 'confidence of their Indian co-religionists'. In Paris Jamal al-
Din al-Afghani advised him not to mention the Arabian caliphate and say
nothing against the Sultan while in India.[64] On his first trip to India in 1879,
his British hosts, however, had not found Blunt's ideas about Arab independence uncongenial. They would after all form the embryo of Britain's 'Arab
nationalist' policy during the Great War, though at this point Blunt failed to
weigh up their potential for arrogation into the system of imperialism.[65] In the
meantime, India had awakened in him his first anti-imperialist stirrings:

He could not reconcile the 'forward' policy favoured by Simla with the poverty of the people, and he attributed the inconsistency to the influence of imperialism. He thought empire synonymous with exploitation and he distrusted the connection with trade and finance. These were the views put forth in *Ideas about India* which he published in 1885.[66]

Among the British in India in 1883, Blunt's reputation as an agitator of Islamic revolution had gone before him. The combination of an anti-imperialist stance and the applause of the Muslim community proffered to Blunt what for the next decade or more proved a recurring temptation: making 'profession of Islam, and perhaps attaining to lasting honour in Mohammedan regard'.[67] Blunt had high hopes of converting the Nizam of Hyderabad and his Muslim subjects to the cause of Islamic reform but noted the British Resident favoured a policy of keeping the Hyderabad notables 'ignorant of modern thought': supporting the religious reactionaries over the liberals was precisely what Britain was doing in Egypt, he noted.[68] For the moment Blunt could only confide to his diary: 'The Muslims have no better friend than I'. But within a matter of a few years, according to Elizabeth Longford, he had swapped Egypt for Ireland, and his 'new Nationalist friends' there became 'substitutes' for Urabi, al-Afghani and Abduh. Now the East had become 'an irritant'.[69] On one level, perhaps, 'his attention toward those whom he supported savoured too strongly of the beneficent lord and master.'[70] Nevertheless, Blunt maintained a continuity of regard for his favoured causes as he did for his mistresses. In point of fact, the East was his first and most enduring love, as time would show.

One personal outcome of Blunt's fidelity to the Egyptian national cause – his attempt to mitigate the consequences of the invasion by endeavouring to get justice for the defeated nationalists – was his short-term banishment from the country. This did not reduce his activism in the least. Throughout the Gordon episode, in between 'trying his Arabs on the race courses at Sandown and Newmarket' and meeting the ex-Khedive Ismail whom he loathed, he continued to lobby Gladstone, consult with Jamal al-Din, and even set himself up (a proposal backed by W.S Stead's *Pall Mall Gazette*) as an emissary to the Mahdi.[71] For his first biographer, though he might scorn 'the political game [...] he enjoyed the excitement and importance of being at the centre of the fray and also of stirring it up.'[72]

Behind the politics of the Gordon debacle Blunt recognised the same high-up treachery that he had exposed in the move to invade Egypt. The aim was the strengthening of British control over Egypt and the means the deception of Gladstone. Blunt was convinced that Gordon had been duped into agreeing to the Khartoum mission by Liberal imperialists in Gladstone's cabinet, and that full powers had secretly been acceded to him by Lord Wolseley at the War Ministry. He threw his efforts into the cause of retrieving Gordon and settling the Sudan issue peacefully, but that would have meant handing the country to the Mahdi, a policy that became virtually impossible as war fever grew in Britain. News of the fall of Khartoum and

Gordon's death for a moment quieted this war fever and brought 'applica-
tions [...] to Blunt from numerous high quarters, usually indirectly, to inquire
about means of communication with the Mahdi.' Then, 'stirred to white fury'
by a British victory at Suakin accompanied, it was reported, by army
atrocities against the native population, Blunt furiously lobbied MPs to
protest in parliament.[73]

The diary entries in *Gordon at Khartoum* (1911) record Blunt's quite
astounding hatred for the British military manoeuvres of the time. His anger
against Britain's military involvement in Sudan stretched to praying for her
defeat. After the battle of Abu Klea in January 1885, he celebrated the deaths
of nine British officers, and branded the English soldiers 'mere murderers':

> I confess I would rather see them all at perdition than that a single Arab more should die.
> What are they? A mongrel scum of thieves from Whitechapel and Seven Dials, com-
> manded by young fellows whose ideal is the green room of the Gaiety – without beliefs,
> without traditions, without other principle of action than just to get their promotion and
> have a little fun. On the other side men with the memory of a thousand years freedom,
> with chivalry inherited from the Saracens, the noblest of ancestors, with a creed the
> purest the world ever knew, worshipping God and serving him in arms like the heroes of
> the ancient world they are. It is over the death of these that we rejoice.[74]

Again, when the British advance in eastern Sudan was halted, the diary
cheers on Osman Dinga, the Mahdi's emir in the region: 'If there is a God in
heaven he will prevail against the hosts of Mammon'; the abandonment of
Suakin was 'the greatest victory of the [Islamic] Faith since the siege of
Vienna'.[75] Such alienation from the social realities of nineteenth century
Europe led Tidrick to remark, à propos of the little kingdoms Blunt built for
himself at Crabbet and Shaykh Obayd: 'he created for himself [...] a world of
the past, a reminiscence of the golden age of the squirearchy.'[76] The diary
passage quoted above would appear to fuse Islam with an aristocratic,
chivalric code whose day was clearly passing in the face of the advance of
modern European imperialism. But alongside passages celebratory of the
medieval set-up at Shaykh Obayd, other diary entries show denunciations of
imperialism in an Urquartian mode:

> there were only two policies on which party lines could run, the first of Imperialism,
> which meant a bid for the Empire of the world, a gambling venture which would entail the
> sacrifice of everything we have of value at home, personal liberty, freedom from con-
> scription and financial prosperity; the other Anti-imperialism, which meant letting the
> world alone and leaving the colonies to work out their own destinies without our interfer-
> ence, and the same for Ireland.[77]

This diary entry from 1901 underscored the persistence of Blunt's anti-
imperialism, but at the same time it signalled his declining faith in the
possibilities of a reformed Islam. Tidrick and Assad instance Siwa as the
climactic in Blunt's relationship with Islam. It is true this incident left him
despondent about religion in general and convinced there was '*no* hope
anywhere to be found in Islam'.[78] On at least two earlier occasions he had
failed to take the leap of faith. The first was in Ceylon in 1883. The second he

recorded during his visit to Sta Sophia in Constantinople in 1884 where he wished he could join in the Islamic prayer 'but only looked on from the gallery'.[79] However, as already indicated in chapter 1, it could be argued that Blunt's pessimism related as much to the contemporary political situation of the Islamic countries as it did to his own spiritual problem. Up till the Siwa incident, the personal and the political had always been intertwined as far as he was concerned. After this moment, the former is perhaps best assigned to a private interior space. As far as the latter was concerned, in the first decade of the twentieth century Blunt's involvement in the politics of Islam and the anti-imperialist struggle showed little sign of abating.

Blunt and Cromer: the debate continues

1. The Gordon Debacle

Blunt's account of Britain's occupation of Egypt might be read as a subtle re-shaping of the core Urquartian theme of treachery/ betrayal. In that case his argument with Cromer over the Gordon mission extends the dual motif. Vindicating Gordon and attacking Cromer's duplicitous record of the Gordon episode in *Modern Egypt* meant a further undermining of the imperial enterprise in Egypt and Sudan. But because he possessed a civility beyond Urquhart, whose single-minded obsession with Palmerston was undoubtedly personal, Blunt rarely lost sight of Cromer as the imperial enemy. Their debate was conducted at a distance of a quarter of a century from the events under consideration, at least as far as the Gordon episode was concerned. By this time, both had entrenched battle positions that belied the fact that there had been a moment, as Blunt's diary entries show, when their relations had been amicable if formal. As far as Egypt is concerned, although entirely outside of the events of 1881-82, Cromer receives Blunt's opprobrium, indeed becomes the prime accused, for his part in the transformation of a temporary occupation into a permanent one.

Writing in 1911, four years after Cromer's reign in Egypt had come to an end, Blunt credits all of the former pro-consul's most important actions with a consistency commensurate with an imperialist grand design. The Mahdi crisis of 1884 forms the core around which the second volume of the 'Secret History' series, *Gordon at Khartoum*, is constructed. The text adopts the same format of diary entries and post facto commentary as the first volume. Blunt uses his diary account to tease out his earlier positions, where necessary re-aligning them according to the 'finished' anti-imperialism of his later years. His message is also carried over from *The English Occupation of Egypt*, and gives the narrative its strength. At its heart is his sense of the intensification of imperialist aggression against the Islamic *umma*, and again, it is this long-term teleological view that constitutes its challenge.

The Egyptian defeat at Tel al-Kabir had ramifications all over the Muslim world: it claimed immediate effect at Istanbul where Sultan Abdul Hamid concentrated power in his hands and was able to 'crush what remained of the constitutional party and the party of religious liberalism.' Reaction was also strengthened in Persia, while in North Africa religious thought formed along the lines of 'fiercely bitter hatred of Christendom', the Sanusiyyah responding to the French invasion of Tunisia by arms. Above all, 'the English invasion of Egypt was answered by Mohammed Ahmed's appearance in the Soudan as Mahdi.'[80] To Baring in the autumn of 1883, Blunt had represented unavailingly the vital importance of establishing a native administration in Egypt. In *Gordon at Khartoum*, he argues that a moderate Islamic government in Cairo led by Urabi might have come to terms with the Mahdi. Both the Urabist and the Mahdist movements were closely analogous being the 'natural rebellion of a people against long misgovernment' taking on a religious complexion when Europe intervened to prop up a tyrant ruler. The difference between the two was that the Mahdists were fanatical and reactionary, whereas Urabi's supporters were 'enlightened men, representing the humaner and more progressive side of Islam'. How ironic that 'Liberal England' had chosen to strike the latter down. The wrong committed was not so much that a free and national government had been destroyed, but that Britain's armed intervention 'struck everywhere at the aspirations of liberal Islam'. In short, the Sudan crisis when it came was entirely of Europe's making ('Europe itself was the sole responsible cause of the trouble.')[81]

Cromer's personal culpability in all this was very great on account of his underwriting and amplification of the terms of the occupation. His involvement in the Gordon episode, though it might superficially appear otherwise, was part of the grand design to make the incorporation of Egypt into the empire permanent and, in addition, to gain a firmer footing in Africa by bringing Sudan under British control. In *Modern Egypt*, Cromer exonerates himself of all blame attaching to Gordon's mission other than the part that accrued to him for agreeing to Gordon's appointment in the first place. Even then, for emphasis, he points out he only yielded to Granville's proposition on the third time of asking. His being the last to accept Gordon is thereby turned into a virtue. And as is often the case in *Modern Egypt*, Cromer valorises his own professionalism by making this a warning and a homily that officials be prepared when really necessary to stand up to public opinion 'in these democratic days'.[82] Responsibility for the Gordon tragedy therefore rested not with him (as had been argued by Gordon's family) but on a weak if over optimistic Liberal government borne along by popular emotion stirred up by the *Pall Mall Gazette*.

In order to support his argument, Blunt supplies a sub-text to the policy of evacuation, which he implies Baring never intended to go along with. He links the consul-general with the imperialist, largely Whig faction in Gladstone's cabinet who, according to Blunt, were the force behind the original occupation and were now intent on its indefinite maintenance. They were responsible for getting up an agitation in the press that inflamed public opinion and thereby pressurised Gladstone and Granville into sending Gordon to Sudan. Baring's part in Gordon's mission was to further this design by advising the British government to send an English officer to Khartoum, ostensibly to evacuate the garrison, but in reality to establish British influence there. Blunt focuses on Cromer's omission from his official narrative of 1908 of a crucial qualifying adjective from a contemporary dispatch.

Originally Baring had recommended that an English officer be sent to Khartoum; in *Modern Egypt* he dropped the word *English* in order to imply he intended an Egyptian to fulfil this task. For Blunt, Baring's part in Gordon's mission was vital: he insisted on Gordon proceeding to Khartoum via Cairo in order that he might receive instructions from the Khedive and Baring. For his part, Baring confirmed in a letter to Granville that Gordon should been given the 'widest discretionary powers as regards the best manner of carrying out the policy [of evacuation].' However, he attempts to exonerate himself of responsibility in his commentary: 'It mattered little what instructions General Gordon received, because he was not the sort of man to be bound by any instructions.'[83] Blunt's response is an outright challenge. Baring's instructions left Gordon with the widest possible leeway once he reached Khartoum, whereas in his memoir Cromer had 'the face now to come forward and charge Gordon with overstepping his authorized programme.'[84] Blunt's accusation is therefore that Cromer suppressed the true 'secret history' of the Gordon affair, which was about sending an 'English Officer' to 'Sarawak the Sudan'.[85] This was implicit in the excision of the word 'English' from his original despatch:

> I recommend this dispatch to the renewed attention of historians, for in it lies not only the demand for new absolute powers to be undertaken by England in Egypt, but also in regard to the Soudan, the germ of that claim, afterwards enforced upon the Khedive in 1899, that Egypt should abandon the Soudan, leaving it to England to decide what later should be its status. The Egyptian Government was to withdraw its troops, but "an English officer of high authority" was to be sent to Khartoum, not only to insist upon withdrawal, but also to provide the Soudan with a new government. One cannot help thinking that Cromer may have already contemplated what he afterwards carried out, the appropriation of the great Nile provinces to England herself.[86]

By phrases such as 'germ of that claim' and 'may have already contemplated' Blunt lends to the Gordon episode an organic significance as part of a teleological narrative of British imperialism in North Africa and the Near East. From the vantage point of 1911, the narrative comprehends the 'veiled' protectorate set up by Cromer in Egypt, Kitchener's revenge on Sudan in 1898, and the 'theoretical equality of the condominium' of Anglo-Egyptian Sudan.[87] In each of these imperial advances, Cromer's part was instrumental. But was Blunt exaggerating? On the details of the Gordon affair Blunt got it more or less right. Cromer's purposive suppression of the 'English' officer was later proven; as regards the intentionally open instructions Baring was supposed to have given Gordon, Owen confirms these made Gordon's mission 'wider than most of Gladstone's cabinet had intended'. Overall, Owen concludes, those figures in power who were involved in the Gordon affair afterwards suffered 'collective amnesia', Baring included.[88]

2. The Management of Egypt

> We did not come here with any promise of immediate evacuation [...] Egypt is capable of reform and regeneration but not by good advice. No oriental country except Japan has accepted reform but by compulsion. There is no argument but 'you must.'
>
> Milner, quoted in Marlowe, *Milner: Apostle of Empire*, p. 19.

Blunt's counter-imperialist narrative construed from a post-Cromer perspective probably conflates Baring's first few years in Egypt with the entrenched imperialism of the 1890s onwards, giving retrospective meanings to his actions in 1883-84. Cromer, says A.G. Hopkins, arrived at this point after passing through several earlier stages:

> The evolution of Baring's attitude towards Britain's presence in Egypt is instructive because it illustrates both the changing balance of forces within the Liberal party and the process by which an anti-imperialist became an apologist for empire.

In 1883, Baring 'planned only a sort stay in Egypt'. By 1885, having embarked upon reforms,

> he was devising a justification of Britain's continued presence on the grounds that further 'good works' were needed; and by 1887 [...] he had come to believe that, since the scope for improvement was infinite, no precise date for withdrawal could be fixed. By the 1890s Baring had changed his mind about evacuation and envisaged a long period of British rule which had no set limit.[89]

In practice, the shifts in Baring's political positioning probably affected but marginally the actual way in which Egypt was governed. There is in fact a consistency in how, as Lutfi al-Sayyid puts it,

> Baring's reports on Egypt helped the British government to prolong the occupation. His accounts of the incompetence of the Egyptian ruling class, his repeated assurances that 'I do not believe that there are a dozen people in the country who really wish us to go', and the assumption that if England evacuated Egypt then a power-vacuum would be created – one that France would hasten to fill – all pointed in the direction of a semi-permanent occupation.[90]

By 1892 Cromer (who was that year elevated to the peerage) had settled into the autocratic mode by which he would continue to govern Egypt for the next fifteen years. Towards the end of that year, a number of factors helped him consolidate Britain's and his own position in Egypt. The accession of the young Khedive Abbas II on the death of his father Tawfiq led to a brief power struggle from which the consul-general would emerge victorious. The return of a Liberal government, which some had thought might terminate the occupation, in fact facilitated Cromer's successful struggle with Abbas because the new Foreign Minister, Lord Rosebery, was a Whig imperialist who supported Cromer to the hilt.

A third favourable element was the publication of Alfred Milner's *England in Egypt* – 'a eulogistic, not to say euphoric, account of the very moderate benefits which the British occupation had brought to the people of Egypt.'[91] According to Owen, Cromer had learned from the Sudan debacle the vital need 'to balance appeals to his political masters with a more direct manipulation of those on whose votes their own power depended.'[92] Recognising the importance of influencing public opinion, Cromer 'prompted and promoted' Milner to write a book that contributed to a new pride in British imperial achievement in Egypt.[93] Milner had just completed three years as an official in the Egyptian Ministry of Finance during which time he published several articles in the British press extolling the benefits to Egyptians of the occupation. *England in Egypt* is an exercise in propaganda that not only elevates the British imperial administration in Egypt (in which, in spite of its title, several Scots played prominent roles) but specifically valorises the guiding hand of Cromer himself.

Blunt opined later on: 'It was a combination of Baring, and of Milner, acting under his direction in the London Press, with Rosebery, that prevented an honest solution of the Egyptian question when the Liberals [...] returned to power.'[94] Milner knew Cromer's regime from the inside and was even talked of as his successor. He therefore brought to the composition of *England in Egypt* the correct political orientation, journalistic skills acquired during his period on *The Pall Mall Gazette*, and nurture in the ideology of the so-called 'New Imperialism'.[95] It was apposite that such a rising star of imperialist governance should be the articulator of a discourse derived from the imperator himself, later to be filtered through the Egyptian narrative of Auckland Colvin and the memoirs of Edward Malet, and then returned to the source of its provenance in the inscription of *Modern Egypt*.[96] It was Milner's book that first justified the British occupation of Egypt, and indicated its optimum future course. Indeed, as Blunt noted later, Milner's work 'too candidly revealed the nature of the Baring policy, unveiling to nakedness the "Veiled Protectorate".'[97] In arguing for a permanent occupation the book 'succeeded in rousing a wave of indignation amongst the Egyptians [when translated into Arabic], for this was the first time that such a policy had been openly advocated – and by someone who had served in the Egyptian government.'[98]

As far as a late nineteenth-century English reading public was concerned the appeal of the book is not difficult to see. It incorporates the cultural arrogance, prejudice and manipulation of fear of an expansionist western power seeking to establish its governance over the Muslim Middle East. This is in part accomplished by projecting the prospect of massacres of indigenous Christian Europeans as a *raison d'être* for the installation of European power in the first place. The civilising role of Europe as a foil to indigenous disorder is then proposed alongside the notion of the 'civilised world' as the arbiter of correct standards of international behaviour. Embedded but barely concealed within all of these assertions of western superiority is the threat of force to establish its will and the contemptuous dismissal of all indigenous efforts toward self-determination. The veiled protectorate painstakingly rescued Egypt from the tyrannical inheritance of the family of Muhammad Ali and the complex mesh of the capitulations, conflicting authorities and interests vying with one another in a land apparently irreversibly penetrated by European influence. Milner frequently re-iterates Cromer's assertion that the ordinary Egyptians wanted Britain to stay, instancing the stability and opportunities for future prosperity brought about by Cromer's financial reforms, as well as the re-organisation and regularisation of the Egyptian army, and the radical improvements in implementation and inspection of the irrigation system which were especially popular amongst the fellahin. Milner's argument installs all the main planks in the imperial platform on which subsequent justifications of British rule in Egypt would stand. Britain's initial intervention brought salvation to a land set on the road to anarchy, facilitating against all odds a potential revival of Egypt under a governance that was in all but name a protectorate.

The non-interventionist principles of the Gladstone epoch demurred to acknowledge an open protectorate even though such a mode of operation would have lightened Cromer's task. The capitulations could have been swept away and the scope of the occupation's systems of military, political and administrative power clearly delimited and the new governing power properly empowered to govern, had Britain possessed the strength of will to proclaim a formal protectorate. For the vagaries of men like Granville and Dufferin, Milner had little time. Granville's compulsory but whispered advice to the Egyptians was a 'charming euphemism' that elided the realities of imperialist intervention. 'The advice of an armed man in possession of your property is apt to be something more than a mere recommendation; it is an order.' Behind the bland 'optimistic forecasts of the Dufferin epoch', Milner implies, was the mindset of a now discredited era. The 'theory of our limited liability for the management of the affairs of Egypt' was the 'fiction which destroyed Hicks and his ten thousand men' in the Sudan.[99] Milner was allowed the space to ironise the old laissez-faire Liberalism out of which Cromer had grown, announcing in its stead a new imperialism valorised on the ground by Cromer's record in Egypt, now elevated post facto into a form of manifest destiny.

As Cromer would later do himself in *Modern Egypt*, Milner then proceeds to disable all alternatives to the 'romance' and 'fairytale' of the English engagement with Egypt and the Sudan. The standard British denunciations of the different strata of would-be native government are rehearsed. At the head of the Urabi movement had been 'an absolutely uneducated' man, a demagogue ignorant of the complexities of the Egyptian problem, whose power base resided in 'fanatical school-men and ignorant peasants'. The movement's 'great destructive force' was its 'ominous and misleading watch-cry of "Egypt for the Egyptians"'. Men from the old regime like Nubar and Riaz who continued under the British were scarcely better qualified to rule. They chaffed at 'a great deal too much guidance', or confronted the British and fell; either way, they were corrupt and 'despot[s] at heart' or 'medieval in character'. As a class, the Turco-Circassians were only superficially civilised and though the native Egyptian country shaykhs were noble, they were ignorant and given to the abuse of power. As for external Islamic influences, Ottoman Turkey exercised a merely nominal suzerainty: the extent of the Sultan's remit in Egypt began and ended with his religious role. (The continued presence of his political representative, Mukhtar Pasha, was, however, still 'a perpetual nuisance, which may at any moment become a danger').[100]

Given that Britain had gained a foothold in Egypt, every effort is made to justify its consolidation and continuance. Against odds that Milner takes great pains to stack up, the British administrators – above all Baring – emerge as men specially qualified for the task of bringing order to a country he dubbed in his opening chapter, quoting the authority of Herodotus, the 'land of Paradox'.[101]

> It needed a back as broad as that of Sir Evelyn Baring to bear the accumulated weight of all the work, worry, and misconstruction which attended that hard, uphill struggle to improve administration while preserving solvency [...] Baring, Vincent, Moncrieff – these were the men who bore the burden and heat of those early days of stress, and who deserve the chief credit for the ultimate unexpected success of our unpromising experiment in the civil government of Egypt.[102]

In the case of the irrigation engineers, critics were silenced and respect and even the affection of the native Egyptian were won, but only because, Milner re-iterates, the engineers had 'a power behind them, which ensures their advice being followed'. No doubt the French would have accomplished similar feats, but they had tried and failed under khedival government. Britain had taken the nettle by the hand: 'European skill [...] is necessary for the regeneration of Egypt. But European skill is useless without European authority. Wherever you turn, that cardinal fact stares you in the face.' The colonial technicians, with their 'sound technical knowledge, untiring industry, absolute contempt for hardship or misrepresentation and the most perfect impartiality' manifested the superiority of the Anglo-Saxon imperialist cadres, and the irrigation achievement itself becomes a metonym for the entire imperialist project in Egypt. A racial pride that is typical of the new school of imperial thinking cannot but break through: 'The qualities of the race have triumphed'.[103] Britain was not in Egypt as a master alone, but to teach by practice. The oriental either wanted to be master or to be told what to do. Egyptians needed to be shown what to do, and also to practice doing it. Such tutelage could only benefit the colonised population, because, a refrain that Cromer had masterminded and would again take up in *Modern Egyptians*: 'Our interests in Egypt are absolutely identical with those of the Egyptian people'.[104]

Milner turns this narrative of celebration to rhetorical effect by posing the questions: 'How can the work of reform be maintained and consolidated? How can the country be kept steadily advancing along the road of European civilization, on which it is now fairly launched, and prevented from slipping back into chaos?' In the answer is the embedded rationale of *England in Egypt*: 'there is no guarantee that Egypt may not thus slip back, except the maintenance, for a considerable time longer, of the controlling influence of some civilized Power.' This entailed the indefinite postponement of Egyptian self-determination. Native representation was ruled out until a distant future. For Egypt to continue 'advancing along the road of European civilization' every measure should be taken to prevent reforms from being lost, of the country 'slipping back into chaos'.[105] Much still needed to be done; no date could therefore be set for withdrawal.

Milner's book contains, then, some of the key motifs of the imperialist creed. Its strategic political message is that the bad old days of laissez-faire in foreign policy are over. Interventionist imperialism gets things done. The moribund oriental system of government must be set in abeyance and Egypt placed under the tutelage of superior Anglo-Saxon administrative and technical know-how, either voluntarily or by imposition, under a never far beneath the surface threat of violence. In arguing that British interests coincided with those of Egypt, that the interest of European bondholders was never 'the inspiring motive of our policy', Milner occludes the re-configuration whereby Cairo had replaced Istanbul as the focus of Britain's eastern policy. Discoursing on Britain's moral duty to make good the withdrawal from Sudan by a war of re-conquest Milner lets slip the issue of imperial strategy by warning that 'failing to recognise the great importance of Uganda, we shall abandon our hold on that region'.[106]

From the late 1880s and through the 1890s, the period during which Cromer strengthened Britain's management and control over the country, Blunt wintered annually at Shaykh Obayd. His differences with Cromer continued to centre on the latter's refusal to allow Urabi to return to his native land, and his deaf ear to the establishment of a National Government, instead using Egypt for 'highly paid posts for not very capable Englishmen'.[107] Blunt established friendly relations with the Khedive Abbas, and a former political enemy Riaz Pasha, largely because each was anti-British. He considered Cromer had got the better of the Khedive through the latter's own mistakes; seeing a diminution in Abbas's optimism and self-confidence Blunt expressed a perceptive fear that the Khedive would degenerate into 'the shifty intriguer' his father had been. In the nineties Blunt continued to talk of evacuation as though it were still a possibility even though it was apparent that Cromer's grip had grown stronger, particularly after the showdown with Abbas. Alive to the wider context of British imperial aggrandisement in South Africa as well as Sudan, and to the constraints on that imperialism coming from other, competing European imperialisms, Blunt accepted developments in a fatalistic spirit, telling his cousin George Wyndham in

1898 that the Empire was 'a poor cockney affair invented hardly twenty years ago to the ruin of our position as an honest *Kingdom* at home.'[108] His was a lone voice raised in a letter to the *Daily News* attacking Kitchener's massacre of the Khalifa's forces at Omdurman the same year.

3. Denshawai

The relative truce between Cromer and Blunt in the 1890s eventually foundered over another issue of imperialist violence – the 1906 affair at Denshawai, one of the *cause célèbres* of British anti-imperialism. The vengeance perpetrated against the Egyptian village was for Blunt, writing his pamphlet *Atrocities of Justice under British Rule in Egypt* (1906), the culmination of a series of incidents in which judicially sanctioned executions and beatings of Egyptian peasants constituted an 'immense disgrace to the English name'. Demanding that 'somebody be called to account for it', and dismissing the possibility that influences outside his control were to blame, Blunt alights on Cromer as the public defender and ultimate sponsor of the executions. Cromer's conduct over the Denshawai affair laid bare the evils of his rule in Egypt. For, even though he had been absent on leave when the sentences were delivered and carried out, he had 'cynically' connived in 'a judicial crime of the extremest'. In fact, while dealing with effectively the final 'insincerity' and 'lapse from public virtue' of the man on whom Blunt was subsequently to heap so much responsibility for the perversion of Egypt under British occupation, this pamphlet is the original of the denunciations of Cromer and British imperialism to be found in the 'Secret History' series. The Denshawai case, the pamphlet suggests, changed for good Blunt's view about Cromer. As the personification of British prestige: 'His fame is a European one; nay, one world-wide. He has been a great benefactor even to Egypt, the land he has sullied with this last mad act of violent oppression.'[109]

Effecting a *J'accuse* style condemnation of officialdom, Blunt threatens to promulgate the 'Denshawai miscarriage of injustice' by having his pamphlet translated into French so that British imperial rule might be shown to be on a par with that of Czarist Russia or King Leopold's Congo. By publishing it in Arabic, he could expose the emptiness of British justice throughout the East.[110] The judgement on the Egyptian peasants is subverted by turning the pronouncement of guilt against Cromer and the entire British empire. In this instant Blunt adopts a humanitarian discourse that joined him within a growing disquiet at home over Britain's overseas suppression of indigenous movements for self-representation. Cromer himself seems to have been aware of the new currents, associated with the election of a popular Liberal Government. In 1907 he writes to Grey of 'the supposed sympathy in England with the ultra/ opposition here' adding: 'I know the difficulties of reconciling an Imperial policy with democratic tendencies at home.'[111] Though, after 1904, he was banished from Egypt for good (this time not by the government authorities but by ill health) Blunt, needless to say, was in close contact with the Egyptian 'ultra-opposition' nationalists led by Musta-pha Kamil. In Parliament, the newly formed Egyptian Committee asked 'a dozen or so questions a week'. With Denshawai, Blunt showed once more that he was 'still capable of exercising a considerable influence'.[112] His agita-tions from the late 90s onwards, involving letters to the *Daily News*, *Times*, and *Manchester Guardian*, alongside his composition of pamphlets, now bore fruit as at last he became visibly situated within a collective anti-imperialist tendency. More specifically, his publicising of the Denshawai atrocity can be seen as a preparation for other campaigns against conservative policies in the East, notably E.G. Browne's Persia campaigns.

The keynote of Blunt's polemic is the dishonouring of notions of British justice by a corrupting imperialism embodied in the person of Cromer. Though he had great abilities as an administrator and an economist, and had in earlier years helped judicial reform in Egypt, his rule had of late become dictatorial. Denshawai crystallised the systemic breakdown of justice in a situation where civil law had been made subservient to political advantage. In a powerful passage Blunt wires into the new qualms about the legality of Milner-type justifications of imperial violence:

> Sir Edward Grey has said that the British Empire cannot be carried on if the doubtful acts of its officials abroad are to be criticised at home and their injustices denounced. It is a grave saying and one which, if true, would lead to but a single conclusion. If of a truth the deeds of our officials cannot bear the light, if they are indeed deeds of darkness, then the British Empire, which exists, Sir Edward Grey tells us, by the world's ignorance of these things, deserves to go the way of other Empires where justice has been flouted and the common right of humanity denied. It were best, then, to paraphrase Mr. Gladstone's well-known utterance about India thirty years ago, that the British Empire with all its crimes upon its head should 'perish'.[113]

The 'deeds of darkness' that Blunt proceeds to expose are a series of cases, going right back to the occupation of Egypt itself, when 'English military power in Egypt [was used] to punish natives for crimes against Englishmen, according to military ideas of law, and by irregular means'; when an 'astonishing disproportion between offence and punishment [was] shown in cases where Englishmen were concerned'.[114]

For the reader of the future 'Secret History' series a familiar figure emerges from these narratives, one who has painstakingly researched the evidence that he may embarrass political chauvinism as it goes about its business. A righteously angry Englishman, he tirelessly lobbies official figures – sometimes as important as Prime Minister Gladstone – invoking liberal nostrums of justice and, at least in the early days, often gaining redress. That figure is of course Blunt. After 1895, incidents involving violence against British soldiers were to be dealt with under a decree which stipulated that where soldiers had been in uniform and in the performance of their military duties natives could be tried in special courts. These were presided over by both British and native judges, semi-military law operated, and draconian punishments up to the level of crucifixion were allowed. The tribunals were increasingly invoked during the period of Cromer's degeneration into dictatorial modes. A special tribunal had been called for in the Denshawai case by General Bullock and Cromer had assented. The process this set into motion had eventuated in the

> iniquity of the hanging of four natives and the scourging of eight others, besides the infliction of varying terms of penal servitude ranging up to life imprisonment, for a so-called 'assault' on five English officers under circumstances of the strongest provocation last month at a village in the Delta.[115]

Blunt's argument is that the British officers attacked at Denshawai were not performing their military duty but were involved in a pigeon shoot. The prosecution manufactured the charge that the killing of one of the officers was premeditated; the two native judges on the tribunal were subservient to the three British ones; the proceedings were hastily conducted, compounded by language difficulties, and the defendants were given only thirty minutes to defend themselves. Finally, the verdict was pre-determined since gallows were ordered four days before the trial began. The pamphlet's delineation of the events surrounding the Denshawai case culminates in a detailed eye-witness account by a French journalist of the punishments of flagellation and execution, terminated by the expression 'Civilisation has triumphed!'[116]

Conclusion: Blunt, Cromer and the authority of Imperialism

> Most of all, [Modern Egypt] must have reflected the spirit of its age: a pride not only in empire but also in the management of subject races with all the skills and fortitude and knowledge that Edwardians were persuaded went in it.
> Owen, Lord Cromer, p. 362

This chapter has centred on Blunt's dispute with Lord Cromer over the authority of British imperialism in Egypt. First of all, it has examined Cromer's *Modern Egypt* and Blunt's *Secret History of the English Occupation of Egypt* in terms of the arguments surrounding Britain's occupation of Egypt in 1882. Cromer, it was argued, utilises an Orientalist discourse in justifying the intervention and its continuance, while Blunt's opposition to imperialism in the name of the potentiality and authenticity of Islamic reform and self-renewal raises possibilities of what might be termed a counter-Orientalist discourse. Both Cromer and Blunt start out from the common ground of a belief in a European sponsored reform of Egyptian affairs in the name of removing abuses and developing an oriental society. Each, to varying degrees, claims for himself the authority to 'speak for Egypt', desiderating a course for Egypt based on an authority to read that country's needs that is in part self-referential. As the imperial administrator par excellence, claiming ample experience of oriental races, Cromer valorises the professionalism and bureaucratic efficiency that above all characterises his own modus operandi as Britain's consul-general and de facto ruler of Egypt from 1883 to 1907. Blunt's solutions involve himself as sponsor of Egypt's national independence and facilitator of her destiny as an Islamic nation validated by his understanding and promotion of the impending movement of Islamic renewal in the Arab world.

Given the vital difference of executive control that gave Cromer the authority to shape events (Blunt's claim to the Egyptian nationalists that he possessed an influence with no less a person than the British Prime Minister turned out to be an empty one), it was not surprising that the increasing polarisation of the two men centred around the power that accrued to imperialism, especially its providence to block other narratives and to urge its own indispensability. Adopting a 'prophetic' mode that testified to his position outside of power, Blunt countered Cromer's imperial certainties by an enunciation of judgement on the imperialist enterprise that to a degree was able to enter the Muslim foreboding over the invasion of alien Christian power into the Islamic abode of peace (*dar al-Islam*) and articulated the intervention in Egypt in terms of a threatening European imperialism across the Muslim areas of North Africa with all the potential this represented for a religious 'clash of civilisations'. Cromer, on the other hand, maintained his disdain for Islam at a remove in his argument for and justification of the crushing of the Urabist movement, foregrounding instead such pragmatic aims as the necessity of re-establishing order and the clearing of the ground for 'the gradual introduction of European civilisation into Egypt'.[117] Nevertheless, in the penultimate chapter of the section given over to Egypt before occupation, he summarises the arguments for intervention in the process deriding the potential of the Egyptian national movement and excoriating the influence of 'the Ulema of the El-Azhar Mosque' as 'reactionary', 'antiquated, obsolete and opposed to the commonplaces of modern civilisation'.[118] It was precisely on the progressive reformation of the Azhar that Blunt built his belief in Egypt's potential for regeneration. Equally, it was as on the bankruptcy of European civilisation that he based his denunciation of the invasion, led (as he believed) by the financiers and diplomatists who represented the real power of Europe.

In analysing these two discourses, I would suggest, we can observe not merely the personal antagonism of two Englishmen from broadly the same social class. Cromer's writings have frequently been probed for their contribution to the 'official' discourse of British imperialism and Orientalism, as analysed by Edward Said. Blunt has more often than not been categorised as an eccentric Victorian gentleman of idiosyncratic behaviour and views, made all the more aberrant because, like Cromer, his background was of the kind that normally contributed to the 'gentlemanly capitalism' that upheld the British empire. Instead, the voice he raised in his struggle against imperialism in Ireland and India, as well as in Egypt, helped bolster currents within British society that had grave doubts about empire. Certainly, in the opening decade or so of the twentieth century, Blunt provided a model for the British friends of Persia and Turkey in their agitation against the British Liberal Government's foreign policy in favour of the right of Muslim nations to self-determination.

Dedicated to the deconstruction and reconfiguration of the official narrative, the *Secret History* inscribes the perfidy of the British occupation by adopting a strategy of fusing the public record with off-the-record reportage based upon the author's own direct involvement with people in high places. Blunt claims to have penetrated to the truth behind the workings of British power in Egypt by virtue of inside knowledge facilitated by his intimacy with those diplomats, politicians and civil servants who made the decision in favour of intervention. This becomes a contested site that is integral to Blunt and Cromer's battle over the 'true' history of the British occupation. *Modern Egypt* post-dates *Secret History* by a year. In it, Cromer's method, as we saw, is to occlude Blunt's argument by placing it outside the bounds of authoritative discourse, precisely on account of its author's contravention of accepted establishment practice. Indeed, the reader senses that Cromer's recitation of the official criticisms of the nationalists, especially their leader, Urabi, has already been met by Blunt in his defence of the movement against its European critics. Although *Secret History* claims precedence by virtue of its prior publication, in relation to *Modern Egypt*, it possesses the qualities of a counter-reading, subverting the summative pretensions of the later text, and setting itself up instead as the authentic record of the events it presents. Then, in *Gordon at Khartoum*, Blunt returned to the offensive with a perceptive breakdown of Cromer's protestations of innocence over the Gordon affair.

The polarisation over the occupation of Egypt continued in the debate over Cromer's record as consul-general there. One specific charge that Cromer had made in government Blue Books on the Denshawai affair was that an atmosphere of fanaticism informed the attacks against the English officers. Whether attached to 'ultra'– nationalism or Pan-Islamism (and the terms were frequently conflated by both Cromer and Milner) native 'fanaticism' was a fear both floated in their propaganda, and invariably accompanied representations of the dangers faced by the occupation. In *Atrocities of Justice* this factor is dismissed by Blunt as having no bearing upon the preconceptions of either the Egyptian villagers or the British soldiers on the fateful day in question. It had, he asserted, been added by Cromer as an 'afterthought'.[119] The issue is a fitting one upon which to focus in any summary of these two writers' respective positions.

A comparison between the humanitarian discourse of *Atrocities of Justice* and the political and cultural Euro-centrism of Cromer's *Ancient and Modern Imperialism* fixes ideological formations that are still very much with us. Cromer's brand of imperialism certainly deployed Orientalist notions in its characterisation of subject peoples like the Egyptians and Indians as a medley of diverse cultures, religions and peoples such that to speak of India or of Egypt, as 'a single homogenous nation' was a fallacy. Western thought long ago conceded the right of peoples like the Egyptians and Indians to national self-determination. In doing so it allowed as an inevitable concomitant of decolonisation the dismantling of European communities within the boundaries of the independent emerging states, as was the case in Egypt after 1952. Yet the continuing penetration of such states by western influences testifies to a more subtle imperialism that nevertheless still has its germ in the articulation of the idea of the West's 'civilising mission' enunciated by both Cromer and Milner. 'The country over which the breath of the West', Cromer wrote, 'heavily charged with scientific thought, has once passed, and has, in passing, left an enduring mark, can never be the same as it was before. The new foundations must be of the Western, not of the Eastern type.'[120]

In contrast, Blunt in his foresightedness testifies to another stream of thought that is also still alive today. His advocacy of the cause of oppressed peoples often takes the form of an articulation of their thoughts and perspectives that cuts across the supremacist formulations of the western cultural idea. Right up to the outbreak of the Great War Blunt continued to hold fast to the cause of the Islamic nations in spite of a waning personal adherence to any form of religious truth, and a realization that in an immediate time frame, they must share the general fate of non-European peoples at the hands of European imperialism. His authority as prophet, missionary and chronicler derived from his maintaining of the old aristocratic values, his consciousness of the brotherhood of the human race, and his penetration to the core truths of Islam. By virtue of his status as an aristocrat, he advised, directed, half-commanded the Egyptian leaders, at the same time as he spoke for Egypt at the heart of Europe's power.

Undeterred by the defeat of 1882, Blunt continued to promote Egyptian national self-government, inveighed against British imperialism in Sudan, and in the new century primed his new allies on the necessity of Pan-Islamic solidarity. Through the idiosyncratic vehicle of the English squire, the British imperial establishment stood condemned and the potential for freedom of the Islamic nation was vindicated. In articulating this potential by recourse to Muslim figures and Islamic sources, and in fighting the asphyxiating sway of the imperial narrative, Blunt forged a discourse of counter-Orientalism from within the speech community of Orientalism itself.

4

Travel as Imperial Strategy: Lord Curzon and Britain's Empire in the East

The power that designedly fosters its own weakness, ultimately perishes of the atrophy thus engendered.
Curzon, *Persia and the Persian Question*, 1, p. 386.

Lords Cromer, Milner and Curzon might have been active in different theatres of the British empire but the very fact of their collective designation as Britain's imperial Edwardian proconsuls suggests commonalties. Like Cromer, Milner started off as a Liberal with a concern for social issues, but, coming of a later generation, he merged these into the new radical imperialism of the final decades of the nineteenth century. We have seen how *England in Egypt* and *Modern Egypt* share a common discourse; Milner's book, helping to popularise British imperialism in that country, paved the way for Cromer's summative statement of the case. Neither of these texts can be said to function within the specific genre of travel literature. (However, the three volumes in Blunt's anti-imperialist 'Secret History' series – *English Occupation of Egypt, India under Ripon*, and *Gordon at Khartoum* – are constructed around an English gentleman's diary entries, many of them records of personal travel.) If, like Milner's, Curzon's early writings promote empire as a project of 'romance', they do so within an individualised experience specifically enhanced by the travel frame. With Curzon, travel becomes central to exposition of the imperialist message. And just as imperialist literature on Egypt coheres around the achievement and ideas of Cromer, a cognate literature on Persia, the Persian Gulf and Afghanistan arose around the boundaries and strategic assumptions proposed by Curzon in *Russia in Central Asia* (1889) and *Persia and the Persian Question* (1892). This body of writing was enlarged by the pens of acolytes who came from the generation nurtured in the new imperialism. They include figures like Percy Cox and A.T. Wilson. Cox partly owed his promotion to Curzon, and Wilson in turned owed his to Cox. Both men engaged in travel, but like their master's this was travel for a purpose: mapping out the terrain in which Britain's imperial interests interfaced with the perceived threats of competitors. Reference will also be made to political journalism of the early 1900s, which took as its point of departure Curzon's portrayal of the decrepit Persian State and the 'weak' and 'cowardly' 'Persian character'.

This chapter therefore has the purpose of articulating a 'Cuzonian' school of imperialist travel writing, and linking it with the wider discourse of Orientalism. Here Edward Said's analysis remains of great value, and an attempt will be made to apply it to the context of Curzon's travel writings. Indeed, Curzon advances statements that amount almost to a transparent stereotype of Orientalism. He accomplished this by proposing a travel theory of his own in which he divided the purposes of his travels into two. The motivation for the first was political, and entailed surveying the scope of British interests in the East. The second predicated personal enjoyment of the eastern scene – a category later comprehended by Said in the term *aesthetic Orientalism*. Alongside contemporaries Balfour and Cromer, Curzon certainly seems to fit within that bloc of imperial patronage that sought to inscribe the East within the construct of western knowledge/power which Said termed Orientalism. As enunciations of an aesthetic of travel, or codifications of imperial administration, it might be argued that Curzon's writings rarely digress from Foucault's equation of knowledge and power. Curzon's emphasis is on an unchanging but unstable Orient which could be considered exactly what Said had in mind when he defined Orientalism as 'a static system of "synchronic essentialism"'.[1] Curzon and Cromer thought the stagnation of eastern polities like Egypt and Persia was such as to warrant European governance and control. Both were Islamic nations, and Islam contributed to their decay and general hopelessness. Cromer, Curzon, and their allies and supporters also established the code of the childish, irrational oriental, incapable of governing himself and therefore apt subject for European tutelage, which was essential if the eastern society was to progress. Of course, it was distinctly preferable for such governance to be British.

However, while Curzon's travel writings readily yield themselves to Orientalist analysis, his own individual qualities also emerge within his aesthetic Orientalism, in particular a romantic historicism and sense of occasion which fed into the imperialist aesthetic he developed during his period as Viceroy of India. There still remains the need to problematise the confidence of imperial mastery in Curzon's Orientalism. This can be done by supplying the interior anxieties it seeks to cover by its political/racial logocentrism, particularly as these anxieties relate to the imperial rivalries of the late nineteenth century. These operate within the political climate of late European imperialism in the East. Where Oriental stasis was judged beneficial to Britain's imperial interests (that is, when characteristic of an area over which Britain exercised control) re-iteration of Muslim weakness both justified and supported her imperial provenance (Egypt). But if such weakness was deemed to jeopardise Britain's imperial interests, as evidenced in an area over which British power could not be exercised or maintained (Persia), it became a subject of anxiety. Imperialist strategies for British involvement in Islamic affairs therefore differed according to the degree of control, direct or indirect, Britain might be able to apply.

Curzon and the East

George Nathaniel Curzon came of a long line of Curzons who, in his own words, went 'straight back to a Norman who came over with the Conqueror'. Unlike most of his ancestors, who were 'content to remain in possession of the same [Derbyshire] estate since the twelfth century', George Curzon was marked out for great things, amply fulfilling his prep school headmaster's prophecy that he would 'certainly be a distinguished man in the best sense of the term'.[2] An outstanding career at Eton was followed by five years at Balliol College, Oxford, the 'kindergarten for aspiring politicians and diplomats', attended by future Prime Minister H.H. Asquith, Foreign Secretary Edward Grey, and Alfred, later Lord Milner. The future Viceroy of India began his travels in the East as a young graduate, smarting from the humiliation of gaining only a second class degree. In 1883 he set out for the eastern Mediterranean with the aim of researching the Byzantine Emperor Justinian, the subject of one of Oxford's hardest essay prizes. En route from Naples to Athens he sat on his bunk writing his essay, in between paroxysms of seasickness. Curzon left his party of Oxford friends in Greece, going on to Egypt, where he cruised the Nile, had an affair with an exotic Englishwoman, but resolutely refused to enjoy the seductiveness of Cairo. From there he proceeded to Palestine and Syria, where he 'spent most of the time comparing the sites [...] with the events associated with them in the Bible' – much to the detriment of the former.[3] This was to set a pattern for his subsequent travels in Persia and Central Asia (though not in India) where he continually came across ruins on or near sites celebrated for their former glories. Despite such disappointment, Curzon's travels for a purpose had yielded a result: on his way home via Turkey and the Balkans, he read a copy of *The Times* announcing that his essay on Justinian, dispatched some weeks earlier, had won the Oxford prize. This vindication of the journey through and by the text (for Curzon always read everything written on the target area by other authors ancient and modern, and then endeavoured to supersede them himself) was to set a precedent for his later books on Central Asia and Persia.

Between 1887 and 1894 Curzon made five journeys to the East, including two that took him around the world. His political aspirations were the main motive, the aim being to establish himself as the foremost expert on Asian affairs in so far as they impinged upon the British empire. But he also found the East captivating in a manner that served to accentuate his Orientalism. In 1886, Curzon crossed the Atlantic, traversed eastern Canada, the Mid-West, and sailed from San Francisco to Japan, returning via Hong Kong,

Singapore and Ceylon. Calcutta, seat of an empire not far short of the entire size of Europe, furnished the climactic for his pride in British governance over the East. His aesthetic pleasure was no less fulfilled by the Taj Mahal. In 1888 Curzon journeyed across Central Asia on the newly completed Trans-Caspian Railway, from Uzun Ada on the Caspian, to Merv, Ashkabad, Bokhara and Samarkand, and then on horseback to Tashkent. The following year found him on the same railroad, this time crossing the Persian frontier into Khorassan, travelling from Meshed to Teheran by post horse (the only means of transport through a terrain devoid of roads), south to Bushire, and down the Persian Gulf. His second round the world trip, in 1892, gave Curzon the opportunity to observe China, Japan, and Korea. In 1894, he made his last journey East – to the Pamirs and Afghanistan – prior to his appointment as Viceroy of India (1899). His later career on the Conservative front bench and in government (his last years spent as Foreign Secretary) precluded extensive travel outside Europe.

Curzon's journeys are recorded in three works, each of which consists not only of travel writing, but copious historical research and political analysis on the East. *Russia in Central Asia*, and, *Persia and the Persian Question*, are both framed by a concern with Russia's spreading power in the region, and the putative threat this posed to British India, while *Problems of the Far East* (1896) concentrates on Britain's providential role in that area of the globe. These writings are in several key respects characteristic of Orientalism as delineated by Edward Said. The primary purpose of their publication was to establish for their author an acknowledged expertise on his subject – Asia/the Orient – so furthering a political career that would in turn be founded on a bedrock belief in British imperial dominance over large areas of the East. Curzon's mastery of his oriental subjects was intended to facilitate his imminent participation in Britain's political sway over the regions studied. The peoples of the East, with the exception of the Japanese, towards whom he is at best ambivalent, are presented as unchanging, picturesque, often corrupt, and generally incapable of reforming themselves. This backwardness is both the object of the traveller's censure, and on occasion, the source of his satisfaction. The 'orientals' having long forgotten their past, this is left to the western traveller and scholar to reconstruct. European encroachment on and conquest over their lands is inevitable. The Turkomans of Central Asia, recently so brutally conquered by the Russians, make willing imperial subjects, while the effete and cowardly Persians, steeped in the mire of centuries of 'oriental' decay, represent a conundrum to British imperial strategy given the importance of Persia within the 'Great Game'.

If, in spite of his noble ancestry, there seemed, as Harold Nicolson reflected, to be something of the self-righteous high Victorian bourgeois in his attitude towards empire, it is true that Curzon was himself conscious of a personal trait that lent itself to 'middle-class' efficiency. On his travels around the outposts of the British empire, Curzon had expected first to find 'good administration, good buildings roads and wharves, order and decorum', but was infinitely gratified to discover acquiescence in Britain's providential rule. He attributed the success of the grandiose Durbar that he directed in Calcutta in 1903 'half in earnest and half in jest, [to] his "middle class method".'[4] Government House, the Viceroy's residence in Calcutta, which he and his beautiful American wife Mary (née Leiter) were to grace between 1899-1905, was an Adam Smith creation based on his family seat at Kedleston, Derbyshire.

Curzon's career presaged great promise, but a combination of personal flaws and misfortunes perhaps denied his gifts their full expression. Lacking personal tact he was not always a good manager of men; his pre-occupation with detail often led him to shoulder absurd quantities of work that eventually broke his health. He attracted strong loyalties but his closest friends and colleagues had a habit of knifing him in the back. Curzon's first brief spell in office was as Salisbury's second in the Foreign Ministry in 1891, but his carefully accumulated experience of eastern affairs won him the Indian viceroyalty at the relatively young age of forty. Even this appointment was contested by those who saw liabilities in his advocacy of a forward foreign policy in the East to counteract Russia. The imperial historian, Ronald Hyam, believes 'politically his viceroyalty was disastrous'. Like Cromer, Curzon had no regard for the indigenous people other than as an imperial subject race. He 'spoke of Indians in terms normally reserved for pet animals: at best they were "less than school-children".'[5] The period in India cut the groove of his later political career. Erstwhile friends like the Secretary of State for India, John Brodrick, turned enemy; and ambitious adversaries like Lord Kitchener succeeded in bringing down the disingenuous Viceroy two years into his second term. Curzon returned to England to the political wilderness of the Liberal years under the highhanded Tory leadership of another one time friend, Arthur Balfour, and was passed over as leader in 1911 when the latter resigned to be replaced by the Canadian Bonar Law. With the fall of Asquith in 1916, Curzon – who was this time accused of his own political manoeuvrings – should have been the natural choice for Foreign Secretary, but the dilettante Balfour again stood in his way. The post finally became his in 1919, and with the fall of Lloyd George in 1922, and the death of Bonar Law a year later, the scene was set at last for Curzon to accede to the highest office. But once again, personal enemies, in no less a figure than King George V, and unadventitious circumstances – by now it seemed anachronistic for a Prime Minister to lead a government from the House of Lords – conspired to frustrate arguably the ablest man in politics. Curzon left the Foreign Office after the Conservative defeat of December 1923, and died prematurely sixteen months later. His legacy in India – beyond the renovation of ancient monuments – was swept away by the growing indigenous opposition to imperial rule.

No one could, more premeditatedly, and with greater application, have set out to adopt the East as a career. Harold Nicolson argued that 'most of Curzon's basic convictions, the articles of his faith, were absorbed before he

left Eton in 1878', and that it was as president of the literary society that he
heard Sir James Stephen proclaim: 'There is [...] in the Asian Continent an
empire more populous, more amazing, and more beneficent than that of
Rome. The rulers of that great domain are drawn from the men of our own
people.'[6] Five years later, Curzon embarked on his first journey East. After
doing the sites of Italy and Greece, he went on to Egypt, of which he wrote:
'Here are the same men of the same build and stature, [...] plying the same
business as did their ancestors of five thousand years ago [...] civilisation is
foiled by a country which refuses to be civilised, which cannot be civilised,
which will remain uncivilised to the end.' In Palestine, according to his
biographer, he suffered disappointment – 'disillusionment almost' – at what
he called the 'deformities of modern surroundings' as opposed to the 'original features' recorded in the Bible.[7] Coming from a young man in his
twenties, these assessments bare the stylistic hallmarks, as well as the Orientalist ideology, which characterises Curzon's pronouncements and political
practice thereafter. He carried them with him on his more extensive travels
East, between 1887 and 1894. How exactly did this love for the peoples of
the East present itself? Strikingly good-looking, of statuesque feature and
build, Curzon's other loves were restoring ancient buildings, and women. Just
as he enjoyed attractive women without any wish to waste time in consulta-
tion and discussion with them, Curzon was enchanted by an eastern landscape
or engaged by a loyal oriental retainer. A man of prodigious administrative
thoroughness and scholarly diligence, before composing a travel narrative he
read literally everything that had been written before on the target location.
However, Curzon's main preoccupation appeared to his contemporaries to be
his own ego: 'Never did his energy become more dynamic than when it was
seasoned by the competitive [...] never did his enjoyment of foreign travel
become so acute as when it enabled him to correct the imperfect information
or the erroneous hypotheses of previous travellers.' The East became his area
of political expertise, and upon this he built his political career, the
valedictory to which he sketched out himself on 10 Downing St notepaper
('in the course of some dull session of Cabinet', as Nicolson put it.) 'A
faithful servant of the Empire, he explored the secrets, and loved the peoples,
of the East. A ruler of his country in the Great War, he strove to add honour
to an ancient name.'[8]

Travel as Aesthetic Pursuit

At the height of his political career, as Foreign Secretary, Curzon encapsulated the motivation behind his journeys to the East:

> In my case the purpose was twofold: to see the beautiful and the romantic and,
> above all, the ancient things of the earth – a taste which I probably share with most
> travellers, but which took me preferably to distant Oriental lands; and, secondly, to

see how far the study of these places and peoples would help me to form an opinion of the Eastern responsibilities and destinies of Great Britain.[9]

The passage proposes a distinction which I intend to interrogate – between travel as a pursuit of 'the romantic and the beautiful', and as a means of establishing a knowledge of 'those places and peoples' that would give the traveller an expertise in governing them in the future (in exercising 'the Eastern responsibilities and destinies' of the British empire.) Curzon appears to be arguing for a simple bifurcation between the aesthetic value of travel and the political uses to which practical observation of eastern lands and peoples might be put. Indeed, he goes on to subordinate the second proposition altogether when he claims:

it gave me greater pleasure to be awarded the Gold Medal of the Royal Geographic Society for exploration and research than it did to become a Minister of the Crown; and every moment that I could snatch from politics – before they finally captured and tied me down – I devoted to the pursuit of my old love.[10]

This may be disingenuous, or it may be that Curzon genuinely believed in the aesthetic as a discrete category in his travel project. His travel writings certainly exemplify his aesthetic Orientalism, even if this is ultimately integral to his political programme in the East. It comprehended enjoyment of the East as a scene, as an inspiring spectacle, and its presentation of itself as a mystery and a riddle. As diversion and enchantment, the East afforded opportunities for philosophic reflection on such topics as the racial origins of the European, wonderment at natural landscapes, and contrastive meditations on evidences of ancient civilisations and present decay.

Travelling [...] Eastward, [...] arrested at each forward step by some relic of a dead civilisation, or a glorious but forgotten past, [...] the imagination of the European cannot but be impressed with the thought that he is mounting the stream of ages, and tracing towards its remote source the ancestry from which his own race sprung. His feet are treading in an inverse direction the long route of humanity.[11]

The implications of setting the schema of human progress into reverse in the way Curzon does are not hard to tease out. The East is simultaneously the site of European origin and Europe's primitive Other by virtue of the arrested development caused by its unchanging essence. To support this idea, which is embedded in the passage on Egypt quoted at the beginning, Curzon quotes from the work of his favourite commentator on the Oriental scene, the seventeenth-century traveller Jean Chardin's *Voyages*. According to Chardin: 'In the East they are constant in all things. The habits are at this day in the same manner as in the precedent ages; so that one may reasonably believe that in that part of the world the exterior forms of things (as in their manners and customs) are the same now as they were 2,000 years since.' Curzon finds ample material for reflective contrast with the nineteenth century in such a proposition:

> [...] is it that in the East, and amid scenes where life and its environment have not
> varied for thousands of years, where nomad Abrahams still wander with their
> flocks and herds, where Rebecca dips her water skin at the well, where savage
> forays perpetuate the homeless miseries of Job, western man casts off the slough of
> an artificial civilisation, and feels that he is mixing again with his ancestral stock,
> and breathing the atmosphere that nurtured his kind?[12]

Another authority Curzon cites in *Persia and the Persian Question* is Comte
Arthur de Gobineau's, *Religions et Philosophies dans l'Asie Central* (1865).
Gobineau, the 'father of racist ideology', seems not to have infected Curzon
with his racist theory, except in so far as Curzon appears to endorse the
Aryan origins of Europe in Asia in a passing remark: 'It ought not to be
difficult to interest Englishmen in the Persian people. They are the same
lineage as ourselves.'[13] Gobineau's theory of the decay of Asia may also have
strengthened Curzon's own assessment of the moribund state of oriental
societies, but he certainly did not go along with Gobineau's pessimistic
appraisal concerning the degeneration of Europe's Aryans – not, anyway, as
far as Great Britain was concerned. Nevertheless, the Sphinx-like remark
with which the French Orientalist began *Religions et Philosophies* finds a
resonance within Curzon's own aesthetic Orientalism: 'Tout ce que nous
pensons et toutes les manières dont nous pensons ont leur origine en Asie'.

Gobineau, Michael Biddiss points out, emphasized the magnitude of the
debt Europe owed Asia. (By Asia Gobineau meant Persia and the areas where
Iranian influence had been felt in previous historical epochs.) But he also
wrote: 'Their [Asians'] senility will probably lead us to reflect upon certain
features at present emerging in Europe which do not fail to suggest this same
decrepitude.' His theory of racial decay suggested a European imperialism
over the Orient would corrupt Europe; such domination was 'a very appetiz-
ing dish, but one which poisons those who consume it'. Gobineau 'denied
that the remaining virtues of European civilization were communicable to the
still more moribund Orient.' Nevertheless, 'he always looked back with some
nostalgia' to his oriental experiences. Biddiss concludes that Gobineau's
writings on Persia leant no support to 'an imperialist doctrine'.[14] Clearly,
Curzon absorbed the nostalgia but completely discarded Gobineau's pessimism about empire.

Curzon's aesthetic Orientalism is fed by a romantic re-creation of
oriental sites and scenes (recently excavated by the archaeologists) in terms
of the mythologies that had accreted around them. The mythological geography of Mesopotamia, for instance, contained the Garden of Eden and the
Babylonian tower ('where Daniel prophesied, where Israel wept, where
Alexander perished'), places valorised in the histories of the Jews, the
Classical world, the Arabian Nights, and more recently, European travellers'
tales – 'waters [...] ploughed by the rival argosies of Portugal, Holland, and
Great Britain'. It was crucial that Curzon's own race be situated as the latest
link in this narrative:

If I am there tempted to unravel some few of the threads that have been woven into a web of history, intensely personal to our own country and race, I shall also be able to show that Great Britain sustains, in a less acquisitive and martial age, that prestige which she gained at the dawn of her career of Asiatic conquest, and that the British name is still on these distant waters a synonym for order and freedom.[15]

Curzon's sense of Britain's relation to this imagined history helped lend his romanticism an embodied form during his period as Viceroy of India, when aesthetic Orientalism merged into an aesthetic of imperialism. This was evidenced par excellence in the great Durbar of 1903, a 'spectacle [that] owed its dramatic quality to his artistic temperament, to his sense of the Imperial grandeur of the British Empire, both as an abstract idea and as a concrete reality.'[16] The corollary, however, of making the East all past, aesthetically satisfying as this might be as a refuge from an artificial nineteenth century, was to imprison it within a riddle which could only be read by the trained eye of the western aesthete and man of knowledge, who saw everywhere the juxtaposition of ancient ruin and present desolation and decay.

Indeed, it could be argued, though I do not wish to enlarge on this here, that Curzon's eastern scene differed from that of the European explorers of Africa and the Americas, discussed by Mary Louise Pratt, precisely in so far as that scene was ancient and ripe for reconstruction, rather than virgin and newly to-be-reported-on. The 'imperial eye' in this context is versed in the knowledge of the ages, and the 'monarch of all I survey' feeling contains within it both racial pride of origin, and the empowerment provided by the sense of ultimate placement at the fountainhead of the human civilisation project.[17] 'It is a contrast equally visible in the inanimate and in the human world [...] Majestic ruins that tell of a populous and mighty past rear their heads amidst deserted wastes and vagabond tents.' Looked at in this context, the unchanging character of the East can be brandished as a stick to berate the lethargy and fatalism of the easterner, and exalt the energy of the European. The 'poetry of contrast' between Britain and the East could be viewed in their respective modes of travel: 'Here all is movement and bustle, flux and speed; there, everything is imperturbable, immemorial, immutable, slow.'[18] But stasis meant retrogression: it was not surprising that the traveller passed through towns in Persia that were 'entirely abandoned', with a melancholy confusion of 'tottering walls and fallen towers'; saw citadels and fortified posts 'fallen into irretrievable decay', now 'shapeless heaps of mud', or entered cities whose walls were in ruins or had yawning gaps, and whose cemeteries were dirty and desecrated. The miserable and chaotic conditions of Persia in the North around the Caspian Sea (an area potentially important as a trading centre) revealed Persia's 'congenital inability to help herself'.[19] The decaying oriental scene is thus engaged in painful dialectic with its past, but cannot be allowed to do so alone; without, that is, registering the impact of spreading European hegemony, both cultural and political. Castigated for their backwardness, when the Persians do adopt a western veneer in their capital, this is condemned as 'a city [...] born and nurtured in the East, but

[…] beginning to clothe itself at a West-End tailors', and is compared to 'the insufferable and debauched districts of Galata and Pera'. Korea, 'half stupe-fied by its long repose', is only challenged by the arrival of 'the plenipo-tentiaries of great Powers in its ports to solicit or to demand reciprocal treaties'.[20]

Curzon's aesthetic Orientalism, however real and distinctive it figures in his mind, where it does appear to take on a life of its own, still dissolves into a political taxonomy of the East, the embedded concern of all his travel writings. 'Curzon never allowed his romantic self to submerge the politician, the fledgling statesman, or the missionary of empire.'[21] This remark is exemplified by the pageantry of the Durbar, which satisfied, at one at the same time, Curzon's own imaginative sense of Britain's linkage to the oriental past, and the need to impress on the world (and the oriental) the might of Britain's imperial power.

Travel as imperial strategy

Drawing on Curzon's speeches and addresses post-dating his period as Viceroy of India, Edward Said saw in Curzon's emphasis on study of the Orient that Foucauldian equation of knowledge and power that was central to the Orientalist project: 'From the days of Sir William Jones the Orient had been both what Britain ruled and what Britain knew about: the coincidence between geography, knowledge, and power, with Britain always in the master's place, was complete.'[22] Curzon's travel writings, composed by an aspiring politician in his thirties, exemplify the imperial uses to which knowl-edge acquired through travel could be put. They establish a geography often so nakedly political as largely to deconstruct Curzon's disingenuous claim that he engaged in travel literature as a form of relaxation and escape from the grind of political life. (No sooner had he surveyed the source of the Oxus and explored the Pamirs – for which he was awarded the Royal Geographic Society's Gold Medal – than he was proceeding to Kabul where he achieved the coup of being the first private traveller to be invited to visit the Amir of Afghanistan.) The expertise and publicity (he was a writer of copious letters and articles on Asian issues for *The Times*) derived from his journeys in the East helped Curzon gain his first government post as Under Secretary for India in 1891, and in 1898 enabled him to secure his appointment as Viceroy of India. The recrimination surrounding his resignation from the last post helped sour his career for many years to come. But Curzon never relinquished his political love affair with the East. 'Asia was his speciality, and he inclined to regard all extra-Asian matters as questions well-suited to the capacities of Mr. Lloyd George or Mr. Bonar Law.' This 'was to prove both a useful and a destructive element in his […] career'.[23]

According to John Seeley, two schools of English opinion existed on the empire. Curzon's writings and speeches situate him definitively in the 'bombastic' camp: those 'lost in wonder and ecstasy at its immense dimensions, and at the energy and heroism which presumably have gone to the making of it; this school advocates the maintenance of it as a point of honour or sentiment.'[24] Landing at Hong Kong, Curzon registered 'a thrill of pride for his nationality'. 'The sight [he wrote] [...] of the successive metropolises of England and the British Empire in foreign parts is one of the proudest experiences of travel.' This was 'a responsibility [which] [...] with its associated virtues of duty, sacrifice and justice, dominated his conscience [...] He believed profoundly that God had selected the British Empire as an instrument of Divine purpose.'[25] At the same time though, Curzon's immersion in the imperial enterprise coincided with an 'increasing scepticism about [Britain's] ability to influence events or even to retain the empire.' The 1890s and opening decade of the twentieth century were accompanied by a deepening anxiety including a fear of non-European races, crystallised in 1905 by the Japanese victory against Russia, whose own 'ominous' challenge had been over-estimated.[26]

At the centre of Curzon's imperial geography, and embedded in his travel writings on Central Asia, Persia, or the Far East, was India. 'Even the fortunes of remote Korea are in a manner bound up with the politics of Hindustan [...] Towards her, or into her orbit, a centripetal force, which none appears able to resist, draws every wandering star. Just as it may be said that the Eastern Question in Europe turns upon the dismemberment of Turkey, so the Eastern Question in Asia turns upon the continued solidarity of Hindustan.'[27] His first published exercise in the genre of travel writing, *Russia in Central Asia in 1889*, is a political essay on the expansion of Russia towards the borders of Persia and Afghanistan, her military consolidation of the mainly Turkoman territories, and the strategic response Russia's forward possessions should or should not excite in London and Calcutta. Curzon's text skirts around a fascination with Russian methods of conquest and colonisation which he explicitly compares with British rule in India. In contrast with eastern cities that mimicked Europe, Bokhara in Central Asia remained 'at the present juncture the most interesting and intact city in the East.' Ten miles away the Russians had established a station on their Trans-Caspian Railway, around which a new city, certain to eclipse the old, was building. Bokhara under the Russians was theoretically an autonomous khanate, indirect rule meaning avoidance of the expense of annexation. But Curzon had been there and seen it with his own eyes; he knew very well what was afoot – by a seeming concession to native sentiment, the Russians were in reality playing their own game, 'tolerat[ing] a semi-independent Amir with as much complacency as we do a Khan of Khelat or a Maharaja of Kashmir.'[28]

Beneath their imperial cunning the Russians adopted a ruthless policy in Central Asia expressive of a power that Curzon affects to dismiss as efficient if crude. By its vigour Russia resituated the staid imperial provenance of Great Britain. Of the Russian massacre of Turkomans at Geok Tepe in 1881, he observes:

> A greater contrast than this can scarcely be imagined to the British method, which
> is to strike gingerly a series of taps, rather than a downright blow [...] But there
> can be no doubt that the Russian tactics, however deficient they be from the moral,
> are exceedingly effective from the practical point of view.

The oriental was apt to see 'in the heavy hand of the conqueror the all-powerful will of God', which made his subsequent pacification an easier task.[29] Submerged beneath the surface Orientalism, with its gratification of Curzon's racial pride and its imperial logocentricism, is a destabilising anxiety that derives from his awareness of that project's vulnerability to an alien more vigorous imperial challenge. He affects to dismiss the Russian threat by disclaiming any British interest in the conquered territory, even proffering the hand of friendship as from one imperial power to another. But he also includes belligerent statements by Russian generals on Britain's tyrannical hold over India that are hardly reciprocal, and even quotes an article from the French press which announces Russia's inevitable ejection of the English from India. Curzon's response is to berate the Russians for their lack of finesse 'altogether lacking the moral impulse that induces unselfish or Christian exertion on behalf of a subject people.' He doubts if the Russians, 'though they may have the ability to conquer and the strength to keep, have the genius to build a new fabric out of old materials.'[30] So troubling is the Russian spectre, however, that Curzon accomplishes the rhetorical feat of doubling his Orientalist critique, that is, by stripping Russia of her European race and branding her an oriental power:

> The conquest of Central Asia is a conquest of Orientals by Orientals [...] Civilised
> Europe has not marched forth to vanquish barbarian Asia [...] but barbarian Asia,
> after a sojourn in civilised Europe, returns upon its former footsteps to reclaim its
> own kith and kin.31

In *Persia and the Persian Question*, Curzon repeats his assessment that Russia is in that early stage of imperialism in which 'the lust for new possessions is in excess of every other sentiment'. Inconsistencies in *Persia's* discourse, now accommodating to Russia's motives in her expansion into Central Asia, now condemnatory of her designs on Persia, may incorporate Curzon's personal anxieties and ambivalence, and, equally, his politically-inspired manoeuvres as a self-appointed expert on the East, setting himself up both to solace and to warn. Seistan, an impoverished, unattractive province of eastern Persia, merits an entire chapter because here Russian and British strategic interests appeared to converge if not collide. Curzon's advocacy of an Anglo-Indian railway across Indian Baluchistan to the borders of Seistan mimics Russia's Trans-Caspian Railway but affects to eschew belligerence even as it acknowledges strategic fact. Curzon is coy about the strategic details and floats the railway as a commercial scheme, even broaching the idea of a link up with Russia's. Personally, he claims not to foresee the transportation of troops along its length, but 'the map [...] will assist the reader to form his own judgement'. Conversely, Curzon declares openly that Russia 'regards the future partition of Persia as a prospect scarcely less certain of fulfilment than the achieved partition of Poland.' (Ironically this prophecy would be 'achieved' in Curzon's lifetime, by the Anglo-Russian convention of 1907, an agreement Curzon bitterly opposed. Persia was effectively partitioned by Russia in collusion with the British Liberal Government).

Russia's occupation of Khiva, Merv, Bokhara and Samarkand presaged annexation of the provinces of North Persia 'from west to east'.[32] The scattered warnings of Russia's intent are encapsulated in the final chapter of volume two in a statement Curzon attributes to Peter the Great: 'Hasten the decadence of Persia, penetrate to the Persian Gulf, re-establish the ancient commerce of the Levant, and advance to the Indies, which are the treasure-house of the world.' Consciousness of Russia's master-strategy in Asia therefore spoiled any prolonged state of detached aesthetic pleasure the traveller might have enjoyed in Persia. Instead, Curzon is the British imperial surveyor, scrutinising a corrupt and despotic oriental state bordering Northern India and the warm waters of the Gulf – clinically reporting the precariousness of its fabric and the points most likely to cave in the ramshackle edifice, as Russia looks covetously across from the newly conquered wastes of Central Asia: 'like a man camping in a desolate and stony field divided only by a thick hedge from a spacious pasture, where he sees food for himself, fodder for his beasts [...] What a temptation to break through the hedge and poach on the hidden preserves!'[33]

In Khorasan, Curzon sees 'a succession of points at which Russian interference, influence, or intrigue is being actively pushed forward.' Ever the prospective imperial manager, he desiderates that a 'cardinal axiom of Russian politics in the East [is] that commercial must precede political control' and meticulously checks the bazaar in Meshed for evidence of Russian goods. The decay he sees all around him possesses connotations beyond philosophic meditation on Asia's proverbial ageless decline. *Kashan*: 'A more funereal a place I had not yet seen. Scarcely a building was in repair, barely a wall in tact.' *Isfahan*: 'fallen from its high estate, and now in perpetual sackcloth and ashes'; 'in itself an epitome of modern Iran.' In *Nishapur*, home of the poet Omar Khayyam, the city walls are broken down – why the desultory workmen – who would wish to repair them? 'An enemy could march into Nishapur as easily as he could march down Brompton Road, and would find about as much to reward him as if he occupied in force Brompton Cemetery.'[34] The irony is directed at Persia, but the English reference suggests that, worthless though the Persian scene might appear to a casual observer, occupation of Persian soil is no remote eventuality, and any loss of her national sovereignty would constitute a grave setback for Great Britain. The lesson is spelled out in the book's last chapter: 'I can see no reason why a Russian army of 10,000 men should not be in bloodless occupation of Meshed within three weeks of the commencement of hostilities.' The landscape acquires a strategic focus, as the traveller probes Persia's woefully exposed northern defences. Mounted on a donkey, a solitary Curzon almost succeeds in penetrating the mountain fort of Kelat-i-Nadiri, only to be halted a few metres from the entrance by the shouts of a ragbag soldiery. They claim if he was a Russian they would have shot him – 'though how they could have guessed my nationality when they never saw me, or have shot at all when they were fast asleep, I did not needlessly vex them by asking.'[35] Oriental unchangableness, decay, and European encroachment are here fixed ineluctably within the bounds of Britain's imperial interests.

Alone of all the eastern peoples whose acquaintance Curzon made on his travels, the Japanese appeared to subvert the theses of Orientalism; and this sets up a further anxiety in Curzon's narrative. Not only did the outward evidences of westernisation/ modernisation testify to Japan's exception to the oriental rule, Curzon also noted in the armed forces a strain of discipline that was native and potentially disquieting to the European powers. Scrutinising Japan's attitude toward foreigners decides him that 'the more she has assimilated European excellences the more critical she had become of European defects.' The Japanese temperament displayed 'impetuous Chauvinism' and readiness for war; however, this puerile patriotism might be tempered by the nation achieving international recognition and the maturity that came from 'conscious strength'.[36] As with Russia, Curzon recognises in Japan a potential antagonist that might not play the game in the mature and sedate manner adopted by Great Britain in her great domain in the East. Britain had met Japan's demands for a revision of treaties with foreign powers with a 'conciliatory and generous spirit' born by a 'desire to welcome [Japan] into the comity of nations'. 'A power with whom we share so many common relationships', Japan might be seen as a worthy recipient of Britain's magnanimous sponsorship of reform in the East. In revising their treaty, 'England assisted Japan to strike-off from herself the shackles of a past to which she had proved herself superior, and which is every day fading into a more rapid oblivion.' But within Curzon's imperialist discourse, such phraseology carries split significations: it attempts both to underwrite Britain's imperial primacy as the 'pivot of the situation – no slight proof of her commanding influence on the destinies of distant Asia', at the same time as it betrays a submerged anxiety and fear of a new, more vigorous and threatening challenger.[37]

Fixing the Oriental Subject

According to Said, the eighteenth century move towards classification of nature and man into types, associated pre-eminently with Linnaeus and Buffon, aided descriptions of the oriental. 'When an Oriental was referred to, it was in terms of such genetic universals as his "primitive" state, his primary characteristics, his particular spiritual background.' In the discourse of Curzon's contemporaries, Balfour and Cromer, Said argues that the oriental is represented as 'irrational, depraved (fallen), childlike, "different"; [...] the European is rational, virtuous, mature, "normal".'[38] The political ramifications of dealing with the oriental polity, nominally independent, but in reality enmeshed in the system of imperial *realpolitik*, is what exercises Curzon chiefly in his representations of 'orientals'. On his travels in the East, he never lost an opportunity to make himself known to the local political elite. His portrait of the Persian monarch, Nasir al-Din Shah, had needed to be toned down owing to his entry into Salisbury's short-lived Conservative Ministry of 1891, but Curzon was compensated by the coup of gaining access to the Amir of Afghanistan. This gained him added political capital because it resulted in the establishment of closer diplomatic links with a recalcitrant but in Britain's imperial geography strategically crucial player.

> Turkestan, Afghanistan, Transcaspia, Persia – to many these names breathe only a sense of utter remoteness or a memory of strange vicissitudes and of moribund romance. To me, I confess, they are the pieces on a chessboard upon which is being played out a game for the dominion of the world.[39]

In a key passage in his introduction to *Persia and The Persian Question*, Curzon fixes the oriental subject in the same dualistic terms as the environment of grandeur and decay:

> Splendide mendax might be taken as the motto of Persian character. The finest domestic virtues co-exist with barbarity and supreme indifference to suffering. Elegance of deportment is compatible with a coarseness amounting to bestiality. The same individual is at different moments haughty and cringing. A creditable acquaintance with the standards of civilisation does not prevent gross fanaticism and superstition. Accomplished manners and a more than Parisian polish cover a truly superb faculty for lying and almost scientific imposture. The most scandalous corruption is combined with a scrupulous regard for specified precepts of the moral law. Religion is alternately stringent and lax, inspiring at one moment the bigot's rage, at the next the agnostic's indifference. Government is both patriarchal and Machiavellian – patriarchal in its simplicity of structure, Machiavellian in its finished ingenuity of wrong doing. Life is both magnificent and squalid: the people at once despicable and noble, the panorama at the same time an enchantment and a fraud.[40]

Again, the tone of the last sentence should not mislead us into regarding Curzon's attitude towards the Persians as one of mere aesthetic detachment. As in his portrayal of the Persian landscape, Curzon's dialect of Orientalism inscribes an ambivalence that vacillates between confirmed racial superiority and unease that in competition for power over the oriental subject control could be wrested from Anglo-Saxon hands.

If within the threatened boundaries of Persia there could have but preponderated men like Curzon's servant, an Afghan of Persian extraction – 'a fine specimen of the Asiatic. Courageous and resourceful, a good horseman, with the manners of a perfect gentleman [who] entertained a profound

conviction there was no people in the world like the English.' Or even the
drunken Ilkhan of Kuchan, who had met English travellers before – Curzon
lists four between 1873-80 – and asked them the same suspicious questions.
His ancestors, owing to their rebellious character, had been moved from their
Kurdish area by Shah Abbas to protect the northern border. (Curzon approved
of the strategic transference of whole tribes to defend imperial borders.)
Admittedly, compared to the Persians, the Turkomans, Afghans and Kurds
were known to be warlike people. But the Turkoman tribesmen, a people who
once terrorised Khorasan, had already been incorporated into the Russian
empire with worrying success. They were to be encountered wearing Russian
uniforms in Baku: 'only eight years ago [Russia's] bitter and determined
enemies [...] crossing into Europe in order to salute as their sovereign the
Great White Czar.'[41] The problem with the Persian – 'a coward at the best of
times'– was that he lacked the mettle required to resist any invader. 'There is
not one in a hundred who would pull his sword from the scabbard to vindicate [his country's] independence.'[42]

The Shah, diplomatically presented, was the establisher of as strong,
secure and centralised a regime as could be expected given recent Persia's
history. He was 'the best existing specimen of a moderate despot' disposed
toward reform, if given to adopting fads which were just as soon dropped,
and ruler over a people hostile or inimical to reform. Deferring the myth of
the Persians' Aryan race (attractive to Gobineau and other European writers
on the country) Curzon accounts for the monarch's 'manliness, amounting
almost to a brusqueness of bearing' by contrasting his Turkish blood to the
'smooth and polished Persian'. 'Extremely affable and well-disposed towards
Europeans' as he was (particularly Britain after his reception by Queen
Victoria), the Shah was unfortunately situated between the rivalry of Britain
and Russia.[43] Curzon's instinct was to buttress the authority of the Shah, and
the pro-British politicians around him (though he is often suspicious of the
reputed Anglophile sentiments of some of these.) But the odds were stacked
against Nasir al-Din committing himself to a British alliance:

> Whenever Russia desires to enforce with peculiar emphasis some diplomatic
> demand at Teheran, a mere enumeration of the Russian garrisons within a few
> hundred miles of the Persian capital is enough to set the Council of Ministers
> quaking, and to make the sovereign himself think twice.[44]

In the north of Persia, British power could barely strut as ostentatiously as
Russia's (hence Curzon's concern to make the British embassy building in
Meshed more prepossessing.)

In Afghanistan though, Curzon could celebrate one victorious episode
in the game: his own successful wooing of its amir. A case study of the
civilised barbarian, which inscribes the Orient as 'both magnificent and
squalid; the people at once despicable and noble', Curzon's essay on the
Amir of Afghanistan is a bizarre traveller's tale that revels in paradox. Fixing
the oriental despot according to a recognisable oriental type, Curzon's repre-

sentation at the same time enhances its author's political kudos as self-appointed intermediary between an *outré* tyrant and the British Government. 'In my numerous interviews I flatter myself I succeeded in winning the Amir's confidence.' The Amir exercised his tyrannical power for the good of his country, even as he violated all the codes of humanity.

> In this strange and almost incredible amalgam of the jester and the cynic, the statesman and the savage, I think that a passion for cruelty was one of his most inveterate instincts [...] He confided to an Englishman at Kabul that he had put to death 120,000 of his own people [...] Nevertheless, this monarch, at once a patriot and a monster, a great man and almost a fiend, laboured hard and unceasingly for the good of his country [....] He and he alone was the Government of Afghanistan [...] [In his] colossal but, childish vanity, [...] he cherished the illusion [...] that he had a monopoly of all the talents and was the universal genius of Afghanistan, particularly in all matters of mechanics and arts.[45]

Here was a man of blood who loved scents, colours, gardens, singing birds and flowers. Quotation from his lengthy epistles reveals a rambling oriental prolixity; his English guest is also treated to a rehearsal of his imagined behaviour when presented to Queen Victoria at the Parliament of Westminster. Nevertheless, Curzon is filled to overflow with gratification at being able to deliver the Amir's acceptance of an invitation to visit London. In his celebration of the archetypal oriental tyrant, Curzon can even indulge a criticism of his own country as he half-endorses the Afghan's exercise of a random oriental terror to limit crimes of murder, comparing this to the unpunished murders of English cities. Curzon's account exudes the confident assurance that the country over which the Amir ruled would one day become the Anglo-Afghanistan protectorate.

Great Britain, Russia, and the politics of Islam

The contrast between indulgent aesthetic delight, and cold assessment of imperial strategy, structures Curzon's attitude towards Islam. He always had an eye for Islamic architecture. The Taj Mahal was the building that most impressed him on his first visit to India - its 'frigid emptiness' gave scope for his imagination where the 'bursting [...] life' of South India did not.[46] On his journey to Tunisia in 1885, Curzon approached the architecture of Kairwan in the same spirit. This 'secluded city' accorded well with his aesthetic predilections: for twelve hundred years it had remained 'inviolate -its sanctuaries undefiled by the foot of Christian or of Jew'. Set apart from the city of Tunis, which had been conquered by the French four years earlier, 'even in her desolation, ravished and forlorn she still retained the halo of sanctity [....] Though the enemy was within her gates [Kairwan] was his superior by reason of a majesty which none could gainsay.'[47] By chance Curzon's visit coincided with that of General Boulanger; the conquest thus personalised contrasts the glorious Islamic past even more starkly with the colonised

present. In fact, through an ironic modification of the strategy of disguise,
Curzon poses as the general's son and is thereby enabled in his desire for
access to mosques that would otherwise have been off-limits. But from being
in a position to bear witness to Islam's stately decline, the western visitor is
abruptly transformed into spectator at a 'horrible rite of self-mutilation'
performed by a marabout and his followers. 'As I witnessed the disgusting
spectacle and the pandemonium of sounds [...] my senses reeled.' On the
point of fainting, Curzon is ushered away by one of his friends.[48] The
contrasts are further muddied: the reader cannot help draw the inference that
what began as an aesthetic reconstruction of 'a mystic fascination' Kairwan
had 'long exercised over [Curzon's] mind', has been replaced by an experience of the sort of dark, unspeakable rites the French occupation had arrived
to put an end to.[49]

   In Persia, Curzon doffed all pretence of being anyone but himself. As a
representative of his country he could not risk detection as a European within
Islamic holy places, such as the Shi'ih pilgrimage shrines at Meshed and
Qum. His predilection for imaginative reconstruction of a glorious past could
not, anyway, be indulged in places teeming with Asiatic pilgrims. But Islamic
Central Asia was a different story. In Samarkand, he conflates a funeral, a
sunset, and the decay of Islam, in one piece of self-referential purple prose.

> Below and all around, a waste of grey sand-hills was encumbered with half-fallen
> tombstones and mouldering graves. Here and there a horsehair plume, floating
> from the end of a rickety pole, betrayed the last resting-place of a forgotten sheikh
> or saint. The only existence of life was supplied by the horses of the mourners,
> themselves out of sight at the moment, which were picketed amid the waste of
> graves. Presently round the corner of the mosque emerged the long line of tur-
> baned orientals, grave and silent. Each mounted his beast without speaking a word
> and rode away.[50]

Against 'the turquoise blue' that 'seemed to encircle the horizon', and the
'glory' of the sunset, quickly replaced by dusk, 'a long cry trembled through
the breathless void. It was the muezzin from a neighbouring minaret, sum-
moning the faithful to evening prayer.' Inscribed by tropes of neglect, decay
and death, its devotees persisting in haunting rituals from a once glorious
past, Islam, Curzon implies, presents no danger to the western imperial
project. It is only an obstacle to those who profess it. 'Western Asia [was] in
the unyielding and pitiless clutch of Islam, which oppose[d] a Cyclopean wall
of resistance to innovation or reform.'[51] Particularly galling was the success
with which Russia had pacified her own Muslim subjects. The Muslims of
Transcaspasia had benefited by their interface with European imperial power.
The once brutally courageous, barbarian Turkomans had been subdued and
incorporated into Russia's imperial war machine as loyal auxiliaries. The
people had tasted the uses of western technology too. In Bokhara, the
railway, originally denounced as satanic by the clergy, afforded the spectacle
of 'Mussulman passengers crammed to suffocation, just as they are in India

the infantile mind of the Oriental deriving an endless delight from an excitement which he makes not the slightest effort to analyse or to solve.'[52]

Curzon's image of Islam is a simple one. The religion is a cause of atrophy, an enemy of progress. Allied with the 'infantile Oriental mind', Islam created a problem of no mean magnitude for Britain. In as strategically sensitive a state as Persia, Britain's interests were hardly served by the country's backwardness, for it encouraged Russia's aggression, and this in turn endangered Britain's hold on India. Any rejection of western modernisation is therefore dismissed as mere fanaticism. The would-be innovator, Nasir al-Din Shah, was hampered by 'a sense of powerlessness against the petrified ideas and prejudices of an Oriental people', but had also shown 'commendable independence of the fanatical element among the *mullas* and *mujtaheds* of Islam'.[53] Ominously, in Meshed, Curzon found the local population resigned and respectful towards their encroaching northern neighbour. Russia's contract with Muslim backwardness in Persia was that it consistently blocked all attempts at reform. In contrast, Britain – which did 'not covert one square foot of Persian soil' – despite past vacillations, would need to establish a future policy that guided Persia along the pathway of 'material expansion and internal reform'. The British had established the telegraph system there in an act which Curzon presents as one of entirely benevolent disinterest.

Curzon's assessment of the reform issue looks forward to the early years of the next century in which Britain's interests in Persia led her to sponsor reform – until the Anglo-Russian convention caused her withdrawal of this support. But his more profound long-term failure was perhaps his misreading of Persian resistance to western encroachment, which he dubbed purely reactionary and fanatical, and unrelated to popular patriotism. For example, he saw the signs of popular anger against foreign commercial monopolies in Persia and opposition to the Shah, but dismissed them as led by the 'retrograde and priestly party'. The mullah-led tobacco protest of 1891 evidenced to 'the manacles of Mohammedan prejudice and superstition' resulting in 'recrudescence of bigotry at the admission of the foreign element upon so large a scale.'[54] It is noteworthy that Curzon makes no mention of Persian oppositional thought; in particular, of the revolutionary Pan-Islamist thinker, Jamal al-Din al-Afghani, substantial English accounts on whom later appeared in Wilfrid Scawen Blunt's, *Secret History of the English Occupation of Egypt* (1907) and Edward Granville Browne's, *Persian Revolution* (1910).

It is significant too that Curzon chose not to devote a section to Islamic beliefs in *Persia*, but instead gave coverage to religious minorities. The Babi movement, in particular, had been noticed by European diplomats (an account of it was included in her Persian memoirs by Lady Sheil, a British diplomat's wife), and interpreted to Britain by the eventual Cambridge Professor of Arabic, E.G. Browne. Curzon does not seem to have met any Babis while in Persia, but his account of them is highly sympathetic, and goes to some lengths to 'correct' misreporting of the sect's aims and doctrines. Discounting political or revolutionary motives, Curzon defines Babism as 'a religious movement whose primary object is a revolt against the tyranny and fanaticism of the Koran, and against the growing laxity of Mussulman practice.' He foregrounds reformist tenets, such as emancipation of women, which he takes as Christian-inspired, disuse of the veil, and abolition of polygamy. In fact, Curzon reads Babism as a challenge to the religious status quo in Persia, doubling the probable number of its acolytes, and opining 'a time may conceivably come when it will oust Mohammedanism from the field in Persia.'[55] While his account may be located in a western desire to see Islam reformed, a counter-reading might see it as a further exercise in European Orientalism. Additionally, he may have seen the benefits for Europe, and Great Britain in particular, in a diminution of the role of Islam, and its superseding by a movement he took to be sympathetic to 'Europeanisation', and which he may have thought would strengthen the ramshackle Persian state, in the process offering a stronger resistance to Russian penetration.

So far this chapter has concentrated on discussion of Curzon's travel writings in categories that accord with his own. What Curzon calls travel for love of 'the beautiful and the romantic [...] the ancient things of the earth' I have comprehended in the term 'aesthetic Orientalism'; while his study of those 'people and places' that helped him form 'an opinion of the Eastern responsibilities and destinies of Great Britain', has been contextualised in the phrase, 'travel as imperial strategy'. Curzon himself comes across – in the jargon of today – as a driven man. He adopted the entire sphere of the East as the subject of his mastery. The aim was the construction of a political career from the expertise he had gained on his travels, as reported in his writings. There can be little doubt, however, that the East, especially the Islamic Near East, generated a personal response in Curzon. As he wrote: 'Do we ever escape from the fascination of a turban, or the mystery of the shrouded apparitions that pass for women in the dusty alleys?'[56] Aesthetic Orientalism merges into an imperialist aesthetic. The magical sites and scenes of the East to which Curzon responded with such satisfaction engaged his imagination the more as they were caught up in Britain's imperial dominion; each sanctified the other and underwrote his sense of providential endorsement for Britain's presence there. At the performative level, this aesthetic was expressed in the processions of exotically accoutred natives at the 1903 Durbar. Then again, as much as his romantic sensibility was engaged by an 'oriental scene', Curzon's ego was at stake when he set himself up as an expert on/explainer of 'the Orient'. In his criticism of oriental decay he was perhaps little different from the majority of his class of contemporaries. To the standard nineteenth-century Orientalism he brought the imperial anxieties of his time. Gobineau had been a diplomat in Persia in 1855-56, and again in 1862-63.

During both his visits his dominant international concern was to contain Russian expansion: 'If the Persians [...] unite with the western powers, they will march against the Russians in the morning, be defeated by them at noon and become their allies by evening. All courses seem to me to have the same upshot'.[57]

Given the sharpening of imperial rivalries of the last decades of the century, it is not surprising that there should have been a shift in Curzon's writings from the Orientalist attitude towards Persia, to a fearfulness of being deprived of conquest by the Russians.

Curzon returned from his second round the world trip in 1893 to tell his constituents at Southport:

Rightly or wrongly [...] it appears to me that the continued existence of this country is bound up in the maintenance – aye I will go further and say even in the extension of the British Empire [...] India is [...] the strength and the greatness of England [that makes] you feel that every nerve a man may strain, every energy he may put forward, cannot be devoted to a nobler purpose than keeping tight the cords that hold India to ourselves.[58]

This was typically the rhetoric of high imperialism. We might say that Curzon's travels had provided him with the rationale for his forthcoming stint as Viceroy of India; but it could equally be argued that they had merely confirmed him in his allegiance to the rule of Englishmen proclaimed by Sir James Stephen in his Eton speech fifteen years before. In fact, the travel writings belong with a body of work that stretched over a lifetime, and found Curzon attempting, as Foreign Secretary in 1920, to implement a policy towards Persia already implicit in his two volumes on that country published in 1892. By then, however, though Czarist Russia was no more and its Bolshevik successor lay in quarantine, Britain was too weak to make of Persia another protectorate as she had Egypt in 1914. And Curzon's claim to be writing not 'a work of travel [...] [but] an authoritative work (I trust) of permanent value, which will be read and referred to, twenty, fifty, and perhaps more years hence,' reads as a statement replete with all the ironies of the imperial project itself.[59]

The Curzon version

Persia is still the country of Haji Baba.
Robert Byron, *The Road to Oxiana*, p. 85.

It is easy with hindsight to consign Curzon's imperial idea to the dustbin of history. In terms of time its provenance may have been brief; yet what we might term 'the Curzon version' with respect to Britain's control of its empire in the East was a significant factor within the imperial world picture of the first two decades of the twentieth century. Coinciding with the high noon of Britain's imperial sway and anxiety, this brand of Tory imperialism, as far as Curzon's own political career was concerned, might well have counted

against him in the minds of those Tory grandees who diluted their imperialism with a sizeable dash of soda.[60] Curzon's ideas on: favouring a forward
policy in the East, defining and mapping out of the areas of potential conflict
with Russia, and trenchantly foregrounding the weaknesses of eastern states
like Persia, reverberate within the discourse of influential and aspiring supporters of empire in the first two decades of the twentieth century. This
process was helped both by his travel writing and speeches, and by the fact
that Curzon's patronage during his time as Viceroy of India extended to like-
minded officers in the field. Indeed, we could say this amounted to a discourse or sub-discourse of its own. The 'Curzon version' may be construed as
a discursive formation built out of Curzon's public pronouncements on the
relationship between Britain and the East, in which, Said notes, the relationship is delineated 'in terms of possession [...] of a large geographical space
wholly owned by an efficient colonial master.'[61] As well as the travel writings, which continued to be quoted, Curzon's miscellaneous desiderata contributed to his status as an authority on the 'eastern character'.

An example of the latter is to be found in an introduction, published in
1895, to James Morier's *Hajji Baba of Ispahan*, in which Curzon utilises his
Orientalist's expertise to vouch for the accuracy of Morier's representation of
the Persian character. 'No man could have written or could now write such a
book unless he were steeped and saturated, not merely in Oriental experience,
but in Oriental forms of expression and modes of thought.'[62] Curzon sketches
in detail the diplomatic missions to Persia that gave Morier the opportunity to
penetrate the culture and its people, providing originals for the work's court
characters, historical events and many of its fictional incidents, as well as
giving his imprimatur for the authenticity of Morier's descriptions of tribal
life. His account portrayed 'a people, light-hearted, nimble-witted, and
volatile, but subtle, hypocritical, and insincere; metaphysicians and casuists,
courtiers and rogues, gentlemen and liars, *hommes d'esprit* and yet *incurable
cowards*.'[63] Curzon specifically emphasises the book's perfect rendition of
the corrupt Persian character that, he argues, persisted from Morier's day to
his own. 'The intrinsic merit of the book [is] as a contemporary portrait of
Persian manners and life, [...] also [...] the fidelity with which it continues to
reflect, after the lapse of three-quarters of a century, the salient and unchanging characteristics of a singularly unchanging Oriental people.'[64] The national
vices of 'treachery, deceit, and falsehood' substituted prowess with 'the
sword and spear'. Morier revelled in his 'tales of Persian cowardice' using
one character as the mouthpiece for the putative words of a real Persian
commander: 'O Allah, Allah, if there were no dying in the case, how the
Persians would fight!'[65] Even were the Persians to be 'blotted out as a
nation', Curzon insists, Morier's 'immortal book' would remain, not merely
as a satire, but as an 'historical document', an epitome of 'modern and
moribund Iran', portraying with 'unrivalled humour and accuracy' a people
once important in Asian affairs, though 'now in their decadence'.[66] We shall
see that the characteristics inscribed in *Hajji Baba*, especially those marked

out and re-iterated by Curzon's commentary, continued to form the picture British writers, journalists and political commentators entertained of Persia and the Persians. Even as redoubtable a defender of the Persian national spirit as Edward Granville Browne was forced to contend with this image as he struggled to assert the Persians' facility for political and social change.

We can see some of the key features of the Curzon version in Valentine Chirol's, *The Middle Eastern Question or Some Political Problems of Indian Defence*, published in 1903. The authority of Curzon is invoked from the beginning. En route to becoming the foreign editor of *The Times*, Chirol reshuffled the titles of two of Curzon's travel books for this work, and for an earlier one entitled *The Far Eastern Question*. Chirol begins by formulating the central issue of his text firmly within the Curzonian mould. His mentor had defined the Middle Eastern Question 'with the authority belonging alike to his intimate knowledge of Asiatic countries and peoples and to the high office he holds under the Crown.'[67] This question was part of the wider issue of the future of Asia, set against European expansion into the continent and the consequences this held for India's security. Persia, which Chirol had recently visited, still retained the same crucial role within this wider picture that Curzon had assigned to it; in fact the country was still powerless to resist the external forces acting upon her: 'Persia herself remains to-day exactly the same inert organism that Lord Curzon described in 1889-90'.[68]

According to Chirol, Britain only woke up to the strategic significance of Persia within the Asiatic scheme of things towards the end of the previous century, just at the time Curzon wrote about it. Russia's expansion into Central Asia challenged Britain's position as the 'greatest European power in Asia'. Construction of the Trans-Siberian railway and the stirrings of Japan (again reported by Curzon) reconfigured Persia as one link in a long chain stretching from Constantinople to Peking. 'Great Britain and Russia still stand alone and almost face to face in Persia, in the presence of a sick-bed more desperate perhaps than that of any other Asiatic monarchy.' Chirol's immersion within the Curzon version is evident in his detailed evidencing of Russia's strategic proximity to Persia and its ascendancy (at the expense again of Britain) in commercial matters. He also emphasises the utter ineptitude of the Persian army which, given that the Persian soldier was little more than a coolie in uniform, must (quoting Curzon) in typical Hajji Baba fashion 'degenerate on the least provocation into a rabble'.[69]

The desuetude of the Persian state in all its aspects had been manifested on the occasion of the preparations for the Shah's return from Europe. An 'illustration of Persian medievalism', the spectacle epitomised the extremities of splendour and penury Curzon had iterated in *Persia and the Persian Question*. To begin with the road from Rasht to Teheran along which the Shah's factotums and lackeys passed had been constructed by the Russians. 'It was a wonderful succession of *tableaux vivants*, embodying the whole story of what "Eothen" terms the glory and the havoc of the East – more especially the havoc.'[70] The affair emblazoned the Shah's profligacy; just as his father Nasir al-Din had done, Mozaffar al-Din was bankrupting his country by the loans that financed his European tours. The spectacle itself was 'a vivid reminder of the fateful writing on the wall, translated on this occasion into Russian characters'.[71] Chirol accounts for Persia by referring to its 'Oriental system of government', going back to Xerxes and Darius. Such a system, in which sale of office and robbery of the native population led to chronic disturbance and chaos, could only be righted by a 'strong man', of which history afforded preciously few examples. 'As for the merits or de-merits of the system, it is one to which [the Persians] have been accustomed for centuries, and the vast majority know and can conceive of no other.'[72]

Persia was stuck in the oriental bind; the modern world would not allow her to work out her own destiny free of interference. This fatalistic appraisal is supported by Gobineau's theory of race degeneracy, and the evidence of the malign power of Islam, which set a 'profound gulf between the Persian and the European mind'. The only hope for Persia was that such discontent would favour 'some great religious movement such as Babism was'. Taking his lead once more from Curzon, Chirol inflates the number of Babis even above the figure of his master, over-estimating Babi strength at 'nearly one and a half millions or 20 per cent of the total population'.[73]

Percy Cox, Arnold Wilson, and the cult of Pax Britannica

Valentine Chirol represented an important strain of imperialist discourse that would continue to report the Orient in a Curzonian manner in the British press. Two other figures to emerge as reporters of the East from the *Times* academy were David Fraser (see next chapter) and Philip Graves (see chapter six). A further quarter where Curzon's ideas found reception was among the servants of empire, in figures like Percy Cox, Curzon's man in the Gulf and later ambassador to Persia, as well as Cox's protégé, Arnold Wilson, who stepped into Cox's shoes and became acting British civil commissioner in Baghdad from 1918-20. Cox was appointed British resident at Bushire in the Persian Gulf when he was forty years old. His biographer Philip Graves pictured him as 'tall, spare, blond and blue-eyed, with an almost Welling-tonian nose that was none the less commanding for being somewhat out of line.'[74] Cox was a 'politico' who had moved from his position in the Indian Army to become a temporary assistant political resident in British Somaliland Protectorate at Zeila. His Bushire appointment (1904), as well as his earlier one as political agent and consul at Muscat (1899), were both Curzon's doing. The two men had first met when Curzon came on a hunting trip to Zeila. Cox subsequently gained the consent of the Sultan of Muscat to send his eldest son to Curzon's grandiose 1903 Durbar at Calcutta.

During his period at Muscat, Cox saw off the French and the Turks, doing battle with troublesome pirate tribesmen, unruly Arab sheikhs, weak and corrupt Persian officials. By the time he moved on he could mark down as his main achievement that he left the Gulf a British lake.[75] He came at a particularly sensitive stage in Britain's long-nurtured hegemony over the area. Having superseded the Portuguese and the Dutch, by the end of the eighteenth century 'England had attained a position in the Gulf to which none of her competitors could then lay claim.'[76] Trade and protection of the route to India were the pillars upon which she built her expansion. In his speech to the trucial chiefs on his visit to the Gulf in November 1903, Curzon articulated these British interests with a characteristic rhetorical flourish:

> We were here before any other Power, in modern times, had shown its face in these waters. We found strife and we have created order. It was our commerce as well as your security that was threatened and called for protection. At every port along these coasts the subjects of the King of England still reside and trade. The great Empire of India, which it is our duty to defend, lies almost at your gates. We saved you from extinction at the hands of your neighbours. We opened these seas to the ships of all nations, and enabled their flags to fly in peace. We have not seized or held your territory. We have not destroyed your independence, but have preserved it. We are not now going to throw away this century of costly and triumphant enterprise; we shall not wipe out the most unselfish page in history. The peace of these waters must still be maintained; your independence will continue to be upheld; and the influence of the British government must remain supreme.[77]

Curzon's speech contains a story of pacification – 'we found strife and created order' – in which Arabs of the Gulf played the part of the unvoiced Other. These Arabs, particularly of the tribe of the Qawasim, lived along the coast around Ras al-Khaimah in modern day United Arab Emirates, and were cast as pirates, supported by the rising power of the Wahhabis of Najd. Britain's engagement in a war against 'piracy' at the end of the eighteenth and beginning of the nineteenth centuries was represented by one of Curzon's epigones as less about 'our rights and privileges' in the Gulf, and 'more about our responsibilities'. In defeating the Arab 'pirates' and inscribing a Pax Britannica in a general treaty of peace in 1820, it was not Britain's own protection alone that she sought, 'she was solicitous for the common good, and was securing other nations as well as herself.'[78]

An alternative view is that the East India Company, wishing to take over the Gulf Arabs' share of trade with India, lobbied the British Government to intervene against the danger of 'pirates' to international shipping until the situation of 1820 was effected. Curzon may not have invented, but he was instrumental in disseminating this tale of empire. Sultan Muhammad al-Qasimi, in *The Myth of Arab Piracy in the Gulf*, charges Curzon with having as Viceroy of India commissioned a history of the Arabian Gulf and peninsular which promoted this 'deliberate misrepresentation of history'. He argues that this narrative was still in partial currency in historical accounts written up to the 1960s. Curzon adopted it himself in *Persia*, writing: 'Early in this

century Arab corsairs desolated [the Gulf's] slopes and swept its waters with
piratical flotillas [...] The pacification of the Persian Gulf in the past and the
maintenance of the status quo are the exclusive work of this country.'[79]

During his term of duty in Muscat, Cox would travel extensively in the
interior. On one occasion he encountered an Arab tribe living in the vicinity
of the northern coast of Oman:

> These shepherds were asked how they could wander afield unarmed. They replied
> that they had no need of weapons since their enemies could not penetrate to their
> mountain haunts and the Christians (i.e., the English) gave them immunity by sea.
> I found this sentiment agreeably prevalent ... in all the out-of-the way places
> visited in these waters ... Natives to whom the explanation 'Angrez' (English) in
> reply to queries who we were, of itself conveyed nothing, invariably followed up
> their first question by inquiring whether we belonged to the nation 'who kept the
> sea,' and on finding that we did, endeavoured to show their respect and friendli-
> ness for us forthwith. On such occasions one could not but be possessed for the
> moment by the spirit of pride of race and by the kindred hope that this honourable
> heritage the Pax Britannica or ... 'Keeping of the sea' might not be shared with
> any, at all events in our generation.[80]

By the 1890s, the Gulf was susceptible to the eddies spread by the international situation in other areas of the globe.[81] Besides taking action against the
French desire to establish a coal station in Muscat, Cox had to function within
an atmosphere that feared Russian southward expansion, reassertion of Turkish claims, and the projected Berlin-Baghdad railway. As far as the Gulf was
concerned, he was required to exercise a decisive influence upon the affairs
of the Sultanate of Muscat, the Trucial States, Bahrain and Kuwait. The tribal
chiefs of each of these Gulf territories had signed a treaty not to give control
of any of their lands to any outside power save Great Britain. The Amir of
Kuwait had signed a 'secret treaty' in 1899, since nominally his land was
under the suzerainty of Ottoman Turkey. This was the dispensation by which
the British (or 'Angrez' as Cox reports in the remarks above) kept the sea,
refusing to share it with any other. The statement that Cox consolidated British power in the Gulf, affirmed by his own diaries and by the testimony of his
chief, was no mean achievement in the British imperial scheme.

The political resident at Bushire also had the remit of reporting on the
situation in southern Persia and was responsible to the Ambassador in
Teheran. Cox's reports on the deteriorating situation there following the
Persian revolution would highlight the need for a British intervention that
eventually came in 1911. Bushire, it should be noted, is situated on the
Persian side of the Gulf, about two hundred English miles from Basra. Sir
Percy had exceedingly friendly relations with the Arab Shaykh of Mohammerah whose writ ran above that of the Persian authorities in the lands around
the Karun River, in which oil would soon be discovered. With the Persians
themselves, as was the case with other British imperial managers, his experience was not to be so happy. Like many other British colonisers, travellers
and visitors to the Middle East, Sir Percy got on better with the relatively
simple, uncivilised Arab Bedouin than with his more tricky city cousin, and

the complex, emotionally volatile people of Iranian race. The chief political resident in the Gulf, Sir Percy was also consul-general for the province of Fars, of which the provincial capital was Shiraz. After the Anglo-Russian carve-up of Persia he became the senior British representative in the British 'sphere of influence'. A taciturn and thorough administrator, with a large quotient of patience and tact, Sir Percy found the Persian ruling class frequently corrupt, or if otherwise, hamstrung and ineffective. 'In the Gulf ports we have a civilised and capable Governor,' he wrote. 'Originally belonging to Fars, but educated at University College, London; takes his *Times* and knows English as well as you or I. This man is a Persian if you scratch deep enough but would be a good and useful Governor if he had any force at all at his command.'[82]

The problem was: during almost the entire period of Sir Percy's residency, which ended in 1914, Persia was either undergoing the throes of her first revolution, or suffering from the effects of the Russian-led reaction. Inevitably, in such a situation, disorder and confusion prevailed, particularly in the south of the country, Sir Percy's area of jurisdiction. The resident and consul-general was, like most officers of the British army in India, a Tory by inclination, and the Persian experiment in constitutionalism left him cold. According to his biographer, the Persians lost British sympathy because they were incapable of combining liberty with order or tolerance – a classic riposte which could be equally applied to the revolution in France more than a century before (and was by the political philosopher, Edmund Burke.) In 1909, Cox ordered British naval forces to land in Bushire for the 'protection of the country'. He also advocated British military intervention in the south of Persia to offset the anarchy and brigandry and to make sure the roads, but his advice was ignored.

Just as he had himself been discovered and promoted by Curzon, Cox kept under his wing a singularly promising and energetic young officer on secondment from India, who he made his personal assistant, 'almost his alter ego'.[83] The young man would in a very short time fully repay his mentor's confidence. Arnold Wilson established for himself a reputation as a prodigious mapper of the terrain surrounding the Karun river and the lands bordering the Persian Gulf, boasting later that his reports contained 'six or seven volumes, covering all S.W. Persia'.[84] Where Curzon's travel writings were intended to establish him as an authority on the East and so advance his political career, Wilson's intelligence work in S.W. Persia was not designed to keep him in the Persian Gulf, but expedite his promotion in colonial India. In the Great War, he would distinguish himself in reconnaissance and behind-the-lines commando-style raids in southern Mesopotamia, creating a particular appeal for young officers, to many of whom he must have seemed the authentic hero of the adventure stories of their schooldays.

Wilson's diary of his exploits, in *South-West Persia*, does often capture the heroic, derring-do of the tales of empire so popular among British schoolboys before the war. 'I grew a beard, partly to save trouble when travelling, partly because most Persian tribesmen grew beards. When travelling in tribal territory I often dressed as a Persian.'[85] This Sir Percy would never have done, even as a young man. He had certainly undertaken journeys in the interior of Oman of a type to compare with any other European traveller in that area to date, even his redoubtable predecessor as consul at Muscat, S.B. Miles.[86] But there was a difference between his and the rising generation of young imperialists who had either taken *Kim* to heart, or, in the case of T.E. Lawrence, had read too much medieval romance. On his travels through Persia a generation before, the aspiring Curzon, avoided anything that might compromise his nationality. He travelled as that superior being, the future British imperial manager. His journeys were training for his eventual role of India's Viceroy and he expected to be received as such wherever he arrived. Like Kim, the young Wilson was able to spot a specimen of the superior ruling caste when he saw one, and was ready to do business with him. He found the Governor of Juwun: 'Tall, handsome, and powerfully built, intelligent and genial, like many of the dominant class in S. Persia, he seemed to belong to a different race from the cultivators and townsfolk.'[87] Again, like Kipling's hero, he would mix freely with all races and classes – talking on board ship to Indians, Persians, Arabs, and a young English engineer in the boiler room who was full of enthusiasm for his profession. Inevitably, this meant being out of sorts with the Liberals and Socialists back home who had never experienced the esprit de corps of the Indian Army. But democratic mixing with the ranks, and wearing foreigners' exotic clothes had its limitations. This was not the same as going native in the sense of diluting one's commitment to the imperial mission for the sake of partial entry into an inferior culture. The British consul at Mohammerah had done that, marrying a Persian woman whilst a junior clerk. 'He had three or four children, none of whom were worthy of him'. His wife and the younger children lived 'behind the screen' as the Persian custom was in another part of the house.[88]

It is safe to assume that despite differences of style, politically Percy Cox and A.T. Wilson (who were after all of similar background) entertained precisely the same imperial allegiances. Wilson wrote: 'Before the Great War my generation served men who believed in the righteousness of the vocation to which they were called, and we shared their belief. They were the priests, and we the acolytes, of a cult – *pax Britannica* – for which we worked happily, and if need be, died gladly. Curzon, at his best, was our spokesman and Kipling, at his noblest, our inspiration.'[89] This meant Wilson saw eye to eye with Cox when it came to Persia. For the young Wilson, Persian nationalism was a natural phenomenon 'with roots and a tradition as old as Persia itself'; but the Parliament (*majlis*) in Teheran would not work because it had 'no roots in the soil and no tradition'.[90] Just as it would be argued that Persians could not possibly exploit their own oil themselves, it was almost a fact of nature that Persia's corrupt, self-seeking politicians could never function according to constitutionally correct principles. 'Were there any deep-seated popular desire for change' (Wilson wrote in 1909, at the height of the struggle between the constitutionalists and the reactionaries) 'there would be a great explosion, but the scramble for the sweets of office is too blatant, and political movements in the towns smell of Tammany rather than of the Commune.'[91] The type that actively engaged in politics was necessarily lower than the governing class who one either recognised as belonging to a superior caste (like oneself) with which one could do business, or wrote off as genial rascals of the corrupt old order. What was unallowable, both to Sir Percy and his protégé, was that people who were scrambling for the sweets of office, or who lacked the discipline of order and tolerance to go with their new found love of liberty, should emerge as the men of the hour. You no more wished to deal with this kind of native, than you desired to share 'keeping of the sea' with any other power. Sir Percy had said it: however laudable the order which the British brought to the Gulf, its real basis was jealousy of all rivals, and for most British diplomats and imperial administrators in Persia, that was the bottom line. By 1913, Cox was able to argue Britain's case with a weak Persian government for – to use his own phrase – 'policing the Gulf'.[92]

Like their illustrious mentor Lord Curzon, Tory imperialists such as Cox and Wilson had not liked the Anglo-Russian convention, but this was not because it destroyed liberal and radical dreams of a constitutional Persia. For Curzon, Persia only existed in so far as it exemplified the static Orient evoked in the phrase of his favourite writer on the land, the French Protestant Chardin: 'in the East they are constant in all things. The habits are at this day in the same manner as in the precedent ages'. Curzon found in Persia delectation for his aesthetic Orientalism, but, much more important, an arena of an imperial struggle that he found all absorbing. After all, Persia, along with Afghanistan and Russian Central Asia, were pieces on a chessboard upon which a game was being played out for the dominion of the world. Persia was part of the larger world of Asiatic politics, in which, for a British imperialist, India overshadowed all other considerations. Curzon's disciples understood as well as he that control of Persia must never pass to Russia.

> We in India [Wilson wrote] wanted a strong and independent nation on our western border and on the shore of the Persian Gulf, but preferred a highly decentralized regime, independent of Russia, to a centralized regime under the thumb of St. Petersburg.[93]

That was code for: we want to go on pulling the strings in south Persia, and paying off our friends in Teheran.

For a brief interlude during the Great War, it seemed as if Curzon's hopes for Britain's empire in the East might be realised. Both Cox and Wilson played active, possibly crucial roles in forwarding this project. Cox returned to the Gulf in 1914 with the Indian Expeditionary Force 'D' as chief political officer, subsequently becoming one of the architects of Britain's expansion into Mesopotamia, assembling and training 'an admirable team of political and administrative officers which included Wilson and was joined later by Gertrude Bell.'[94] From the War Cabinet, Curzon sent Cox a eulogy of his role to date: 'Nobly have you carried out the missions with which I entrusted you 18 years ago... you have made yourself the King of the Gulf. When the war is over we shall consolidate that Kingdom and see that no one snatches the crown away.'[95] When the war finally did end, Cox was despatched to Teheran to negotiate an Anglo-Persian treaty that Persia would eventually reject as demeaning to its national sovereignty, while in Baghdad, Wilson was doing his level best to annex Iraq to the British empire – an act that in the event was a signal failure: Britain's power in the world had reached its apogee, and its tide was on the ebb.

Conclusion

This chapter began by suggesting two specialisms of imperialist literature cohering around the areas of Egypt, and Persia/ Afghanistan. Cromer and Milner wrote on the former, and Curzon and his acolytes on the latter. It was argued that the writings on both areas are to be located within the discourse of Orientalism proposed by Said, and indeed bear out a connection between this discourse and the project of imperialism in the East in the nineteenth and early twentieth centuries. Curzon's brand of Orientalism displays a slight variation on Milner and Cromer's in that the area of the East on which he reported was not under direct British control, as was Egypt, but instead registered a fault-line between British and Russian imperialisms. This situation gave rise to anxieties that in turn led to the weaknesses of the eastern people(s) concerned, though fixed by the usual Orientalist categories, to become accentuated. Egyptians could be declared unfit for self-government and the lack happily supplied by British governance; but the same character weakness in the Persians de-stabilised rather than confirmed British imperial interests, since, nominally self-governing, Persia was in reality in danger of becoming a mere satrap of Russia. In addition, Curzon declared an aesthetic pleasure in eastern landscape, peoples, and culture, which can hardly be said to find an echo in the pronouncements of Cromer. This aesthetic quality – joined to the imaginative Orientalism of a writer like Kipling – helped enthuse and inspire the deeds and writings of empire of a younger generation of Tory imperialists. Lastly, Curzon's colourful delineation of 'the Persian character' struck a particular chord with certain journalists, in the process perpetuating a 'popular' strand of Orientalist discourse.

Blunt may be said to have single-handedly opposed Cromer's record in Egypt before Denshawai; but was there anyone to contest the production of Persia thus far presented, to raise a voice in opposition to this Orientalist orthodoxy? The answer is affirmative, but it was perhaps not inflected in quite as polarising a manner as Blunt's in the debate over Egypt. In the literary field at least, Edward Granville Browne often appeared to labour in

Persia's favour in an isolation comparable to Blunt's. But rather than engage in direct contention with the Curzonite imperialist 'reading' of Persia and the Persian question, Browne chose to adopt an alternative delineation. In an odd way, in the face of the British government's foreign policy re-alignments of the first decade of the new century, Browne's liberal nationalist project for Persia almost came to convergence with the Tory imperialist one. Where Browne did confront a spin-off of the latter was in his replacement of the Hajji Baba image with a trans-historical, heroic Persian national spirit that periodically renewed itself. Initially founded on an implicit endorsement of Gobineau's Aryan theory, and Browne's deep personal response to the Frenchman's chronicling of the Babi movement, this led to an eventual identification with the Persian revolution so doctrinaire as to cut Browne off almost entirely from the British liberal-radical mainstream. It is to Browne's battle with the British establishment over Persia that we will now turn.

5

Edward Granville Browne
and the Persian
'Awakening'

Edward Granville Browne's reputation in the first decade of the last century as a fervent proponent of Persian nationalism and supporter of what he called the core remaining independent Muslim nations makes him, alongside his mentor Blunt, one of the foremost anti-imperialist voices of the time. A professional Orientalist, Browne owned precisely those qualifications necessary for making him the most coherent figure within the counter-Orientalist tendency. He was capable of developing a narrative of an eastern awakening which, stretching from Egypt through Turkey to Persia, incorporated the protégé Muslim nations of Blunt, Urquhart and Browne himself. A founder member of the Ottoman Society, he rubbed shoulders with its secretary, the Turcophile Marmaduke Pickthall, and was a frequent contributor to Blunt's agitations on behalf of Egyptian nationalism. With H.F.B Lynch, he became the prime mover behind the Persia Committee formed in October 1908. Browne's fluency in Arabic, Turkish and Persian empowered him to proclaim a linkage between the Egyptian nationalists, the Young Turks, and the Iranian constitutional revolutionaries, while *The Persian Revolution of 1905-1909*, which was serialised in Persia, can be said to have 'influenced the very course of events it covered in its pages'.[1] Browne's defence of Persia at all costs and 'almost continuous antagonism to his own government and establishment' has been linked to the personal wealth which made possible an independence of thought and action that was sometimes 'arbitrary and cranky'. His support for the nationalist cause in Persia was considered uncritical even by some of his allies.[2]

I will argue that there was something quixotic in Browne's partisanship for the Azali sect of Babism, as well as in his penchant for the extravagant and shocking that impelled him as a young man to consort with the more outlandish elements in Persian society. No doubt like Blunt (who was ostracised by Society as a result of his position on Egypt, and was gaoled in Ireland for his resistance to the land legislation), Browne too enjoyed acts of extremity and self-dramatisation. But I shall still argue the significance of

both in creating a discourse that challenges Edward Said's negative estimation of resistance to imperialism from within the imperial metropolis.

In *Culture and Imperialism*, Said wrote: 'Certainly there were late-
nineteenth century intellectuals (Wilfrid Scawen Blunt and William Morris)
who were totally opposed to imperialism, but they were far from influential
[...] In other words, there was no overall condemnation of imperialism until –
and this is my point – after native uprisings were too far gone to be ignored or
defeated.'[3] The Iranian scholar Mansour Bonakdarian has challenged Said's
marginalisation of dissent by referring to British writers and intellectuals who
raised the standard of revolt against the imperialist politics of their day.
Citing the case of Edward Granville Browne – whom he notes Said mentions
only once in passing – Bonakdarian claims: 'By denying Browne and others
like him their dissenting voices, it tends to historically sterilize Orientalist
contributions to the anti-imperialist campaigns early in the [twentieth]
century.' As evidence, he asserts; 'It is also questionable whether a crowd of
reportedly 6,000 who attended the 1912 meeting of the [Persia] Committee
[in London] for condemning the Iranian policy of the British Government
[...] indicates that "they were far from influential".'[4] The fact that Browne's
sustained criticism of his government's imperial policies in Ireland and the
East was routinely dubbed 'idealistic' by an establishment newspaper like
The Times indicates that far from being a negligible voice, some felt it
necessary to rubbish the Cambridge professor's voice.[5] A.T. Wilson, writing
in 1911, claimed: 'no one in British official circles in Persia pays any heed to
Browne's politics'.[6] This clearly underestimated Browne's influence, at least
at the start of the Persian revolution, with diplomats in the British Legation in
Teheran, some of who were Browne's former pupils. Browne himself
associated the anti-constitutionalist position with the 'Anglo-India environment' that had helped form Wilson.[7]

It was, however, on Persia that Browne's most cherished labours were
bestowed. His sole visit in 1887-88 realised one of the great pieces of
Victorian travel literature, *A Year Amongst the Persians* (1893). The journey
also set him on a path of search in the cause of Persia's national and spiritual
awakening that led eventually to his wholehearted immersion in the revolution of 1905-11, the course of which is partially inscribed in the groundbreak-
ing, *Persian Revolution 1905-1909* (1910). Browne's discourse of Iranian
national identity derives from those linguistic-racial formulations pioneered
in German national thought of the early nineteenth century, and, as applied to
Iran, from the theories of 'the Father of Racism', Comte Arthur de Gobineau
– ideas which may initially have developed to find the European a noble
ancestor in the East, but which subsequently played their part in the construction of racist, imperialist ideology.[8] In addition, several of the key Urquartian
motifs entered Browne's writings: an ambivalence towards European-led
modernisation of Persia, and, less surprising given the circumstances of the
first Persian revolution, the charge of Britain's betrayal of small eastern
nationalities. Moreover, the politics of Great Britain and the international

scene immediately prior to the First World War drew a vociferous anti-imperialist Liberal like Browne into potential tactical alliance with arch-imperialist-exponent of Orientalism, the Tory Lord Curzon.[9]

Browne's Persian Travels: the Making of an Orientalist

> In Persia Browne realized himself fully for the first time; the year of seeing and talking lasted him throughout all the remaining years of his life; the fire which Persia kindled in his heart would prove inextinguishable.
> A.J. Arberry, *Oriental Essays, Portraits of Seven Scholars*, p. 171.

Unlike Curzon, Browne's 'desire for the Orient' was framed by neither the ambition of the imperial politician nor the aristocrat's aesthetic Orientalism (Blunt pronounced him 'the least aesthetic of men').[10] He wrote:

> It was the Turkish War with Russia in 1877-88 that first attracted my attention to the East [...] At first sight my proclivities were by no means for the Turks; but the losing side, more especially when it continues to struggle gallantly against defeat, always has a claim on our sympathy [...] I would have died to save Turkey, and I mourned the fall of Plevna as though it had been a disaster inflicted on my own country.[11]

In time Browne was to speak of Persia – not Turkey – as, after his own, the country he loved better than any nation in the world. Finding in himself proficiency for oriental languages, he learnt Turkish and then Persian with the aid of idiosyncratic tutors. Though his upper middle-class, non-conformist parents (Sir Benjamin Browne was for many years head of a North East engineering and shipbuilding company) pointed him in the direction of engineering and later medicine, Browne continued to follow the promptings of a heart turned east. When he passed his second MB at Cambridge, his father sponsored his trip to Constantinople in 1882. In an age when the eastern consular service recognised only European and not oriental languages as subjects of examination, Browne was advised by a Cambridge professor: 'If you have private means which render you independent of a profession, then pursue your Oriental Studies'.[12] Fortunately, the luxury of a considerable family fortune, and his innate abilities, made this an option Browne could pursue. He therefore set out for Persia in 1887, a freshly elected fellow of Pembroke College with a year's dispensation to perfect his knowledge of Persian.

Browne's journey was underwritten by a secret mission, a yearning after a new oriental cause that was not, however, greatly dissimilar to the one that had first stirred his partisanship of the Turks. Having acquired an interest in Sufism, he had graduated on to the history and beliefs of the Babis – the sect that would also attract the attention of Curzon. The source of information for both travellers was Gobineau's *Religions et Philosophies dans l'Asie Centrale* (1865). This account fired the impressionable young academic with a romantic attachment to a persecuted, but courageously resilient Iranian religious movement. In the French traveller and diplomat's redaction the Babis' Shi'ih millennial milieu was dissolved into a narrative of a Muhammadan messiah whose tragic martyrdom, and that of his followers, paralleled that of Jesus and his disciples.[13] The image of Persia supplied in *A Year Amongst the Persians* may sparkle with Browne's iridescent infatuation for the Persian character in its many variant aspects, but there is a deeper structure raised upon two polar narratives from Gobineau. The first is the genus of the 'pure' Persian, embedded within which is the myth of the Indo-European 'Aryan' race fathered by European racial theory projected on to Iran by Orientalists, pre-eminently Gobineau himself.[14] Second, and connected to the first, is the central paradigm of the tableau of the martyred prophet of Shiraz, Ali Muhammad, or 'the Bab', whose sufferings and eventual execution are figured as a return of the spirit that attended past Persian greatness. These two narratives, which may be said without distortion to form two halves of the work, (albeit ones which continue to intersect) are joined by an effort of construction that is central to Browne's later career both as Orientalist and political polemicist. Attraction to Persia is mediated by his affinity for the 'subtle' 'vivacious', 'versatile' 'clever' Persian genus.[15] This attraction is in turn intensified and valorised by the heroic, self-sacrificing example of the Bab and his followers at the hands of the Turkic Qajar dynasty which usurped the seat of the ancient, 'authentic' Aryan rulers of Iran. Asleep but not dead, the Persian people themselves await the cause that will accomplish their national awakening.

The early chapters of *A Year Amongst the Persians* treat Browne's progress through Turkey, Persian Azerbaijan, and the northern areas of the country surrounding the capital Teheran. Browne reads the terrain, especially its human inhabitants, in terms of the racial division of Persia into a Turkic north and a Persian south. This fissure is articulated in political terms by setting the Turkic Qajar dynasty against the 'pure' Persian people over which it rules. In addition, the landscape is decoded for evidences of a decay and pseudo-modernization both of which are interpreted according to the abdicated responsibilities of the Shah and his family. The narrative builds to its first climax as Browne reaches the authentic Persian heartland in Fars province, voices his apostrophe at the degradation of Persia's ancient glories as evidenced by the vandalised ruins of Pasargadae and Persepolis, then transforms grief into epiphany on the traveller's approach to the panorama of a verdant Shiraz. Nearing the frontier between Turkey and Persia, Browne and his unnamed travelling companion encounter a Belgian. He informs them: 'I have travelled in many lands [...] and have discovered some good qualities in every people, with the exception of the Persians, in whom I have failed to find a single admirable characteristic.' The servant who accompanies the travellers is an old Turk whose 'religious and national prejudices caused him ever to regard [the Persian] with unconquerable aversion', while the Turkish muleteers averred 'the Persians were the wickedest, most faithless, and most dishonest people in the world'.[16] It is not until Qazvin that the Turkish preponderance recedes, giving Browne the opportunity to remark: 'Here, indeed, a marked change was observable in the people, who appeared much brighter, more intelligent, and more amiable than the natives of Adharbayjan.'[17] No sooner is the transition from Turk to Persian effected than Browne has cause to extend the division by indulging in the first of a series of criticisms of Nasir al-Din Shah. Though they might offer modern creature comforts, the guest-houses along the route from Qazvin to Teheran, apparently built by order of the Shah after his visit to Europe, are exorbitantly priced and staffed by insolent servants. This 'chaos of luxury' elicits in Browne a meditation on 'the unhappy effects produced in Eastern lands by the adoption of Western customs'.[18] A perhaps more crucial importation – again the doing of the Shah – was the railway between the small town of Shah Abdul-Azim and the capital. This was torn up some while after Browne's visit by a hostile crowd reacting to the death of a man who had fallen from a moving train. Browne sees in this event, not the action of a bigoted populace opposed to a modernising monarch (as Curzon might have done), but a merited sentence on one of the Shah's plentiful fads. The Shah did

> everything in his power to prevent the diffusion of those ideas which conduce to true progress, and his supposed admiration for civilisation amounts to little more than the languid amusement which he derives from the contemplation and possession of mechanical playthings and ingenious toys.[19]

In his condemnation of these aspects of false innovation, Browne's comments evince a split between an Orientalism protective of the 'authentic' ways of a native people; and a liberal anger against an eastern tyrant whom he believes is the chief obstacle to the development of a naturally resourceful nation. In the same spirit, Browne charges the rulers of Persia with complicity with time in allowing the glories of the land's illustrious past to crumble into ruins, aided by the depredations of ambitious ministers who plundered them to erect their own monuments. 'Would that some portion of that money which is spent in building new palaces in the capital, and constructing *mihman-khanes* [guest-houses] neither beautiful nor pleasant, were devoted to the preservation of the glorious relics of a past age!' But the East's Ozymandiases thought too much of their own vainglory to concern themselves with these. 'And so it goes on – king succeeding king, dynasty overthrowing dynasty, ruin added to ruin; and through it all the mighty spirit of the people "dreaming the dream of the soul's disentanglement," while the stony-eyed lions of Persepolis look forth in their endless watch over a nation which slumbers, but is not dead.'[20]

As regards this historical moment, however, there *was* blame to attribute. Browne's earlier remarks about the Shah's insincere projects suddenly

merge into the discourse of race as he launches a sustained attack against the
Turkic Qajar dynasty as usurpers of the throne of Cyrus and Shapur, the great
ancient kings of Persian race.

> I wish to insist on the fact that the reigning dynasty of the Kajars are essentially of
> Turkish race, because it is often overlooked, and because it is of some political
> importance [...] The whole history of Persia, from the legendary wars between the
> Kiyanian kings and Afrasiyab down to the present day, is the story of a struggle
> between the Turkish races whose primitive home is in the region east of the
> Caspian Sea and north of Khurasan on the one hand, and the southern Persians, of
> almost pure Aryan race, on the other [...] Ethnologically, therefore, there is a
> marked distinction between the people of the north and the people of the south – a
> distinction which may be most readily apprehended by comparing the sullen,
> moody, dull-witted, fanatical, violent inhabitants of Adharbayjan with the bright,
> versatile, clever, sceptical, rather timid townsfolk of Kirman. In Fars, also, good
> types of the Aryan Persian are met with, but there is a large admixture of Turkish
> tribesmen, like the Kashka'is, who have migrated and settled there.[21]

Although he admits 'intermixture' has taken place, Browne still adheres to
his Turkic north/Persian south binary. This Manichean division climaxes in a
historicism that traces the struggle backwards of a millennium:

> Thus it happens that to-day the Kajars rule over the kinsmen of Cyrus and Shapur,
> as ruled in earlier days the Ghaznavids and Seljuks [both Turkic dynasties]. But
> there is no love lost between the two races, as anyone will admit who has taken the
> trouble to find out what the southern peasant thinks of the northern court, or how
> the Kajars regard the cradle of Persia's ancient greatness.[22]

Separation of Persian and Turk is not the only racial determinism inserted
into this reading of late nineteenth-century Iranian cultural and political
geography. Once again, Gobineau is the source of Browne's declaration that
the Persian Sufis employed a mysticism inherent to their race in rebelling
against the letter of the Qur'an. Browne is indeed unashamed in his
reiteration of the European Orientalist nostrum that Iranians had never accustomed themselves to the role of Islam, brought into their land by a prophet of
detested Arab race:

> Truly it seemed that a whole nation had been transformed, and that henceforth the
> Aryan Persian must not only bear the yoke of the Semitic "lizard-eater" whom he
> had formerly so despised, but must further adopt his creed, and almost, indeed, his
> language.[23]

On reaching Shiraz two of Browne's most cherished obsessions were
realised. Here was the home of the 'pure' Persians of Aryan myth ('its
inhabitants are, amongst all Persians, the most subtle, the most ingenious, the
most vivacious, even as their speech is to this day the purest and most
melodious').[24] Shiraz had also been the birthplace and youthful home of the
Bab. No wonder then that Browne wrote: 'Words cannot describe the rapture
which overcame me as, after many a weary march, I gazed at length on the
reality of that whereof I had so long dreamed, and found the reality not
merely equal to, but far surpassing, the ideal which I had conceived.'[25] Now

the search for the residuum of the Bab's heritage, already begun in Isfahan, could be resumed and more clearly focussed. The axis of the narrative shifts from the racial to the spiritual as the western traveller becomes embroiled in the religious politics of a sect which, surrounded by a prejudiced and antagonistic majority population, had been persecuted enough to be forced underground, but was now itself split into two hostile factions. One of the prime motivations behind Browne's journey to Iran had been to investigate the fate of the followers of the Bab and re-live the movement's Calvary. His route through Persia was punctuated by its stations-of-the-cross. At Tabriz, he re-imagined the site of the Bab's execution by firing squad; at Zanjan, he searched the terrain for the configuration of one of the Babi militants' last stands; in Isfahan, he had made first contact with latter-day followers of the sect; and, at Shiraz, he would be introduced to the new direction the Babi community had taken. Here he discovered there was a new leader, Mirza Husayn Ali-i-Nuri, known as Baha'ullah, and that only a tiny number had followed the Bab's designated successor, Mirza Yahya, known as Subh al-Azal. Although the majority faction were now calling themselves Bahais, true to his devotion to the Bab, Browne continued to refer to them as Babis (the minority faction he termed Azalis).

The apprentice-Orientalist's attempts at retrieving the pristine narrative of the Bab, who had been executed in 1850, and many of whose followers had perished in mass bloodletting two years later, falters in the face of the new realities. Shiraz taught Browne that Gobineau's narrative was no longer sacrosanct.

> Now, I found, the Bab's writings were but little read even amongst his followers, for Beha [Baha'ullah] had arisen [...] and it was with his commands, his writings, and his precepts that the Babi messengers went forth from Acre to the faithful in Persia.[26]

When prompted to open his heart, Browne

> proceeded to set forth what I had heard of the Bab, his gentleness and patience, the cruel fate which had overtaken him, and the unflinching courage wherewith he and his followers, from the greatest to the least, had endured the merciless torments inflicted on them by their enemies.[27]

But the Bahais were concerned not with the Bab, only with convincing Browne of Baha'ullah's claim to be the new messiah. Though their debate with him engaged his faculty of reason, the part of Browne's mind that had been colonised by Gobineau's account of Babism refused to succumb to the subtle rationalising of his new acquaintances. 'Those events of which Gobineau's vivid and sympathetic record had so strongly moved me' were apparently cherished with more ardour by the British would-be Orientalist than by his Persian hosts.[28] The ramifications of this discovery would provide a number of twists and turns in Browne's subsequent career as an Orientalist and promoter of Persia's awakening, some of which I shall touch on below.

For the moment, I shall return to Browne's stay in Kirman, for the confusion he experienced there also played a part in his later attitude to the Babis.

Browne's own narrative now enters a phase of opium-induced phantas-magoria as he travels from Yazd to Kirman, and there engages votaries of the two Babi groups, their mutual enemies, the Shaykhis, mainstream Shi'a, freethinkers, and Sufi Kalandars. This interface with the spectrum of Persian religious expression appears to confirm that 'in Iran, things are *never* what they seem'.[29] Later Bahai writers have regretted that Browne took a wrong turn in going to Kirman where not only Azalis, but Bahais of – to put it mildly – an unorthodox hue, broke the spell of their pious co-believers of Isfahan, Shiraz and Yazd.[30] Browne's own remarks suggest he found in the southern city a dimension to the Persian character he had all along been desirous of encountering. Within a garden placed at his personal disposal, Browne met 'that object which, since my arrival in Persia, had been ever before me, namely, to familiarise myself with all, even the most eccentric and antinomian, developments of the protean Persian genius.'[31] The traveller's own personality is seen in his wish to be the sole European in the city; his enjoyment of having the reputation, contrary to the other 'firangis', of one who 'goes after religions'; his indulgence in 'all that is wildest and strangest in the poetry of the Persians'. By means of an opium addiction initiated to remove the pain of opthalmia, Browne half-willingly penetrates 'that vision of antinomian pantheism which is the world of the Kalandar'.[32] The dialogue below is no fantasy, but though Arberry considered it 'a typical scene'[33] – he may have been thinking of the quality of vividness *A Year Amongst the Persians* demonstrates overall – Browne surely intends its extravagance to shock his more staid Victorian readers:

> Then Fathu'llah, the minstrel, broke in. 'O Hazrat-i-Firangi!' he exclaimed, 'all these ideas and thoughts about God which you have, yea, your very doubts and wonderings, are your creatures, and you are their creator, and therefore above them, even according to the verse you quote, "Exalted is God above that which they allege!" [...] When His Holiness[...] the Bab[...] was asked "What are the Firangis?" he replied, "They are Spirit." You are to-day the Manifestation of Jesus, you are the Incarnation of the Holy Spirit, nay did you realise it, you are God!'[34]

Browne's simultaneous fascination with and repulsion from the blasphemous extravagances of his Azali/Bahai companions might be represented as a split-ting of the self along the fault-line of his English forebears' Christian re-spectability, and an urge to subvert convention that would lead him further than others in his bitter arraignment of the British government in the name of Persian national freedom.

Towards the end of his Persian journey, Browne reached the fort of Shaykh Tabarsi in Mazindaran, a province of northern Iran. Here his original project of recovering the spirit that animated the Bab and his early followers achieved partial restitution. Barely two generations ago, hundreds of Babis had been slaughtered in this vicinity. A peasant guide led the solitary traveller on, believing him 'to be at heart a Babi come to visit the graves of the martyrs of my religion'. After leaving him there for a while he returned and affirmed Browne was 'now a Haji'. Browne inwardly agreed that he had 'accomplished this final pilgrimage'. A short while later, having said farewell to his Persian servant, finding himself on a Russian steamer crossing the Caspian Sea, he felt 'for the first time for many months, [...] with a sudden loneliness, a stranger in the midst of strangers'.[35] Europe and the age of modernity would soon reclaim the English Babi.

A little more than Orientalism: retrieving authentic Babism

> It is about the Bab, especially, and Kurrat'ul-'Ayn and the others, not about Beha, that I want to hear [...] Beha may be very well, and may be superior to the Bab, but it is about the Bab that I want to hear.
> *Year Amongst the Persians*, p. 514.

After his return to Cambridge in 1888, Browne set about deepening his scholarship on the Babi movement. In 1890, he went to the East to visit the leaders of both Babi factions, Azal in Cyprus, and Baha'ullah in Akka, Palestine. Publications of introductory material had appeared in 1889, and in the next decade two historical accounts in English translation. Then a gap opened during which Browne devoted his time to writing a history of Persian literature. But in 1910, and again in 1918, he published further material on both Azalis and Bahais.[*] In foregrounding the formative elements in Browne's construction and reconstruction of Babism and its offshoots, some important conclusions may be reached concerning his attitude towards a favoured eastern people (the Persians); his personality as an Orientalist with a specific 'desire for the Orient'; and his belief in the conditions of possibility of a Persian national awakening in the late nineteenth and early twentieth centuries. The last issue is specially germane to a study build around the articulation of western travellers and Orientalists' ideas about a reformation of the Muslim *umma* and the potential of its states and peoples to engage with the modern world inaugurated by western political, economic, and technological hegemony. We shall also find that, as with other British figures with pro-eastern sympathies scrutinised so far, Browne's writings register a split between engagement with an ideal aspect or cause of an eastern society, and a European idea and/or ego that asserts itself over, and is integral to, the formulation or representation of that ideal.

Browne's successive publications on the Babi movement document a trajectory of concerns, including his increasingly partisan involvement in the issue of the succession to the Bab, and the establishment of a canonical

---

[*]   See bibliography and below for these publications.

textual rendition of Babi history in the teeth of efforts, as he supposed, to elide, smooth out and re-write it from a later perspective. Reading through the series of introductions, annotations and appendices attached to his translations of the various Persian texts that aspired to represent – or which Browne re-configured to represent – that authentic history, is a repetitious, digressive, and on the face of it, recondite, activity. Yet around Browne's assemblage of this textual record accumulate certain key axioms, which subsequent critics and defenders have largely missed. These are connected to the dual narrative, derived from Gobineau, already mentioned. Gobineau's word is consistently cited to lend authority to the positions his disciple takes up. Embedded in these is a predilection for an essential Persia that, while it stresses the archaic and the primitive, does not propose a condition of stagnation and stasis, but, on the contrary, projects a recurrence of revival and re-awakening of an ancient spirit of patriotism, heroism, and self-devotion. Babism was a movement that embodied precisely these constituent qualities, and therefore evidenced to a hope of renewal, a conviction that Persia might have been slumbering, but was not dead. Browne's investment in 'getting the history right' was a mark and expression of his faith in this proposition, and, passionate as his espousal of causes invariably became, we should not be surprised to find that such a formulation, enclosing as it did his own 'desire for the Orient', eventuated in an urge to project Babism as the realisation of a deeply-held personal object. The result, which we have already seen in the making in his travel writing, was to favour the unadulterated story of the Bab, and to this end, to exalt the claims of the Bab's appointed successor, Subh al-Azal, with his conservative interpretation of the Babi tradition, over the innovative tendencies of Baha'ullah. Crucial in this regard was Browne's belief that Azali Babism maintained a Persian locus as its area of concern, along with foundation traits of the Bab and his followers that Browne took to be specifically Persian. The Bahai narrative of Babism was not only revisionist in its weighting and prioritising of the new 'manifestation' of Baha'ullah over the Shirazi prophet, it also smoothed out the milieu of his activity and transposed its focus from Persia to a cosmopolitan arena beyond its borders.[36]

Some of these considerations are present in Browne's introduction to *A Traveller's Narrative*, a text he brought back from his visit to Akka in April 1890 and published with notes and introduction the following year. Here his interest in the Babi movement is explained in the following terms:

> To the student of religious thought it will afford no little matter for reflection; for here he may contemplate such personalities as by lapse of time pass into heroes and demi-gods still unobscured by myth and fable; he may examine by the light of concurrent and independent testimony one of those strange outbursts of enthusiasm, faith, fervent devotion, and indomitable heroism – or fanaticism, if you will – which we are accustomed to associate with the earlier history of the human race; he may witness, in a word, the birth of a faith which may not impossibly win a place amidst the great religions of the world. To the ethnologist also it may yield food for thought as to the character of a people, who, stigmatised as they often

have been as selfish, mercenary, avaricious, egotistical, sordid, and cowardly, are yet capable of exhibiting under the influence of a strong religious impulse a degree of devotion, disinterestedness, generosity, unselfishness, nobility, and courage which may be paralleled in history, but can scarcely be surpassed. To the politician, too, the matter is not devoid of importance; for what changes may not be effected in a country now reckoned almost as a cypher in the balance of national forces by a religion capable of evoking so mighty a spirit? Let those who know what Muhammad made the Arabs, consider well what the Bab may yet make the Persians.

But to myself, and I believe to most others who have been or shall be brought to consider this matter, the paramount interest thereof lies in this, that here is something, whether wise or unwise, whether tending towards the amelioration of mankind or the reverse, which seemed to many hundreds, if not thousands, of our fellow-creatures worth suffering and dying for, and which, on this ground alone, must be accounted worthy of our most attentive study.[37]

Browne's apologia for inquiry into Babism directs questions at academic professionalism – 'student of religious thought', 'to the ethnologist', 'our most attentive study' – as well as political expediency and personal curiosity, to elicit a rationale for research. But each category is brought up against the same embedded proposition, one Browne would continue to reiterate in his writings on Babism. The Babis' fervent devotion and indomitable heroism, unselfishness, nobility and courage evidenced to the rebirth of a people otherwise stigmatised in the crudest type of Orientalism as selfish, mercenary, in all ways corrupt. An equation of the Bab and the Persians with Muhammad and the Arabs caps the implied racial argument and answers to its own rhetoric. Already there is evidence of Browne's interest in the political revival of Persia, although here it is incorporated in – or at the moment not emphasised above – the spiritual renaissance he felt Babism proffered to that land. In this early piece of his writing we can already see a predisposition for a mix of dispassionate, academic discourse with language that is fervent and engaged. The former is notable in the use of qualification ('may not impossibly', 'wise or unwise') and an apparent effort of objectivity ('examine by the light'). But this soon dissolves into Browne's own fiercely subjective desire for the Orient – a longing for a cause 'worth suffering and dying for', juxtaposed against the anomie of western modernity whose colourless phraseology ('towards the amelioration of mankind or the reverse') is employed in order that it might be undermined. It may well have been precisely this impassioned encoding within Browne's study of Babism that upset his more staid Orientalist colleagues. (This preoccupation with a heterodox oriental religious movement attracted criticism – and some affirmation – from reviewers and fellow Orientalists).[38]

Browne then proceeds to set the enthusiasm of his own methodology squarely before his readers, invoking Gobineau's *Religions et Philosophies* ('this masterpiece of historical composition') to account for his initial romantic interest in the Babis. Ironically, Gobineau had at first quashed his disciple's antecedent romanticising of Sufism by dismissing it as 'Le quiétisme, le beng et l'opium'.[39] These were strongly pejorative terms in Browne's lexicon – the precise qualities he came to admire in the Babis were their courage, pro-activity, and at times violent engagement with the world. Having explained his motivation for studying Babism, Browne then allows scholarly impulse to come into play and his study's chief problematic is activated: no less than the possibility of retrieving an authentic Babi history.

> My impatience, too, was greatly increased; for I reflected that although there must be many still living who had witnessed, or even taken part in, the events of which I was so anxious to discover every slightest detail, each year that passed would materially lessen their number, and render ever fainter the possibility of restoring the picture in its entirety.[40]

Browne uses Gobineau's *Religions et Philosophies* as his master text. Although this left off events at the Babi holocaust of 1852, it clearly indicated Azal as the Bab's successor. Browne tries to grasp the new realities centred on Baha'ullah's leadership and the effective sidelining of the Bab. When in Persia he had scarcely heard Azal's name mentioned by the Bahais, and he might have remained unaware of his significance were it not for Gobineau's book, and coming across some Azalis in Kirman.[41] (Browne subsequently visited Azal in Cyprus in 1890.) The introduction to *A Traveller's Narrative* demonstrates its translator and editor's bias toward the cause of Azal, but this is balanced by eloquent exposition of the transformational potential of the Bahai development. At this point Browne is torn between the spiritual dynamism that he had personally encountered among the Bahais in Akka, and a tenacious hold on the apostolic succession from the Bab to Azal. Equally significant, particularly for Browne's long term orientation vis-à-vis Persian affairs, was that while he was putting this first Persian text on the history of the Babi movement through the press, he had begun to correspond with Azalis outside of the ambit of Persia and Cyprus. If Gobineau – whose authority in matters of Babi history Browne accepted with quixotic trust – had laid the foundations for his advocacy of Azali Babism, his contact with key Azali intellectuals helped channel the course of his enthusiasm for Persian causes over the coming two decades.

In his next publication on the Babis, the *Tarikh-i-Jadid or New History*, which appeared in 1893, Browne's dependence on an Azali interpretation of Babism is no longer counterweighted. *A Traveller's Narrative* he now knew to be the work of Baha'ullah's eldest son, Abbas Effendi (Abdul-Baha). *The New History* was also a Bahai source, what Browne later described as a '"Bowdlerized edition" of another text, Mirza Jani -i -Kashani's *Nuqtatu'l-Kaf*.[42] His search for a canonical exposition of early Babism had led him to adopt the latter text, which he had found by chance among Gobineau's manuscripts in the Paris Bibliothèque Nationale, as the key to the Babi succession, and a source that steered between the anti-Babi stance of the Iranian court historians and the revisionist distortions of the Bahais. But having already prepared the *New History* for publication, Browne waited another seventeen years before he brought out Mirza Jani's putative text. Nevertheless, in his introduction to the *New History*, he valorised the *Nuqtatu'l-Kaf* as 'the most interesting book, perhaps, in the whole range of Babi literature'.[43] Browne's reading foregrounded the work's picture of a primitive, pristine Babism which, he argued, the Bahais would prefer to be suppressed. What excited him was its representation of a specifically Persian Shi'ih milieu that, whatever its strangeness to the European reader, was the reality of Babism, warts and all:

> There was nothing of caution, compromise or concealment about the Kashani merchant [Mirza Jani]. The Babis of his time looked rather for an immediate triumph over the existing powers culminating in the universal establishment of the True Faith and the Reign of God's Saints on Earth, than for a Heaven of Glory, a far-distant Millennium, or "the Most Great Peace" on which Beha and his followers love to dilate.
>
> {...} The doctrines of the Bab, it is true, formed together a system bold, original, and, to the Persian mind, singularly attractive.
>
> [...] The original doctrine of the Bab, fascinating as it was to Persians of a certain disposition, was utterly unfitted for the bulk of mankind.
>
> [...] Great conceptions, noble ideals, subtle metaphysical conceptions, and splendid, though ill-defined, aspirations do, indeed, exist in the Beyan; but they are so lost in trackless masses of rhapsody and mysticism, so weighed down by trivial injunctions and impracticable ordinances, that no casual reader, but only a student of considerable diligence and perseverance, can hope to find them.
>
> [...] [The Bab's writings] were, for the most part, voluminous, hard to comprehend, uncouth in style, unsystematic in arrangement, filled with iterations and solecisms, and not infrequently quite incoherent and unintelligible to the ordinary reader.[44]

Browne's ambivalence toward Bahai divergences from early Babism and later Azali accounts derives from several standpoints by now well crystallised. Baha'ullah saw the need to file away Babism's grotesqueries, 'to discourage speculation [...] to exalt ethics at the expense of metaphysics [...] to check mysticism [...] and to render [Babism] more capable of becoming [...] a universal system suitable to all mankind.' He downplayed the grievances of the past and 'gradually but steadily [...] eliminate[d] the tinge of Muhammadan, and more especially of Shi'ite, thought which the Babi doctrine still maintained.'[45] Browne's position here is illogical but emotionally consistent. If Babism was to take its place among the religions of the world as he suggested, it could not have done so – as he readily admits – in the inchoate form described above. Baha'ullah's reforms were therefore, as he says himself, 'beneficial and salutary'.[46] For Browne, however, the later reformulation removed the fascination of Babism, particularly for the Orientalist who could tease out significations where the 'ordinary' reader could not. The ordered, settled character of the system of Baha'ullah (charismatic as its creator was) excluded the outlandish elements of the old Babi faith. Most telling, however, was the new orientation toward government. The Bahai

position was conciliatory, whereas Browne's contempt for the Turkic Qajars
who had so ruthlessly persecuted the Babis was nurtured by the Azali hatred
for Nasir al-Din Shah ('the Nero of the Babi faith') which continued
unabated.[47] It was precisely in this area that Kashani's text scored: the Babis

> did not make any profession of loyalty to, or love for, the reigning dynasty; nor did
> they attempt to exonerate the Shah from responsibility of the persecutions which
> they suffered at the expense of his ministers or the Musulman divines, as later Babi
> [Bahai] historians have done. They hated the Muhammadan clergy [...] with an
> intense and bitter hatred [...]; but they entertained for the Kajar rulers an equal
> hatred, which Mirza Jani is at no pains to disguise. To Nasiru'd-Din [...] and to his
> father, Muhammad Shah, such terms as 'tyrant', 'scoundrel', 'unrightful king', and
> 'progeny of Abu Sofyan' are freely applied.[48]

It is difficult to escape the conclusion that Browne's discovery of the
Nuqtatu'l-Qaf fulfilled a profound personal need, whatever its significance as
a history of Babism.[49]

Fuelled in the first instant by Gobineau, Browne's bitterness towards
the Bahais and unbalanced admiration for Azal drew attention as it intensified
to a specific facet of Orientalism. His predilection for the 'conservative' or
'stationary' faction of Babism might be read as a variation on what Said
called 'another aspect of the spiritual crisis of "late bourgeois humanism"':

> When Gibb opposed nationalism in the modern Islamic states, he did so because he
> felt that nationalism would corrode the inner structure, keeping Islam Oriental; the
> net result of secular nationalism would be to make the Orient no different from the
> West.[50]

Browne's opposition to cosmopolitan Bahaism and his predilection for
primitive Babism may be located within a similar desire to Gibb's, that is, to
defend 'the inner structure', to keep the Orient oriental. (But in contrast to
Gibb, Browne later went on to offer his vigorous support for nationalism in
Islamic states). Uncommitted readers may find Browne's adherence to one
side in what – for someone who had been so fired by the story of the Bab –
was a sorry and confusing set of outcomes, a peculiar aberration for a
professional Orientalist to follow. What I have tried to argue is that Browne's
decision to uphold the priority of the Azali case was no arbitrary whim. For
him, it was primitive Babism that had manifested the spirit of heroism and
self-sacrifice that he identified as representing the best that was to be found in
the racially pure Persian character. While he appreciated it was more likely to
succeed in attracting converts than original Babism, Bahaism had adopted a
posture of quietism and turning of the other cheek that slipped out of the old
Babi covenant to rid Persia of the Qajars and enact a reform of *the land of
Persia itself*. In point of fact, the Azali Babis, though they maintained this
hatred of the Qajars as an article of their creed, were prepared to mould the
militancy of the early Babis into a tactical alliance with the hated Shi'ih
clergy as a means of revolutionizing Persia. If, as Abbas Amanat claims,
Browne had been drawn to Persia in 1887 in the hope of encountering in
Babism a movement of religious protest and reform which could rejuvenate a

stagnant Persia, this desire later simply took on a new form as, disillusioned by the direction religious Babism had taken, he beheld the configuration of a new set of conditions in Iran that might enact in the political realm his first dream for Persia.[51]

Narrativizing an Eastern Awakening

> This final effort of an ancient race
> To burst its bondage, cast aside its chain,
> And rise to life 'a Nation once again'.
> Browne, Dedication, The Persian Revolution

The interest in Babism accounted for the first stage of E.G. Browne's career as an Orientalist, a career that rarely deviated from a sustained celebration of the Iranian people. The early line of research remains controversial, both for Bahais, who do not approve of his partisanship for the Azalis, and for the majority of Iranians, who would find his passionate advocacy of what in their eyes was a heretical sect hard to account for. However, this needs to be set against Browne's subsequent labours on behalf of the Iranian national constituency. Browne's own remarks in 1908, at the height of the revolutionary struggle in Persia, appear only to elide the apparent contradiction.

> The main interest of the Babis was to secure the spread of their religion, and as it was a reforming, Puritan faith, he [...] at one time felt that the regeneration of Persia was in their hands. But his sympathy was now transferred to the Constitutionalists, for he felt that their programme was more practical than that of the Babis.[52]

Amanat argues that Browne's early admiration for the revolutionary Babis against Iran's conservative ulama and Qajar state was rekindled by the popular tobacco protest of 1891-92, and by the first signs of the emerging constitutionalist movement in the early 1900s. 'Here no doubt he must have detected a degree of historical continuity with the Babi movement, though he preferred not to acknowledge it openly.'[53] Browne's contact with the Azali Babis in the 1890s may have prepared him for the active role members of this sect subsequently played in the revolution that began in 1905. But it is still not clear from his work up to that date that the line he would take when the revolution broke out would be one of such total commitment to the nationalist cause. My task in this section will be to interrogate Browne's adoption of a new narrative for the Persian awakening, replacing one that valorised a religious and sectarian agency (Babism) with one that pronounced on a national, political reformation (constitutionalism). Viewed from this perspective, Browne emerges as more than a simple exponent of academic Orientalism turned political activist.[54] I shall be arguing that, as seen in his advocacy of Babism, Browne's approach to the Persian revolution entails a split Orientalism. On the one hand, in his endeavour to break away from and

contest the fixed traits ascribed to the Persian national character of the type
sponsored by Curzon and his epigones, Browne would appear to have
spawned a counter-Orientalist discourse. By plotting the movement of this
discourse in some detail, I hope to demonstrate how Browne constructs an
account of the Persian national awakening which, as well as attacking the
official Orientalist version of the Persian predicament, also re-sites some of
his own earlier positions on the Persian racial character. At the same time
however, this discourse is sustained by a narrative of Iran's national origins
and continuing racial specificity that, while it is enabling of the foundation of
an Iranian national movement, is, not unsurprisingly, firmly fixed within the
domain of European Orientalist writing. I shall refer to the claim made by
Mostafa Vaziri that Orientalists (Browne chief among them) deployed
European nationalist historiography to fabricate an Iranian identity that was
subsequently taken up by Iranian nationalists.[55]

Wedged between his first publications on Babism and his writings on
the Persian revolution – and running concurrently with the latter – Browne
had embarked upon the project of writing a literary history of Persia. This, of
all his writings, would stand as his monumental contribution to academic
Orientalism. Conceived less as a history of Persian literature and more a
detailed survey of Iranian culture and thought linked to the politics of each
successive age, A Literary History of Persia spanned almost a quarter of a
century in production, the major part of its author's career – volume one
appeared in 1902, volume two in 1906, volume three in 1920, and the fourth
and final volume in 1924. Amanat stresses the continuity this project represented for Browne's Persian ideal. 'In his study of Persian literature, both
past and contemporary, he seemed to be seeking a paragon of rejuvenation,
one that could remove the dust of exhaustion from the face of an old
culture.'[56] Mostafa Vaziri goes further by placing Browne's work within a
larger Orientalist enterprise of constructing an imagined national identity for
Persia. 'Browne's creative adaptability in linking literature to political history
extended the European vision of history as a linear national progression.'[57] In
fact, he sees Browne's Literary History of Persia as a master-text that
summarises the nineteenth century philological work of the Germans, and
embodies both the Aryan concept and the language issue within the frame of
a national category:

> In any discussion of the turn-of-the-century scholarship, a return to Browne's ideas
> is inevitable. From the period of Browne on, a formative process is evident in
> using the Aryan hypothesis, connecting the Farsi language with Iran (as its home-
> land and its national language) and at times lumping disjointed historical devel-
> opments into a national category, all in the new direction of embryonic Iranian
> nationalism.[58]

Vaziri is concerned to deconstruct the fallacy he sees as implicit within
Browne's national methodological framework. He argues this by referring to
Browne's collapsing of the language issue into the political geography of the
supposed Iranian heartland. The Farsi language flourished in the eastern

Iranian plateau whereas European Orientalists located the western part as the home of 'alleged ancient Aryans'. Also, Farsi had been widely employed by such non-Iranians as Indians, peoples of Central Asia, and later on, others resident in Ottoman lands, who Browne cavalierly dismisses. But 'identification of the Farsi language with Iranian geographical limits was a natural step, given the cultural and political nationalism of Europe'.[59] For Vaziri, not only did Browne and other European Orientalists divide Persia's history along the lines of an ancient and Islamic period, they also provided the aliment for glorification of a pre-Islamic past (and concomitant denigration of Iran's Muslim heritage) which was subsequently adopted by Iranian nationalism of the twentieth century, particularly by the Pahlavis.

In fairness to Browne, it should be pointed out that in his *Literary History of Persia* he is more sophisticated in his observations on race and its implications for nationalism than the young Orientalist who wrote *A Year Amongst the Persians*. For example, he clearly deprecates the kind of 'Aryan' racist bias that Vaziri attributes to the academic Orientalist George Rawlinson – 'Loath to accord to the Jews any priority or excellence over the Aryan peoples, they belittle Moses to glorify Zoroaster'.[60] The 'Semitic influence on Persia' had been great in all periods of its history. While he does adumbrate a periodicity for Iranian history that discriminates between the ancient and Islamic ages, Browne criticises 'the narrower view of Persian literary history' that sees the Persian voice as silenced during the first two centuries of Islam.[61] In fact, he celebrates the 'Semitic' influence on Persian culture and in the preface to volume two states: 'For Islam and the Perso-Arabian civilisation of Islam I have the deepest admiration.'[62]

It is, to use Amanat's term, the pursuit of the grail of rejuvenation that brings life to Browne's European 'vision of [Persian] history as a linear national progression'.[63] Since Browne was not, as Vaziri points out, qualified to speak of Persia's pre-Islamic past with much erudition, it is upon Persia's Islamic literature and culture that he concentrates his hermeneutic. Here he is, not surprisingly, drawn to what he terms 'the Persian Renaissance', an event beginning two centuries after the Arab conquest of Persia that resulted in the production of a literature in the Persian language.[64] The *Literary History* project, the last two volumes of which were finished after the revolutionary interregnum, culminates in the 'modern period' from 1500 onwards (covered by volume four). This highlights the restoration of Persian nationhood by the Safawis after a suspension caused by eight hundred years of Arab, Mongol and Turkish conquests.

Browne then engages the nineteenth century 'fermentations' caused by the Babi insurrection and the stirrings of political revolution.[65] By the time he had reached the middle point of his study, the Persian revolution broke out in the world outside academic Orientalism. Browne, however, already had the scope of his subject, especially a settled periodicity, in view. Owing to the possibilities such a narrative opened up for placing Persia's revolutionary moment within the context of a long, unbroken national history, Browne was

already geared to providing the national idea for the revolution when it
arrived. From the point of view of Persia's national rejuvenation then, the
approach adopted in the *Literary History* encapsulated something more than a
switch of agency from Babism to revolutionary national politics. It confirmed
the Orientalist underpinning of Browne's own faith in the Persian awakening,
which I argued earlier was central to his desire for the Orient. His study
comprehended the recovery of the illustrious past he had envisioned on his
visit to Pasargadae and Persepolis in his year of travel in Persia. By its means
the spirit of the Iranian people as a trans-historical entity had now achieved
representation.

In his preface to *The Persian Revolution*, Browne lays out the unique
qualities of his Persian subject, drawing a parallel with the Greeks, who
because of their ancient renown had been considered worthy of national self-
determination. In a discourse that straddles his own liberal sympathies and a
narrative that seeks to ascribe a linear history to a land, a language and a
people, Browne argues that the uniqueness of the Persian nation should be
recognised and protected.

> Of all the ancient nations whose names are familiar to us Persia is almost the only
> one which still exists as an independent political unit within her old frontiers (sadly
> contracted, it is true, since Darius the Great caused to be engraved on the rocks of
> Bagastana or Bisutun, in characters still legible, the long list of provinces which
> obeyed him and brought him tribute), inhabited by a people still wonderfully
> homogeneous, considering the vicissitudes through which they have passed, and
> still singularly resembling their ancient forbears.[66]

To support this principle examples of Persia's contributions to art, literature
and metaphysics are educed: 'Sufis, Ismailis, the Shi'a, the Hurufis, the
Babis, all alike reflect the subtle metaphysics of the Persian mind'.[67] Evinced
as proof of the potential of the Persian character for devotion to and heroic
sacrifice for a cause, the Babi experience is now incorporated into the Persian
national genus and rewritten into the contemporary struggle for national self-
determination. Browne's promotion of the Persian revolution both counters
the imperialist Orientalism that derided the capricious and corrupt Persians as
incapable of democratic self-government, and by means of a 'nationalist
Orientalism',[68] announces the revival of an eastern people whose national
character had empowered past historical achievements and might do so again.
At the same time though, Browne is fearful of the hegemonic force of a
western imperialism that reduces all national diversity to its own type:
homogeneity and a crude utilitarian notion of 'development'. *The Persian
Revolution* inscribes a coherent response to this force as embodied in the
hostility of the conservative British establishment towards the Persian constitutionalists: 'Powerful interests and prejudices have been against them and
misapprehensions as to their aims and motives have prevailed.'[69]

In addition to writing his history, Browne engaged these interests by a
variety of means (e.g. his activities on the Persia Committee, delivery of
public lectures, composition of pamphlets and letters to the press, direct

contact with nationalists and revolutionaries in Persia and in exile abroad, as well as with pro-Iranian British diplomats in Persia). Bonakdarian summarises the substance of Browne's involvement in the politics of the Iranian revolution:

> As an Oriental expert, he claimed to be making sense of the situation in Iran for the British public and providing an alternative interpretation of the developments intended to correct the "misconceptions" promoted by the Foreign Office and the conservative press. Hence, his task may be characterized as "corrective/ reactive" hermeneutics. In this hermeneutic venture, Browne resorted to what Bakhtin has termed "dialogic discourse," whereby his narrative constructs engaged in a dialogue with malevolent representations of the Iranian revolution both in Britain and Iran, seeking to disarm and eradicate the authority of these alternative accounts.[70]

Bonakdarian's perceptive delineation of Browne presents him as an Orientalist who developed a discourse of 'Persia for the Persians' similar to Blunt's project for the Egyptians. Like Blunt, Browne provided 'a narrative of *native resistance* to both despotism and foreign domination'. He encompassed this by 'making it possible for a particular range among the many voices of the Iranian nation to be heard by the British public'.[71] But whereas Blunt was present in Egypt during some of the key events of the Urabi nationalist struggle, orchestrating the nationalist cause and representing it to the British government, Browne disregarded W.A. Smart's warning at the outbreak of the Persian revolution 'not to write a history of this movement, without coming out here and studying it *sur lieu*. It is no easy thing to understand'.[72] Browne's decision to remain in England where he could edit and arrange the information reaching him from a variety of sources, Persian and English, actively steering the Persia Committee in its campaign, and in particular firing off letters to the press that were highly critical of official policy on Persia, made him as influential a figure as Blunt had been, probably more so. While it is clear that Browne modified his Iranian 'voices' to influence the British public, it was also the case that his publicist activities frequently embarrassed the British government, and succeeded in winning greater support for Persian constitutionalism than Blunt had been able to do for Egyptian nationalism in and after 1882. (Blunt claimed, with characteristic hyperbole, that Browne could justly claim for himself the successful reinstatement of the Persian constitution in July 1909: 'But for him Persia would most certainly have been annexed by Russia, or rather put under Russian tutelage after the precedent of Egypt'.)[73]

The Argument with *The Times*

Browne's major opponent and the chief object of his 'dialogic discourse', as frequently indicated in *The Persian Revolution*, was *The Times*. The paper's main Persia correspondent, David Fraser, left for Iran early in 1909, at a time when the Persian nationalists were attempting to rally after the Shah's coup against the constitution in the summer of the previous year. His account, *Persia and Turkey in Revolt*, was published a short time after Browne's book in 1910 In it, Fraser projects a popular Orientalist portrait of the Persians – one remarkably similar to that of Curzon and his epigones, if politically at variance with the master. (Curzon strongly opposed the Anglo-Russian convention because he believed it ceded too much to Russia.) But it is also readily discernible that a commonality exists between Fraser and Browne's discourses; each works through a semantic field in which lexis largely pertains to a putative 'Persian character', and the viability or otherwise of Iranian self-government. (Not only does Browne cite *The Times* and Fraser in his narrative, Fraser returns the compliment in his). In Fraser's codification, the Persians are 'soft', 'peaceful', 'mild', 'benevolent', and 'gentle'. But these qualities slip quickly into the pejorative: 'effeminate', easily led, child-like, 'ignorant', and 'cowardly'. 'A Persian volunteer is usually a person of no property, no morals, and no courage'; 'firearms to a Persian are like matches to a small child in Europe'; 'Persians are incapable of managing their own affairs without foreign guidance'. As for the Majlis, or Iranian national assembly, this was 'impotent' and its membership 'ignorant, headstrong and irresponsible'.[74]

> There are capable men in Persia [...] It is a pity that such men do not possess more self-confidence and more strength of character, but it is not their fault that some evil genius has looked into the Persian soul and withered some of its courage. There is great natural intelligence in Persia, great versatility, and a remarkable capacity for enthusiasm. With these good qualities go instability, and a vanity that is probably a greater curse to the Persian character than any of its other defects. Nevertheless, I am a believer in the Persian, for his buoyant temperament and high intelligence appeal irresistibly to one's sympathy; one cannot believe but that he will develop generously when his colossal ignorance has been enlightened, and his disposition sobered by contact with the materialities of modern civilisation.[75]

Though he goes to some length to mystify the forces behind the revolutionary outbreak ('a movement with unimportant beginnings expands out of all proportion owing to adventitious circumstances'), Fraser has to account for active elements within it, in contradistinction to the cowardly and inept Persians who 'whatever their ideas may have been [...] certainly never evinced the intention of shedding blood for them'.[76] These he identifies in the form of the Caucasian 'foreigners' who fought alongside their Azerbaijani cousins in Tabriz, and who were responsible for 'foully murdering the Governor [of Rasht] in cold blood', and giving 'the inhabitants [of Meshed] a lesson in revolutionary tactics'.[77] Interestingly, and like Curzon before him,

Fraser finds something to admire in the Turkic peoples, especially those from 'the more virile province of Azerbaijan', who alone credited themselves in defending the constitution during the 1908 coup. 'The handful of Nationalists belonging to the Azerbaijan *anjuman*, who alone fought, showed dash enough to open the ball, and without support could not have been expected to do more than they did.'[78] Another active group were 'turbulent and lawless' tribesmen, particularly the Bakhtiari, who Fraser himself witnessed marching on Tehran to depose the Shah and re-establish the constitution in the spring of 1909, but whose revolutionary credentials he dismisses as based solely on self-interest. The revolutionary forces were thus made up of 'soldiers of fortune' like the Caucasians, and Bakhtiaris who 'had no interest in the question of Constitutional government'.[79]

Outwardly principled in his support for the Anglo-Russian convention (but showing tendencies to slippage into cynicism) Fraser represented all that Browne detested about the Foreign Office/establishment line on Persia. Unsurprisingly, the *Times* correspondent never forgot for long the geopolitical context of the Persians' misguided bid for freedom. He berates Britain's pusillanimous diplomacy in Iran, underscoring Russia's decisive action while maintaining the Foreign Office fiction that her troops had neither interfered with Persia's administration nor occupied her territory. While superficially congratulating the 'smooth working of the Agreement', which was his paper's position, Fraser's instincts lined him up with a Curzonian forward policy.[80] In one of his less guarded passages, he lays open a stock imperialist rendition of the need for a parental hand (replete with stick) to intervene with the 'childish oriental':

> We are a very humanitarian people, greatly given to forwarding the social and spiritual fortunes of others less blessed than ourselves. But it is a futile sort of humanity that allows our own countrymen to be hurt, while at the same time it permits an ignorant country like Persia to continue unchecked in the way that leads to disruption. It would seem as if the sooner we act the parental part towards Persia, the better it will be for Persia in the end and the less troublesome for ourselves in the future.[81]

Again, like Curzon, Fraser cannot but admire the virile approach of Russia. He ends up calling for the creation of a British military presence in the south of Persia to compare with Russia's in the north, and strongly hinting at the need for British intervention there 'to put Persian affairs on a sound footing', before underlining Anglo-Russian co-operation: 'England and Russia hold Persia in their hand, to do with as they will'.[82]

To understand Browne's response to Fraser and the imperialist position he represented, it is necessary to interrogate Browne's framing of the revolutionary movement, in particular his intelligent appraisal of effective tactics vis-à-vis his British audience, and his personal predilections. Browne's overall riposte to Fraser's rubbishing of the Persian character is inscribed in the argument of his preface, already discussed above, in which the nation's illustrious pedigree is set out, and the Babis' courage and valour deployed to represent Persians' willingness to sacrifice themselves in the right cause. According to Amanat: 'To Browne [...] Persian paradigms of martyrdom, particularly when they occur in the cause of a national movement, are a sign of strength at odds with the stereotypes of timidity, irresolution, and deception prevalent in European popular Orientalism of his time.'[83] Browne – again in a similar manner to Blunt in Egypt in 1882 – strenuously endeavours to project a united national movement, cured of the 'fatal tendency to quarrel with one another, and so to play into the hands of their enemies', characterising his Persian protégés as motivated by 'the true patriotic feeling – the power of combined action and personal sacrifice – which so unexpectedly developed itself in a people whose weak points are mercilessly exposed, though unfairly exaggerated, in Morier's *Hajji Baba*, whence most Englishmen derive their ideas of the Persian character.'[84] Within the body of his text, Browne adopts a unifying strategy with respect to social background, clerical and secular parties, religious denominations and ethnic groupings. Browne smoothes over the initially uneasy, and in due course unsustainable, coalition between the Shi'ih higher clergy and the secular nationalists who, as Fraser and later historians point out, were very often anti-clerical and personally irreligious.[85] The old racial and territorial divisions, so openly proposed and polarised, in *A Year Amongst the Persians*, are closed and subsumed within the popular national cause. In particular, the Azerbaijani input – manifest even to a hostile observer like Fraser – is celebrated as an ornament of the constitutional spirit. 'All competent observers seem to agree that the deputies from Azarbayjan, and especially from Tabriz, constituted the salt of the [national] Assembly.' The city of Tabriz was 'the Manchester of Persia', its inhabitants among those who 'best understood and most loved freedom and independence'. The Azerbaijani who assassinated the reactionary Amin al-Sultan is eulogised in quoted Persian verse, one line of which apostrophises him, 'O Turk of Iranian descent'.[86] Browne takes issue with Fraser's charged use of the terms 'foreign' and 'revolutionaries', his over-emphasis of their number, and his distorting characterisation of the Bakhtiaris as 'actuated solely by tribal ambition, innate love of fighting and hatred of the Qajar dynasty'.[87] He then goes on to quote the *Yorkshire Daily Post*'s account of the Sipahdar, or Field Marshall, commanding the nationalist army of the north, implying that other papers besides *The Times* were able to get their facts right. But Browne's careful downplaying of the clergy-secular division, and his preference for eschewing terms like 'revolutionary' and 'nationalist', is done out of sensitivity to those readers who might cast an anxious eye upon Britain's imperial interests in Egypt and India.

> On numerous occasions he was prepared to suppress information that could have proven detrimental to the British public opinion he was striving to mobilize in support of the beleaguered Iranian constitutional movement, thereby undermining his own self-ascribed role as a historian committed to the goal of objectivity.[88]

To his sensitivity toward British public opinion may also be added Browne's own personal unease with some of the republican, anti-imperialist, secular-radical ideas fostered within Tabrizi groups by Social Democratic theorists and activists of the Russian Caucasus. No hint is made of the secret societies who 'wrapped their innovative thought in religious cloaks in an attempt to attract the olama to their cause', or indeed of the Azali Babis who adopted a similar tactic as well as playing a prominent part in the early years of the revolution, sometimes in the guise of clerics.[89]

What Browne does to counter the anti-constitutionalist stance of *The Times* and its backers is to construct carefully out of the sources and documents at his disposal a narrative of awakening in which voices from within Persia receive space to vindicate their own cause, emphasising, as Bonakdarian points out, the thesis that the revolution was self-generated and self-nurtured. The Iranian press is quoted copiously as an open challenge to *The Times*'s assertion 'that "the free Press of Persia proved to be as mischievous and as dangerous as it proved to be in other Oriental lands"'.[90] A drama is played out episode by episode, as the Persian people of light are collectively pitted against the evil Shah and his courtiers, waging 'the old, old battle against the powers of tyranny and darkness'.[91] Browne constructs a grand narrative in a by now conservative, nineteenth-century mode that recalls Michelet and Carlyle:

> an ancient and talented people, long oppressed and downtrodden, long schooled to servitude and silence, but now suddenly awakened to new hopes and conscious powers, and resolute not to suffer the cup of Freedom, as yet hardly tasted, to be dashed from their lips; a people clearly conscious of the manifold perils overshadowing them, betrayed by those to whom they had a right to look as their natural protectors against foreign invasion, half mad with anger and terror, yet resolutely groping their way through the triple darkness of Anarchy, Bankruptcy, and Chaos towards the Light which they would fain share with other happier nations.[92]

The spectre of foreign invasion and the motif of betrayal lays open the area in which Browne clashed with Fraser and his ilk in the most strident way. Amanat goes so far as to suggest Browne was 'tormented by the prospects of his own country condoning Russia's hostility towards the Persian revolution'.[93] Browne is clear in his own mind about the limitations of any British threat, but, using the words of one of his English correspondents in Persia, makes a play for British sympathies at home:

> 'One Englishman said to me, "Could not the Times be stirred up to write the truth on the state of affairs in Persia? [...]" "There is no question of difference of opinion between Englishmen who know the Persians. Cannot public opinion at home be roused, or is England still so obsessed by the fear of Germany that she must stoop to bargain with so horrible a Government as the Russian?"'

Although Browne's approach is considered in answering the criticisms of *The Times* point by point, he condemns the newspaper for 'its consistent sympathy with reaction', for its anti-liberal bias, and for the 'purely opportunist [...] considerations [that] govern its utterances'.[94] On the Anglo-Russian

convention he knew he could make capital out of the disquiet with which the
agreement was viewed by the Curzonite Tory imperialists. To this end he
later adopted an argument that had the potential of joining radicals with
Curzonites. Britain's traditional policy of buttressing an independent Persia
as a buffer state between the British and Russian empires had been sacrificed.[95] Browne also responded to Fraser's demand for an intervention that
wasn't an intervention by pointing out the reality of Russian aggression in
Europe as well as Persia. To do this he invoked a foundational Liberal
discourse that went back to Gladstone and Bright. It was Britain's mission to
protect weaker nations. Immediately after the constitution had been granted,
England's popularity had been widespread in Persia. All that was lost after
she had joined hands with Russia. Connecting the cause of constitutionalism
in Persia with the Liberal's hostility toward Russian reaction, Browne
juxtaposes Russia's vicious repression of the Baltic States alongside Grey's
determination to live with a former enemy. (The Foreign Secretary said the
Czar was 'a kind, moral family man, who as an English squire, would be
much respected in the parish'.)[96]

> Still, political exigencies must, apparently, even in the case of a Liberal
> Government, over-ride mere humanitarian sentiments and the Government organs
> in the Press had to put the best face they could on the matter, gracefully ignore the
> courts-martial, the hangings, the farm-burnings and the prison tortures of [the] new
> ally, and simulate, at least, some enthusiasm for 'Holy Russia,' which seems to
> wield so strange a hypnotic influence over a certain number of prominent English
> Liberals.[97]

Nationality and Pan-Islam

A further issue to be added to those outlined above is the relationship
between the Persian national 'awakening', and the wider eastern awakening
associated with Pan-Islamism. Browne's situation of Persia within such a
trend is at first hesitant, but later becomes a necessity. In 1902, in a lecture
entitled 'Pan-Islamism' (a subject he claimed was chosen for him), he raised
objections to the use of the term – 'I am not quite sure what it means; and, in
the second place, I am still less certain whether any such thing really exists.'[98]
In the East, race or nation was not as important as religion, clan or family,
and he doubted if a concept created after the pattern of European movements
(Pan-Hellenism, Pan-Germanism etc.) could be applied to the Orient. Interestingly, given that he had in the 1890s met both Jamal al-Din al-Afghani and
the Persian Armenian publicist, Malkum Khan, Browne has nothing to say at
this point about figures he would so purposively build into the first chapter of
his *Persian Revolution* as instigators of the Pan-Islamic ideal. His lecture
steers a diachronic course through Islamic history in pursuit of a trend or
movement the existence of which he is uncertain of. All of which might
appear to substantiate the claim that Browne's political activism was only

sparked from a disengaged academic Orientalism by the events of 1905. What the lecture does foreground, however, is a fear of European imperialism spreading throughout the East: 'We talk in the West of the "Yellow Danger," the "Black Danger," and the like; but what are these when compared with the "White Peril" which threatens Asia?'[99] According to Amanat, it was precisely this emotion that lay behind Browne's readiness to condone, in *The Persian Revolution*, 'Afghani's Pan-Islamic hegemony [...] as a legitimate answer to Europe's aggression.'[100] By the time he came to write this narrative nine years later, Browne had come to believe that a Pan-Islamic front was vital for the defence of the East against western imperialism, whereas at the start of the decade he had doubted the relevance of the term. Now he was fully alive to the need, if not for a substitute for the campaign of the Persia Committee to convince the British public of the wrong being allowed by their government in Persia, then at the very least a parallel strategy which might defend Persia's freedom by advising Persians and Muslims of other lands to join one another in a defensive mutuality. To this end, Browne started to construct a wider narrative of eastern awakening against the encroaching power of the imperialist West.

In his portrait of Jamal al-Din al-Afghani, which provided a national context out of which a Persian awakening might grow, Browne not only gave the lie to Fraser's denial of initiative to the Iranians themselves in their struggle for a constitution, he also linked the revolution to a wider, Pan-Islamic movement in the East. The originator of both movements was Afghani. 'To write his history in full would be to write a history of the whole Eastern Question' encompassing Afghanistan, India, and to a greater degree, Turkey, Egypt, and Persia. Afghani is credited with being the 'chief agent in bringing about the Egyptian Nationalist movement', and it is he 'to whom the present Constitutional Movement in Persia in large measure owes its inception'.[101]

In *The Persian Revolution*, Browne defines the Pan-Islamic trend as the awakening of Muslim countries to a common danger. He quotes an article he had himself written on Afghani on his death in 1896, inscribing the thinker's 'great ideal' as 'the desire to unite in one mighty nation all the Muhammadan peoples, and to restore the ancient power and glory of Islam.'[102] In practical terms, in *The Persian Revolution* Afghani is conceived of as a lover of Islam who fought the tyranny of the Shah and desired to bring about the unity of Muslim nations to counter the imposition of the West. In her biography of Afghani, who she presents as a different person to the figure portrayed in both Browne's and standard Muslim accounts, Nikki Keddie notes that Browne derived his picture of Afghani from several Arabic renditions that scarcely problematised his legend. Afghani was a more complex figure than Browne either realised or cared to credit.[103] Amanat too sees Browne's portrait of Afghani as a tailored one. Browne speaks of the Pan-Islamic movement in broad terms (according to what Amanat calls 'his own brand of Islamic idealism') missing out key factors. Clerical-secular tensions were one, and, in order to promote Afghani's 'anti-despotic stance', Browne occludes his readiness to enlist in the support of Pan-Islam a despotic reactionary like Ottoman Sultan Abdul Hamid.[104]

The strange point about Browne's remarks on Afghani, which I think have been overlooked, is that Keddie's picture of him as a dissimulating opportunist who may have lacked orthodox religious belief himself but who invoked Islam in order to unite the peoples of the East as a response to western imperialism, does contain striking similarities with Browne's own position. This may be crystallised as follows: where Keddie believes Afghani smoothed out the tensions between Islamic reformers and traditionalists, encouraging instead a 'religious-radical alliance', Browne may be said to have adopted a comparable tactic.[105] As far as Afghani was concerned:

> there is a constant stress on the power of the state and community. This is not to say that Afghani was not a reformer, or that he did not really hope for a diminution of absolutism and an increase in equality, justice, and consent of the governed; but when there was a potential conflict between these goals and Afghani's primary goal of rebuilding a strong Islamic state capable of withstanding Western encroachments, he consistently opted for the later.

Keddie contextualises this decision by referring to the European occupations of Tunisia, Egypt and Central Asia, and Iran's reduction 'to a virtual Western protectorate'.[106] Browne too refers to a 'core' of remaining Muslim states that (in 1909) had still to be fully colonised by Europe, this in the context of a project he personally furthered, that of mutual support and self-help between the two revolutionary Islamic states, Turkey and Persia. He believed these states – in part thanks to Afghani – now understood each others' 'common hopes and fears' when before they had been divided according to their respective Sunni/Shi'ih sectarian positions.[107] Browne may have adopted what amounts to an Azali Babi mode of procedure in advocating a clerical-secular nationalist alliance in Persia; when it came to the existence of a wider Pan-Islamic narrative, he built this around Afghani, at the same time endeavouring to make this good in reality by acting on Blunt's encouragement and bringing the Persians and Young Turks together. Though Browne 'failed to bring about a strong and durable solidarity between the Iranian constitutionalists and the Young Turks', this did not prevent him from continuing to educe parallels between the national struggles of Egypt, Turkey and Iran, and the common threat of European imperialism.[108] He continued to argue that:

> The bright hopes born in Turkey in 1908 and in Persia two years earlier have, indeed, been sorely dimmed, when not entirely extinguished, less through faults or shortcomings of the patriotic elements in these countries than through the Machavellian cynicism and materialistic greed of the Great Powers of Europe, who least of all desired any real reform in the lands which they had already marked down for their spoliation.[109]

Probably the clearest statement of linkage between the struggles for independence and resistance to European imperialism of these Muslim states is made in the *Press and Poetry of Modern Persia* (1914). In his preface to this collection of translations from poems and press articles from Iran, Browne also quotes from the literature of and makes reference to the national 'revivals' of Egypt and Turkey. Here he takes the opportunity of writing an acid appraisal of the 'unhappy antipathy which has grown up in recent years between West and East.'[110] In some ways, his preface is an afterword on the revolutionary period itself, which, following the Russian intervention that resulted in the closure of the Majlis in Tehran in December 1911, had effectively been terminated. Synchronous events at Tabriz had called forth another pamphlet, *The Reign of Terror at Tabriz: Britain's Responsibilities* (1912), exposing Russian atrocities in the city and incorporating eye-witness accounts and gruesome photographs of patriots hanging from scaffolds. A few months later, further Russian activity in the pilgrim city of Meshed leading to the sacking of the shrine and the killing of pilgrims and inhabitants 'was the culmination of these horrors, and produced an indescribably painful impression throughout the Muslim world.'[111] Browne's decision to merge Iranian, Egyptian and Turkish patriotic poetry into a common statement of resistance to European imperialism has to be seen in the context of this continuing tendency in Morocco and Tripoli in 1911-12, with the effective partition of Persia looming, albeit overshadowed by the deteriorating international scene.

Another catalyst to the production of *The Press and Poetry of Modern Persia* was a curious incident that Browne himself described. This might be said to disclose the aporia at the heart of his career as an Orientalist. At the end of a lecture on Persian literature several members of the audience expressed surprise 'at learning that there was modern poetry to speak of'. Already the author of two volumes on Persia's classical literature and thought, Browne embodies in his riposte all the contradictions embedded in his life's work as Orientalist and professor who played at politics:

> This determined me to devote some attention to the refutation of a pernicious error chiefly attributable to the rarity of intimate relations between the literary worlds of Europe and Asia, but fostered and encouraged to some extent by those who desire for political reasons to represent such Asiatic peoples as the Persians as entirely decadent and degenerate, whereas in fact they have during the last eight years shown a vitality which, under happier circumstances, had it been unimpeded by malignant external forces entirely beyond the control of the Persian people, would, I am firmly convinced, have ultimately effected the moral and material regeneration of the country.[112]

Few were so well qualified as Browne was to recognise, in the writings of professional Orientalists, representations of a pre-modern East as ancient in heritage as it was without 'vitality' or culture in the age of modernity. His entire point of departure, if it could be summarised, had been his urge to promote the first part of the proposition, while standing the latter on its head. He maintained 'an unshakable faith in the ability of the Iranian people to effectively guide their own destiny'.[113] If the revolution was dead, long live the revolution.

Browne's grasp of the terrain contested by European conquering nations and the colonised or endangered Muslim states is as sophisticated in its grasp of ideological fields dividing them as any other account of the period. He can articulate the triumph of *realpolitik* over principle by recourse to Arabic maxims and by adopting a polemical idiom excoriating British Liberalism (the 'veteran "Liberal"' who relinquishes both Mill and his love of liberty on assumption of office in the newly formed Liberal Government is of course Grey.)[114] A quotation from *Modern Egypt* denying to Islam the power of self-reformation, backed up by the authority of the Orientalist Muir, is refuted by Browne and characterised as 'calculated to wound Muslim sentiment'. Cromer's ignorance of Egyptian culture is demonstrated by his dismissal of the poet and prominent patriot, Mahmud Sami Pasha al-Barudi, as 'illiterate'.[115] Browne devotes much space to a virtually unobtainable volume of Egyptian patriotic verse, whose proscription had led to its author fleeing the country and the imprisonment of two nationalists who contributed to its preface. His choice of *Wataniyyati* ('My Patriotism'), from whose preface, a manifesto for nationalist poetry, he quotes extensively, cannot fail to foreground Browne's insurrectionary intentions, especially since it refers several times to the notorious Denshawai incident in which four Egyptians were executed for beating armed and marauding British army officers. Browne not only chooses to refer to what was controversial and current, in promoting patriotic verse from 'the conquered and helpless nation' he gives voice to silenced resistance and, equally important, makes the appropriate connections too. (Yeats's *Kathleen ni Hoolihan* is referred to as an example of 'that [patriotic] verse wherein Ireland stands supreme'.)[116] A chronology of nationalist awakening is also set down. The 'Young Ottoman' Turks of the 1860s/70s who drew 'their ideas, both political and literary, from France' are cited as likely precursors of the eastern awakening, with its watchwords '"the Fatherland" (*Watan*), "the Nation" or "People" (*Millat*), and "Liberty" (*Hurriyat*).' Browne argues that these words were passed on to Persia and the Arabic-speaking lands 'so that the humblest patriots who died on the Russian gallows at Tabriz in January 1912 cried with their last breath "*Yashasun Watan*" or "*Zinda bad Watan*" in the full sense of "Vive la Patrie!"'[117]

Conclusion

Working out of a tradition of nineteenth-century historiography as he did, Browne could hardly have been expected to problematise the dubious European gift of nationalism to the East. As it was, he endeavoured to excise as much as he could of the European influence behind the eastern national 'awakenings'. In the lecture *Pan-Islamism*, Browne acknowledged Islam's non-privileging of particular races (except perhaps the Arabs), stating how it tended to the creation of a unity based on a common faith rather than nationality. Keddie stresses the importance reformers placed upon the common Islamic cultural tradition providing 'an identification with a supra-national community'.[118] Browne adopted a similar approach when appealing for unity among national reformers in Muslim states. All the evidence points to the fact that he used Islam as a political rallying tool as did the other secular reformers, eliding the issue of reform in order to keep the traditional-ists on board. Browne smoothed out, as did Afghani, the disconnections between traditionalist clergy and secular nationalists in the name of a national, anti-imperialist front. He may not have got himself embroiled in the kind of labyrinthine intrigues and apparently contradictory positions into which, as Keddie shows, Afghani and his Azali Babi accomplices fell follow-ing this course. Their questionable tactics raised the issue: 'were Pan-Islam and appeals to the clergy effective paths to the modernization and regenera-tion of Iran?'[119] While it did not countenance the inclusion of Abdul Hamid within a Pan-Islamic movement (the Sultan was anyway neutralised for good in 1909) Browne's narrative of a Persian awakening might be charged with occluding the truth that 'the clergy were not really reformers, and that encouragement of their leadership perhaps in the long run slowed the process of reform'.[120] Browne's interest in the possibilities of religious reform waned with his enthusiasm for Babism. Instead, he convinced himself that the genius of the Persian nation would somehow find its way toward a new beginning. As long as it could sever itself from the Qajar absolutism forced upon it by the Russians (the higher clergy, that other evil in the demonology of primitive Babism, having thrown in its lot with the nation) Persia had the resources to guide itself, becoming a trans-historical reality that must eventually win through because predestined to do so.

Browne's position on the eastern awakening was arguably as fragile as Curzon's on British imperialism. The diplomat and ambassador to Iran, Reader Bullard, pointed out many years ago that Browne was a nineteenth century Liberal whose creed of internationalism scarcely survived the cala-mity of the Great War.[121] But from an Iranian perspective the standing of Browne the anti-imperialist has perhaps proved more enduring.[122] What Browne, Blunt and even David Urquhart shared – a bitter narrative of Britain's moral turpitude and betrayal of trust where her foreign policy in the East was concerned – has remained alive and well in Iran. The Iranian historian, Firuz Kazemzadeh wrote in 1968:

> It was in September 1907 that the modern Persian image of England crystallized [...] However, it was not any single act of dishonesty that mortified the Persians. What shocked and oppressed them was the atmosphere of uncertainty and hypo-crisy that Sir Edward Grey managed to create, and the sudden realization that Britain was not the moral force they had believed her to be. Justifiably or not, most Persians would, from then on, be prepared to believe only the worst of England [...] The image of a cynical people totally indifferent to the sufferings of the rest of

mankind [...] would survive the departure of British power from the Middle East, Indian independence, and the decline of Britain to the rank of a secondary power.[123]

A contemporary British reader might well be repulsed by such a picture, but were they to read the writings of Edward Granville Browne, they might obtain a better understanding of why others think this to be so.

6

Marmaduke Pickthall, Turkey and the Governance of Islam

The term *renegado*, once employed to designate individual, often high-ranking, Europeans who chose exile in the Ottoman empire and conversion to Islam, seems hardly to apply to Marmaduke Pickthall. Son of a Suffolk Anglican clergyman, by upbringing a Disraelian Tory and a supporter of the British empire in India and Egypt, Pickthall's name will be familiar to those conversant with English translations of the Holy Qur'an. His youthful journeys in Syria and Palestine in 1894-95 laid the foundations for his lifetime's engagement with Islam and the East. Financed by his mother as a compensation for his failure to secure a position in the Levant consular service, this period of his life serves as a prelude, vitally formative it is true, for the later ones when the centre of his world shifted to Istanbul and then to India. In the words of Peter Clark, Pickthall's best modern interpreter:

> He did not pass this time with the small earnest British community but wandered around Greater Syria, living roughly in villages and khans, learning the dialects, absorbing the values of the local culture, picking up local legends and the oral traditions of the previous generation. As he wrote twenty years   later, he 'ate native meals and slept in native houses following the customs of the people of the land in all respects. And I was amazed at the immense relief I found in such a life. In all my previous years I had not seen any happy people. These were happy people.' He returned to Jerusalem to see his family friends, perhaps irritating them by talking only to the servants in colloquial Palestinian Arabic.[1]

In Damascus, one moment perhaps encapsulated the attenuated yearning for a consummation that might envelop the young traveller's entire experience in Syria. 'He learnt to read Arabic and delighted in the city with its strong Islamic traditions, then enjoying a stability and prosperity as a major Ottoman provincial capital. In his youthful enthusiasm he sought to embrace Islam, but was dissuaded by the *shaikh al-ulama* at the Umayyad Mosque. "Wait till you are older," the old man advised, "and have seen again your native land. You are alone among us, so are our boys alone among the Christians. God knows how I should feel if any Christian teacher dealt with a son of mine otherwise than as I now deal with you.'"[2]

Pickthall's youthful journeys around Palestine and Syria provided the inspiration for his most successful and enduring novel, *Said The Fisherman* (1903), as well as for *Oriental Encounters* [1918](1927), an autobiographical collection of episodes set in the region. In 1907, he visited Egypt where he stayed in the house of a British official and 'met other imperial servants and publicists'.[3] A year later, he and his wife Muriel made a more protracted visit to the Middle East during which time they visited Egypt, Lebanon, Syria and Palestine. Further novels and articles on Egyptian and Near Eastern themes followed, including an introduction to J.E. Hanauer's *Folklore of the Holy Land* (1907) and a novel about the Urabi revolution, *Children of the Nile* (1908). But his Turkish sojourn, between March and July 1913, confirmed the predilections on which Pickthall's later conversion to Islam (1917) were based. A newly found conviction of Turkey's crucial importance within any scheme to reform the Muslim world led him into bitter opposition to Britain's Turkish policy. His adherence to the Young Turk cause acquired an unmoveable quality that would deliver him to the limits of opposition to his country's wartime policies by his open advocacy of a separate peace with Turkey.

This strange streak of dissidence is perfectly encapsulated in the title of Anne Fremantle's biography of Pickthall, *Loyal Enemy*. The reasons behind so profound a dislocation of a Victorian gentleman from a 'solidly professional, middle class, assured and [until the death of his father] comfortable' family background are complex.[4] In part they can be observed in a collection of pieces Pickthall wrote for the *New Age* periodical soon after his return from Istanbul, and eventually published in book form as *With the Turk in Wartime* (1914). Composed *en scène*, this piece of writing takes its place among a longer series of articles Pickthall wrote for the *New Age* from 1912 until 1919. (A year later he left Britain for India.) For the most part political essays, they embody a dual discourse that both addresses England and mediates the Muslim world, seeking to convince and correct, as well as, on occasion, apologise for England's crass mistreatment of the foremost Islamic nation. There was a remarkable facility in Pickthall's journalism – a capacity for reworking over and over again in incisive phrases a central narrative strand according to political exigencies of the moment. His fiction from *The Children of the Nile* onwards also invariably packed a political moral, and did not lack influential admirers in its time. According to E.M. Forster, the oriental tales (which all have Islamic settings) are seemingly infused with an insider's vision of the Orient and Islam.[5] Neither are the politics an artificial distortion: the very quality of 'insideness' lends to Pickthall's novels on the East a sympathy with the culture and praxis of his Muslim characters that spills out into the politics of great events.

In addition, those novels set in modern times probe the interaction of traditional eastern social norms with an ever more invasive western presence. But Pickthall's politics are as idiosyncratic in his fiction as they are in his political journalism. Although consistent in their own terms, to the student they pose obvious problems. Why is a revolutionary politics advanced in the instance of one Islamic society – Turkey – while the validity of a religio-nationalist struggle in another – Egypt – is denied? And how can the exercise of British imperial self-interest be valorised in the Egyptian context, and yet denounced in its operation in Turkey? For the modern reader the conundrum might be arcane. Pickthall was, after all, neither a great thinker of his time nor an influential one. Yet the stance he adopted might have prevented his achieving a more prominent position in, at the very least, British historical memory. Through his knowledge of two eastern languages and experience gained through eastern travel, Pickthall might have been an obvious candidate for that sphere of his nation's war activity that would win others conspicuous applause. But his choice of the Turks as the vanguard for a revolutionised Islam was his unquestionable disqualification from that gambit of fame. Instead, he continued even after the Great War in his agitation in favour of the Young Turks. Yet although Pickthall's chosen route may have delivered him into historical oblivion, it is of no small significance for the direction of the present essay. For this trajectory raises vital issues about the direction of the different forms of pro-Islamic politics I have been addressing so far, and it is these that I shall in due course attempt to address.

Confessions of a Turcophil: Pickthall's Turkish sojourn and Britain's Young Turk Policy

> By infamous unbridled tongues and dumb deceit,
> Through pulpits and the Stock Exchange the Balkans do their work,
> The preacher in the chapel and the hawker
> Feed on the dying Turk.
> Aubrey Herbert

Pickthall's advocacy of the primacy of Turkey's reform role as 'the one hope of the Islamic world' led him into collision with the Liberal Government, its pro-Balkan-Christian radical critics, and, during the Great War, the whole thrust of his nation's war endeavour. The pro-Turk opinions of his articles are set against the background of war in the Balkans, internecine strife within Istanbul between the CUP (Committee of Union and Progress) and the Ottoman Union Liberal party, and Turkey's later involvement in the First World War on the side of Britain's enemies. 'The most significant personal impact on Pickthall of these four months in Turkey [writes Peter Clark] was that, with prejudices reinforced, he became politicized as never before.'[6]

With the Turk in Wartime begins with an unintended, unless it be a subliminal, metaphor. The boat on which the Englishman is travelling gets stuck in a pea-soup fog on the Bosphorous, further agitating all the European passengers, already in a state of nervous anticipation over their reception in a wartime capital. But Pickthall, having seen off an unpleasant and oily Levantine Christian who had assumed he was a spy, suddenly experiences a momentary vision of Istanbul bathed in light, only for the clouds of vapour to encircle the ship once more. It is not too farfetched to discern a symbolism in this: the capital of the Ottoman empire to which the Englishman had travelled was engaged in a war for its survival. Pickthall was near to despair on account of a personal identification with the cause of Turkey that seemed to have foundered on the rocks of his compatriots' prejudices towards all the Young Turks stood for. His support for Turkey intensified during his four-month stay, quickly taking on the character of a vision of Turkey's lustre. Soon to be obscured once more by the fog of the First World War, it would nevertheless sustain him for many years to come. In Britain, Pickthall's fierce support for the revolution left him isolated and frustrated, sustained only by a small group of pro-Turkish travellers, diplomats and eccentric political figures. The British government appeared to have abandoned all semblance of being Turkey's traditional help and stay. Radical opinion, which had at first been sympathetic at the outbreak of revolution in July 1908, soon swung round to the cause of the Balkan League. Their victories in the late autumn of 1912 had 'produced a wave of enthusiasm in Western Europe, which was by no means confined to the parties of the Left.'[7] Certainly, some radical opinion – well represented in a Left-leaning periodical such as the *New Age* – enthused in their rediscovery of a gude auld cause. 'Many "pacifists" were so far excited by the prospect of the collapse of Turkish rule in Europe that they claimed this was no ordinary war but a Christian crusade of defence and liberation and therefore worthy of their support [...]. The spirit of Gladstone was abroad and Radicals rejoiced.'[8]

Pickthall may not have been alone in naming the war against Turkey a crusade. But he showed his own disdain for the pseudo-Christian connotations of this particular conflict by adding the epithet 'black' to denote the anything but holy nature of the Balkan States' enterprise. His five articles under the heading 'The Black Crusade' were published on the eve of the trip to Istanbul (November-December, 1912) and subsequently appeared as a pamphlet from the New Age Press. They embellish a message that was straightforward enough: the traditional image of the unspeakable Turk preying upon Christian victims was not only a cliché – it needed to be reversed.

> It is natural [...] that Serbs and Bulgars, Greeks and Monetengrins should deal in priestly benedictions and Te Deums when preparing for a slaughter of mere Unitarians. But when one hears (as I did lately) in an English church, the Turks compared to Satan, the Bulgarian advance to that of Christian souls assailing Paradise, one can only gasp. Are we really in the twentieth century?[9]

The Balkan States, backed by the Powers of Europe, were engaged in a destructive and vengeful exercise in which Turkey had the right to proclaim herself the wronged party. Pickthall has difficulty in deciding who is the more blameworthy: the greedy unprincipled Balkan states or Great Britain, the cowardly betrayer of her former friend and of her own once noble aspirations. Reversing the lazy encoding of vocabulary such as 'crusade', 'fanaticism', 'atrocities', Pickthall lambastes the stock-in-trade clichés of the British press he so detested:

> A plague upon the blessed word 'Bulgaria.' It has brought out automatically, as the cuckoo from the clock, 'our fellow-Christians,' 'horrible atrocities,' 'sacred name of Gladstone,' and 'unspeakable' Turk – a whole array of pseudo-pious catch-words as in-apposite to the present conflict as 'Abdul the Damned.' The same newspapers and individuals who 'danced with garlands' to the Young Turk deputies with delirious joy, are now the cruel foes of Turkey. Why? There is no answer but the blessed word 'Bulgaria.'[10]

Behind the crusading rhetoric of the British papers lay the reality of an opportunist war *par excellence*. Bulgaria, Greece and Serbia could only have sunk their differences and joined in their crusade against Turkey because of their common hatred of Islam, in particular, their fear of the idea of Muslim progress. They had resolved to strike now in order to make sure that a revived Ottoman empire led by the Young Turks would never have the power to pacify that empire's European provinces. Edward Grey's pusillanimous policy of neutrality barely disguised British and wider European hypocrisy: 'Turkey was made to honour her obligations under the Treaty [of Berlin] but the European Powers made no effective protest when Bosnia and Herzogovina were annexed by Austria, Bulgaria declared her independence, Italy invaded the province of Tripoli and the Balkan Christian states invaded European Turkey.'[11] Philip Graves, the *Times* correspondent in Turkey, later noted how the Christian victories were received by an 'outburst of enthusiasm' throughout Europe, and how this 'led Mr Asquith in his Guildhall speech of November 9 [1912] to express the view that "the victors were not to be robbed of the fruits that had cost them so dear." Turks and not Turks only, found the British Prime Minister's attitude a little indecent when the five Powers had insisted that the victors were to go unrewarded a month and a day before his speech.'[12]

For Pickthall, Britain's broken pledges were all the more galling because, he argued, she before all others should have understood the importance of a reforming Turkey as a bridge between East and West. This idea he would re-iterate over and over and it is integral to the Turkish narrative to which he subscribed. Britain's failure to recognise and nurture the crucial role Turkey as 'the last great Moslem power' was linked to an explanation of the long term causes of Turkey's putative 'fanaticism'.[13] Pickthall's point was that Muslims and Christians had lived side by side in the Ottoman empire until the nineteenth century. However, Muslims had never been happy under Christian rule; the massacres that seemed to exemplify the charge of Muslim fanaticism had been flamed in the previous century by European interference in Ottoman affairs upsetting the balance between Muslim and Christian. Advancing 'the Nasarene at the expense of the Mohammedan' had been at

the root of the 1860 massacres of Christians in Syria.[14] The chief victims
were not so much the Christians but rather the Ottoman Muslims, specifically
the poorer ones: evicting Turkey from Europe was no solution. After that
what lay in store for the Muslims of Asia?

If convictions such as these burnt into Pickthall's heart and mind as he
approached the capital of the Ottoman empire, he was to see there the CUP
attempting to regain Edirne/Adrianople from Bulgaria, and eagerly work at
rehabilitating the empire. 'I saw the remarkable change which was wrought in
five months – months of infinite depression for the Turks – and with a
country bankrupt.'[15] The keynote of *With the Turk in Wartime* is its vindication of the Turkish character and the vital nature of the work the Young Turks
were carrying out in the teeth of Europe's aggression:

> Our self-righteousness is principally to blame for the horror which has filled the
> East upon the recrudescence of the wicked old crusading spirit in our midst, duly
> reported by the Turkish and Indian Press, at a time when Turkey was deserving of
> all human pity. We had talked as if fanaticism were extinct in England.[16]

In his introduction, Pickthall arraigns western Europe and above all Britain
for forfeiting all 'moral claim' to the allegiance of the East. Britain, once the
exemplar for 'universal toleration, for a nationality which should be independent of religious differences' had largely inspired the eastern awakening.
Now with the rest of Europe she shrank back in horror 'as did Frankenstein
before his monster, trying frantically but in vain to wreck their work.'[17]

Pickthall also arrived in Istanbul with no little prejudice against the
Christian communities of the Ottoman empire. He certainly was not the first
western traveller to find the Pera district gaudy and squalid, and to delight in
the traditional wooden buildings of the city, with its azure setting and its
miraculous skyline of mosques. On his entry to Istanbul his political antenna,
however, had already tuned to the presence of warships in the Bosphorus.
According to Philip Graves:

> These vessels and those of other Powers had been lying off the
> Turkish capital since the early days of the Balkan War, when it
> was feared that the Bulgars might reach the city and that the Turks
> would massacre the Christians and then escape to Asia![18]

With The Turk in Wartime confirmed Pickthall's earlier articles in laying
before his fellow countrymen the perspective of every Turcophile, and also
some neutrals, that the real endangered entity in the Balkan strife was not the
eastern Christian but Turkey herself.[19] As the vehicle for a precarious Islamic
renewal, embattled on all sides against the Powers of Europe, Turkey represented 'the head of a progressive movement extending throughout Asia and
North Africa', and 'the one hope of the Islamic world'.[20] As for the true
fanatics – they were the newly emerging, predominantly Christian, former
states of the Ottoman empire. In Pera, Pickthall observed battle-worn Ottoman troops returning from the front being sneered at by the Levantine
Christian population who wished nothing but ill to the empire. These stood in

no peril, and hardly needed warships to protect them. They were to him nothing less than an open fifth column at the heart of Ottoman power, flaunting their fanaticism with impunity against the beleaguered Muslims. Pickthall was brought into closer alignment with the Committee of Union and Progress by his insistence on receiving from the Turkish Government an accurate figure for the Muslim victims of atrocities at the hands of the Bulgarians and Serbs in Macedonia and Thrace. Typically, his report clashed with that of Philip Graves who took a balanced view of the 'atrocity stories' claimed by both sides. Pickthall argued that the silence of the British papers on the massacre of Muslims in the Balkans was part of their bias against the Young Turks. Graves, on the other hand, responding to the claim of the veteran pro-Balkan Christian journalist Edwin Pears that the press had adopted a 'conspiracy of silence' in favour of the Young Turks responded: 'British journalists had been most indulgent to Young Turkey in 1909' and that he had been the first to leave that 'conspiracy'.[21]

Pickthall could not wait to get out of his hotel in Pera to the suburbs where his contacts found him lodging with a German lady, Frau Eckerstein, who since her childhood had lived in Turkey and was a vehement supporter of the Committee of Union and Progress. His daily routine now consisted of catching a steamer to Istanbul, and it was upon this boat that he met members of the political intelligentsia commuting to the capital, and was able to try out his rapidly improving Turkish. The Istanbul to which he journeyed was a troubled place. The Turks were not only in the depths of a struggle with the advancing Bulgarians, whose army was no more than thirty miles away at Chatalja during much of Pickthall's stay. The country was also passing through a revolution, and was split between two bitterly contesting parties, the Unionists, or Committee of Union and Progress (CUP), and the Union Liberals or Decentralization Party. Their division rent the capital and reached to the suburbs where Pickthall now lived. He found that most of his neighbours, belonging to the upper echelons of Ottoman society, were natural followers of the more cosmopolitan Liberals, and thus bitter enemies of the Committee. Power swung between the two parties, but under both the war had progressed disastrously, capped by the siege of Edirne. On the eve of Pickthall's arrival, Graves wrote:

The [Liberal] Government decided to abandon Adrianople [...] But on January 23, before they had drafted their acceptance of the terms, a small body of officers, accompanied by a band of Committee bravi, and led by Enver Bey, Jemal Bey Vali of Adana, and Talaat Bey, broke into the Sublime Porte and killed Nazim Pasha, the Minister of War, and Mahmud Shevket Pasha became Grand Vizier.[22]

The 'second' revolution was, however, barely a few months old when the admired General Mahmud Shevket was assassinated in reprisal for the death of Nazim. A few days before, Pickthall had had the chilling experience of a meeting with a member of the Decentralization Party who warned him a coup was in the offing. He then had the equally testing task of being present while

his Liberal friends exulted at the death of a man he considered a patriot and
the firm, controlling hand vital for Turkey's survival. A few months after
returning to Britain, Pickthall summed up the tragedy for Turkey of this party
strife in an article in the prestigious *Nineteenth Century and After*:

> There are well-intentioned men to-day in Turkey who have inherited a trick of
> plotting from the old regime; who cannot yet conceive the mere ideal of a
> patriotism which shall include various opinions [...] Their presence makes a
> certain harshness necessary in the attitude of either party when in power; which
> harshness, in its turn, begets the lust for vengeance.[23]

He then instanced the preparations made by the 'reactionary party' to avenge
the death of Nazim Pasha by murdering five hundred CUP men. The
assassination of Mahmud Shevket Pasha might have been all the conspirators
could manage, but: 'This anti-patriotic feud among the ruling classes, causing
men of talent and of prowess to sulk in dudgeon when their country had most
need of all her sons, is the most disheartening fact in recent Turkish
history.'[24]

Accounting for Pickthall's politics at this moment in his career is no
facile task. He was a regular contributor to a Left-inclined periodical, writing
chiefly in the defence of Turkey, and, on occasion other threatened Islamic
nations such as Persia and Morocco. There can be no doubt that Pickthall's
politics were modulated by his contact with orientals. He found the ordinary
Turks, as he had the Arabs of Syria and Palestine, simple and endearing. He
wrote to his wife Muriel: 'There is something extraordinary sweet and gentle
about the menservants and labourers here – all the poor people – the very
opposite of the sanguinary character which English people commonly ascribe
to the Turks. I am quite sure that you will fall in love with the whole race.'[25]
At the same period he wrote to a Muslim friend:

> The reports of danger run by Europeans are all rubbish. The indifference of the
> Europeans and the Levantines to the whole tragedy would justify a massacre; but
> the weakness of the Turks is, they have no fanaticism, but are trying hard to be like
> Europeans.[26]

What drew Pickthall into such close identification with the Young Turks? A
reading of his earlier novels and political comments after his visit to Egypt in
1907 would suggest that the upholder of Cromer and the British empire might
find common cause with the CUP's Liberal enemies, who were pro-British
and indeed reputed to be the favourites of the British embassy in Istanbul.
They were predominantly elite figures from the old regime who retained a *de
haute en bas* attitude towards the masses and looked with contempt on the
inexperience and lower class of the CUP leaders and their acolytes. Pickthall
wrote:

> I said that I should call the Liberals the Cosmopolitan, the Unionists [of the CUP]
> the Nationalist Turkish party; that the latter seemed to me to wish to raise the
> common people to intelligent participation in the work of government; while the
> former wished, without malevolence towards the subject people, to keep things

pretty nearly as they were, securing their own status as the ruling class, and figuring as wardens of the Powers of Europe over savage hordes; but that the fierce reactionary attitude recently assumed by the Liberals, in my opinion, put them out of court.[27]

Pickthall's identification with the CUP against the Ottoman Liberals crystallised around his conviction that they were the party that was most in touch with the Turkish people. As for the CUP's policies and principles, Pickthall stressed their Islamic modernism at the same time as he dismissed criticisms levelled against them by their Ottoman enemies as well as by contemporary British observers. Interestingly, for a Tory gentleman, Pickthall is not shy to instance 'the look of socialism' and republicanism of the Young Turks' programme, cause, he argued, for the Powers to welcome 'every symptom of reaction' since their revolution.[28] He rarely addresses familiar charges concerning the high proportion of freemasons and Jewish adherents amongst the Young Turks, or that their leaders used Muslim symbols while being without belief themselves. But he was able to agree that their ignorance and inexperience contributed to the CUP's policy 'blunders'.

Pickthall understood but underplayed the fact that the Young Turk leaders' employment of crude Ottomanising measures not only destroyed any residual support they may have held among the Balkan Christians, but also alienated fellow Muslims especially among the Albanians and Arabs. Because he always foregrounded the CUP's Pan-Islamism, he remained curiously unaware that to harness this with Turkism made their programme suspect to many.[29] His own celebration of Turkish ethnicity – of Turks as an aristocratic, 'white' European race – does not place him too far off the Turkish nationalist Gokalp's pronouncement 'we belong to the Turkish nation, the Muslim religious community and the European civilization'.[30] For Graves, the incompatibilities of the CUP programme were just cause for Britain's alienation from the Young Turk regime. He was under few illusions with respect to the British embassy's own policy blunders in Istanbul specifically referring to the highly indiscreet association of some of its diplomats with elements involved in the reactionary coup attempt of April 1909. Nevertheless, he remained convinced that: 'A Government who ran such unnecessary risks by their treatment of their minorities, their attitude towards neighbouring states, and their encouragement of Pan-Islamism would have been a liability to the Triple Entente.' Britain's leaving of Turkey in the lurch, if that is the right phrasing, could partly be accounted for by Grey's dithering. More hard-headed was the proposition that: 'On the British side, what statesman, what soldier who feared war with Germany could hesitate had he to choose between an Anglo-Turkish and an Anglo-Russian military alliance in the event of a European conflict.'[31] Graves' position returns repeatedly to what he understood to be the policy failings of the Young Turks and as a result their liability, not least to their own country. He wrote to Noel Buxton in 1911: 'I object to the Young Turk policy first and foremost because it makes for political disturbance and weakens the Turks.'[32] With

Graves, however, one can never entirely escape the patronising double-bind
that seems to run through the reports of his other colleagues on the *Times*
foreign desk as well. The oriental nations were damned whatever they did;
whether they chose obscurantism or revolution it made no difference.

In contrast, Pickthall passionately declaimed against the British
government's ditching of the cause of reform in Turkey by accusing the
Liberals at home of being the true fanatics and betrayers of the traditional
policy of friendship and protection of Turkey. Well into the Great War he
continued to argue that Britain had made a great strategic mistake by not
firming up an alliance with Turkey which, after the failed Gallipoli campaign,
appeared all the more desirable now the Turks had demonstrably held on to
the impregnable fortress of Istanbul. Admitting his powerlessness to
influence his government's policy toward Turkey, he had nevertheless laid
out Turkish grievances for any who cared to hear. These related specifically
to the behaviour of the Powers. They had intervened in Turkish affairs and
failed to honour their own international treaties (for example the Treaty of
Berlin broken by Austria's unilateral annexation of Bosnia Herzegovina in
1908). Over the Balkan wars they had applied double standards – no
territorial acquisitions by either side while in reality backing the Balkan
League. Their charge of Muslim fanaticism might be turned against
themselves: by their promotion of the empire's Christians at the expense of
the Muslims they had stirred Muslim resentment. Finally, on the issue of
Turkish reform the Powers had displayed their rankest hypocrisy: when the
Young Turks did begin to implement reform their treatment of Turkey
became even harsher.

Pickthall's views line up with those of the respected historian of modern
Turkey, Feroz Ahmad. Among general points of agreement, the following
might be noted. 1) Non-Turkish communities in the empire would not give
their support to the Turkish revival, while the Powers had no interest in
seeing reforms succeed but wished instead to pursue their carve up of the
Ottoman empire. 2) Britain was involved in the anti-CUP machinations
especially the March 1913 assassination of Mahmud Shevket and coup
attempt. 3) The Young Turks would have preferred an alliance with Britain
but were forced to choose the Triple Alliance. 4) The CUP began a Turkish
social revolution realising the status quo was no longer viable – their
modernisation policies further clashed with the interests of the Powers.[33]
Back in Britain, Pickthall joined other sympathisers with Turkey to form in
January 1914 the Anglo-Ottoman Society. His enthusiasm for the Young
Turks had been confirmed by his Turkish sojourn. So too was his conviction
that Britain had betrayed the cause of progress and self-sufficiency in Turkey,
deciding instead, out of obeisance to Russia, to side with the parties of
reaction. Alienated by an anti-Turk sermon in his Suffolk home village, 'he
slipped quietly from the church and from Christianity'.[34] A combination of
political identification with the Turkish people, and a profound
disillusionment with his own, helped crystallise the attraction to Islam first

experienced in Syria as a young man that began with his learning of Arabic and his sharing in the equality and simplicity of ordinary Muslims. A few short years after his visit to Turkey, this deep attraction could no longer be gainsaid: Pickthall declared his faith in Islam.

Egypt, Turkey, and the British empire

In sh'Allah, now that the Inkliz have won, things will be settled, and the land will prosper.
Children of the Nile, p. 252.

Your enemies are frightened of Islamic progress far more than they have ever been of what they call 'fanaticism'.
Pickthall, *New Age*, 26 December, 1912.

In his defence of beleaguered Turkey and indictment of his own government, Marmaduke Pickthall had stumbled into a discourse of betrayal that recalls the other anti-imperialist voices of this study. Yet the irony was that this Englishman was an upholder of the British empire who unrelentingly banged on the tub of Disraelian Toryism, claiming that he had remained loyal to his country's traditional policy towards the East. From this position, Pickthall could argue for reform in Turkey and beneficent British control of Egypt without seeing any inconsistency. What is interesting about Pickthall's attitude toward nationalist politics in Egypt was that so long as the British brought efficient and impartial rule – which he believed Cromer assuredly had – he saw no need for Egyptians to demand a government of their own nationality and race. Pickthall's enthusiasm for revolutionary Turkey modulated his Tory imperialism in a strange way. Crucially, he would throw his loyalism overboard in his support of the Young Turk revolution. But as far as Egyptian nationalism was concerned, putting aside a sympathy he entertained toward any Islamic nation, he continued to remain tone-deaf. How was it that Pickthall's stance on Egypt 'coincided with that of the more imperially minded British officials of Cairo'?[35] First of all, there is ample evidence from his writings to show that Pickthall's attitudes on Egypt in 1907 – which filter through *Children of the Nile* – were only later modified to the extent that they became merged into his fixed personal narrative on the East. This was built upon Britain's betrayal of Turkey, the Allies' plans for the partition of the Ottoman empire, and the emergence of what he called 'the Arab Question'. That said, a comparison of the political discourse of two novels separated by a decade and a half would show a shift in tone that, politically, might be characterised as a movement from quietism to revolutionary activism.

The environment of revolutionary fervour in Pickthall's last novel, *The Early Hours* (1921), contrasts markedly with indifference to the political status quo of the earlier *Children of the Nile* (1908). This disjunction might be the result of their different subjects – the Urabi revolt as opposed to the

Young Turk revolution – and different investments of authorial sympathy. Or
the shift could be accounted for by other factors, such as Pickthall's engagement with a vision of a reformed Islamic polity in the later novel as opposed
to a previously static one. In terms of the framing of the two narratives, there
are obvious similarities. In his political fiction, Pickthall frequently adopts the
device of a main protagonist whose fate causes him to fall in with one party
in a key historical incident or series of events. In *Children of the Nile*, this is
the young student Mabruk who is recruited as a spy for the national party by
a Turkish notable Omar Effendi. Mabruk's father is a village *omdeh* or
headman linking him with the ordinary Egyptian peasantry. But the Frankish
education Mabruk has received as a student of medicine in Cairo sets him
apart from the fellahin who the author describes as 'a gentle, smiling race,
subject to anger just as children are, not without guile, but before all things
sociable, whose fathers had tilled the soil of the delta from the days of
Noah.'[36] Peter Clark argues that Pickthall's sympathies were with the ordinary people of Islam whose faith was capable of withstanding the political
intrigues of the day. 'Commitment to the world of Islam and detachment
from strife for advancement or temporal gain becomes a common theme in
Pickthall's later Islamic thinking.'[37] By investing the fellahin with this
political quietism Pickthall aligns himself, albeit for different reasons, with
the apolitical peasantry of Cromer's *Modern Egypt*.[38] This is in spite of the
fact that, as Clark again points out, Pickthall was very much alive to the
changes occurring within Egyptian society during the period in which his
narrative is set. In contrast to the hard-pressed and often cynical peasantry,
the Urabist forces are presented as opportunist and scheming and, as Cromer
argued in *Modern Egypt*, unrepresentative of the ordinary peasantry, unless
they are enlisted in the ranks of the army. In that case, Jack Cade-like, they
envision the world turned upside down: 'then every soldier man will be a lord
in the province of Masr – Arabi Bey, our friend, will see to that'.[39] The
mantle of disapproval in Pickthall's novels and political articles invariably
falls upon the clever opportunists – Said the fisherman is one, so too are
Mabruk, Urabi and his 'so-called' nationalist followers, and also the new
breed of British rulers, especially those at the Foreign Office. In *Children of
the Nile*, the opportunist nationalists appeal to Muslim prejudice against foreigners in the hope of recruiting the *ulama*, and at the same time pose to the
Franks 'as ardent champions of the civilization of Europe and its so-called
progress'. Mabruk's Turk employer, Omar Effendi, is in reality not so much a
proponent of the national cause as an opportunist cynic who reserves his most
pitiless excoriation for his 'closest friends'. 'Indeed, while working for the
revolution with unsparing zeal, the Turk had a sneer for the cause, and all to
do with it.' Omar Effendi also acts as Pickthall's own cynical alter ego,
whose running commentary on the nationalist campaign ridicules it and never
fails to attribute to its leaders self-seeking motives, and, in the case of Urabi
himself, 'credulity' for 'giving ear to the disquisitions of some renegade
Franks'.[40] Interestingly, given his later enthusiasm for the activism of the

Young Turks, Pickthall undercuts the Urabist movement by appealing to the cynical world-weariness of the Egyptian masses whose sympathy with an agenda of change can only be passive and who are ultimately impressed only by superior force.

If the revolt's aims are undermined by its own supporters, what of its opponents? Chief among the latter is a prominent member of the higher *ulama*, Sayyid Muhammad Hafiz. His pronouncements against the revolutionaries incorporate a suspicion of foreigners and the axiom that the order of the Prophet is upset by deeds that fail to manifest the humility demanded of Muslims and sow disorder in the land. The merchant class too 'curse Arabi roundly', fearing the rule of soldiers will create 'a reign of terror' and express the hope that 'the Sultan would interfere' to avert it.[41] During the stand off between Urabi and the British fleet at Alexandria, the ordinary people catch sight of a dignified Khedive and show sympathy for the hopelessness of his cause. (The novel presents the Khedive Tawfiq as a dignified but weak figure.) Curiously, the reasons for the sudden arrival of British warships at Alexandria go unexplained except for terse remarks, delivered from the perspective of an undifferentiated Egyptian vox pop. 'The Franks, by the mouth of their consuls, clamoured for the resignation of the Ministry and Arabi's banishment, simply because the finances of the country had been rescued from the hands of their commissioners.'[42] The English are seen as racially ridiculous infidels with red cheeks. But their presence in Egypt is endorsed, significantly, by the fatalistic fellahin's acceptance of their triumph over Arabi's forces and expectation that they will re-establish order in the land. Pickthall continued to maintain a detached view of the invasion, later accounting for it by Britain's financial interests. Regarding the riots at Alexandria that provided an immediate pretext for British intervention, his novel supports the story that the governor of the city tried to put an end to them but could not get the soldiery to do so because Urabi refused to telegraph consent.[43] Finally, it should be noted that on the slaughter of Urabi's fellahin army at Tel al-Kabir, *Children of the Nile* is silent.

Six years after the publication of *Children of the Nile*, in the thick of his newly acquired faith in the Young Turk revolution, Pickthall's commitment to the British presence in Egypt and denigration of the nationalist argument was apparently unchanged. It is crystallised in an article published in the *New Age* on 26 February, 1914 entitled, 'Concerning Denshawai'. The celebrated case that had so incensed Blunt and deeply troubled liberal opinion in England is here accounted for in a manner that places the blame squarely on 'the murderous attack of the fellahin'. At the same time it exonerates the British soldiers and British controlled Special Court in a language that recalls the unmoveable certainties of imperialist discourse. Pickthall charges that the villagers' attack was 'premeditated', that the 'outrage' was easily 'arranged' by agitators. With the aid of what he claims to be his inside knowledge of the Egyptian fellahin he demolishes the proposition that the villagers were innocent victims by making of them outcasts who were cursed by their immediate neighbours because they kept pigeons. The army uniform becomes a sign of order and credible power and the fact of its assail by the fellahin inscribes the entire episode (in a manner strikingly similar to the way the Special Court saw it) as a test of imperial power over insurgency.

> The Army of Occupation stands for English rule in Egypt; and English rule in Egypt stood at that time for things which did not yet exist in neighbouring lands – things like religious toleration, personal security and some attempt at even-handed justice. The uniform of ruling Powers throughout the East has the same quasi-religious sanctity as has the flag; and its prestige is guarded as jealously.

These two sentences in fact signal a larger narrative into which the imperial dispensation for Egypt feeds. The surprising thing about this is, as already noted, that Pickthall is caught up in the paradox of urging revolution in one society (Turkey) while upholding the status quo in another (Egypt). He sees the ceding of ground to the nationalists in Egypt as a dangerous game pursued by the Liberals at home – a classic Tory imperialist argument. But he also allows himself to lapse into colonial discourse in characterising the native as prone to 'lethargy', the *ulama* as given to the delivery of 'incendiary sermons', and the Muslim population as immersed in debate on the merits of killing Christians, Christian lives being worth less than their own. To cap it all, he endorses Teddy Roosevelt's Guildhall speech – notorious to Egyptian nationalists – arguing that England should 'govern Egypt or get out'.[44]

Signposted but not spelt out in the Denshawai article is Pickthall's belief in a parallel imperialism to that of the British order in Egypt. Religious toleration, personal security and an attempt to deliver even-handed justice did not exist anywhere else in the Islamic Near East in 1906 at the time of the Denshawai incident, but would do after the winning of the constitution by the Young Turks in 1908. In defending both the English occupation in Egypt and the revolution in Turkey, Pickthall believed he was forwarding the same cause. It seemed not to occur to him that demanding freedom for an Islamic people in one instant, but denying it in another, was inconsistent. The Turks, as the aristocracy of Islam, were fit for freedom whereas the Egyptians were not. A reformed Turkish empire under the Committee of Union and Progress would work for similar objectives to the British, or would have, had the British allowed them to. In a telling riposte to C.H. Norman, a critic of his article and along with Bernard Shaw a petitioner on behalf of the Denshawai prisoners, Pickthall uninhibitedly hangs out his colours:

> Why have Humanitarians like Mr. Bernard Shaw and Mr. Norman not been with us in protesting against the most inhuman massacre of modern times, and demanding justice for progressive Turkey – things far more vital to the good of Egypt and the East in general than the Denshawai affair?[45]

A year later, in the same forum, Pickthall wrote an article that not only dealt explicitly with the linkage of Turkey and progressive Islam, a theme on which he had expatiated since *With the Turk in Wartime* and on which he would continue to do for years to come. He also set this within the context of the Turks' connection with 'oriental' races, such as the native Egyptians. In a nutshell, the argument centres on Turkey's power to absorb influences, not always European, and mediate these to the more 'childlike' oriental mind. In the case of Egypt, however, Pickthall adopts a Gobineau-type prospect of racial deterioration:

> One reason why Mohammedan officials now in Egypt are less efficient and enter-prising than they were of old is that the flow of Turkish, Arnaut and Circassian officials into Egypt ceased with the British occupation, and families of those races which have long established in Egypt have lost energy and in other ways deteriorated, acquiring many characteristics of the real Egyptian.

Again, Pickthall toys with imperialist discourse, this time with categories of racial superiority/inferiority, only to soften and perhaps dissolve their binaries in an Islamic direction:

> For the Turkish influence is not that of rulers of an empire only; it is also that of blood-relations of all Muslims. The brotherhood of all believers being an estab-lished principle, colour is not the barrier it is with us [...] An example of real Muslim progress of the Turks, supported by the Western Powers of Europe, a progress that would be expressed in sound Coranic [sic] terms would have roused half of Asia, might even – who can tell? – have wakened Africa.[46]

This promotion of progressive Islam in imperial terms is perhaps not surprising; nor is the utilisation of Orientalist tropes of 'childlike races'. But what it adds up to is the old patronage argument in which Britain's role as sponsor has been vacated as a result of her decision to abandon Turkey. What Britain gave up was not only the Disraelian vision of a British-ruled polyglot eastern empire, but the chance that the Muslim East and the Christian West might cohabit. Now the outlook was grave, for co-operation could not 'take place freely under conquest or a foreign occupation, which makes the conquered bow but hug their prejudices.' Was this observation not as true for the Egyptians as it was for Turkey, or any other Muslim nation?

In his last novel, *The Early Hours*, published in 1921, Muhammad Mar-maduke, as he now was, disclosed the combination of religious conviction and political enthusiasm that had helped make him a Muslim. The novel's hero, Camruddin, fits into the pattern of Pickthall's earlier main protagonists and falls in with one party in a series of key historic events. Through his eyes the reader is brought into the religio-political ideals of the Young Turk revolutionaries, beginning with their struggle to obtain the constitution in 1908, through to the later reverses of the Balkan wars. Camruddin's awaken-ing to activism in the cause of the Young Turks fuses the religious and politi-cal ideals that, in Pickthall's rendition, were the leitmotif for their revolution.

> It was a fact that much was wrong in the Islamic empire. The thought that men were striving for improvement, even to death, now thrilled him like an inspiration. It gave him hope for the revival of Islam, for which all Muslims prayed. The sad and shameful things that happened daily in the empire were all against the teaching of the Sacred Law, they were the product of ambition, lust of power and man's oppression in the realm where God alone was rightful King. [...] As he looked

across the dusky garden to the western glow, he had a vision of a new life for all
mankind.[47]

The 'western glow' might be the inspiration that thrilled the revolutionaries
into believing they could borrow from Europe the springs of progress and
incorporate them into their Islamic faith. The novel in its early parts accurately captures the pro-British sentiments of the revolutionaries. The conspirators struck at the corrupt tyranny of Sultan Abdul Hamid in the belief
that British support might be won. 'By some immediate action we shall make
it known that the Turkish nation is alive and bent on progress, that we abhor
the Government's corruption, and have not sunk to the condition of unthink-
ing slaves.'[48]

Alongside this runs Pickthall's by now long-established anti-eastern
Christian politics. The spies of Abdul Hamid and the cruel neighbour who
eventually defiles Camruddin's family during the massacres of Muslims in
Thrace, all belong to one or other of the Ottoman Christian nationalities.
Historical figures flit across the pages, such as Niazi Bey, the Young Turk
officer whose band of revolutionary soldiers effectively raised the constitutional standard in their march to the mountains above Resna. Pickthall's
pro-revolutionary characters all make exhortatory speeches in favour of the
revolution and have the tendency to sound the same. But he does succeed in
representing through their voices a blend of Islamic modernism and millenarianism that sustained some factions of the Young Turks: their belief that
Ottoman decline was not due to any intrinsic barrier to progress within Islam
itself; that Islam could absorb western science and technology and still
remain what it was. The European Powers controlled the modern world on a
programme of reason that was inimical to Christianity itself and would be
better employed by Islam which 'could have reclaimed and elevated [it] by
giving it religious purpose and a soul'. The 'glory of Islam was not a mere
remembrance. The triumph of Islam was yet to come.'[49]

Pickthall penned *The Early Hours* not longer after the Young Turk
leaders had been on trial for their lives, fugitives or exiles. (By 1922, all of
the triumvirate of CUP leaders, Enver, Tala'at and Jamal were in fact dead.)
Indeed, he quixotically claimed in 1919 that 'the vast majority of thinking
Turks are impassioned partisans of the Committee'.[50] The desperate plight of
both Turkey and Islam are reflected in the novel's title which is derived from
a Qur'anic sura pledging Allah's support for the believers even at the darkest
hour. On another level, however, Pickthall is making a larger claim for the
role of Islam in the modern world. Towards the close of the novel, addressing
the perilous situation faced by the revolution in 1913, a young Imam proclaims:

> Five years ago was born a new, more fervent spirit in Islam, drawing men nearer to
> the Prophet (Allah bless and keep him), and his fortunate companions, away from
> dead tradition of the schools. From that we reasonably date a new beginning. My
> brethren, it is once again the early hours. And that new, faithful spirit which we
> cherish and defend will not be lost, for it is good; it cannot die, for it is part of

Allah's mercy. Here, or elsewhere among the Muslim peoples it will triumph, and in triumph flourish and become a blessing to the world – if Allah wills! Not all the might of all the Christian powers can extinguish it. What matter then though we all suffer, though we die a cruel death, so long as we are servants of the Heavenly will against the Powers of Evil which must pass away.[51]

In his last novel, Pickthall summarised and incorporated many of the ideas and beliefs that had moved him since his embrace of the cause of Turkey. In fact it might be considered one of the key testaments of those British travellers and writers who embarked on an Islamic journey. Pickthall was of course unique among them in arriving at the destination of Muslim faith, and finally severing his hitherto disappointed and embittered ties with Britain and her empire. 'His imperialism failed when put to the test of "my country, right or wrong". With the necessity of facing that issue upon him, he proved, by his fidelity to what he believed was the higher law, his faithlessness to his own country.'[52]

Ottoman Partition and the Caliphate

We must be careful to create and preserve, for as long as may be necessary, the façade of an independent Arab Empire and grant to its titular ruler the appanage of an Imperial State if we are to assuage Moslem pride and reconcile Moslem sentiment to the overthrow of the Ottoman Empire.
Mark Sykes to Arthur Balfour, 11 June 1917, quoted in Adelson, *Mark Sykes*, p. 233

In the section above I contrasted the political quietism of *Children of the Nile* with the revolutionary and spiritual fervour of *The Early Hours*, in the process marking out the different dispensations Pickthall envisaged for Egypt and Turkey. I argued that employment of a variant discourse in the later compared to the earlier novel can be accounted for by juxtaposing the novels alongside statements from some of his articles of the intervening period. From these materials emerged an idiosyncratic intersection of imperialist, Orientalist, and progressive Islamist discourses to which, as ever, the relationship of Turkey to Britain is the master key. I now intend to rotate the figure bounded by the nodal points of Egypt, Turkey and Britain in order to bring them alongside a triumvirate of concerns that figure largely in Pickthall's writings during and immediately after the Great War. These are: British betrayal of Turkey, partition of the Ottoman empire, and the emergence of what Pickthall termed 'the Arab Question'. Together they cohere around what for some was the vital Islamic issue of the time: the question of the caliphate.

During his stay in Cairo in 1907, Pickthall met some individuals who, with respect to Britain's eastern policy, either already had a voice, or would in the course of time possess very significant ones. Of the senior types, Valentine Chirol, was reputed both for his position at *The Times* and for his books on the Middle and Far East. Aubrey Herbert, a son of the Victorian aristocrat Lord Carnarvon who was briefly Conservative Viceroy for Ireland in 1886, would in the next decade be a conspicuous member of a group of Tory MPs who took independent positions on issues like Ireland and eastern policy. Herbert ploughed an individualistic furrow over his support for eastern nationalities, maintaining a close connection with the CUP leaders as well as opposition figures in Turkey. In the war he distinguished himself at Gallipoli where his Turkish language and negotiation skills helped win for both sides a temporary truce to bury their dead. Another member in Herbert's group, and a close friend, was the young satirist and oriental traveller, Mark Sykes. Although a notable pro-Turk before the War, Sykes would adopt the official position once conflict began, becoming in due course a key framer of the British government's Middle East policy. The British negotiator of the notorious Sykes-Picot agreement, he would pursue a policy that eventuated in almost everything 'pro-Turks' like Herbert and Pickthall rejected. During the war, it was Sykes, as a government figure and former Turcophile associate, who corresponded with Pickthall over the matter of the latter's desire to travel to neutral Switzerland to negotiate with Turkey. He also took a hostile position towards Pickthall's and Herbert's appearance on public platforms in 1917 advocating a separate peace with Turkey.[53] The disagreement with Sykes encapsulated both the isolation Pickthall now courted on account of his extreme Young Turk sympathies, and the distance official thinking had moved from the old pro-Ottoman policy of the Victorian political establishment.

In Sykes' case, a key question is raised by his biographer, Roger Adelson: 'why had he shifted from pre-war Turcophilia and anti-Semitism to become a leading champion of the Arabs, Armenians and Zionists?'[54] Addressing precisely this issue in his essay on Sykes in *England and the Middle East*, Elie Kedourie argued that Sykes' support for the Ottoman empire, which went back to his early years as a traveller in the 1890s, drew on 'the traditional reasons which made Englishmen support it in the nineteenth century'.[55] That is: the obstacle it presented in the Middle East to the ambitions of the other European Powers. Politically, Sykes supported the traditional policy of bolstering the Ottoman empire as a bulwark against Russian expansionism. But when increasingly anarchic conditions signalled its imminent break up, as seemed the case immediately before World War One, the new exigencies demanded a change in imperial strategy. Sykes then moved over to support partition of the remainder of the Ottoman empire in Asia by the Entente Powers. If this was the political thinking behind Sykes' shift in allegiances, there were also cultural and what we might even call spiritual reasons too. Like most of the travellers discussed in this study, he was partial to the East for what he considered its preservation of qualities the West had lost. He considered that there was an Ottoman, or rather an eastern way of life retaining all the precious things the West had forsaken in its search for material power and prosperity. Perhaps the most vivid impression that one gathers from [Sykes'] books is that Eastern society is sustained by the age-old consolatory certainties that serve to make life decent and merciful, and to preserve the dignity of the humblest individual.[56]

Syke's generalisations on the culture, politics, and above all races on the eastern scene were made with a similar partiality and individualism to that displayed by the other oriental travellers. Like Blunt, Sykes called himself a Tory Democrat, hating the institutions of bureaucracy run by the middle classes and proposing a natural alliance between aristocracy and men of the soil:

> The East preserved [...] all the qualities which the West had lost. A social order compounded of small, intimate communities; authority hallowed by mercy, descending by small visible degrees from governor to governed; lord and serf, rich man and poor man rooted in the dignities and obligations of their station, owing respect to each other, and moved neither by fear nor contempt; all doing homage in their lives and thoughts to the divine eternal order of which their society was but the mirror. This was what the West once had been and what the East still was [...] Sykes believed in Tory Democracy. Middle class ideals and interests, according to this creed, had overwhelmed European civilisation and destroyed the harmony of classes [...] Sykes' doctrine about the Ottoman Empire is a counterpart of his belief in Tory democracy.[57]

Roger Adelson calculated Sykes spent forty months of his life in the Ottoman empire between 1897 and 1906. During this period he developed a repertoire of public lectures accompanied by lantern-slides in which 'he used pictures to point up the different racial and moral characteristics of Turks, Arabs and Persians'. But although Sykes' travel writings showed some insights, in Adelson's judgement they 'lacked understanding'. 'More maps, photographs, ethnological lists and universal histories could not fill the gaps in his knowledge, nor could thousands more miles of travel.'[58]

Sykes' published works dealing with his journeys in the Ottoman empire are certainly exercises in belated travel writing. They draw on the intertexuality of the oriental travellers' canon, especially in their re-visitation of the themes of eastern authenticity and purity of race. But their denunciations of western-induced corruption and crude racial theorising, present a nastiness all of their own. The travel sections of *The Caliph's Last Heritage* (1915) often are little more than exercises in what Sykes himself termed 'my racial cross-examinations'. In an age which has recently experienced the revival of tribal atavism in the Balkans, and endeavours to keep fresh the lesson of the obscene ends of anti-Semitism, Sykes' pursuit of racial purity in the Near East may possibly appear more sinister than it would have done to his contemporaries. The language find its natural level in discussing 'corruption, vice, disorder and disease', and regularly falls into a register of categorising the 'degraded' peoples through whose territories the traveller moves.[59] Sykes' main problem seems to have been in identifying and separating the mixed populations of the eastern Ottoman domains, especially around

the Euphrates, in Mesopotamia, the farther reaches of eastern Anatolia, and
along the Black Sea littoral. But to what end? Certainly, these writings bear
all the hallmarks of what we would now term colonial ethnography. And
though he possessed no very thorough command of an eastern language, 'to
those people in England who lacked [...] knowledge and training [...] Sykes
appeared to be an expert on the East.' Sykes' travel books, like Curzon's,
demonstrate their author's determination to make his reputation in the East.
Not only was this status desirable to him, he wanted it to come fast, painfully
aware as he was that his 'pro-consular ambitions' would be judged against
figures like Curzon and Cromer, and that the former in particular was a hard
act to follow.[60] If Sykes' travel books hardly equal Curzon's in their straining
after comprehensiveness, they suggest he was trying to shape his material by
means of an authoritative ego while at the same time trying to escape the
ersatz air that hangs about their subject matter. The inclusion of small,
dramatised scenes from the eastern bazaar in *Dar-ul-Islam* (1904) mimic the
offhand tone of Kinglake; the satirical swipe at Blunt's archaism in *the
Caliph's Last Heritage* (1915) implies Sykes is out to settle scores with old
authorities.[61]

Given Sykes' evident urge to seek out a focus for the corruption of the
eastern scene, it comes as no surprise to find in his writing almost from the
beginning a distasteful Other upon which he was able to deposit the loathing
he entertained for modernity. Kedourie demonstrated clearly enough how
Sykes' hatred for the 'Levantine', or 'Gosmobaleet' (Cosmopolit[an]) – the
term he gave to the part-westernised eastern Christian – derived from a
discourse that had begun to emerge in European commentaries on the eastern
scene at around the same time as Palgrave wrote disparagingly of the eastern
Christian sects in his *Essays on Eastern Questions*. The theory behind this
discourse was that 'Eastern civilisation was purer, more spiritual, more
wholesome than Western, and that European greed and viciousness was
destroying the East'. The conduit for this western corruption was through the
West's co-religionists in the East, the non-Muslim Levantines. The eastern
Christians were 'the corrupt element in eastern society, the nefarious carriers
of infection'.[62] In his earliest travel narrative, *Through Five Turkish
Provinces* (1900), Sykes characterised the Armenian in the following terms:
'His cowardice, his senseless untruthfulness, the depth of his intrigue, even in
the most trivial matters, his habit of hoarding, his lack of one manly virtue,
his helplessness in danger, natural and instinctive treachery, together form so
vile a character that pity is stifled and judgement unbalanced.'[63] Of the 1893-
94 massacres of Armenians, Sykes argued in *Dar-ul-Islam*: 'while no excuse
can be made for the conduct of the Turks in slaughtering Armenians, it
should be remembered that massacre is still a recognized method of policy
throughout the East, and until lately in the West.'[64]

Like Sykes, Pickthall saw the eastern Christians as a vehicle of corruption, particularly for their treachery toward the Ottoman State in its time of
need. In fact, he found Sykes' poisonous racial categorisation of the

Armenians so much in sympathy with his own racial ideas on the Ottoman empire that he continued to quote them even after Sykes switched sides.[65] But the separation between Sykes and Pickthall during the Great War was perhaps not as complete as it might at first seem. From the start they had seen Turkey differently. Sykes' view was conservative – he had been one of the few British commentators on the Turkish scene who admired Sultan Abdul Hamid. He may have been looking for a revitalisation of the East, but he 'wanted the East to reach the prosperity of Europe without being contaminated by the ills of Europe'.[66] Sykes subscribed to a nineteenth century image of the Turk which Schiffer argues was a conception derived from Victorian notions of class. This could be seen in the remarks of the traveller John Edwin Davis writing in 1872. 'Davis praised the "old fashioned Turk of the interior of Anatolia" for being "brave, hospitable, truthful, and religious". He was, admittedly, uneducated and prejudiced, yet no more so than ordinary Englishmen. Davis concluded: "There is much that is admirable in the Osmanli pure and uncorrupted – but it is mostly found in the lower classes!"'[67] For Sykes the Turkish soldier showed 'a heroism that no other race can boast'. His admired Turkish character is without gesture, laconic, humourless, not quick in intelligence, and very patriotic: 'there are few Turks who would not lay down their lives for their country', but 'fewer who would save it from internal decay'.[68]

Pickthall, on the other hand, embraced the Young Turks precisely for those qualities that Sykes contemned: their desire to turn Turkey into a modern state, and their ability to represent the entire Turkish population not, like the Liberals, merely an elitist portion. He also rejected the notion that the 'traditional' fatalism of the Turkish masses was a good thing, making his heroes in *The Early Hours* ashamed of the backwardness of their nation during the Hamidian era. *With the Turk in Wartime* pronounced the birth of a new educated spirit among the Turks, embracing love of duty and pride in burdens of responsibility – a patriotic, tolerant, self-reliant trustworthy character was to be theirs. The old Muslim education, medieval in its religion, had ceased to meet the needs of the community. The Turks, Pickthall writes, 'have accepted once and for all the point of view of Europe, and are using every effort to live up to it. All they ask is leave to work out their own problems, and advance to modern progress in the way they understand'. Camruddin, the hero of *The Early Hours*, is represented as hearing 'on every hand [...] the cry for education, sanitation, and improvement of all kinds'.[69] Pickthall would therefore have rejected out of hand Sykes' magisterial comment that 'Orientals hate to be worried and hate to have their welfare attended to – oppression they can bear with equanimity, but interference in their private affairs, even for their own good, they never brook with grace'.[70] Sykes' preferred image of the Turk was static and essentialised. Pickthall's blended the traditional qualities that had made the Turks a nation fated to rule other eastern peoples with a dynamic for change. Syke's own preparedness to swap the Turk for peoples he had formerly condemned may, as Kedourie implied, have merely required a reshuffling of racial essentialisms in order to meet the exigencies of the time. His travel writings, which all date from his Turcophile years, frequently pointed to the superiority of the Turk over the Arab when it came to the practicalities of running and administering a state. In *Dar-ul-Islam*, he drew the appropriate conclusions from the behaviour his Turkish and Arab muleteers demonstrated. Where the Arabs 'raved, shrieked, cursed, and flew into childish passions, were ready to give up in despair, and always required leading', the Turks showed they were from 'a ruling race' by 'stolid, dogged and business-like' attention to their task. Again, *The Caliph's Last Heritage* records a revelation in which some muleteers afforded Sykes 'a glimpse of that rugged and indomitable spirit of the Anatolian Moslem which has carried the Turkish Empire'.[71] During the Balkan wars, Sykes visited Istanbul, wrote letters and articles, and delivered speeches in Parliament, critical of the Powers for failing to reduce the threat to Turkey, and *The Times* for insensitivity to the 'ravages' inflicted by the Balkan powers on the Muslims. At the start of the Great War

> he still regarded Constantinople and the Ottoman Asiatic Empire as of vital strategic concern to Great Britain and the thought that she must never permit their domination by foreign powers. [He] also remained personally committed to the preservation of traditional society in the East.[72]

In reality though, Sykes appreciated that the hour had now come for Britain to implement Palgrave's advice and absorb not only the Ottoman empire's non-Turkish Muslims, but all its non-Muslim subjects in Asia as well. In 1915, under Kitchener at the War Office, Sykes started to plan for the dissolution of the Ottoman eastern domains by the British empire. He now influenced official thinking by presenting his various solutions to the committee responsible for advising the government on Middle East policy, and later as an adviser to the War Cabinet. Progressively, his schemes incorporated his discovery of the suitability of the Arabs, Armenians and Jews to form states that would replace the Ottoman polity.

> The Arabs in particular would recreate the ancient glories of the caliphate [...] in this belief he recommended to the War Committee in July 1916 that 'towards all Arabs…we should show ourselves as pro-Arabs, and that whenever we are on Arab soil we are going to back the Arab language and Arab race'.[73]

These new directions in policy brought forth Pickthall's bitter vitriol, nowhere more starkly than in the British move to back the Arabs and to play the caliphate card. He had, as we saw, gained his first experience of the Middle East as a youth, living a vagabond existence among the Arab population of Syria and Palestine in the last decade of the nineteenth century. The Arabic he had learned during this period helped deepen his understanding of Islam, so that when he became involved in the Muslim community in London during the war, he would give talks 'quoting frequently from the Koran in Arabic', memorably so on the occasion of his public declaration of his Muslim faith in November 1917.[74] Pickthall was therefore no disdainer of the Arabs. But when it came to the governance of Islam, his conviction was simply that the Turks were *non pareille* in the Muslim world. He had written in *With The Turk in Wartime*:

> If progressive Turkey must be crushed, as Europe says, then one day Europe will behold an Arab Empire, with little of the toleration and good temper of the Turks. Much as I love the Arabs and respect their many virtues, I recognise a difference in their mentality, which makes it most desirable, from Europe's standpoint, that the Turks should long remain the leaders of the Muslim world.[75]

As was usually the case, once entered upon a line of reasoning Pickthall rarely gave it up. From now on his position remained more or less the same: the Arabs were likely to stay with the Ottoman empire if Turkish rule remained firm. Should it weaken, the Arabs would secede, and thereby threaten European rule in western Asia and North Africa – 'without the Turkish power to overawe them, [...] nothing under Allah could prevent a melee'.[76] This curious imperialist brand of thinking (curious, because it expressed a sort of Turkish Islamic imperialism refracted through British imperialist eyes) perhaps underestimated the strength of Sunni Arab attachment to the caliphate, especially since the Arab provinces, with the exception of the Hashemite Hijaz, largely remained loyal until the British prized Palestine and Mesopotamia out of Ottoman hands. Nevertheless, at the moment of Turkey's entry into the war on the side of the Central Powers, Pickthall quickly caught the drift on which affairs were moving. His *New Age* article of 29 October 1914 entitled 'Egypt and the Foreign Office' concluded, 'the Arab question' would soon become 'momentous' if Turkey were to be divided up at the closure of the war. By January 1916, he had moved on to the more specific issue of the caliphate, writing: 'this whole idea of interference with the Caliphate is part and parcel of the new – what one may call "allied" – British policy, responsible for the situation we so much deplore.'[77] In that article he set out again the argument for Britain guaranteeing her protection of the Muslims:

> The majority of Muslims still retain some sentimental feeling for the British as their old protectors, some hesitation with regard to Germany, an untried, upstart power. If it could be publicly announced that we have no intention of destroying Turkey, and that the Caliphate shall not in any case be interfered with, as a result of this war, I believe that we should recover by that mere announcement all our Eastern influence.

Pickthall's emphasis on the 'allied' orientation of the new policy was in order to clarify a persistent refrain of his wartime propaganda: the Russians and the French, he maintained, were calling the shots, with the result that Britain, no longer 'really independent', had been so enthralled by her allies as to give up 'our traditional policy' in order to replace it by 'the traditional policy of Russia'. Now Germany was playing Britain's old role as protector of the Muslims and was working towards a Muslim jihad against the British empire. As for the French, they had come up with 'the opinion that the Sherif of

Mecca is the true "overlord of Islam," the Sultan of Turkey a false overlord whose claim is based on violent usurpation.' For the French to propose such an idea was in poor taste given their record of crushing and then corrupting the Muslims under their rule in North Africa. (Ironic this, given the fact that it was the British, initiated by Kitchener while still consul-general in Egypt, who had been secretly discussing the same proposition for more than a year.) Pickthall's refutation of the slur against the legitimacy of the Turkish caliphate might be a tad too glib. But it at least expressed his bottom-line conviction that the Turks held the leadership of Islam out of strength 'considering that the highest rank in El Islam ought to be vested in the greatest Muslim ruler.'[78]

The main argument that Pickthall raised against the British empire's opportunist and belated adoption of Blunt's old argument in favour of an Arabian caliphate was that the Arabs, through their fissiparous, anarchic and fanatic character, disqualified themselves from acceding to the leadership of the Muslim world. In a *New Age* article of November 1914, entitled 'The Arab Question', drawing upon his experience of 'living native' in Syria, he demonstrated his awareness of one line of Arabism centred on the national credentials of the family of the Egyptian khedive, Muhammad Ali. 'I gathered then and subsequently that the Sherif of Mecca was to be the spiritual head of the reconstituted realm of El Islam, the Khedive of Egypt the temporal head.' Pickthall satirically uses the term 'Anglophiles' to link the scheme's advocates with Britain's control of Egypt (rather than her sponsorship of the Sherifian cause, which in late 1914 was barely at the embryo stage) even though its proponents were strongly anti-British.[79] But when at the end of the piece he dismissed the project as 'not English' but 'pure[ly] Egyptian', Pickthall little knew the irony of his words. At this point, though, in spite of his unconcealed cynicism about the caliphate transferring from the Sultan of Turkey to his nominal vassal, he is patently clear about one thing. Britain, in such circumstances, would have the task of taking over the responsibility of all the 'warlike Arabs'. Most significant of all: 'at the same time the head and centre of Islamic life and thought would be removed from a progressive Muslim country near Europe to a Muslim country the reverse of civilised.' For Pickthall, the issue of the caliphate was linked to the arguments we have already seen him set out in favour of Young Turk leadership of a Muslim empire and against an independent Egyptian nationalism. Most of his war articles that either specifically treat or touch upon the 'Arab Question' frame it in terms of the recidivism of creating an Arabian caliphate, both for the domain of Islam, and, no less significantly, for the peace of the post-war world. For example, 'After the Caliphate' (January 1915) argues that Britain's sponsorship of an Arabian caliphate would backfire on her because controlling it 'a succession of relentless tyrants' would in time stir up the Muslims against her.[80] Ann Fremantle succinctly represented Pickthall's private view when she wrote of his dismay at the 'savage tribesmen' who went 'careering through the streets' of Damascus after taking it from the

Turks in 1918. According to her report he 'rejoiced' at the eventual defeat of King Husayn by Ibn Saoud.[81]

Pickthall's analysis, which foresees a Russian occupation of Constantinople, and the allies, each with their own Muslim subjects, competing over the caliphate, is very much stuck in a pre-war – even nineteenth century – mould. Yet at the same time it resonates with foreboding over the difficulties and dangers individuals like Sykes were busily storing up by their spreading game of Chinese-whispers in the corridors of power. For example, 'The Project of Partition' (February 1915) adopts the kind of language Sykes himself was using at the time. It envisages after the war the partition of the Ottoman empire and the end of the old order of buffer states in the East, with 'the whole peninsula of Arabia' included in Britain's 'sphere of influence'.[82] Pickthall's prophecies of dire upheavals on the defeat of Turkey misconstrued, however, the nature of the post-war contention. It was not so much the demise of the last Muslim empire that inflamed the populations of the Near East in the1920s, but the obstacles placed against an insurgent desire for self-determination on the part of peoples newly imbued with the 'principle of nationality'.[83] Perhaps Hisham Sharabi was overstating the case when he wrote: 'The national spirit had already penetrated the core of the Muslim community, and nationalist loyalty had replaced allegiance to the caliphate.'[84] But it was certainly true that there were few mourners when that institution was summarily put to sleep by the vote of the grand national assembly which confirmed the new Turkish Republic in 1924. It was, after all, Sykes' blueprint for a new order in the Middle East that had won the day, at least in so far as the laying of the foundations for new nations in the region were concerned. He had conceived his plans in the spirit of a continuing imperialism, in which the Ottoman empire was to be replaced by British management and control of the Arabs, throwing into his concoction the potent admixture of Zionism. But the dualism behind his thought resided in his adherence to an imperialist creed and archaic, self-regarding attitudes towards eastern traditions, joined with his recognition 'that change was inevitable in the East as well as in the West in the twentieth century'.[85]

The events of 1918 of course represented a massive defeat for Marmaduke Muhammad Pickthall. The stream of his political articles on eastern subjects for the *New Age* petered out in 1919. Old themes reappear in the last ones, including the by now entirely anachronistic imagining of Disraeli's eastern policy expanded into a near divine dispensation of co-operation between the British and Ottoman empires. 'Within a period of fifty to a hundred years the British Empire should have become a perfect league of nations, evolved naturally, exempt from barriers of creed and even colour, an example to the world.'[86] Putative British moves to hand the caliphate to the Arabs trigger the old wound of Britain's betrayal of Turkey. The policy is condemned as 'disastrous […] to the British Empire and humiliating to the British name.'[87] The Arabs of al-Hijaz had been guilty of robbing pilgrims to Mecca and were not popular among Muslims, unlike the Turks who were 'the representatives of law and order, the punishers of marauders, and protectors of the pilgrimage.' All Asia regarded the British 'with horror' for what they had allowed to happen to Turkey. Pickthall's bitterness towards the Arab revolt would resurface sixteen years later in a review of T.E. Lawrence's *Seven Pillars of Wisdom* entitled 'The End of a Legend'. In this he repeated his charge that the Arabs of al-Hijaz were marauders won over by British gold and the desire of booty to sack Damascus. 'Where is the Arab Empire he imagined? The dream has vanished [...] But it was bound to vanish, for it was untrue to life, made up of personal ideas and not of noted tendencies.'[88] Pickthall's agitation over the caliphate briefly revived on his removal to India, where he accepted a post in the State of Hyderabad. The Muslim Nizam for whom he worked had aspirations of his own to the title of caliph which he hoped to strengthen by connecting his dynasty with the now deposed Ottoman imperial family. Also in India, for a brief moment in the 'twenties Pickthall was in contact with the Khilafat movement. Founded before the war around the issue of Pan-Islam and the defence of Turkey, it kept alive Muslim concerns for the caliphate in an alliance with Indian nationalist demands.[89] Pickthall's identification with the Indian Muslims and Gandhi's nationalist ideas, even if marginal, would have kept alive his reputation among the British as a traitor to his country.

T.E. Lawrence and the Myth of Betrayal

In 1926, T.E. Lawrence published a limited edition of his narrative of the wartime Arab revolt, *Seven Pillars of Wisdom*. Although he was by now, thanks to the efforts of the American journalist and publicist Lowell Thomas, a hero-celebrity, Lawrence had already embarked on the years of self-effacement that only ended with his death in 1935. Thomas's book, *With Lawrence in Arabia*, appeared in 1925 and helped embellish the Lawrence myth, the limited release of *Seven Pillars* notwithstanding. The imperial historian John Mackenzie has argued that this myth needs 'to be set into its proper tradition, that of the nineteenth-century imperial hero'.[90] Lawrence is of interest to the narratives followed thus far for several reasons. First, from his undergraduate days in greater Syria spent in pursuit of material for his thesis on Crusader castles, and in the years on archaeological digs in the same region immediately antecedent to the First World War, he was something of a traveller. His were not journeys on a grand scale. It is debatable whether his later flurries criss-crossing al-Hijaz and the Sinai desert during the campaigns of 1916-18 qualify him to join the ranks of the great Arabian travellers. What we can say is that Lawrence aspired to this connection. When it came to writing *Seven Pillars* he was influenced both in his style by the literary corpus created by travellers like Charles Doughty, for whom he wrote a preface to the second edition of Doughty's *Arabia Deserta*, and Blunt, whose ideas on the Bedouin he absorbed.

Seven Pillars revisits the Arabian travellers in some key aspects. According to Kathryn Tidrick, Lawrence reproduced those elements of their writings that together comprised the 'English Romance with Arabia'.[91] This constituted an escape from modern western civilisation accomplished by romantic, upper-class Tory English travellers who hated the advances of middle-class bureaucratisation at home. Their travel writings privileged the 'unspoiled' desert *bedu* over his cousin the semi-sophisticated town-dweller, and, more importantly, designated the tribal sheikhs as the aristocracy of Arabia. As analogues to Lawrence, Tidrick would have us read Burton, Palgrave, and especially Blunt.[92] What Lawrence achieved was a fusion of the romance with a political cause – that of Arab nationalism. This he centred not on the urban middle class and intelligentsia, who in reality were most attracted by the nationalist idea, but on the 'authentic' natural leaders of the Arabs, as embodied in the Hashemite (or Sharifian) rulers of al-Hijaz. These Lawrence claimed to have managed in furtherance of his own political idea. 'I meant to make a new nation, to restore a lost influence, to give twenty millions of Semites the foundation on which to build an inspired dream-palace of their national thoughts.'[93] The imperial grandiloquence is even more marked in the comment by his friend Robert Graves. 'He, a foreigner and an unbeliever, inspired and led the broadest national movement of the Arabs that had taken place since the great times of Mohammed and his early successors, and brought it to a triumphant conclusion.'[94]

Another aspect linking Lawrence with the subject of this book is the flipside of his 'triumph'. Between 1919 and 1922, while he was writing *Seven Pillars*, he was intimately connected with working out the cause of the Hashemites – the creation of an Arabian kingdom/kingdoms, which for him was synonymous with Arab nationalism itself. Far from inscribing a victory, *Seven Pillars* is riddled with personal guilt on Lawrence's part for his involvement in the deception perpetrated on the Arabs by the post-war settlement. More important for the Lawrence myth, he vicariously took upon himself the blame for his country's betrayal of his Hashemite protégés. This drawing of shame upon himself partly accounted for Lawrence's complete withdrawal from public life after the composition of his great work, or so the myth ran. The triumph was therefore also a fraud, or rather, depending on which perspective we regard the issue, a bit of both. From the vantage point of the year 1919-20, the Treaty of Versailles and the imposition of the ramifications of the wartime Anglo-French Sykes-Picot agreement had left the Hashemite cause that Lawrence had himself championed in Paris (replete with Arab dress) in apparent disarray. Faisal had been thrown out of Damascus by the French, and the extent of the Arab kingdom ruled over by his father, King Husayn, was greatly diminished in scope from initial expectations with the French taking over control of Syria and Lebanon, and Britain ensconced in Palestine and Iraq. Yet a year later, Lawrence's influence over Colonial Secretary Churchill at the Cairo Conference seemed in part to retrieve the situation with the establishment of British-sponsored Hashemite entities in Iraq (under Faisal) and Transjordan (under his brother Abdullah). John Mackenzie synchronises the emergence of the Lawrence myth with this moment, and sees some connivance in it by both Churchill and Lawrence's old colleagues of the Arab Bureau in Cairo, the remnant of whose policy was being implemented. In all events, 'the growing attachment [on the part of Britain] to the Arab world, by turns patrician, romantic and escapist, coincided with the gradual extension of British power into the Middle East – an extension that took for granted that these traditional rulers should be sustained and supported'.[95] Lawrence had played his part in an imperial progression after all. Why, then, the talk of betrayal?

Elie Kedourie was the first historian to challenge accepted wisdom behind Britain's sponsorship of the Arab sheikhs and emirs. He construed Britain's post-war Hashemite policy as a volte-face in thinking on the Middle East that was prepared to jettison her traditional support for the Ottoman empire in exchange for the 'ignorant and lunatic fantasies' of the Arabists.[96] 'In his opinion the English (meaning the British political establishment), having succeeded in destroying the Ottoman Empire, had brazenly proceeded to invent a national history for the system of Arab nation-states they themselves had artificially created on its ruins – a phoney history which had to be exposed for what it really was.'[97] Lawrence and the Arab Bureau were, according to this thesis, the opportunistic manipulators of an eccentric theory pioneered by Arabian travellers like W.S. Blunt. (But it was as far back as to David Urquhart, writing at first in the 1830s, that Kedourie traced the genealogy of ideas on eastern authenticity of which Lawrence was a belated exponent.) For Kedourie, in *Seven Pillars* Lawrence parroted clichés on the rottenness of Turkey and declared his faith in the justice of the Arab cause in order to underwrite his actions in helping to bring about Ottoman destruction. 'Besides, there was good faith involved, his own honour and good name. Should the British Government betray, for the sake of imperialist interests, the Arab national movement, he himself would be dishonoured.'[98] Yet in reality, Lawrence knew all about the Sykes-Picot agreement, and – contrary to his argument in *Seven Pillars* – so did King Husayn and Faisal. Lawrence was well aware he was dealing in duplicity, and so were the Hashemites, and the British Government. Who or what then did Lawrence betray? John Mackenzie and Peter Sluglett concur that his 'chief complaint was not against Britain's manifest destiny to rule Arabs (who were to become "our first brown dominion") but against Britain's pusillanimity in sharing this destiny with the French'.[99] Alternatively, Kedourie saw him as being motivated by an abstract moral ideal – but not Arab nationalism, for he felt the Arabs were incapable of uniting around such an idea. Lawrence was a 'partisan doctrinaire', who 'believed neither in the Sharif, nor Faisal, nor in the Arab national movement [...] He was a doctrinaire empty of doctrine, and a partisan without a party. [...] What interested him rather were his own sensations, and to see how he could manipulate events'.[100]

British connection with oriental nations and a linkage to imperialism has been one of the key areas of this inquiry. Urquhart has been represented as the initiator of a school that encompasses many of the celebrated nineteenth-century British travellers to the Middle East, into whose camp the imperialist Lawrence strayed in writing *Seven Pillars*. Lawrence's use of the betrayal idea is important because it constitutes a further connection between him and some of the other Middle East travellers discussed in this book. We saw that England's perfidy towards an eastern cause it should have honoured and promoted is a recurrent motif in the writings of certain travellers from Urquhart onwards. If Lawrence proclaimed himself a great leader of the Arabs, Urquhart was celebrated in his lifetime as a patron of the Ottoman Turks. But, paradoxically, 'Lawrence of Arabia' is perhaps the best known popular example of a British traveller who empathised with the East. His case, or rather the myth that surrounds him, exemplifies a number of the key threads connecting a good proportion of the travellers discussed. These are: putative identification with a particular Muslim people, pleading of their 'cause' at home, and the proposition that British contact had in some way let them down. Adapting an oriental trope, we might say that for true gold to exist, fool's gold must too.

Conclusion

At the start of this chapter it was suggested that Pickthall's case would be helpful in my endeavour to define – or perhaps problematise would be a better word – the direction taken by the different forms of pro-Islamic politics discussed in this book. The comparisons made between him and Herbert on the one hand, and Mark Sykes on the other, will have demonstrated that Pickthall, extreme Turcophile as he was to the last (our at least to 1924, the year the caliphate ended), nevertheless possessed a 'spiritual home' in a tradition of pro-Ottoman thinking that was by no means negligible between 1830 and 1926. In the latter year the Hungarian Felix Valyi, a close associate of Pickthall's, wrote an excellent (if unintended) valedictory of the tradition in *Spiritual and Political Revolutions in Islam*. According to Valyi, the West was arrogant in its technological success and failed to understand the spirit of Asia, particularly its moral power, whereas the hope of 'a spiritual unification of the world' rested on the transformation of Asia, and above all of Islam.[101] Turkey, now as of old, remained the key to Asia. Urquhart had been the first to preach absolute non-intervention in Ottoman affairs, and fulminate against the wrong thinking behind the nineteenth-century reforms Europe forced upon Turkey. He had called for the preservation of Turkish traditions free from foreign interference, but recommended the admission of Turkey into the

European system. The failure of the Tanzimat reforms was substantially the result of an 'incessant meddling, amounting to a regular tutelage over Islam'.[102] But there had been positive moments that might have spared the antagonism of Europe and the Ottoman East. Anglo-Saxons had a gift for leadership, and the British empire could have adopted a spiritual emphasis rather than a materialistic concentration on dividends as its guiding idea. Britain could have been an impartial mediator between Christianity and Islam. Disraeli's policies, for one, had fostered 'brotherly collaboration' between the two.[103] Unfortunately, beginning with Palmerston, the Liberals adopted a policy of enmity towards Islam that in practice meant acting as the unconscious ally of Csarist Russia. This modus operandi was entrenched by Gladstone and renewed under Edward Grey. A further opportunity to mend fences by exploiting the pro-British sentiment behind the Young Turk revolution had been squandered. And once again, between 1920 and 1923, Britain had favoured a policy of greater Greece rather than backing Turkey. History might have laid the ruin of Islamic civilisation at the door of the Turks; in reality, as the organisers, assimilators, and doers of Islam, the Turks had preserved it. Now they were, in the form of Mustapha Kemal, ready to show the way forward with a new brand of Islamic modernism.[104]

After the Turcophile, the second strand of thought adopted by our pro-Islamic western thinkers was Blunt's earlier Arabian caliphate idea. (The Pan-Islamic one espoused by Blunt and Browne in the early 1900s was the third). The apparent fruition of the Arabian tendency, if Kedourie is to be believed, was what he called 'The Chatham House version' – that is, the narrative of Arab self-determination favoured by the so-called 'Arabist' branch of Britain's early twentieth century foreign policy establishment. As we have just seen, this was the narrative Lawrence built into his *Seven Pillars of Wisdom*, together with the motif of Britain's betrayal of the Arabs. Because of its close association with power, the Arabian caliphate is at best an ambivalent legacy for an anti-imperialist like Blunt to be associated with. In fact, it might almost provide justification for the Turcophile argument propounded by Pickthall, until one remembers that he would have been more than glad for this to have been adopted as an establishment idea. According to Edith Finch, Blunt the Pan-Islamist had, in 1914, 'feared particularly the dismemberment of the Ottoman Empire and the fate of Islam, should Constantinople fall into the hands of Russia.'[105] But he also wrote of T.E. Lawrence to Cunningham-Graham in the summer of 1920: 'I first heard of him as being among the tribes of N.W. Arabia between Egypt and the frontier with Palestine I used to know so well. It will be a rarity to have a talk with anyone who shares my views, as you tell me he does, on Eastern affairs. He seems to have carried out a dream I had of helping to establish an Arabian Caliphate forty or more years ago.' Was this, as Cunningham-Graham's biographers suggest, an example of 'Blunt's self-deluding egotism,' a product of his decline into dotage?[106] Then again, what might Lawrence have learned from reading Blunt? A skill perhaps in manipulating an old narrative of betrayal and incorporating it into his deceiving account of the 'revolt in the desert' that Blunt in his dotage credulously believed had helped to establish an Arabian caliphate?

As for Pickthall, his standing in the mid 1920s, when his novels were still receiving plaudits from E.M. Forster and D.H. Lawrence, is admirably summed up by Peter Clark:

> He had no disciples. After the First World War his time in India was tantamount to self-exile from Britain. He was unable to salvage his 'unpatriotic' reputation with his right-thinking countrymen. He was a conservative, a monarchist and a traditionalist and so had nothing in common with the body of left-wing opinion that had opposed the war. The causes he supported soon became lost, unfashionable or dead. After the First World War nobody – not even in Turkey – wished to champion the Young Turks. Pickthall had been hostile to the Arab Revolt and had no sympathy for the Arab states that emerged after the war. He was critical of British imperialism in India but supported it in Egypt. He regretted the passing of the Caliphate, a cause that soon died. He had no sympathy for the massacred Armenians and in India his enthusiasm for monarchy and for the world of the Nizam of Hyderabad seems quixotic and anachronistic today.[107]

This may appear as futile a tale as Blunt's and his Arabian caliphate. But both Pickthall and Blunt, in spite of their differences as to who to back in the affair of the Islamic succession, and who should lead the Muslims and the thrust of Islamic renewal, at least agreed on one thing. Islam was a force of great significance still, with a positive part to play if an effort were made by the West to understand it, and to promote sympathetically its incorporation into the modern world. Of course, there was and is no such monolith as Islam, no more than there is a monolith of Christianity. But there are peoples and nations that follow Islamic beliefs and consider themselves Muslim. Wilfrid Scawen Blunt, Marmaduke Pickthall, as well as E.G. Browne, each in their different fashion, attempted to lead their compatriots in the direction outlined above, and we might continue to study their example today.

Envoi

This study has attempted to sketch out a terrain upon which nineteenth- and early twentieth-century British travellers and imperialist administrators constructed at times overlapping and more frequently divergent discourses about the Middle East. Some of these travellers found qualities and characteristics of eastern societies that they felt in certain points to be superior to, or lacking in western Europe. For these, it required no great exertion to advance towards advocacy of a particular aspect or aspects of an eastern spiritual/political cause. Their engagement in turn raised issues as to the impact of European power on the East. To the sympathetic travellers idealism concerning the potential helping hand their country might extend toward the freedom of a favoured eastern nation turned to cynicism as the malign nature of that power was revealed. Where it ought to have supported progress and reform, it provoked reaction and occupation instead. Condemning this, they delivered appeals to a time when a disinterested British upholding of international order could be said to have operated. It followed that Britain had 'betrayed' its 'natural' role as sponsor of smaller or weaker nations. The fact of this ideal period's continual re-location in a more favourable past indicated both its chronic instability in, and mythical importance to, each of the narratives in question. In actuality, anti-imperialist and pro-imperialist travellers, or those who manifested tendencies toward both positions, operated out of similar terrains. The argument that Britain stood in close affinity to the East owing to its love of liberty and its disinterestedness vis-à-vis territorial acquisition might, and has been suggested, sometimes did extend to proposals for British patronage that could easily slide into imperialism. The balance was set between, on the one hand, identification with an oriental cause and people to the degree that the failure of British sponsorship entailed its advocate's rejection of his own government, class and even nation. An opposite position was to argue that Britain's sponsorship and protection of a given people acted in their own interests and must therefore always be considered a priori. Choosing and naming an oriental people itself involved participation in that specifically European language game of 'spot the race/nation', imbricated as it was in nineteenth-century notions of racial hierarchy and historical valorisation. Curzon's pride in the superiority of the British and the providence of their imperial mission finds its antithesis in Blunt's privileging of non-European races over the degenerating imperial whites of western Europe. Mark Sykes' swapping of the Turks for the Arabs, Armenians and Jews was negated by Marmaduke Pickthall's loyalty to the former and turning his back on his own country.

Positioning with respect to the belief-system of Islam might be asserted as a decisive variant between imperialist and anti-imperialist discourses. Cromer, Curzon and the other imperialists, according to this perspective, showed little respect for Islam per se, while the pro-Islamic activists – Urquhart, Blunt, Browne and Pickthall – each celebrated and to varying degrees participated in the specific Islamic qualities of the nations they espoused. But categorising fixed positions in this manner elides intersections of class, race and nation among imperialists and pro-Islamic writers. The upper class backgrounds of Blunt, Sykes, and Aubrey Herbert, seemed to predispose them toward encounters with manifestations of Muslim civility in contradistinction to the middle class arrivism and corruption of the masses in their own society which they saw undergoing importation into the East.[1] Cromer, Browne and Pickthall were locked into an ideological debate about the propensity for reform or stagnation within the Islamic nations. Cromer's attacks on Islam may draw their reductive character from his chauvinism and lack of an oriental language. But Browne's Islamic interests were deflected to the extent that he was ready to espouse first the Babi heresy and later the political opportunism of al-Afghani and his Azali Babi fellow agitators in the cause of revivifying the Persian nation. Urquhart and Palgrave both negotiated the history and presence of Islam in the modern world while entertaining ambiguous orientations with regard to imperialism, and cosmopolitan predilections with respect to race.

The issue of the West's interface with the Islamic world still remained of central importance to the writings of all the figures I have been discussing. These are all in one way or another addressed to the response of Muslim nations of the Middle East to the impact of modernity and spread of a western presence within their lands. The period 1830-1926 coincided with the build up to the age of high imperialism and the approaching sunset of Britain's empire even as she enjoyed her moment in the Middle East. Issues precipitated by this period remain embedded in the East-West encounter today. Islamic reform lay at the heart of what was known in the nineteenth century as the 'Eastern Question', cutting across the discourses of both imperialists and those who were sympathetic to Islam. But the modernisation of Muslim societies has been connected intimately with western political strategies, from the beginning of the Tanzimat up to the so-called democratisation of contemporary Iraq. In 1882, an evolving Islamic society was denied an opportunity to begin the process of reform by its own agency.[2] Cromer's assemblage of the apparatus of efficient administration in Egypt called forth, in spite of Blunt's prompting in the direction of partnership with the West, what Milner called an 'experiment' in progress, but one in which the native population were placed firmly under western tutelage. Felix's Valyi's statement: 'To-day the hope of a spiritual unification of the world depends above all upon the transformations that may be looked for sooner or later in the soul of Asia, and in particular in the soul of Islam,' may have elicited varying degrees of assent among the travellers and imperialists whose writings I have been reviewing.[3]

Imperialists like Cromer and Curzon gave little or no indication that the nations of the Islamic world were to be engaged with as potential partners in the building of a world society. They viewed the forces of imperialism as irresistibly hegemonic. The evidence of Muslim decline, perhaps deepened by historical reading, and buttressed by new theories of racial supremacy derived from Gobineau and Darwinism, was enough to convince the imperial traveller that the nations and 'petty peoples' in their path had no choice but to accommodate themselves as best they could, their best course being to embrace the civilising ways of their conquerors. For others, specifics of a Muslim past, intersecting with more general characteristics of pre-modernity, triggered visions of oriental authenticity, renaissance, and even possible schemes of world spiritual renewal. Being embedded within a nineteenth-century construction of politics that left him more than half-wedded to an imperial world view paradoxically enabled Marmaduke Pickthall in imagining the disintegration of the last Muslim empire in terms of the ramifications this had for the fracturing of Muslim identities, and the dangers these might present to future world peace. In the long run, these prognostications may have proven more 'realistic' than the Allies' precipitate decision to wind up Turkish suzerainty in the East after the Great War and their break up of the Middle East into arbitrarily conceived 'nations'. Any assessment of the significance of the 'School of Urquhart Orientalists' would need to set what Kedourie considered to be its utopian impracticality against the imperialist *realpolitik* behind the eastern policies adopted by the western powers after the Congress of Berlin in 1878.

In what other ways could Britain have defrayed what Kedourie called her 'responsibilities' toward the Ottoman empire? Why were Blunt's representations on behalf of native Egyptian involvement in Cromer's governments so contemptuously dismissed, and why did Grey constrict Britain's national interest out of such obsessive fear of Germany that the democratic experiments of Muslim nations like Iran and Turkey were cynically sacrificed? Why was the refrain of oriental decadence invariably sounded when tentative steps were made toward modernisation by Middle Eastern peoples? Do the travellers, fallible as their attempts were to represent eastern nations, at least signal a sense of the cynicism and betrayal their peoples entertain towards western meddling in their affairs? In the context of the 'strangling of Persia', the American economist Morgan Shuster, writing to Browne in 1911, articulated a habitual western double-standard:

> You, I believe, are rated by that esteemed London *Times* as a 'dreamer' and 'sentimentalist'. From their smug editorials I take it they consider any man who dares to look further than his own pantry or larder as stamped with this seal, and that they publicly uphold a far different code of ethics and morality in dealing with a whole nation or people from that which they would be willing to countenance in transactions between private individuals or business corporations.[4]

I find it curious to observe in the anti-imperialist politics of writers like Blunt, Browne, and even the Tory Pickthall, affinities with an emerging 'Islamic response to imperialism' that one might encounter in the pronouncements of figures as various as Jamal al-Din al-Afghani, Hassan Banna, and Ruhollah Khomeini. Whatever this says about the orientations of such voices, if they do indeed possess common strands, this in itself might be said to diminish, albeit in very small part, the astringent binaries that some would have us believe represent intrinsic fault lines between 'Islam and the West'.

Notes

Introduction

1. See Albert Hourani, Foreword to Kathryn Tidrick, *Heart Beguiling Arabia*, p. xiv-xv, and Edward Said, *Orientalism, Western Conceptions of the Orient*.
2. Philip Darby, *Three Faces of Imperialism, Britain and American Approaches to Asia and Africa 1870-1970*, p. 51.
3. *ibid.*
4. Billy Melman, 'The Middle East/Arabia: "the cradle of Islam",' p. 106.
5. David Urquhart, *The Spirit of the East: A Journal of Travels through Roumelia*.
6. John Darwin, 'An Undeclared Empire: The British in the Middle East, 1918-39', p. 163, p. 166.
7. Elie Kedourie, *England and the Middle East, The Destruction of the Ottoman Empire 1914-1921*, p. 26.
8. On the gender issue see Lisa Lowe, *Critical Terrains, French and British Orientalists*; Billie Melman, *Women's Orients, English Women and the Middle East*; Reina Lewis, *Gendering Orientalism*. On colonialism and cultural hybridity, see Homi Bhabha, *The Location of Culture*; Robert Young, *Colonial Desire: Hybridity in Theory, Culture and Race*.
9. Rana Kabbani, *Europe's Myths of Orient*; Ali Behdad, *Belated Travelers, Orientalism in the Age of Colonial Dissolution*.
10. For example, see Albert Hourani, *Arabic Thought in the Liberal Age 1789-1939*, and *Europe and the Middle East*.
11. See especially Abbas Amanat, Introduction to Edward Granville Browne, *The Persian Revolution, 1905-1909*; Mansour Bonakdarian, 'Edward Granville Browne and the Iranian Constitutional Struggle: From Academic Orientalism to Political Activism'.

Chapter 1

1. Peter Sluglett, 'Formal and Informal Empire in the Middle East', pp. 419-22.
2. Elie Kedourie, *England and the Middle East*, p. 9.
3. William Cleveland, *A History of the Modern Middle East*, p. 83.
4. M.E.Yapp, *The Making of the Modern Near East*, p.111.
5. Yapp, *Modern Near East*, p. 136.

6. Cleveland, *Modern Middle East*, p. 90.
7. Yapp, *Modern Near East*, p. 114.
8. M.S. Anderson, *The Eastern Question*, p. 216.
9. Yapp, *Modern Near East*, pp. 117-18 .
10. E.J. Hobsbawm, *Industry and Empire*, p. 130.
11. P.J. Cain and A.G. Hopkins, *British Imperialism: Innovation and Expansion 1688-1914*, p. 398.
12. E.G. Browne, 'The Persian Constitutional Movement', pp. 323-24.
13. Lord Cromer, *Modern Egypt*, 2, p. 391.
14. According to Zara Steiner (*The Foreign Office and Foreign Policy*, pp. 131-32) both Sir Edward Grey, and his permanent under-secretary at the Foreign Office, Arthur Nicolson, 'had an exaggerated respect for Russia'. Nicolson 'felt, even when the Anglo-Russian convention had been negotiated, that a Russian absorption of northern Persia could not be avoided [...] Grey, too, had made his basic decision but he was made acutely uncomfortable by Russian behaviour in Persia [...]'.
15. Cain and Hopkins, *British Imperialism*, p. 417.
16. Yapp (*Modern Near East*, p. 172) sees 'some truth' in the argument that 'it suited the interests of Russia and Britain to preserve Iran as a weak buffer between them and that by their constant interference they handicapped Iranian development, aligning themselves with conservative groups and contributing to the downfall of reformers.'
17. Cleveland, *Modern Middle East*, p. 173, pp. 165-66.
18. Cain and Hopkins, *British Imperialism*, pp. 42-3.
19. John Darwin, 'Imperialism and the Victorians: The Dynamics of Territorial Expansion', p. 614.
20. Paul Kennedy, 'Continuity and Discontinuity in British Imperialism', p. 29, p. 34.
21. Robert Young, *Postcolonialism: An Historical Introduction*, p. 29.
22. D.K. Fieldhouse, *The Colonial Empires*, pp. 209-10.
23. Sluglett, 'Formal and Informal Empire', p. 418.
24. M.E. Chamberlain, 'British public opinion and the invasion of Europe', p.8, p. 23.
25. A.G. Hopkins, 'The Victorians and after: a reconsideration of the occupation of Egypt, 1882', p. 384.
26. See Roger Owen, 'Egypt and Europe: from French expedition to British occupation'.
27. Wilfrid Scawen Blunt, *Gordon at Khartoum*, p. 3.
28. Anthony J. Morris, *Radicalism against War, 1906-1914*, p. 258-59.
29. Morris, *Radicalism against War*, p.187.
30. Morris, *Radicalism against War*, p. 275.
31. Morris, *Radicalism against War*, p. 354.
32. E.M. Foster, *Abinger Harvest*, pp. 303-4.
33. Kedourie, *England and the Middle East*, p. 26.

34. A.J.P. Taylor, *The Troublemakers: Dissent over Foreign Policy, 1792-1939*.

35. See Young, *Postcolonialism*, pp. 73-87.

36. See Miles Taylor: 'The old radicalism and the new: David Urquhart and the politics of opposition, 1832-1867'.

37. Karl Marx, *The Eastern Question*, p. 24.

38. Kedourie, *England and the Middle East*, pp. 27-8.

39. Kathleen Tidrick, *Heart Beguiling Araby*, p. 124. It is the argument of this study that both Kedourie and Tidrick overemphasise this stage in Blunt's thought which, coming before his involvement in Egyptian nationalist politics, was gradually dropped in favour of endorsement of Islamic reform and, later still, agitation on behalf of nationalist anti-imperialist movements across the Middle East.

40. Interestingly, Blunt had shown full awareness of this danger in *The Future of Islam*, where he also envisaged the partition of the Ottoman empire with apparently few regrets. The text proposes that the British empire protect an Arabian caliphate in Mecca, and seems to envisage the Muslim world in retreat embracing a quietist spiritual stance. This position contrasts with Blunt's later promotion of a decidedly political and militant Islam in the *Secret Histories* and elsewhere.

41. Thomas Assad, *Three Victorian Travellers*, p. 81.

42. Earl of Lytton, *Wilfrid Scawen Blunt*, p. 138.

43. Ali Behdad, *Belated Travelers: Orientalism in the Age of Colonial Dissolution*, p. 94.

44. Mansour Bonakdarian, 'Edward Granville Browne and the Iranian Constitutional Struggle', p. 16, ftn. 27.

45. On Hajji Baba and 'the Persian character' see the below, chapters 4 and 5.

46. Edward Granville Browne, *The Persian Revolution, 1905-1909*, p. 187.

47. Albert Hourani carried 'the Liberal Age' with respect to Arabic thought through to 1939 (*Arabic Thought and the Liberal Age, 1789-1939*). Wilfred Cantwell Smith, (*Islam in Modern History*) was inclined to see the liberal project in the East as for practically purposes over by 1918.

48. The most prominent Orientalist of his time in the field of Persian and Arabic, Browne received no public honours. C. Edmond Bosworth ('Edward Granville Browne', p. 77, ftn. 3) rather disingenuously notes the omission of a posthumous appreciation of Browne from the British Academy's *Proceedings*.

49. See Mostafa Vaziri, *Iran as Imagined Nation*. The topic is discussed more fully in chapter 5.

50. Forster, *Abinger Harvest*, p. 279.

51. For a recapitulation of this narrative, see Felix Valyi, *Spiritual and Political Revolutions in Islam*, pp. 24-34.

52. See M.S. Anderson, *The Eastern Question*, introduction.

53. Hourani, *Arabic Thought*, p. 49.

54.   Wilfred Cantwell Smith, *Islam in Modern History*, p. 35.

55.   Smith, *Islam in Modern History*, p. 46.

56.   Seyyed Hossein Nasr, *Traditional Islam in the Modern World*, p. 81. At the beginning of the twentieth century the American missionary Samuel Graham Wilson adopted a similar categorisation of tendencies in the Muslim world. See his *Modern Movements Among Moslems*, pp. 50-1.

57.   H.A.R. Gibb, *Modern Trends in Islam*, pp. 64-5.

58.   Edward Said, *Orientalism*, p. 280.

59.   Arnold Toynbee and Kenneth Kirkwood, *Turkey*, pp. 42-3.

60.   Hourani, *Arabic Thought*, p 95.

61.   Hourani, *Arabic Thought*, p. 88.

62.   On al-Tahtawi's impressions of France, besides Hourani's *Arabic Thought*, see Paul Starkey, 'Egyptian Travellers in Europe'.

63.   Hourani, *Arabic Thought*, p. 81.

64.   Serif Mardin, *The Genesis of Young Ottoman Thought*, p. 319.

65.   Mardin, *Young Ottoman Thought*, p. 117, p. 60.

66.   Hourani, *Arabic Thought*, p. 104.

67.   Hourani, *Arabic Thought*, p. 111.

68.   Concerning Abduh's overall reform effort Gibb stated (*Modern Trends*, p. 29, p. 32): 'among the main body of Muslims, whether conservatives or reformers, it has never been fully accepted', all attempts at Islamic modernism being hindered by 'the struggle against the pervasive influences of European culture and civilization'.

69.   Gibb, *Modern Trends*, p. 63.

70.   On the question of al-Afghani's orthodoxy or heterodoxy see Hamid Algar, *Religion and State in Iran 1785-1906*, Elie Kedourie, *Afghani and 'Abduh: an essay in religious unbelief*, and most importantly, Nikki Keddie, *Sayyid Jamal ad-Din 'al-Afghani': a political biography*, and *Iran: Religion, Politics and Society*.

71.   Hamid Enayat, *Modern Islamic Political Thought*, p.7.

72.   Hamid Algar, *Malkum Khan*, p. 17.

73.   Algar, *Malkum Khan*, p. 15, p. 17.

74.   Algar, *Religion and State,* discounts a significant influence of Jamal al-Din's on either the tobacco protest of 1891-92, or the constitutional revolution. For Smith (*Islam in Modern History*, p. 54) 'there is little in twentieth century Islam not foreshadowed' in al-Afghani. To him was the merit of being 'the first Muslim revivalist to use the concepts "Islam" and "the West" as connoting correlative – and of course antagonistic – historical phenomena'. For a sourcebook that widens the scope of Islamic modernism beyond the figures I have discussed, see Charles Kauzman, ed. *Modernist Islam, 1840-1940.*

75.   Wilson, *Modern Movements*, pp. 121-2, p.123.

76.   Juan R.I. Cole, 'Iranian Millenarianism and Democratic Thought in the Nineteenth Century', p. 7, pp. 10-11, p.12. 'Close and cordial relations developed between the Bahai leaders in Acre and reformists such as the

Young Ottomans', p. 13. Cole distinguishes between the direction taken by the 'pacifist, gradualist Bahais' and the radical group 'that included political revolutionaries like Sayyid Jamal al-Din', p. 20. Cole's thesis on the Bahai faith and nineteenth century reformism in the Middle East is developed at greater length in his, *Modernity and the Millennium*.

77. Hourani, *Arabic Thought*, p. 155.
78. See Sylvia Haim, 'Blunt and Al-Kawakibi'.
79. See Keddie, *Jamal ad-Din 'al-Afghani'*; and Algar, *Malkum Khan*.
80. Hourani, *Europe and the Middle East*, p. 93. Hourani (p. 91) saw Blunt's first involvement with eastern politics as beginning at a crucial period: 'in the 1870s great changes were taking place, and there still seemed something for a man of good will to do in order to ensure that they went the right way.'
81. Kedourie, *England and the Middle East*, p. 27. The contamination of the Ottomans by Byzantium is also put forward by Mark Sykes in *The Caliph's Last Heritage*.
82. Kedourie, *England and the Middle East*, p. 28.
83. This line is also followed by Tidrick, *Heart Beguiling Araby*, p. 126.
84. Blunt, *Gordon at Khartoum*, p. 284.
85. Blunt, *Secret History of the English Occupation of Egypt*, p. 81.
86. Blunt, *Secret History*, p. 85.
87. Blunt, *Secret History*, p. 82.
88. Edith Finch, *Wilfrid Scawen Blunt*, 122.
89. Blunt, *Secret History*, p. 101.
90. Blunt's disillusionment in this plan is usually explained by reference to the incident at Siwah in 1897. See Assad (*Three Victorian Travellers*, pp. 87-8) and Tidrick (*Heart Beguiling Araby*, p. 131) who characteristically gives this a racial twist. After this he discounted any hope coming from Islam believing he had 'made a romance about these reformers' but now saw this had 'no substantial basis' (Blunt, *My Diaries*, p. 276). But it is clear from *My Diaries* that this despair was linked to a disillusionment Blunt claimed Muhammad Abduh shared about imperialist expansion, Abdul Hamid's reactionary hold over Islam, and the failure of the reform movement.
91. In one of his first articles on Babism Browne gave the following reasons for the movement's growth: 1. Its argument that it fulfilled prophecies relating to the advent of the twelfth Imam 2. Its appeal to those who desired the reform and progress of their country 3. The appeal of its doctrines to Sufis 4. The personal attraction of the Bab and Baha'ullah. Browne, 'The Babis of Persia'; reprinted in Momen, *Selections from the Writings of E.G. Browne*, pp. 163-64.
92. Keddie, *Jamal al-Din 'al-Afghani*, p. 6.
93. Browne, *Persian Revolution*, pp.12-13.
94. Browne, *Persian Revolution*, pp. 29-30. For Browne's understanding of the term 'Pan-Islamism', see below, chapter 5.

95.   See Keddie, *Jamal al-Din 'al-Afghani'*, p. 7. Algar (*Malkum Khan*, p. 61) compares Malkum's activities in Baghdad with those of the exiled Babis. Al-Afghani, whose opinion of Babism was not a high one, according to a conversation he had with Browne, nevertheless collaborated with members of the Azali Babi group in Istanbul On this relationship see Keddie, *Iran: Religion, Politics and Society*, chaps.1 and 2. When it came to tactically condoning allegiances between erstwhile enemies, such as the Babis and the Shi'ih *ulama*, out of revolutionary exigency, Browne appeared to shadow Jamal al-Din himself (see below, chapter 5).

96.   Kedourie, *England and the Middle East*, p. 19, p. 16.

97.   Kedourie, *England and the Middle East*, p. 26.

98.   David Urquhart, *Spirit of the East*, p. xxviii.

99.   Gertrude Robinson, *David Urquhart*, p. 67.

100.   Urquhart, *The Military Strength of Turkey*, pp. 3-4.

101.   This issue, for example, is raised by both Yapp (*Modern Near East*) and Cleveland (*Modern Middle East*).

102.   Peter Clark, *Marmaduke Pickthall: British Muslim*, pp. 23-4.

103.   Clark, *Pickthall*, p. 34.

104.   Clark, *Pickthall*, p. 32.

105.   Albert Hourani, *Europe and the Middle East*, p. 93. On how an Islamic frame of mind helped form Muslim and Arab travellers to the West see, in addition to Hourani, *Arabic Thought*, Nazik Saba Yared, *Arab Travellers and Western Civilization*.

Chapter 2

1.   See Nebahat Avcioglu, 'David Urquhart and the Role of Travel Literature in the Introduction of Turkish Baths to Victorian England'.

2.   Gertrude Robinson, *David Urquhart*, p. 39; Charles Webster, *The Foreign Policy of Palmeston*, 1. p. 530; Frank Edgar Bailey, *British Policy and the Turkish Reform Movement*, p. 16.

3.   DNB, 1899; Robinson, *Urquhart*, p. 35.

4.   David Urquhart, *The Spirit of the East, a Journal of Travels through Roumelia*, pp. 35-6.

5.   See Andrew Wheatcroft, *The Ottomans*, p. xxix.

6.   Bailey, *British Policy*, p. 80.

7.   'The 1830s saw the genesis of a mass Russophobia which created the image of Russia as a sort of hereditary enemy of Britain.' Eric Hobsbawm, *The Age of Revolution*, p. 134.

8.   G.H. Bolsover, 'David Urquhart and the Eastern Question', p. 445.

9.   Bolsover, 'Urquhart and the Eastern Question', p. 446.

10. Urquhart's recommendations on the collection of the poll tax were even considered by Sultan Mahmud. Bolsover, 'Urquhart and the Eastern Question', p. 448.

11. Bolsover, 'Urquhart and the Eastern Question', p. 456.

12. Quoted in Margaret Jenks, 'The Activities and Influence of David Urquhart', p. 109.

13. Bolsover, 'Urquhart and the Eastern Question', p. 465. Giving a negative assessment of Urquhart's part in this, Webster (*The Foreign Policy of Palmerston*, 1, p. 530) wrote: 'so far from helping Ponsonby, Urquhart did his best to undermine his position at Constantinople, in England, and in Palmerston's confidence.'

14. Robinson, *Urquhart*, p. 52.

15. Edwin Muir, *The Mohammedan Controversy*, pp. 1-5.

16. Urquhart, *Spirit of the East*, 1, pp. 347-48.

17. Jenks, 'Activities and Influence', pp. 169-70.

18. Urquhart, *Spirit of the East*, 1, p. x.

19. Urquhart, *Spirit of the East*, 1, p. 6. Peter Trudgill (*Sociolinguistics*, p. 24) writes of the Whorf-Sapir hypothesis: 'The hypothesis is approximately that a speaker's native language sets up a series of categories which act as a kind of grid through which he perceives the world, and which constrains the way he categorizes and conceptualizes different phenomena.'

20. Urquhart, *Spirit of the East*, 1, p. 355.

21. Urquhart, *Spirit of the East*, 1, p. xxvii.

22. Wheatcroft, *The Ottomans*, p. 179.

23. Michel Foucault, *Power/Knowledge*, p. 119. On the epistemic shift from sixteenth century 'similitude' to eighteenth century rationality, see Foucault, *The Order of Things*.

24. Urquhart, *Spirit of the East*, 1, pp. 198-99.

25. *ibid.*

26. David Urquhart, *Turkey and its Resources*, pp. 120-21.

27. Urquhart, *Turkey and its Resources*, pp. 121-22. Curiously, given his vehement denigration of the minister's policies, Urquhart's views on reform were not very dissimilar to Palmerston's. Neither, for example, believed in pressing a constitution on Turkey. On Palmerston's attitude to reform, see Bailey, *British Policy*, pp. 153-56.

28. Urquhart, *Turkey and its Resources*, p. 90. This restoration of the ancient rule was essentially Blunt's first programme for Middle Eastern renewal. Kedourie believed this to be the essential element in the thinking of the 'School of Urquhart', and its signal impracticality.

29. It is useful, when reviewing the entire issue of eastern 'authenticity' to bear in mind Timothy Mitchell's caveat when contrasting the North African Kabyle villagers' house with the Egyptian model dwellings on the imported French plan of the 1840s. Mitchell (*Colonising Egypt*, p. 49) writes: 'Because the purpose of such examples is to make visible

our assumptions about the nature of order by contrasting them with a kind of order whose assumptions are different, I run the risk of setting up this other as the very opposite of ourselves [...] These sort of self-contained, pre-capitalist totalities acquire the awful handicap [...] of having to satisfy our yearning for a lost age of innocence.'

30.   Urquhart, *Spirit of the East*, 1, p. 104.
31.   Urquhart, *Spirit of the East*, 2, p. 205.
32.   Urquhart, *Spirit of the East*, 1, p. 351, p. 353.
33.   Bernard Lewis, *The Emergence of Modern Turkey*, p. 104.
34.   Urquhart, *Spirit of the East*, 1, p. 354.
35.   David Urquhart, *The Military Strength of Turkey*, p. 120, p. 123. On the changes European-style uniforms brought to the Ottoman army see Lewis, *Ottoman Turkey*, pp. 101-3.
36.   Urquhart, *Military Strength*, p. 139, p. 31.
37.   Robinson, *Urquhart*, p. 53.
38.   Robinson, *Urquhart*, p. 73.
39.   See John Rodenbeck, 'Dressing Native'.
40.   J. Hillis Miller, *Victorian Subjects*, pp. 315-16.
41.   Urquhart, *Spirit of the East*, 1, pp. xi-xii.
42.   Urquhart, *Spirit of the East*, 1, p. 348. Palgrave's well known remarks (*A Narrative of A Year's Journey through Central and Eastern Arabia*, 1, 265), concerning the necessity for the oriental traveller to learn an oriental language, make a similar assumption to Urquhart: 'A Christian and an Englishman may well traverse Arabia [...] without being ever obliged to compromise either his religion or his honour; but for this, perfect acquaintance with Eastern customs and with at least one Eastern language, together with much circumspection and guardedness in word and deed, are undeniably required.'
43.   Urquhart, *Spirit of the East*, 2, pp. 273-74.
44.   Urquhart, *Spirit of the East*, 1, pp. 350. Italics in text.
45.   Edward Said, *Orientalism*, p. 196.
46.   Urquhart, *Turkey and its Resources*, p. 21.
47.   Urquhart, *Turkey and its Resources*, pp. 29-30.
48.   Urquhart, *Spirit of the East*, 1, p. xxv. On the Arab origins of Islam, Urquhart wrote: 'Within the lifetime of a man, though in lands of a population, wild, ignorant, and insignificant, it spread over a greater extent than the dominions of Rome.' *Spirit of the East*, 1, pp. xxv-xxvi.
49.   Urquhart, *Spirit of the East*, 1, pp. 323-34; 1, pp. 89-90, ftn. 106.
50.   Urquhart, *Turkey and its Resources*, pp. vi-vii; *Spirit of the East*, 1, p. 90.
51.   Urquhart, *Turkey and it Resources*, p. 74; Urquhart, *Spirit of the East*, 2, p. 19.
52.   Urquhart, *Turkey and its Resources*, p. 76.
53.   Urquhart, *Turkey and its Resources*, p. 135.
54.   Urquhart, *Turkey and its Resources*, pp. 136-37.

55. Urquhart, *Turkey and its Resources*, p. 81.
56. Urquhart, *Turkey and its Resources*, p. 133.
57. Urquhart, *Turkey and its Resources*, p. 134.
58. Bailey, *British Policy*, p. 119.
59. Bailey, *British Policy*, pp. 162-64.
60. David Urquhart, *Lebanon: A History and a Diary*, 2, p. 39.
61. For Marx (*The Eastern Question*, pp. 25-6) sympathetic as he was to Urquhart's diagnosis of the danger to Europe of reactionary Russia gaining a hold on Turkey, the evident flaw in the Scot's economic reasoning was that the traders in Turkey were 'certainly not Turks'. They were Greeks, Armenians, Slavs and Franks. 'Remove all the Turks out of Europe, and trade will have no reason to suffer'. Marmaduke Pickthall (*Islam and Progress*, p. 30) endorsed the pre-capitalist character of trade in the Ottoman empire, but he pointed out that Muslims were forced to devote their energies to war owing to 'attacks made on them by Christian powers [...] Whereas their Christian subjects, exempt from military service, have been able to devote themselves continuously to the peaceful art of self-advancement.'
62. Miles Taylor, 'The old radicalism and the new: David Urquhart and the politics of opposition', p. 39.
63. William Maehl, 'David Urquhart', p. 508.
64. Jenks, 'Activities and Influence', p. 205.
65. Maehl, 'Urquhart', p. 509.
66. David Urquhart, *The Edinburgh Review and the Affghan* [sic] *War*, p. 53.
67. M.S. Anderson, *The Eastern Question*, p. 91.
68. Urquhart, *The Affghan War*, p. 16.
69. Webster, *Foreign Policy of Palmerston*, 1, p. 780.
70. Robinson, *Urquhart*, p. 15.
71. Taylor, 'Old radicalism and the new', p. 39.
72. Maehl, 'Urquhart', p. 510.
73. Jenks, 'Activities and Influence', pp. 278-80.
74. Urquhart, *Lebanon*, 2, p. 173.
75. Urquhart, *Lebanon*, 2, p. 21.
76. Urquhart, *Lebanon*, 2, p. 68.
77. Urquhart, *Lebanon*, 2, p. 36, p. 35.
78. Urquhart, *Lebanon*, 2, p. 31, p. 7.
79. Urquhart, *Lebanon*, 2, p.10, p. 38, p. 20.
80. Urquhart, *Lebanon*, 2, pp. 86-7.
81. Urquhart, *Lebanon*, 2, p. 90.
82. Urquhart, *Spirit of the East*, 1, pp. 302-3.
83. Robinson, *Urquhart*, p. 62.
84. David Urquhart, *The Pillars of Hercules*, 1, p.55.
85. Urquhart, *Spirit of the East*, 1, p. 302. Emphasis in text.

86. Urquhart, *Spirit of the East*, 2, pp. 152-54. On the progressive down-grading of British optimism with respect to the Ottoman empire, from the hopes generated by the 1838 free-trade treaty to the wholesale revision after 1876, see A.G. Cain and P.J. Hopkins, *British Imperialism: Innovation and Expansion*, pp. 397-411.

87. In announcing the conversion, the *Morning Post* confused Gifford's name with that of Francis, prejudicing the latter's career at a crucial moment. See Mea Allen, *Palgrave of Arabia, The Life of Gifford Palgrave*, pp. 132-33.

88. Blunt, *My Diaries*, p. 173.

89. Francis Palgrave, preface to W.G. Palgrave, *A Vision of Life*, quoted in Allen, *Palgrave of Arabia*, p. 270.

90. The DNB (1895), for example, leaves the impression that Palgrave's jesuitical 'repugnance to Mohammedanism' continued after his de-conversion from Rome. Palgrave claimed (in *Central and Eastern Arabia* 1, p. 179, p. 266) that he and his travelling companion 'were known to all for Christians' in Hayil, while in Riyadh they were probably construed as lax Muslims. However, in his letter to Gladstone, (Allen, *Palgrave of Arabia*, p. 272) Gifford wrote 'that he had lived for some time in Egypt as a Mohammedan and frequented the "Azhar" himself.' In 1867 he wrote (in *Ulysses: or Scenes and Studies in many Lands*, p. 216) of having been moved by a particular Islamic recitative: 'I have heard it often in crowded mosques, and never without a thrill at the deep, united, concentrated belief it implies.'

91. Allen, *Palgrave of Arabia*, p. 272.

92. Allen, *Palgrave of Arabia*, p. 290. It is clear that Palgrave hoped for Cairo whilst waiting there after his abortive mission to rescue the British consul in Abyssinia in1866. At the height of the Eastern Crisis of 1876 he coveted Istanbul. In both instances he was palmed off with insignificant postings – Philippines and Bangkok respectively. In 1882, Palgrave lobbied Gladstone forlornly for the post of British minister in Cairo soon to be filled by Evelyn Baring. (Note Gordon's statement of the time: 'Give me Gifford Palgrave and I will govern the Arabs!' Allen, *Palgrave of Arabia*, p. 257). In arguing its subject had 'not attained the full developments of its early promise', the *Athenaeum* obituary (3181, 13 October 1888) opines: 'Certainly those who knew Gifford Palgrave's special qualifications would not have expected that a man with such complete command over Eastern matters would have ended his days as official representative of the British Government in South America.' (Palgrave died in Montevideo).

93. Kathryn Tidrick, *Heart Beguiling Araby*, p. 88. Tidrick sees in Palgrave's life and thought the two 'parallel obsessions' of race and mysticism.

94. Palgrave, *Central and Eastern Arabia*, 1, p. 194.

95. Palgrave, *Central and Eastern Arabia*, 2, p. 261, 1, p.175.

96. Allen, *Palgrave of Arabia*, p. 219.
97. W.G. Palgrave, *Essays on Eastern Questions*, p.19.
98. Palgrave, *Essays*, p. 27.
99. Palgrave, *Essays*, p. 41, p. 31. 'The decline of the *sipahis* (feudal chiefs) as a class, and the gradual replacement of *timar* (grants of land) by *iltizam* (tax farmers) in the country, are among the most frequently cited causes of Ottoman decline.' Lewis, *Ottoman Turkey*, p. 91.
100. Palgrave, *Essays*, pp. 69-70.
101. Palgrave, *Essays*, p. 109, p. 130.
102. Palgrave, *Essays*, p. 122.
103. Palgrave, *Essays*, pp. 131-32.
104. Palgrave, *Essays*, p. 162.
105. Tidrick, *Heart Beguiling Araby*, p. 106.
106. W.G. Palgrave, *Herman Agha, An Eastern Narrative*, p. 17.
107. Ronald Hyam, *Britain's Imperial Century*, p. 178.

Chapter 3

1. An emphasis on the Blunts' desert travels of the 1870s is found in Ali Behdad's *Belated Travelers: Orientalism in the Age of Colonial Dissolution*, and Kathryn Tidrick, *Heart Beguiling Araby, The English Romance with Arabia*.
2. See Thomas Assad, *Three Victorian Travellers*, and Tidrick, *Heart Beguiling Araby*.
3. *Ali Behdad*, Belated Travelers, *p. 93*.
4. Edith Finch, *Wilfrid Scawen Blunt*, pp. 61-2.
5. Albert Hourani, *Europe and the Middle East*, p. 91.
6. Finch, *Blunt*, p. 112
7. Elizabeth Longford, *A Pilgrimage of Passion, The Life of Wilfrid Scawen Blunt*, p. 157. By 1896, the year the Blunts made their 'last' and 'perhaps the hardest' of their many desert journeys together, Blunt viewed the Royal Geographical Society as 'the precursor and instrument of Europe's penetrations and conquests against the wild races of mankind.' The expedition to the Egyptian Eastern desert was to prepare accurate maps, but for private use. Finch, *Blunt*, p. 294.
8. Roger Owen, *Lord Cromer*, p. 4. The term 'gentlemanly capitalism' is discussed by P.J. Cain and A.G. Hopkins in *British Imperialism, Innovation and Expansion*, ch.1.
9. The Marquess of Zetland, *Lord Cromer*, p. 56.
10. Owen, *Cromer*, p. 48.
11. Owen, *Cromer*, pp.114-15.
12. Zetland, *Cromer*, p. 89.
13. Owen, *Cromer*, p. 156.

14.   Owen, *Cromer*, pp. 90-91, p. 118.
15.   Cromer, *Modern Egypt*, 1, p. 39.
16.   Zetland, *Cromer*, 62.
17.   Owen, *Cromer*, p. 125.
18.   Owen, *Cromer*, p. 126.
19.   Tidrick, *Heart Beguiling Araby*, p. 128.
20.   W.S. Blunt, *The Future of Islam*, pp. 202-3.
21.   W.S. Blunt, *The Secret History of the English Occupation of Egypt*,
      p. 150.
22.   Blunt, *Secret History*, p. 153.
23.   Cromer, *Modern Egypt*, 1, p. 256.
24.   *ibid.*
25.   Cromer, *Modern Egypt*, 1, p. 279.
26.   Cromer, *Modern Egypt*, 1, p. 343.
27.   Edward Said, *Orientalism*, pp. 38-9; Cromer, *Modern Egypt*, 2, pp. 146-
      53.
28.   Mansfield, *British in Egypt*, p. 14.
29.   Sir Auckland Colvin, *The Making of Modern Egypt*, p. 9.
30.   Cromer, *Modern Egypt*, 1, p. 58, p. 49.
31.   Cromer, *Modern Egypt*, 1, p. 57, p. 59.
32.   Cromer, *Modern Egypt*, 1, p. 165.
33.   Cromer, *Modern Egypt*, 1, pp. 150-1.
34.   Cromer, *Modern Egypt*, 1, pp. 344-45. Malet's own account of his
      period in Egypt (*Egypt 1879-1883*), which was published posthumously
      by his family, vacillates between parroting the 'official' narrative estab-
      lished by Cromer and attempts to vindicate his own personal role.
35.   Longford, *Pilgrimage of Passion*, p. 126.
36.   Blunt, *Secret History*, p. 6
37.   Assad, *Victorian Travellers*, p. 78.
38.   Blunt, *Secret History*, p. 67.
39.   Hourani, *Europe and the Middle East*, p. 93.
40.   Hourani, *Europe and the Miuddle East*, p. 94. Blunt's ideas on the
      caliphate influenced the pioneer Arab nationalist thinker al-Kawakibi,
      according to Sylvia Haim. See her 'Blunt and Al-Kawakibi'.
41.   Nikki Keddie, *An Islamic Response to Imperialism*, p. xvi.
42.   Blunt, *Secret History*, p. 62.
43.   Blunt, *Secret History*, p. 74.
44.   Blunt, *Secret History*, p. 92.
45.   Blunt, *Secret History*, p. 39, p. 76.
46.   Blunt, *Secret History*, pp. 76-7.
47.   Blunt, *Secret History*, pp. 75-6.
48.   Blunt, *Secret History*, p. 28.
49.   Daniel Crecelius ('Nonideological Responses of the Egyptian Ulama to
      Modernization', p. 167) argues there has been 'an incredible over-

emphasis upon the importance' of al-Afghani, Abduh, and his disciple Rashid Rida.

50. M.E. Yapp, *The Making of the Modern Near East*, p. 226. 'When the British cabinet first decided to occupy Egypt, it did so with no thought beyond rescuing the Egyptian monarch from the nationalists, restoring his authority, effecting rapid reforms in the administration, and then retiring from Egyptian political life.' Afaf Lutfi al-Sayyid, *Egypt and Cromer*, p. 28.

51. Cromer, *Modern Egypt*, 1, p. 13

52. Cromer, *Modern Egypt*, 1, p. 247, p. 297.

53. Cromer did, as Frederic Harrison pointed out, accept that Urabi did 'in some respects' lead '*a bona fide* national movement' (*Modern Egypt*, 1, p. 249). But Harrison asks (*Autobiographical Memoirs*, p. 172) of Cromer's tale of wars, trials, riots and coups d'etat: 'Does this read like peace and progess?' According to Donald Malcolm Reid ('The 'Urabi revolution and British conquest', p. 218) while 'the slogan "Egypt for the Egyptians" underlines the proto-nationalist strand [in the Urabi revolution] this was not conceived in narrow ethnic terms and coexisted easily with religio-political appeals to jihad and professions of loyalty to [Sultan Abdul Hamid].' The preponderance of 'the very rich' among the opponents of Urabi 'suggests a social edge to the revolution'.

54. Cromer, *Modern Egypt*, 1, p. 331.

55. Blunt, *Secret History*, p. 166.

56. Mansfield, *British in Egypt*, p. 22.

57. Blunt, *Secret History*, p. 164.

58. Blunt, *Secret History*, p. 247, p. 264.

59. Blunt, *Secret History*, p. 222.

60. Blunt, *Secret History*, pp. 286-87.

61. W.S. Blunt, *Gordon at Khartoum*, p. v.

62. Blunt, *Secret History*, p. 70.

63. Finch, *Blunt*, p. 181.

64. W.S. Blunt, *India under Ripon*, p. 8, p.13.

65. Finch (*Blunt*, p. 112) wrote: 'Ideas of Arab independence were agreeable to the official view because the Sultan of Turkey had begun to alarm India by pan-Islamic propaganda and had asserted a claim of sovereignty over the Persian Gulf ports which for many years past had been under a kind of protectorate exercised by the Indian navy.'

66. 'Blunt', *DNB*.

67. Finch, *Blunt*, p. 182. On board the ship to Ceylon, his first port of call, Blunt had passed his time reading the Qur'an, which he described as 'a great consolation in circumstances such as ours' i.e. surrounded by English passengers – mostly tea-planters and settlers in India - against whom he felt he might 'arise and proclaim a *jehad*'. Blunt, *India*, p. 16.

68. Blunt, *India*, p. 68.

69. Longford, *Pilgrimage of Passion*, p. 201, p. 228, p. 239.

70. Finch, *Blunt*, p. 174.
71. Shane Leslie, *Men were Different*, pp. 258-59.
72. Finch, *Blunt*, p. 174.
73. Finch, *Blunt*, pp. 199-200.
74. Blunt, *Gordon*, p. 362.
75. Blunt, *Gordon*, p. 404.
76. Tidrick, *Heart Beguiling Araby*, p. 125.
77. Blunt, *My Diaries*, pp. 429-30. During the Mahdi crisis Blunt delivered a similar message to the Russian agent in London who asked him what was to be done 'when the East won't be quiet and we come into collision'. Blunt told him: 'The West should retire'. *Gordon*, p. 425.
78. Blunt, *My Diaries*, 276; italics in text. Blunt's extension of his own religious agnosticism to Muhammad Abduh was believed by Hourani to be too absolute. Hourani, *Europe*, p. 98.
79. Blunt, *Gordon*, p. 313.
80. Blunt, *Gordon*, p. 80.
81. Blunt, *Gordon*, p. 79.
82. Cromer, *Modern Egypt*, 1, p. 438.
83. Cromer, *Modern Egypt*, 1, p. 446, pp. 447-78.
84. Blunt, *Gordon*, p. 198-99.
85. Blunt, *Gordon*, p. 169.
86. Blunt, *Gordon*, p. 157.
87. Mansfield, *British in Egypt*, p. 79.
88. Owen, *Cromer*, pp. 193-95.
89. A.G. Hopkins, 'The Victorians and Africa: A Reconsideration of the Occupation of Egypt', p. 388.
90. Al-Sayyid, *Egypt and Cromer*, p. 65.
91. John Marlowe, *Cromer in Egypt*, p. 176.
92. Owen, *Cromer*, p. 249.
93. Hopkins, 'The Victorians and Africa', p. 367.
94. Blunt, *My Diaries*, p. 61.
95. John Marlowe, *Milner: Apostle of Empire*, p. 20.
96. Hopkins, 'The Victorians and Africa', pp. 367-68.
97. Blunt, *My Diaries*, p. 85.
98. Al-Sayyid, *Egypt and Cromer*, p. 101.
99. Alfred Milner, *England in Egypt*, p. 33, p. 81, pp. 85-6.
100. Milner, *England in Egypt*, pp. 18-19, p. 129, p. 132, p. 155, p. 154.
101. Herodotus, *The Histories*, II, 35-7.
102. Milner, *England in Egypt*, p. 103, p. 108.
103. Milner, *England in Egypt*, pp. 285-86, p. 438.
104. Milner, *England in Egypt*, pp. 40-1, p. 436.
105. Milner, *England in Egypt*, p. 426.
106. Milner, *England in Egypt*, p. 444, p. 202.
107. Blunt, *My Diaries*, p. 213.
108. Blunt, *My Diaries*, p. 137, p. 290. Italics in text.

109. Blunt, *Atrocities of Justice under British Rule in Egypt*, pp. 64-5.
110. Blunt, *Atrocities*, pp. 10-11. 'The pamphlet was translated into Arabic and published in two Cairo newspapers in early October [1906]. A leader in the *Manchester Guardian* used its contents to point out that the original decree setting up the Special Tribunal referred only to attacks on soldiers going about their duty.' Owen, *Cromer*, p. 338-39.
111. Marlowe, *Cromer in Egypt*, p. 269.
112. Owen, *Cromer*, pp. 344-45, p. 340.
113. Blunt, *Atrocities*, p. 12.
114. Blunt, *Atrocities*, p. 15.
115. Blunt, *Atrocities*, p. 36.
116. Blunt, *Atrocities*, p. 62.
117. Cromer, *Modern Egypt*, 1, p. 328.
118. Cromer, *Modern Egypt*, 1, pp. 325-26.
119. Blunt, Atrocities, p. 55.
120. Cromer, *Ancient and Modern Imperialism*, p. 120. In 1913 Cromer stated his view ('The Capitulations of Egypt', p. 8) that the capitulations needed to be removed, but added that 'Egypt can never become autonomous in the sense in which the word is understood by the Egyptian nationalists. It is, and will always remain, a cosmopolitan country.' Two years later, he argued that 'both sound policy and justice point to the conclusion that [...] [the foreign residents] should be considered as Egyptians.' *Abbas II*, p. xix. Owen (*Cromer*, p. 394) dismisses this as 'the pretence that the foreign communities had just as much a claim to representation as the local population.'

Chapter 4

1. Edward Said, *Orientalism*, p. 240.
2. David Gilmour, *Curzon*, p. 1, p. 10.
3. Gilmore, *Curzon*, p. 23, pp. 36-7.
4. Earl of Ronaldshay, *Life of Curzon*, 1, p. 133; 2, p. 254.
5. Ronald Hyam, *Britain's Imperial Century*, pp. 184-5.
6. Harold Nicolson, *Curzon: The Last Phase*, p. 12. For a discussion of Sir James Stephen's imperialism and its influence, see Michael Edwardes, *The High Noon of Empire*, chap.1.
7. Ronaldshay, *Curzon*, 1, p. 81, p. 87.
8. Nicolson, *Curzon*, pp. 6-7, p. 19.
9. Lord Curzon of Keddleston, *Tales of Travel*, p. 3.
10. Curzon, *Tales*, p. 4.
11. G.N. Curzon, *Russia in Central Asia in 1889 and the Anglo-Russian Question*, pp. 138-39.
12. G.N. Curzon, *Persia and the Persian Question*, 1, pp.12-13.

13. Curzon, *Persia*, 1, p. 5.

14. Comte de Gobineau. *Les Religions et Les Philosophies dans L'Asie Centrale*, p. 405; Michael Biddiss, *Father of Racist Ideology, The Social and Political Thought of Count Gobineau*, p. 183, pp. 188-89.

15. Curzon, *Persia*, 1, p. 11. Italics mine.

16. Ronaldshay, *Curzon*, 2, pp. 254-55.

17. See Mary Louise Pratt, *Imperial Eyes, travel Writing and Transculturation*.

18. Curzon, *Persia*, 1, p. 14, p. 275.

19. Curzon, *Persia*, 1. p. 255, p. 386.

20. Curzon, *Persia*, 1 p. 306; G.N. Curzon, *Problems of the Far East*, p. 86.

21. Edwardes, *Empire*, p. 24.

22. Edward Said, *Orientalism*, p. 215.

23. Nicolson, *Curzon*, p. 23, p. 27.

24. J.R. Seeley, *The Expansion of England*, pp. 340-41. The other school in Seeley's schema, 'the pessimists', is readily identifiable with the 'Little Englander' tradition.

25. Nicolson, *Curzon*, pp. 13-14.

26. See Hyam, *Imperial Century*, pp. 192-97.

27. Curzon, *Problems*, p. 9. 'Every movement in Turkey, every new symptom in Egypt, any stirring in Persia or Transoxiania or Burmah or Afghanistan, we are obliged to watch with vigilance. The reason is that we have possession of India.' Seeley, *Expansion*, p. 222.

28. Curzon, *Russia*, p. 153, p. 157.

29. Curzon, *Russia*, p. 86.

30. Curzon, *Russia*, pp. 401-2.

31. Curzon, *Persia*, p. 392. Arminius Vambery, the Hungarian Orientalist, who declared himself 'a zealous defender of British interests in Asia', wrote (Vamberry, *His Life and Adventures*, p. 358, p. 361, pp. 362-63):

    > Russia [...] more easily assimilat[es] the semi-civilized and barbarous Asiatics to the spirit of the bulk of the Russian people [...] In spite of the undeniable progress of modern Russia, her sons are nevertheless still imbued with the true Asiatic spirit. [...] Russia conquers in order to Russianize and to absorb all the various nationalities in the large body of the Russian people, whilst England conquers in order to civilize, to give the unhappy nations in Asia for a while an education, and to let them afterwards loose, matured in liberal institutions, able to take care of themselves.

32. Curzon, *Persia*, 1, p. 216, p. 238; 2, p. 593, p. 594.

33. Curzon, *Persia*, 1, p. 601, p. 217.

34. Curzon, *Persia*, 1, p. 201, p. 205; 2, pp. 14-15, p. 25, p. 39; 1, p. 261.

35. Curzon, *Persia*, 2, pp. 592-93; 1, p. 130.

36. Curzon, *Problems*, p. 45, p. 48, p. 49.

37. Curzon, *Problems*, pp. 68-9. Hyam (*Imperial Century*, p. 194) writes: 'In 1916 Lord Cromer wrote that the West still had scarcely even yet recovered from the "profound astonishment" at the emergence of Japan as a highly civilised and very powerful nation.' The Anglo-Japanese alliance of 1902 hastened the actual decline of British power in the Far East.

38. Said, *Orientalism*, p. 120, p. 40. By calling upon the authority of He-rodotus on the great continuity in Persian character, Curzon associates himself with a tradition of western discourse on oriental rulers and ruled traced back to the Persians' ancient enemy. 'By far the most important element in the Greek view of the Persian Empire was its symbolization of the abjectness of the individual under autocracy; for when a Greek wished to take stock of the values inherent in his own civilization he could always assess them by their opposites as revealed in the lot of the subject peoples in the Persian Empire.' A.J. Arberry ed., *The Legacy of Persia*, p. 327.

39. Curzon, *Persia*, 1, pp. 3-4.

40. Curzon, Persia, 1, p. 15. Italics mine.

41. Curzon, *Persia*, 1, pp. 117-18; *Russia*, p. 133.

42. Curzon, *Persia*, 1, p. 277; 2, p. 628.

43. Curzon, *Persia*, 1, p. 391, p. 395, p. 396, p. 401. On the Shah's recep-tion in England see Denis Wright, *The Persians among the English*. Despite Curzon's bowdlerising of his portrait of the Shah, *The Echo* (June 2, 1892) still thought it 'no less correct than unpleasant – a callous barbarian in a state of childhood with all the caprice of child-hood.' Ronaldshay, *Curzon*, 1, p. 155.

44. Curzon, *Persia*, 2, p. 593.

45. Curzon, *Tales*, p. 83, pp. 51-4, 65.

46. Edwardes, *High Noon*, p. 24.

47. Curzon, *Tales*, pp. 15-16.

48. Curzon, *Tales*, p. 31, p. 35. Curzon refers in a footnote to Edward Lane's report on coal-eaters in Cairo in *Modern Egyptians*, chap.25. Arguably, this reinforces the genre of writing Curzon is himself indulg-ing in. Of Lane, Said (*Orientalism*, p. 162) wrote:

   > As rapporteur his propensity is for sadomasochistic colossal tid-bits: the self-mutilation of dervishes, the cruelty of judges, the blending of religion with licentiousness among Muslims, […] and so on.

49. Curzon, *Tales*, p. 15.

50. Curzon, *Russia*, p. 275.

51. Curzon, *Problems*, pp. 7-8.

52. Curzon, *Russia*, p. 155.

53. Curzon, *Persia*, 1, p. 401, p. 405.

54. Curzon, *Persia*, 2, p. 619, p. 618, p. 629. Curzon had himself – less disinterestedly – invested in exploration of Persian oil, a move he

prematurely pronounced a net loss and failure (Gilmore, *Curzon*, p. 76.)
On the tobacco protest see Nikki Keddie, *Iran: Religion, Politics and Society*, pp. 58-60, *passim*.

55. Curzon, *Persia*, 1, p. 502-3.
56. Curzon, *Persia*, 1, p. 13.
57. Biddiss, *Father of Racist Ideology*, p. 182.
58. Ronaldshay, *Curzon*, 1, pp. 192-93.
59. Ronaldshay, *Curzon*, 1, p. 157.
60. Balfour, for example, 'disapproved of any territorial expansion which did not serve clear and precise British interests. Accordingly, his government [in 1902] forced a showdown over Curzon's aggressive "forward" policies as Viceroy towards Afghanistan and Tibet.' (Denis Judd, *Balfour and the British Empire*, p. 18.) Looking at Curzon's latter period in government between 1916-1919, John Fisher comments (*Curzon and British Imperialism in the Middle East*, pp. 294-99): 'The strength of opposition to Curzon's involvement in foreign affairs within the Foreign and India Offices was indicative of the extent to which his policies were identified with a bygone era of British imperialism in the east.'
61. Said, *Orientalism*, p. 213.
62. Curzon, Introduction to James Morier, *Hajji Baba of Ispahan*, p. x.
63. Curzon, *Hajji Baba*, p. xxiii.
64. Curzon, *Hajji Baba*, p. ix.
65. Curzon, *Hajji Baba*, p. xii.
66. Curzon, *Hajji Baba*, p. xiv, pp. xxiii-xxiv.
67. Valentine Chirol, *The Middle Eastern Question or Some Political Problems of Indian Defence*, p. 5.
68. Chirol, *Middle-Eastern Question*, p. 7.
69. Chirol. *Middle-Eastern Question*, p. 16, p. 18, p. 43.
70. Chirol. *Middle-Eastern Question*, p. 32, p. 35.
71. Chirol, *Middle-Eastern Question*, p. 36
72. Chirol. *Middle-Eastern Question*, p. 89, pp. 92-3.
73. Chirol. *Middle-Eastern Question*, p. 93-4, p. 123.
74. Philip Graves, *The Life of Sir Percy Cox*, p. 64.
75. Graves, *Percy Cox*, p. 173.
76. Arnold. T. Wilson, *The Persian Gulf, An Historical Sketch*, p. 179.
77. Wilson, *Persian Gulf*, p. 192. Ironically, Curzon (*Persia*, 2, p. 443) had already staked Britain's claim to Oman in 1892: 'Oman may be justifiably regarded as a British dependency. We subsidize its ruler; we dictate its policy; we should tolerate no alien interference. I have little doubt myself that the time will some day come when, as these petty native states crumble before the advance of friendly civilisation, a more definite possession will be required, and the Union Jack will be seen flying from the castles of Muscat.'
78. Wilson, *Persian Gulf*, p. 195, p. 210.

79. Sultan Muhammad al-Qasimi, *The Myth of Arab Piracy in the Gulf*, p. xiii; Curzon, *Persia*, 2, p. 398.
80. Graves, *Percy Cox*, pp. 77-8.
81. Briton Cooper Busch, *Britain and the Persian Gulf*, chap. 1.
82. Graves, *Percy Cox*, p. 167.
83. John Marlowe, *Late Victorian: The Life of Sir Arnold Talbot Wilson*, p. 44.
84. A.T. Wilson, *South-West Persia: A Political Officer's Diary*, p. 37.
85. Wilson, *South-West Persia*, p. 29.
86. Samuel Barrett Miles, an Arabist, diplomat and traveller, was the author of many articles and several books on Oman and its environs.
87. Wilson, *South-West Persia*, p. 7.
88. Wilson, *South-West Persia*, p. 17, p. 21.
89. Wilson, *South-West Persia*, p. viii.
90. Wilson, *South-West Persia*, p. 9,
91. Wilson, *South-West Persia*, p. 85.
92. Graves, *Percy Cox*, p. 164.
93. Wilson, *South-West Persia*, p. 10.
94. Graves, 'Cox, Percy Zachariah', *DNB*.
95. Graves, *Percy Cox*, p. 231.

Chapter 5

1. Abbas Amanat, Introduction to E.G. Browne, *History of the Persian Revolution, 1905-1909* (1995), p. xii.
2. G.M. Wickens, Browne, Edward Granville, i. 'Browne's Life and Academic Career', p. 484; Mansour Bonakdarian, 'Edward Granville Browne and the Iranian Constitutional Struggle', pp. 29-30.
3. Edward Said, *Culture and Imperialism*, p. 241.
4. Bonakdarian, 'Browne and Iranian Struggle', pp. 10-11, ftn 13.
5. 'Even as late as 1914 Browne was responding to the charge of the Foreign Office and *The Times* that he and his cohorts were "sentimentalists".' Bonakdarian, 'Browne and Iranian Struggle', p. 30, ftn. 63.
6. John Marlowe, *Late Victorian*, p. 57.
7. E. Denison Ross, *Both Ends of the Candle*, p. 62. On Browne's diplomatic links see Mongol Bayat, *Iran's First Revolution*, pp. 243-46, and Mansour Bonakdarian, 'Selected Correspondence of Edward Granville Browne and contemporary reviews of *The Persian Revolution*', in E.G. Browne, *The Persian Revolution* (1995).
8. See Leon Poliakov, *The Aryan Myth, A History of Racist and Nationalist Ideas in Europe*.

9.   On the Radicals' alliance with Curzon see A.J. Anthony Morris, *Radicalism against War*, pp. 258-59.

10.   Blunt, *My Diaries*, p. 658.

11.   Browne, *A Year Amongst the Persians*, p. 8.

12.   Browne, *Year Amongst the Persians*, p. 3. Sources for Browne's life and career: R.A. Nicholson, *A Descriptive Catalogue of the MSS belonging to E.G. Browne*; E. Denison Ross, *Both Ends of the Candle*, and 'A Memoir' in, E.G. Browne, *Year Amongst the Persians*; Arberry, *Oriental Essays*; Wickens 'Browne's Life', and (basically a summary of the above) C. Edmond Bosworth, 'Edward Granville Browne 1862-1926'.

13.   While Browne was among the first in Britain to respond to the story of the Bab, in France, it has been argued, the Bab's disciples 'realised a dream that obsessed the generation of nineteenth century French Romantics from Saint-Simon to Pierre Leroux and Auguste Comte [...] this religion which in its beginnings appeared a simple attempt at the reform of Islam, was called on to become a universal religion.' 'Notice', Comte Arthur de Gobineau, *Oeuvres*, 2, p. 1078.

14.   Browne, *Year Amongst the Persians*, p. 109. On Gobineau's ideas, see Michael Biddiss, *Father of Racist Ideology, The Social and Political Thought of Count Gobineau*.

15.   Browne, *Year Amongst the Persians*, p. 109, p. 287.

16.   Browne, *Year Amongst the Persians*, p. 25, p. 24, p. 38.

17.   Browne, *Year Amongst the Persians*, p. 84. Compared with the Turkic Azerbaijanis the people of Qazvin were also 'more pleasing in countenance, more gentle in manners, and rather darker in complexion' (p. 85).

18.   Browne, *Year Amongst the Persians*, p. 87.

19.   Browne, *Year Amongst the Persians*, p. 99.

20.   Browne, *Year Amongst the Persians*, pp. 238-39

21.   Browne, *Year Amongst the Persians*, p. 109

22.   Browne, *Year Amongst the Persians*, pp.109-110.

23.   Browne, *Year Amongst the Persians*, p. 134. Browne indicates Gobineau's *Religions et Philosophies*, chap. 3, as a source for such ideas. Hourani pointed out: 'Gobineau in his book on the inequality of human races [*Essai sur l'Inégalité des Races Humaines* (1853-55)] put forward a similar thesis [to Renan]. Islam was created by the Arab race because it could not be absorbed into the civilisations already existing. In the same way, other races were never really absorbed into Islam: they remained true to themselves and in the end reasserted their own culture.' *Europe and the Middle East*, p. 61. Biddiss (*Father of Racist Ideology*, p. 186) quotes Bernard Lewis's remark that Gobineau represented Shi'ism as 'a reaction of the Indo-Persians against Arab domination – against a constricting Semitism of Arab Islam'.

24.   Browne, *Year Amongst the Persians*, p. 287.

25. Browne, Year Amongst the Persians, p. 284.

26. Browne, *Year Amongst the Persians*, p. 329.

27. Browne, *Year Amongst the Persians*, p. 330.

28. Browne, *Year Amongst the Persians*, p. 328.

29. Nikki Keddie, *Iran, Religion, Politics and Society*, p. 26. What is perhaps really striking about the affinity between *A Year Amongst the Persians* and *Religions et Philosophies* is both writers' fascination for a Persian aptitude for metaphysical speculation, however extreme: 'La première de toutes les affaires, a leur sens, et je parle ici de la disposition générale parmi eux, c'est de général le plus possible et avec le plus de détails possibles les choses supernaturelles [...] Chacun, a vrai dire, en Asie, a l'esprit ecclésiastique.' Gobineau, *Religions et Philosophies*, pp. 408-9.

30. See Hasan Balyuzi, *Edward Granville Browne and the Baha'i Faith*, chap.1.

31. Browne, *Year Amongst the Persians*, p. 475-76.

32. Browne, *Year Amongst the Persians*, p. 499, p. 550, p. 530.

33. Arberry, *Oriental Essays*, p. 168.

34. Browne, *Year Amongst the Persians*, pp. 537-8.

35. Browne, *Year Amongst the Persians*, p. 618, p. 620.

36. In his introduction to *Kitab-i-Nuqtatu'l-Kaf* (p. lii), Browne wrote: 'Baha'ism, in my opinion, is too cosmopolitan in its aims to render much direct service to [the Persian] revival. "Pride is not for him who loves his country", says Baha'u'llah, "but for him who loves the world". This is a fine sentiment, but just now it is men who love their country above all else that Persia needs.'

37. Browne, Introduction to *A Traveller's Narrative, written to illustrate the episode of the Bab*, pp. viii-ix).

38. Browne's researches into Babism were applauded by R.A. Nicholson (*Descriptive Catalogue*, p. x.) who felt in the long term they would be 'the most original and valuable of all his contributions to our knowledge of Persia'. Another of his protégés, E. Denison Ross (*Both Ends of the Candle*, p. 54), considered it a matter for regret that Browne should have 'devoted so many years to the minutest inquiries into this subject for he might have been turning his vast knowledge to more useful account.' Browne was particularly stung by a hostile review in the *Oxford Magazine*. See Balyuzi, *Browne and Baha'i Faith*, pp. 58-60; Moojan Momen, *The Babi and Baha'i Religions, 1844-1944*, pp. 35-6.

39. Browne, *A Traveller's Narrative*, p. x; Gobineau, *Religions et Philosophies*, p. 454.

40. Browne, *Traveller's Narrative*, p. xi.

41. Browne, *Traveller's Narrative*, p. xvi.

42. Browne, Introduction to *Kitab-i-Nuqatu'l-Kaf*, p. xxxv.

43. Browne, Introduction to *Tarikh-i-Jadid or New History*, p. xxviii.

44. Browne, *New History*, pp. xvi-xvii, p. xiii, pp. xxv-xxvii.

45. Browne, *New History*, p. xxv.

46. *ibid*.

47. *ibid*.

48. Browne, *New History*, p. xvii.

49. According to Denis MacEoin this work 'deserves to retain its reputation as the earliest comprehensive internal history of Babism.' He states, however, that 'there is internal evidence which argues strongly against Mirza Jani having been the author of this history.' *The Sources for Early Babi Doctrine and History*, p. 151, p. 148.

50. Said, *Orientalism*, pp. 262-63.

51. Amanat, Introduction to *Persian Revolution*, p. xiii. The Azali/Bahai split clearly contributed to Browne's eventual disaffection. In the words of one of his former students: 'From what he told me I judge that the essential nobility of Babiism in its first form would have made a much deeper mark on his life if later developments of the faith, and the defects of some of the Babis he knew, had not disappointed him.' J.B. Atkins, quoted in Momen, *Babi and Baha'i Religions*, pp. 34-5. Browne was further dismayed by the split between Baha'ullah's sons, Abdul Baha and Mirza Muhammad Ali. See his *Materials for the Study of the Babi Religion*. After Gobineau, Browne was not entirely alone among Orientalists in his passionate espousal of the Bab. The Frenchman, A-L-M Nicolas, possessed a similar zeal for the Bab's memory and an antagonism to the later developments the movement took. But he did not throw in his lot as Browne did with the Azalis. See Momen, *Babi and Baha'i Religions*, pp. 98-103.

52. Browne, 'The Persian Constitutionalists', p. 13.

53. Amanat, Introduction, p. xiv.

54. As implied, for example, by Bonakdarian in 'Browne and Iranian Struggle'.

55. See Mostafa Vaziri, *Iran as Imagined Nation: the Construction of National Identity*, pp. 119-30.

56. Amanat, Introduction, pp. xiii-xiv.

57. Vaziri, *Iran as Imagined Nation*, p. 105.

58. Vaziri, *Iran as Imagined Nation*, p. 110.

59. Vaziri, *Iran as Imagined Nation*, p. 111.

60. E.G. Browne, *A Literary History of Persia*, 1, p. 29.

61. Browne, *Literary History*, 1, p. 36, p. 204.

62. Browne, *Literary History*, 2, p. x.

63. Amanat, Introduction, p. xiii; Vaziri, *Iran as Imagined Nation*, p. 105.

64. Browne, *Literary History*, 1, p. 340; 2, p. 4.

65. Browne, *Literary History*, 4, p. 156.

66. Browne, *Persian Revolution*, p. xiii.

67. Browne, *Persian Revolution*, p. xiv.

68. Vaziri, *Iran as Imagined Nation*, p. 107.

69. Browne, *Persian Revolution*, p. xx.

70. Bonakdarian, 'Browne and Iranian Struggle', p. 11.

71. Bonakdarian, 'Browne and Iranian Struggle', p. 16. Italics in text.

72. Bonakdarian, 'Selected correspondence of Edward Granville Browne and contemporary reviews of *The Persian Revolution*'.

73. Blunt, *My Diaries*, p. 671.

74. David Fraser, *Persia and Turkey in Revolt*, p. 101, pp. 290.

75. Fraser, *Persia and Turkey*, pp. 290-91.

76. Fraser, *Persia and Turkey*, p. 27, p. 20.

77. Fraser, *Persia and Turkey*, p. 50-51.

78. Fraser, *Persia and Turkey*, p. 8, pp. 42-3.

79. Fraser, *Persia and Turkey*, p. 34, p. 138, p. 142.

80. Fraser, *Persia and Turkey*, p. 279.

81. Fraser, *Persia and Turkey*, p. 283.

82. Fraser, *Persia and Turkey*, p. 290, p. 291.

83. Amanat, Introduction, p. xix.

84. Browne, *Persian Revolution*, p. 339.

85. Fraser, *Persia and Turkey*, pp. 276-77; Keddie, *Iran*, pp. 60-62.

86. Browne, *Persian Revolution*, p. 146, p. 248, p. 154.

87. Browne, *Persian Revolution*, p. 299.

88. Bonakdarian, 'Browne and Iranian Struggle', pp. 14-15.

89. Bayat, *Iran's First Revolution*, p. 105; Keddie, *Iran*, pp. 13-52. For tactical reasons, Browne played down the contributions of Azalis to the constitutionalist cause in his *Persian Revolution 1905-1909*. However, in his introduction and commentary to *Materials for the Study of the Babi Religion* (1918), he named some of the key Azali revolutionaries. He also wrote: 'Indeed, as one of the most prominent and cultivated Azalis admitted to me some six or seven years ago, the ideal of a democratic Persia developing on purely national lines seems to have inspired in the minds of no few leading Azalis the same fiery enthusiasm as did the idea of a reign of the saints on earth in the case of the early Babis' (p. xix). For the part played by Azali Babis in the Persian revolution of 1905-11, see Keddie, *Iran*, chaps. 1, 2, and 3; Bayat, *Iran's First Revolution*, pp. 53-70.

90. Browne, *Persian Revolution*, p. 128.

91. Browne, *Persian Revolution*, p. 164.

92. Browne, *Persian Revolution*, pp. 159-60.

93. Amanat, Introduction, p. xxiii.

94. Browne, *Persian Revolution*, p. 343, p. 226, p. 246, p. 252.

95. See Browne, *The Persian Crisis of December 1911*. Curzon himself deplored the 1907 Anglo-Russian convention: 'It gives up all that we have been fighting for for years, and gives it up with a wholesome abandon that is truly cynical in its recklessness. Ah, me, it makes one despair of public life. The efforts of a century sacrificed and nothing or next to nothing in return.' (Ronaldshay, *Curzon*, 3, p. 38.) In 1911, H.F.B. Lynch tried to recruit Curzon for a revived Persia Committee,

while in the same year Browne wrote (unsuccessfully) to Curzon asking him to preside over a public meeting organised by the Committee. Lord Lamington, a Curzonite Tory, did preside as President of the revived Persia Committee. (Bonakdarian, 'The Persia Committee and the Constitutional Revolution in Iran', pp. 196-98.) Browne's 'Chronology of The Persian Revolution', which he appended to *The Press and Poetry of Modern Persia* (p. 332, p. 334) notes for 15 November 1911 and 7 December 1911 'eloquent' speeches made by Curzon at The Persia Society Dinner in London and in the House of Lords respectively.

96. G.M. Trevelyan, *Grey of Fallodon*, p. 190.
97. Browne, *Persian Revolution*, p. 194.
98. Browne, *Pan-Islamism*, p.1.
99. Browne, *Pan-Islamism*, p. 24.
100. Amanat, Introduction, pp. xix-xx.
101. Browne, *Persian Revolution*, p. 12, p. 29.
102. Browne, *Persian Revolution*, p. 97.
103. Keddie, *Sayyid Jamal ad-Din 'Al-Afghani', A Political Biography*, pp. 4-6.
104. Amanat, Introduction, pp. xix.
105. See Keddie, *Iran*, pp. 57-63.
106. Keddie, *An Islamic Response to Imperialism: Political and Religious Writings of Jamal ad-Din 'Al-Afghani'*, p. 41.
107. Browne, *Persian Revolution*, p. 250.
108. Bonakdarian, 'Iranian Constitutional Exiles and British Foreign Policy Dissenters', pp. 176-77. Browne sponsored a meeting between the Iranian revolutionary leader, Sayyid Hasan Taqizadeh, and the Young Turk, Ahmed Riza, at the National Liberal Club in November 1908. Bonakdarian concludes: 'In spite of Browne's tireless efforts, however, the Young Turk endorsement of the Iranian constitutional movement did not extend beyond negligible rhetorical pledges' (pp. 183-84). For Blunt's advice to Browne on co-ordinating the efforts of both Turkish and Persian revolutionaries, see *My Diaries*, p. 624. Browne was critical of the Turcification policy of the Young Turks (Bonakdarian, 'Browne and Iranian Struggle', p. 32).
109. Browne, Introduction to Grace Elison, *In A Turkish Harem*, pp. xvi-xvii.
110. Browne, *The Press and Poetry of Modern Persia*, p. xxvi.
111. Browne, *Press and Poetry*, p. 336.
112. Browne, *Press and Poetry*, p. xv.
113. Bonakdarian, 'Browne and Iranian Struggle', p. 30. Browne concluded his chronology of events in *Press and Poetry* (p. 330): 'However dark the horizon and ominous the outlook, Persia, in name at least, still remains an independent and undivided country.'
114. Browne, *Press and Poetry*, p. xxvii.

115. Browne, *Press and Poetry*, p. xxxi.
116. Browne, *Press and Poetry*, p. xxxiii.
117. Browne, *Press and Poetry*, pp. xxxvi-xxxvii.
118. Keddie, *Islamic Response*, p. 43.
119. Keddie, *Iran*, p. 38.
120. Keddie, *Iran*, p. 39.
121. Reader Bullard, *The Camels Must Go*, p. 49.
122. As John Simpson (*Inside Iran, Life Under Khomeini's Regime*, p. 7) points out, a street named after Browne still existed in Teheran in the 1980s.
123. Firuz Kazemzadeh, *Russia and Britain in Persia, 1864-1914, A Study in Imperialism*, p. 502.

Chapter 6

1. Peter Clark, 'A Man of Two Cities: Pickthall, Damascus, Hyderabad', p. 282. The embedded quotation is from Pickthall, *Oriental Encounters*, p. x.
2. Clark, 'Man of Two Cities', p. 283. The embedded quotation is from 'The Black Crusade', *New Age*, 5 December, 1912.
3. Clark, *Marmaduke Pickthall: British Muslim*, p. 15.
4. Clark, *Pickthall*, p. 8.
5. E.M. Forster, *Abinger Harvest*, pp. 275-92.
6. Clark, *Pickthall*, p. 27.
7. Philip Graves, *Briton and Turk*, p. 173.
8. Anthony J. Morris, *Radicalism against War*, p. 350.
9. Pickthall, 'The Black Crusade', *New Age*, 7 November, 1912.
10. Pickthall, 'The Black Crusade', New Age, 14 November 1912.
11. Clark, *Pickthall*, pp. 20-1.
12. Graves, *Briton and Turk*, p. 173.
13. Pickthall, 'The Black Crusade', *New Age*, 28 November, 1912. See also Pickthall, 'The Outlook in the Near East', *Nineteenth Century and After*, December, 1912.
14. Pickthall, 'The Black Crusade', *New Age*, 28 November. On the sectarian integration in the eastern Ottoman empire, see Bruce A. Masters, *Christians and Jews in the Ottoman World: the Roots of Sectarianism*. Cambridge, Cambridge University Press, 2001.
15. Pickthall, 'Six Years', *New Age*, 31 December 1914.
16. Pickthall, *With the Turk in Wartime*, p. 53.
17. Pickthall, *With the Turk*, pp. ix-xi.
18. Graves, *Briton and Turk*, p. 180.
19. Aubrey Herbert, who arrived in Istanbul a few weeks earlier than Pickthall in late February 1913, noted in his diary: 'Bosphorus bleak

and cold. Many apathetic Turks. Guns on the point. Passengers silent
[...] Impression is Constantinople may be lost.' Margaret FitzHerbert,
The Man who was Greenmantle, A Biography of Aubrey Herbert,
p. 114.

20. Pickthall, *With the Turk*, p. 170.

21. Graves, *Briton and Turk*, p. 177, p. 153. In 1913, although Aubrey
     Herbert spoke to all sides on the Turkish political scene, he felt reprov-
     ing eyes when he dined with the CUP leaders and when he returned to
     England was angry that none of the newspapers would print pro-Turk
     letters. FitzHerbert, *Greenmantle*, p. 115.

22. Graves, *Briton and Turk*, p. 174.

23. Pickthall, 'The Hope of Muslim Progress', *Nineteenth Century and
     After*, September 1913.

24. *ibid*.

25. Ann Fremantle, *Loyal Enemy*, p. 211.

26. Fremantle, *Loyal Enemy*, p. 213.

27. Pickthall, *With the Turk*, p. 144.

28. Pickthall, *With the Turk*, p. 152.

29. Graves, *Briton and Turk*, pp.151-52; Pickthall, *With the Turk*, p. 114.
     On the issue of the groups and interests among the Young Turk leaders,
     including their freemasonry and the Jewish element, see A.L. Macfie,
     The End of the Ottoman Empire, pp. 29-30, p. 34.

30. William L. Cleveland, *A History of the Modern Middle East*, p. 136.

31. Graves, *Briton and Turk*, p. 152, p. 160.

32. Graves, *Briton and Turk*, p. 155. Another of the Buxtons, Charles
     Roden, had at first welcomed the revolution of 1908, witnessing the
     early days at close hand (*Turkey in Revolution*, p. 137): 'I cannot resist
     the impression that what has triumphed in this Revolution has been an
     extraordinary moral force.' But the career diplomat, Andrew Ryan, then
     a young dragoman in Istanbul, later considered the Young Turks (*Last
     of the Dragomans*, p. 68) 'imperilled their success by their chauvinism'.
     Their policy of 'extreme centralization and of Turkification of subject
     races' within the empire, and their 'suspicion of foreign powers and
     their jealous hostility towards foreign interests in Turkey' were crucial
     mistakes that lost them support.

33. Feroz Ahmad, *The Young Turks, The Committee of Union and Progress
     in Turkish Politics*. See also his, *The Making of Modern Turkey*, chap.
     3. As news of the Armenian massacres began to filter out, Pickthall
     took up an uncompromising and frankly unpleasant position of exon-
     erating the Young Turks. See below, note 65.

34. Fremantle, *Loyal Enemy*, p. 227.

35. Clark, *Pickthall*, p. 17.

36. Pickthall, *Children of the Nile*, p. 45.

37. Clark, *Pickthall*, p. 86.

38. The unchanging Egyptian peasant is also a feature of narratives of Egyptian fiction of the early twentieth century, although this is arguably a projection of the bourgeois background from which Egyptian writers came. See Jeff Shahlan, 'Writing the Nation: The Emergence of Egypt in the Modern Arabic Novel'.

39. Pickthall, *Children*, p. 150.

40. Pickthall, *Children*, p. 207, p. 240. Pickthall surely intends to include Blunt among the renegade Franks. Clark points out (*Pickthall*, p. 83) that the novel slots in chronologically to the debate between Cromer and Blunt (discussed here in chapter 3.)

41. Pickthall, *Children*, p. 248.

42. Pickthall, *Children*, p. 239, p. 208, pp. 250-51, p. 301, p. 286.

43. On the financial reasons for Britain's intervention, see 'The Case of Egypt', *New Age*, 7 January 1915. For the view that held the governor culpable, possibly following the Khedive's orders, see Blunt, *Gordon at Khartoum*, pp. 20-21.

44. On contemporary nationalist responses to Roosevelt's speech see Browne's preface to his, *Press and Poetry of Modern Persia*.

45. Pickthall, Letter, *New Age*, 12 March. Italics mine.

46. Pickthall, 'Nature and the Doctrinaire', *New Age*, 25 March 1915.

47. Pickthall, *The Early Hours*, pp. 50-1.

48. Pickthall, *Early Hours*, p. 70.

49. Pickthall, *Early Hours*, p. 63, p. 75.

50. Pickthall, 'For the Defence', *New Age*, 19 June 1919.

51. Pickthall, *Early Hours*, p. 270.

52. Fremantle, *Loyal Enemy*, p. 231.

53. Although he took part in the Gallipoli campaign, Herbert maintained a pro-Turk profile throughout the war and like Pickthall would have pursued a secret initiative for a separate peace with Turkey had the authorities allowed. See Fitz-Herbert, *Greenmantle*, p. 150, pp. 192-4; Fremantle, *Loyal Enemy*, p. 276; Clark, *Pickthall*, pp. 31-2. Sykes' response to the attitude of his former allies was one of infuriation. (Roger Adelson, *Mark Sykes: Portrait of an Amateur*, p. 211.)

54. Adelson, *Mark Sykes*, p. 11. According to one of his colleagues, 'Mark Sykes was the chief motive force in London behind the British Government's Near Eastern policy in the War. He inspired both the Arab and Jewish policies and was chiefly responsible for securing their adoption by Ministers at home.' Shane Leslie, *Mark Sykes: His Life and Letters*, p. 288.

55. Elie Kedourie, *England and the Middle East*, pp. 67-68.

56. Kedourie, *England and the Middle East*, p. 70.

57. Kedourie, *England and the Middle East*, p. 71. Kedourie's assessment is re-stated by Tidrick and generalised by David Cannadine. Cannadine's argument (*Ornamentalism*, p. xix, p. 10) is that the promoters of the British empire were as much concerned with '"construction of

affinities" on the presumption that society on the periphery was the same as, or even on occasions superior to, society in the metropolis' as they were with 'exclusivity' and 'otherness'. The British empire 'was first and foremost a class act, where individual social ordering often took precedence over collective racial othering.'

58. Adelson, *Mark Sykes*, p. 105, p. 123.
59. Sykes, *The Caliph's Last Heritage*, p. 370, p. 337.
60. Adelson, *Mark Sykes*, p. 123, p. 106.
61. Sykes, *Caliph's Last Heritage*, p. 300.
62. Kedourie, *England and the Middle East*, p. 74.
63. Sykes, *Through Five Turkish Provinces*, p. 54.
64. Sykes, *Dar-ul-Islam*, p. 77.
65. Pickthall took issue with Sykes over his former hostility towards the Armenians in the Spring of 1916. In a letter to *The Times*, Sykes had distanced himself from Captain Dixon-Johnson's pamphlet, *The Armenians,* which quoted from Sykes' earlier criticism of the Armenians ('Sir Mark Sykes and the Armenians', *New Age*, 4 May 1916). See also Valyi, *Spiritual and Political Revolutions*, p. 144, pp. 191-94. On Pickthall's own 'racist' view of the Armenians, see Clark, *Pickthall*, pp. 30-31, p. 33.
66. Adelson, *Mark Sykes*, p. 110; Kedourie, *England and the Middle East*, p. 81.
67. Reinhold Schiffer, *Oriental Panorama, British travellers in Nineteenth Century Turkey*, p. 250.
68. Sykes, *Dar-ul-Islam*, p. 107, p. 65.
69. Pickthall, *With the Turk*, p. 176, p. 170; Pickthall, *Early Hours*, p. 217. Charles Buxton's representation (*Turkey*, p. 29) of the 'old Turk'- if he ever existed – was precisely the one rejected by the heroes of *The Early Hours*. 'Resigned, fatalist, religious, happy-go-lucky, hospitable; content either to sit cross-legged, enjoying his cigarettes and his wives, or, if need be, to rise and slay the infidel at the pleasure of the "Padishah" [...] the perfect individualist, caring neither the one way nor the other for his neighbours or his government, letting the world go by as it pleased.'
70. Sykes, *Dar-ul-Islam*, p. 104.
71. Sykes, *Dar-ul-Islam*, p. 104; *Caliph's Last Heritage*, p. 377.
72. Adelson, *Mark Sykes*, p. 157, p. 176.
73. Kedourie, *England and the Middle East*, p. 79.
74. Peter Clark ('A Man of Two Cities', p. 285) quotes a witness from that occasion: 'With his hands folded on his breast, and an expression of serene contentment on his face, he [Pickthall] recited that famous prayer which concluded the second chapter of the Holy Koran. When he sat down, every one of his hearers felt that they had lived through, during that one shot hour, the most remarkable period in [their] life.'
75. Pickthall, *With the Turk*, p. 198.

76. Pickthall, *With the Turk*, p. 122. On the emerging Arab sense of separateness from the Ottoman empire, see C.E. Dawn, *From Ottomanism to Arabism*.

77. Pickthall, 'The Last Chance', *New Age*, 6 January 1916.

78. Pickthall's argument (*ibid.*) that the last Arab incumbent of the caliphate had 'of his own free will abdicated in favour of the Ottoman conqueror' Selim I is rather disingenuous. In practice, Enayat (*Modern Islamic political Thought*, p. 13) argued, after the last of the four rightly guided caliphs who immediately succeeded Muhammad, Sunnis allowed the 'prestige of rulers rested [...] on sheer force'. Regarding the jihad which the Turkish caliph had proclaimed on Britain in 1915, Mansfield (*The Arabs*, p. 125) notes that the caliph was widely seen as having been reduced to a 'mere figurehead' of the Young Turks. His proclamation did not stop tens of thousands of Indian and Arab Muslims fighting on the side of the Entente. On the theocratic aspects behind the calpihate issue, see Enayat, *Islamic Political Thought*, chap. 2.

79. Pickthall, 'The Arab Question', *New Age*, 5 November 1914. The early, seminal historian of Arab nationalism, George Antonius, included the Muhammad Ali dynasty as potential sponsors of a specifically Arab movement. See *The Arab Awakening*, chap.2. Of the members of the House of Muhammad Ali, Pickthall was particularly antagonistic towards the Khedive Abbas II, accusing him, post-Cromer, of corrupting Egyptian political life through his power of patronage ('Egypt and the Foreign Office', *New Age*, 29 October 1914).

80. Pickthall, 'After the Caliphate', *New Age*, 28 January 1915.

81. Fremantle, *Loyal Enemy*, pp. 269-70.

82. Pickthall, 'The Project of Partition', *New Age*, 18 February 1915.

83. E.J. Hobsbawn, *Nations and Nationalism since 1780*, p. 131.

84. Hisham Sharabi, *Governments and Politics of the Middle East in the Twentieth Century*, pp. 19-20.

85. Adelson, *Mark Sykes*, p. 301.

86. Pickthall, 'The League of Nations and the British Empire', *New Age*, 3 April 1919.

87. Pickthall, 'The Act of God', *New Age*, 24 April 1919.

88. Pickthall, 'The End of a Legend', p. 667.

89. Clark, 'A Man of Two Cities', pp. 286-88. On the Khalifat movement see Wilfred Cantwell Smith, *Modern Islam in India*, pp.195-207.

90. John M. Mackenzie, 'T.E. Lawrence: The Myth and the Message', p. 151.

91. This is the subtitle of Kathryn Tidrick's, *Heart Beguiling Araby*.

92. Tidrick, with some hyperbole, calls Lawrence 'Blunt's most devoted, perhaps only, disciple' (*Heart Beguiling Araby*, p. 126).

93. T.E. Lawrence, *Seven Pillars of Wisdom*, p. 23.

94. Robert Graves, *Lawrence and the Arabs*, p. 50.

95. David Cannadine, *Ornamentalism*, pp. 72-73.

96. Kedourie, *England and the Middle East*, p. 28.

97. Kamal Salibi, 'Elie Kedourie: A Tribute', p. 1.

98. Kedourie, *England and the Middle East*, p. 96.

99. Peter Sluglett, 'Formal and Informal Imperialism in the Middle East', p. 426; Mackenzie, 'Myth and Message', pp. 158-59.

100. Kedourie, *England and the Middle East*, p. 101, p. 105.

101. Valyi, *Spiritual and Political Revolutions*, p. 20.

102. Valyi, *Spiritual and Political Revolutions*, p. 32.

103. *ibid.*

104. An ingenious if sycophantic solution to Turkish revival and the issue of the caliphate was enunciated by Valyi (*Spiritual and Political Revolutions*, p. 74): 'If enlightened Moslims [sic] in their majority would accept the standpoint of Turkey with regard to the Khalifate, if Mustafa Kemal were accepted as the real leader of modern Musulman thought, if deep in the Moslim soul, the Idjma, the decision has already been made to confer upon Angora the right to direct the reformation of Musulman institutions, and to interpret the Khalifate in accordance with the new social and spiritual aspirations of Islam, let us bow to the choice of the Musulman elite, and do not let us play the game of the ignorant crowds.' However, William Cleveland (*History of the Modern Middle East* p. 177) sees the abolition of the caliphate as the inauguration of Ataturk's secularisation project: 'Secularism was a central element in Ataturk's platform, and the impatient Westernizer pursued it with a thoroughness unparalleled in modern Islamic history.'

105. Edith Finch, *Wilfrid Scawen Blunt*, p. 347.

106. Cedric Watts and Lawrence Davies, *Cunningham-Graham, A Critical Biography*, pp. 264-65.

107. Clark, Introduction to Marmaduke Pickthall, *Said the Fisherman*, p. 7.

Envoi

1. See David Cannadine, *Ornamentalism*, pp.72-3.

2. 'The British invaded in order to ensure that a process of state formation did not succeed in creating a new sort of stable order that would end European privileges and threaten the security of European property and investments.' Juan Ricardo Cole, *Colonialism and Revolution in the Middle East*, p. 17.

3. Felix Valyi, *Spiritual and Political Revolutions in Islam*, p. 20.

4. E.G. Browne, *The Persian Crisis of December, 1911*, p. 17. See also Morgan Shuster, *The Strangling of Persia*.

Bibliography

Adelson, Roger. *Mark Sykes, Portrait of an Amateur*. London: Cape, 1975.

Ahmad, Feroz. *The Young Turks, The Committee of Union and Progress in Turkish Politics 1908-1914*. London: Oxford University Press, 1969.

— *The Making of Modern Turkey*. London: Routledge, 1993.

Algar, Hamid. *Religion and State in Iran 1785-1906*. Berkeley: University of California Press, 1969.

Mirza Malkum Khan, A Study in the History of Iranian Modernism. Berkeley: University of California Press, 1973.

Allen, Mea. *Palgrave of Arabia, the Life of William Gifford Palgrave 1826-1888*. London: Macmillan, 1972.

Al-Qasimi, Sultan Muhammad. *The Myth of Arab Piracy in the Gulf*. London: Croom Helm, 1986.

Al-Sayyid, Afaf Lutfi. *Egypt and Cromer, A Study in Anglo-Egyptian Relations*. London: Longman, 1968

Amanat, Abbas. *Resurrection and Renewal: The Making of the Babi Movement in Iran, 1844-1850*. Ithaca: Cornell University Press, 1989.

— Introduction to E.G. Browne, *History of the Persian Revolution, 1905-1909*, [1910] repr. New York: Mage, 1995.

Anderson, M.S. *The Eastern Question, 1774-1923: A Study In International Relations*. London: Macmillan, 1966.

Antonius, George. *The Arab Awakening*. Beirut: Librairie du Liban, 1955.

Arberry, A.J., ed. *The Legacy of Persia*, Oxford: OUP, 1953.

— *Oriental Essays, Portraits of Seven Scholars*, 1960.

Assad, Thomas J. *Three Victorian Travellers, Burton, Blunt, Doughty*. London: Routledge and Kegan Paul, 1963.

Avoioglu, Nebahat. 'David Urquhart and the role of Travel Literature in the introduction of Turkish Baths to Victorian England', in *Interpreting the Orient: Travellers in Egypt and the Near East*, ed. Paul and Janet Starkey. 69-80.London: Ithaca, 2001.

Badawi, Zaki. *The Reformers of Egypt: a Critique of Al-Afghani, 'Abdu, and Ridha*. London: Slough: Open Press, 1976.

Bailey, Frank Edgar. *British Policy and the Turkish Reform Movement, A Study in Anglo-Turkish Relations 1826-1853*. New York: Howard Fertig, 1970.

Balyuzi, Hasan M. *Edward Granville Brown and the Baha'i Faith*. Oxford: George Ronald. 1970.

Bayat, Mongol. *Iran's First Revolution, Shi'ism and the Constitutional Revolution of 1905-1909*. New York: Oxford University Press, 1991.

Bhabha, Homi K. *The Location of Culture*. London: Routledge, 1994.

Behdad, Ali. *Belated Travelers: Orientalism in the Age of Colonial Dissolution*. Durham N.C.: Duke University Press, 1994.

Biddiss, Michael D. *Father of Racist Ideology, The Social and Political Thought of Count Gobineau*. London: Weidenfeld and Nicholson, 1970.

Blunt, Lady Anne Noel. *A Pilgrimage to Nejd, The Cradle of The Arab Race, A Visit to the Court of the Arab Emir*. 2 vols. London: John Murray, 1881.

Wilfrid Scawen Blunt. *The Future of Islam*. London: Kegan Paul, Trench, 1882.

— *Atrocities of Justice under British Rule in Egypt*. London: Unwin, 1906.

— *Secret History of The English Occupation of Egypt, Being a Personal Narrative of Events*. London: Unwin, 1907; repr. New York: Alfred A. Knopf, 1922.

— *India under Ripon: A Private Diary*. London: Unwin, 1909.

— *My Diaries 1887-1914*. 1 vol. edn. London: Secker, 1932.

Bolsover, G.H. 'David Urquhart and the Eastern Question, 1833-37: A Study in Publicity and Diplomacy', *Journal of Modern History*, 1936, 8, 444-467.

Bonakdarian, Mansour. 'The Persia Committee and the Constitutional Revolution in Iran', *British Journal of Middle Eastern Studies*, 1991, 18, 186-207.

— 'Edward Granville Browne and the Iranian Constitutional Struggle: From Academic Orientalism to Political Activism', *Iranian Studies*, 1993, 26, 7-32.

— 'Iranian Constitutional Exiles and British Foreign Policy Dissenters', *International Journal of Middle East Studies*, 1995, 27, 175-191.

— 'Selected correspondence of Edward Granville Browne and contemporary reviews of *The Persian Revolution 1905-1909*', in E.G. Browne, *The Persian Revolution 1905-1909*, [1910] New York: Mage, 1995.

Boroujerdi, Mehrzad. *Iranian Intellectuals and the West: The Tormented Triumph of Nativism*: Syracuse, N.Y.: Syracuse University Press, 1996.

Bosworth, C. Edmond. 'Edward Granville Browne 1862-1926', in *A Century of British Orientalists 1902-2001*, ed. C. Edmund Bosworth. 74-87. Oxford: British Academy and Oxford University Press, 2001.

Browne, Edward Granville. 'The Babis of Persia'. I: Sketch of their History, and Personal Experiences amongst them. II: Their Literature and Doctrines. *Journal of the Royal Asiatic Society*, 1889, 21, pp. 485-526, 881-1009; repr. in *Selections from the Writings of E.G. Browne on the Babi and Baha'i Religions*, Mojan Momen, ed. Oxford: George Ronald, 1978.

— Introduction and notes, *A Traveller's Narrative, written to illustrate The Episode of the Bab*. Vol.2. Cambridge: Cambridge University Press. 1891.

— *A Year Amongst the Persians*. Cambridge: Cambridge University Press, 1893; repr. London: A.C. Black, 1950.

— Introduction, *The Tarikh-i-Jadid or New History of Mirza 'Ali Muhammad the Bab*. Cambridge: Cambridge University Press, 1893.

— *Pan-Islamism*. Cambridge: Cambridge University Press, 1902.

— 'The Persian Constitutionalists', *Proceedings of the Central Asia Society*, 1908, 21.

— *The Persian Revolution of 1905-1909*. Cambridge: Cambridge University Press, 1910.

— Introduction, *Kitab-i-Nuqtatu'l-Kaf, The Earliest History of the Babis compiled by Haji Mirza Jani of Kashan*. Lyden: E.J. Brill, 1910.

— *The Persian Crisis of December, 1911; How it arose and whither it may lead us, compiled for the use of the Persia Committee*, 1912.

— *The Reign of Terror at Tabriz, England's Responsibility*. Manchester: Taylor, Garnett, Evans, 1912.

— *The Press and Poetry of Modern Persia*. Cambridge: Cambridge University Press, 1914.

— Introduction to Grace Ellison, *In A Turkish Harem*. London: Methuen, 1915.

— 'The Persian Constitutional Movement', *Proceedings of the British Academy*, 1917-18, 8, pp. 311-30.

— Introduction. *Materials for the Study of the Babi Religion*. Cambridge: Cambridge University Press, 1918.

— *A Literary History of Persia*, 4 vols: 1. *From the Earliest Times until Firdawsi*; 2. *From Firdawsi to Sa'di*; 3. *Under Tartar Dominion, A.D. 1265-1502*; 4. *In Modern Times, A.D. 1500-1924*. Cambridge: Cambridge University Press, 1928.

Bullard, Reader. *The Camels Must Go. An Autobiography*. London: Faber & Faber, 1961.

Busch, Briton Cooper. *Britain and the Persian Gulf, 1894-1914*. Berkeley, CA: University of California Press, 1967.

Buxton, Charles Roden. *Turkey in Revolution*. London: Fisher Unwin, 1909.

Cain, P.J. and Hopkins, A.G. *British Imperialism: Innovation and Expansion 1688-1914*. London: Longman, 1993.

Cannadine, David. *Ornamentalism*. London: Penguin, 2002.

Chamberlain, M.E. 'British public opinion and the invasion of Egypt', *Trivium*, 1981, 16, 5-27.

Chirol, Valentine. *The Middle Eastern Question or Some Political Problems of Indian Defence*. London: John Murray, 1903.

Clark, Peter. *Marmaduke Pickthall: British Muslim*. London: Quartet, 1986.

— Introduction to Marmaduke Pickthall, *Said the Fisherman*. London: Quartet, 1986.

— 'A Man of Two Cities: Pickthall, Damascus, Hyderabad', *Asian Affairs*, 1995, 25, 281-292.

Cleveland, William L. *A History of the Modern Middle East*. Boulder: Westview, 2000.

Cole, Juan Ricardo. 'Browne, Edward Granville, ii. "Browne on Babism and Bahaism".' *Encyclopaedia Iranica*, ed. Yershater Ehsan, vol. 4. London: Routledge and Kegan Paul, 1990.

— 'Iranian Millenarianism and Democratic Thought', *International Journal of Middle East Studies*, 1992, 24, 1-26.

— *Colonialism and Revolution in the Middle East: Social and Cultural Origins of Egypt's 'Urabi Movement*. Princeton: Princeton University Press, 1993.

— *Modernity and the Millennium, the Genesis of the Baha'i Faith in the Nineteenth Century Middle East*. New York: Columbia University Press, 1998.

Colvin, Sir Auckland. *The Making of Modern Egypt*. London: Seeley, 1906.

Crecelius, Daniel. 'Nonideological Responses of the Egyptian Ulama to Modernization', in *Scholars, Saints, and Sufis, Muslim Religious Institutions since 1500*, ed. Nikki R. Keddie. 167-209. Berkeley, CA: University of California Press, 1978.

Cromer. Earl. *Modern Egypt*, 2 vols. London: Macmillan, 1908.

— *Imperialism Ancient and Modern Imperialism*. London: John Murray, 1910.

— 'The Capitulations of Egypt', *The Nineteenth Century and After*, 1913, 1-10.

— *Abbas II*. London: Macmillan, 1915.

Curzon, George N. *Russia in Central Asia in 1889 and the Anglo-Russian Question*, London: Longman, Green, 1889; repr. London: Frank Cass, 1967.

— *Persia and The Persian Question*, 2 vols. London: Longman, Green, 1892; repr. London: Frank Cass, 1966.

— Introduction to James Morier, *Hajji Baba of Ispahan*. London: Macmillan, 1895.

— *Tales of Travel*, London: Hodder and Stoughton, 1923.

Daly, M.W. 'The British Occupation, 1882-1922', in *The Cambridge History of Egypt*, vol.2, *Modern Egypt, from 1517 to the end of the twentieth century*, ed. M.W. Daly. 239-251. Cambridge: Cambridge University Press, 1998.

Darby, Philip. *Three Faces of Imperialism, Britain and American Approaches to Asia and Africa 1870-1970*. New Haven: Yale University Press, 1987.

Darwin, John. 'Imperialism and the Victorians: The Dynamics of territorial Expansion', *English Historical Review*, June 1997, 614-642.

— 'An Undeclared Empire: The British in the Middle East, 1918-39', *Journal of Imperial and Commonwealth History*, 1999, 27, 2, 158-176.

Dawn, C. Ernest. *From Ottomanism to Arabism, Essays on the Origins of Arab Nationalism*. Urbana : University of Illinois Press, 1973.

Edwardes, Michael. *The High Noon of Empire*, London: Eyre and Spottis-wood, 1965.

Elgood, P.G. 'Blunt, Wilfrid Scawen 1840-1922', *DNB*, 1937.

Enayat, Hamid. *Modern Islamic Political Thought*. London: Macmillan, 1982.

Fieldhouse, D.K. *The Colonial Empires: A Comparative Survey from the Eighteenth Century*. London: Macmillan, 1966.

— *Colonialism, 1870-1945: An Introduction*. London: Weidenfeld and Nicolson, 1973.

Finch, Edith. *Wilfrid Scawen Blunt: 1840-1922*. London: Jonathan Cape, 1938.

Fisher, John. *Curzon and British Imperialism in the Middle East 1916-19*, London: Frank Cass, 1999.

Fitzherbert, Margaret. *The Man who was Greenmantle, A Biography of Aubrey Herbert*. London: John Murray, 1984.

Forster, E.M. *Abinger Harvest*. Harmondsworth: Penguin, 1967.

Fraser, David. *Persia and Turkey in Revolt*. London: Blackwell, 1910.

Fremantle, Anne. *Loyal Enemy*. London: Hutchinson, 1938.

Foucault, Michel. *Power/Knowledge, Selected Interviews and Other Writings 1972-1977*, ed. Colin Gordon, trans. Loin Gordon *et al.* New York: Pantheon, 1980.

— *The Order of Things, An Archaeology of the Human Sciences*. London: Routledge, 2000.

Gibb, H.A.R. *Modern Trends in Islam*. Chicago: University of Chicago Press, 1947.

Gilmore, David. *Curzon*. London: Macmillan, 1995.

Gobineau, Arthur Comte de. *Les religions et Les Philosophies dans l'Asie Centrale*. Paris, 1865; repr. in *Oeuvres*. Vol. 2, Paris: Gallimard, 1983.

— *Gobineau: Selected Political Writings*, edited and introduced by Michael D. Biddiss. London: Jonathan Cape, 1970.

Graves, Philip. *The Life of Sir Percy Cox*. London: Hutchinson, 1941.

— *Briton and Turk*. London: Hutchinson, 1943.

— 'Cox. Sir Percy Zachariah 1864-1937', *DNB*, 1949.

Graves, Robert. *Lawrence and the Arabs*. London: Jonathan Cape, 1927.

Haim, Sylvia. 'Blunt and Al-Kawakibi', *Oriente Moderno*, 1955, 35, 132-143.

Harrison, Frederick. *Autobiographical Memoirs*. London: Macmillan, 1911.

Herodotus, *The Histories*, trans. Aubrey De Selincourt, revised with introductory matter and notes by John Marincola. Harmondsworth: Penguin, 1996.

Hobsbawm, E.J. *Industry and Empire*. Harmondsworth: Penguin, 1969.

— *The Age of Revolution, 1789-1848*. London: Abacus, 1977.

— *Nations and Nationalism since 1780: Programme, Myth and Reality*. Cambridge: Cambridge University Press, 1990.

Hopkins, A.G. 'The Victorians and Africa: A Reconsideration of the Occupation of Egypt, 1882', *Journal of African History*, 1986, 27, 363-391.

Hourani, Albert. *Europe and the Middle East*. London: St Anthony's/ Macmillan, 1981.

— *Arabic Thought in the Liberal Age 1978-1939*. Cambridge: Cambridge University Press. 2nd edn. 1983.

— Foreword to Kathryn Tidrick, *Heart Beguiling Araby: The English Romance with Arabia*. 2nd edn. London: I.B. Tauris, 1989.

Hyam, Ronald. *Britain's Imperial Century, 1815-1914, A Study of Empire and Expansion*. London: Macmillan, 1976.

Jenks, Margaret H. 'The activities and influence of David Urquhart, 1833-56, with special reference to the affairs of the Near East', unpublished Ph.D thesis, University of London, 1964.

Judd, Denis. *Balfour and the British Empire: A Study in Imperial Evolution 1874-1932*. London: Macmillan, 1968.

Kabbani, Rana. *Europe's Myths of Orient: Devise and Rule*. London: Longman, 1986.

Kauzman, Charles, ed. *Modernist Islam, 1840-1940: a Sourcebook*. New York: Oxford University Press, 2002.

Kazemzadeh, Firuz. *Russia and Britain in Persia, 1864-1914, A Study in Imperialism*. New Haven: Yale University Press, 1968.

Keddie, Nikki R. *Sayyid Jamal ad-Din 'al-Afghani', A Political Biography*. Berkeley, L.A.: University of California Press, 1972.

— *Iran, Religion, Politics and Society*. London: Frank Cass, 1980.

— With Y. Richard. *Roots of Revolution, An Interpretive History of Modern Iran*. New Haven: Yale University Press, 1981.

— *An Islamic Response to Imperialism, Political and Religious Writings of Jamal ad-Din 'al-Afghani'*. 1966: 2nd edn. Berkeley, L.A.: Unversity of California Press, 1983.

Kedourie, Elie. *England and the Middle East, The Destruction of The Ottoman Empire, 1914-1921*. London: Bowes and Bowes, 1956.

— *Afghani and 'Abduh : an Essay on Religious Unbelief and Political Activism in Modern Islam*. London : Frank Cass, 1966.

Kennedy, Paul. 'Continuity and Discontinuity in British Imperialism 1815-1914', in *British Imperialism in the Nineteenth Century*, ed. C.C. Eldridge. 3-38. London: Macmillan, 1984.

Khomeini, Ruhullah. *Islam and Revolution, Writings and Declarations of Imam Khomeini*, trans. and annotated by Hamid Algar. Berkeley : Mirzan Press, 1981.

Kiernan, V.G. *The Lords of Human Kind: European Attitudes to the Outside World in the Imperial Age*. London: Weidenfeld, 1969.

Kinglake, Alexander. *Eothen, or Traces of Travel Brought Home from the East* Oxford: 1844: repr. Oxford University Press, 1982.

Lane, Edward William. *Manners and Customs of the Modern Egyptians*, London and the Hague: East-West Publications, 1981.

Lawrence, T.E. *Seven Pillars of Wisdom: A Triumph.* London: Jonathan Cape, 1940.

Lewis, Bernard. *The Emergence of Modern Turkey.* 2nd edn. London: Oxford University Press, 1968.

Leslie, Shane. *Men Were Different.* London: Michael Joseph, 1937.

Longford, Elizabeth. *A Pilgrimage of Passion, The Life of Wilfrid Scawen Blunt.* New York: Alfred A. Knopf, 1980.

Lewis, Reina. *Gendering Orientalism: Race, Femininity and Representation.* London: Routledge, 1996.

Lowe, C. J. *The Reluctant Imperialists.* London: Routledge and Kegan Paul, 1967.

Lowe, Lisa. *Critical Terrains: French and British Orientalisms.* Ithaca, NY: Cornell University Press, 1991.

Lytton, Earl Noel. Wilfrid Scawen Blunt: A Memoir of His Grandson. London: Macdonald, 1961.

MacEoin, Denis. *The Sources for Early Babi Doctrine and History, A Survey.* Leiden: E.J.Brill, 1992.

Maehl, William H. Jr. 'Urquhart, David', in *Biographical Dictionary of Modern Radicals*, eds. Joseph Baylen and Norbert J. Grossman. vol. 2, 1830-1870, 506-12. Hassocks: Havester, 1981.

Mackenzie, John M. 'T.E. Lawrence: The Myth and the Message', in *Literature and Imperialism*, ed. Robert Giddings. 150-181. Houndmills: Macmillan, 1989.

— *Orientalism: History, Theory and the Arts.* Manchester: Manchester University Press, 1995.

Malet, Edward. *Egypt 1879-1883.* London: John Murray, 1909.

Mansfield, Peter. *The British in Egypt.* New York: Reinhart, Holt and Winstone, 1971.

— *The Arabs*, 3rd edn. Harmondsworth: Penguin, 1992.

Mardin, Serif. *The Genesis of Young Ottoman Thought.* Princeton, N.J.: Princeton University Press, 1962.

Marlowe, John. *Late Victorian, the Life of Sir Arnold Talbot Wilson*, London: The Cresset Press, 1967.

— *Cromer in Egypt.* London: Elek, 1970.

— *Milner: Apostle of Empire.* London: Hamish Hamilton, 1976.

Marx, Karl. *The Eastern Question. A reprint of letters written 1853-1856 dealing with the events of the Crimean War*, eds. Eleanor Marx Aveling and Edward Aveling. London, 1897; repr. London: Frank Cass, 1969.

Masters, Bruce A. *Christians and Jews in the Ottoman World: the Roots of Sectarianism.* Cambridge: Cambridge University Press, 2001.

McLean, David. *Britain and her Buffer State, The Collapse of the Persian Empire, 1890-1914.* London: Royal Historical Society, 1979.

Melman, Billie. *Women's Orients: English Women and the Middle East, 1718-1918, Sexuality, Religion and Work*, 2nd edn. London, Macmillan, 1995.

—   'The Middle East/Arabia: "the cradle of Islam"', in *The Cambridge Companion to Travel Writing*, eds. Peter Hulme and Tim Youngs. 105-121. Cambridge: Cambridge University Press, 2002.

Miller, J. Hillis. *Victorian Subjects*. London: Harvester Wheatsheaf, 1990.

Milner, Alfred. *England in Egypt*. Edwin Arnold, 1892.

Mitchell, Timothy. *Colonising Egypt*. Berkeley, CA.: University of California Press, 1988.

Momen, Moojan. *The Babi and Baha'i Religions 1844-1944: Some Contemporary Western Accounts*. Oxford: George Ronald, 1981.

—   ed. *Selections from the Writings of E.G. Browne on the Babi and Baha'i Religions*. Oxford: George Ronald, 1987.

Morris, Anthony J. *Radicalism against War, 1906-1914: The Advocacy of Peace and Retrenchment*. London: Longman, 1972.

Muir, Edwin. *The Mohammedan Controversy, and other Indian articles*. Edinburgh: T.T. Clark, 1897.

Nasr, Seyyed Hossein. *Traditional Islam in the Modern World*. London: Kegan Paul International, 1987.

Nicolson, Harold. *Curzon: The Last Phase 1919-1925, a Study in Post-war Diplomacy*. London: Constable, 1937.

Nicholson, R.A. *A Descriptive Catalogue of the Oriental MSS belonging to the Late E. G. Browne*. Cambridge: Cambridge University Press, 1932.

Owen, Roger. 'Egypt and Europe: from French expedition to British occupation', in *Studies in Theories of Imperialism*, eds. Roger Owen and Bob Sucliffe. 195-209. London: Longman, 1971.

—   *Lord Cromer, Victorian Imperialist, Edwardian Proconsul*. Cambridge: Cambridge University Press, 2004.

Palgrave, William Gifford. *Narrative of a Year's Journey in Central and Eastern Arabia (1862-63)*. London: Macmillan, 1865.

—   *Essays on Eastern Questions*. London: Macmillan, 1872.

—   *Hermann Agha, an Eastern Narrative*. New York: Holt and Williams, 1872.

—   *Ulysses: or Scenes and Studies in many Lands*. London: Macmillan, 1887.

Pickthall, Marmaduke. *Said the Fisherman*. London: Methuen, 1903.

—   Introduction to J.E. Hanauer. *Folklore of the Holy Land: Muslim, Christian and Jewish*. London: Duckworth, 1907.

—   *Children of the Nile*. London: John Murray, 1908.

—   'The Black Crusade', *New Age*, 7, 14, 21, 28 November, 5 December, 1912.

—   'The Outlook in the Near East', *Nineteenth Century and After*, December, 1912.

—   'The Hope of Muslim Progress', *Nineteenth Century and After*, September, 1913.

—   'Concerning Denshawai', *New Age*, 26 February, 1914

—   *With the Turk in Wartime*. London: J.M. Dent, 1914.

—   'Egypt and the Foreign Office', New Age, 29 October, 1914.

—   'The Arab Question', *New Age*, 5 November, 1914.

—   'Turkish Independence', New Age, 5, 12 November, 1914.

—   'Six Years', *New Age*, 26 November, 3, 10, 17, 24, 31 December, 1914.

—   'The Case of Egypt', *New Age*, 7 January 1915.

—   'After the Caliphate', *New Age*, 28 January, 1915.

—   'The Project of Partition', *New Age*, 18 February, 1915.

—   'Nature and the Doctrinaire', *New Age*, 25 March, 1915.

—   'The Last Chance', *New Age*, 6 January, 1916.

—   'Sir Mark Sykes and the Armenians', *New Age*, 4 May, 1916.

—   'The League of Nations and the British Empire', *New Age*, 3 April, 1919.

—   'The Act of God', *New Age*, 24 April 1919.

—   'For the Defence', *New Age*, 19 June, 1919.

—   *Islam and Progress*. Lahore: Muslim Book Society, 1920.

—   *The Early Hours*. London: W. Collins, 1921.

—   *Oriental Encounters, Palestine and Syria 1894-1896*. New York: Alfred A. Knopf, 1927.

—   'The End of a Legend', *Islamic Culture*, October, 1935.

Poliakov, Leon. *The Aryan Myth, A History of Racist and Nationalist Ideas in Europe*, trans. Edmund Howard. London: Chatto & Windus for Sussex University Press, 1974.

Porter, Dennis. *Haunted Journeys, Desire and Transgression in European Travel Writing*. Princeton, N J: Princeton University Press, 1991.

Pratt, Mary Louise. *Imperial Eyes, Travel Writing and Transculturation*. London: Routledge, 1991.

Reid, Donald Malcolm. 'The 'Urabi Revolution and the British Conquest, 1879-1882', in *The Cambridge History of Egypt*, vol.2, *Modern Egypt, from 1517 to the end of the Twentieth Century*, ed. M.W. Daly. 217-238. Cambridge: Cambridge University Press, 1998.

Robinson, Gertrude. *David Urquhart: Some Chapters in the Life of a Victorian Knight-Errant of Justice and Liberty*. Oxford: Blackwell, 1920.

Rodenbeck, John. 'Dressing Native', in *Unfolding the Orient*, eds. Paul and Janet Starkey. 65-100. Reading: Ithaca, 2001.

Ronaldshay, Earl. *The Life of Curzon*. 3 vols. London: Ernest Benn, 1928.

Ross, E. Denison. *Both Ends of the Candle, the Autobiography of Sir E. Denison Ross*. London: Faber and Faber, 1943.

—   'A Memoir', in Edward G. Browne, *A Year Amongst the Persians*. London: A.C. Black, 1950.

Ryan, Andrew. *The Last of the Dragomans*. London: Geoffrey Bliss, 1951.

Said, Edward W. *Orientalism, Western Conceptions of the Orient*, London: Routledge Kegan Paul, 1978.

—   *Culture and Imperialism*. London: Chatto and Windus, 1993.

Salibi, Kamal. 'Elie Kedourie: A Tribute', *Middle Eastern Studies, A Thirty Volume Index 1964-1994*, comp. Frances A.S. Perry. 1-4. London: Frank Cass, 1994.

Schiffer, Reinhold. *Oriental Panorama, British Travellers in Nineteenth Century Turkey*. Amsterdam: Rodopi, 1999.

Searight, Sara. *The British in the Middle East*. London : Macmillan, 1969.

Seeley, J.R. *The Expansion of England, Two Courses of Lectures*. London: Macmillan, 1911.

Shahlan, Jeff. 'Writing the Nation: the Emergence of Egypt in the Modern Arabic Novel', *Journal of Arabic Literature*, 2002, 33, 211-47.

Sharabi, Hisham. *Governments and Politics of the Middle East in the Twentieth Century*. London: Van Nostrand, 1962.

Sheil, Lady. *Glimpses of Life and Manners in Persia*. London, 1856.

Shuster, W. Morgan *The Strangling of Persia. A Personal Narrative*. New York: Greenwood, 1968.

Simpson, John. *Inside Iran, Life under Khomeini's Regime*. New York: St. Martins Press, 1988.

Slugglett, Peter. 'Formal and Informal Empire in the Middle East', in *The Oxford History of the British Empire*, vol 5, *Historiography*, ed. Robert W. Winks. 416-436. Oxford : Oxford University Press, 1999.

Smith, Wilfred Cantwell. *Modern Islam in India, A Social Analysis*. London: Victor Gollanz, 1942.

— *Islam in Modern History*. New York: Mentor, 1957.

Starkey, Paul. 'Egyptian Travellers in Europe', in *Travellers in Egypt*, eds. Paul and Janet Starkey. 280-86. London: I.B. Tauris, 1998.

Steiner, Zara S. *The Foreign Office and Foreign Policy, 1898-1914*. Cambridge: Cambridge University Press, 1969.

Sykes, Mark. *Through Five Turkish Provinces*, London: Bickers, 1900.

— Dar-ul-Islam, A Record of A Journey Through Ten of the Asiatic Provinces of Turkey. *London: Bickers, 1904*.

— *The Caliph's Last Heritage, A Short History of the Turkish Empire*. London: Macmillan, 1915.

Taylor, A.J.P. *The Troublemakers: Dissent over Foreign Policy, 1792-1939*. London: Hamish Hamilton, 1957.

Taylor, Miles. 'The old radicalism and the new: David Urquhart and the politics of opposition, 1832-1867', in *Currents of Radicalism: Popular Radicalism, Organized Labour, and Party Politics in Britain, 1850-1914*, eds. Eugenio F. Biagini and Alastair J. Reid. 23-44. Cambridge: Cambridge University Press, 1991.

Tidrick, Kathryn. *Heart Beguiling Araby, The English Romance With Arabia*. 2nd edn. London: I.B. Tauris, 1989.

Toynbee, Arnold J. and Kenneth P. Kirkwood. *Turkey*. London: E. Benn, 1926.

Trevelyan, G.M. *Grey of Fallodon, Being the Life of Sir Edward Grey*. Longmans, Green: 1940.

Trudgill, Peter. *Sociolinguistics*. Harmondsworth: Penguin, 1983.

Urquhart, David. *Turkey and Its Resources: Its Municipal Organization And Free Trade*. London: Saunders and Ottley, 1833.

— *The Spirit of the East, A Journal of Travels through Roumelia*. 2 vols. London: Henry Colburn, 1838.

— The Edinburgh Review and the Affghan War, letters re-printed from the Morning Herald. *London: James Maynard, 1843.*

— *The Pillars of Hercules, or, A Narrative of Travels in Spain and Morocco in 1848*. 2 vols. London: Richard Bentley, 1850.

— *The Lebanon: A History and A Diary, notes taken on the spot, 1849-1850*. 2 vols. London: Thomas Cantley Newby, 1860.

— *The Military Strength of Turkey*. London: Diplomatic Review Office, 1868.

Valyi, Felix. *Spiritual and Political Revolutions in Islam*. London: Kegan Paul, Trench, Trubner, 1925.

Vambery, Arminius. *His Life and Adventures*. London, 1914; repr. New York: Arno Press, 1973.

Vaziri, Mostafa. *Iran as Imagined Nation: the Construction of National Identity*. New York: Paragon House, 1993.

Watts, Cedric, and Davies, Lawrence. *Cunningham Graham, A Critical Biography*. Cambridge: Cambridge University Press, 1979.

Webster, Charles. *The Foreign Policy of Palmerston, 1830-41. Britain, the Liberal Movement and the Eastern Question*. 2 vols. London: Bell and Sons, 1951.

Wheatcroft, Andrew. *The Ottomans*. London: Viking, 1993.

Wicken, G. M. 'Browne, Edward Granville, i. "Browne's Life and Academic Career",' in *Encyclopaedia Iranica*, ed. Yershater Ehsan. London: Routledge and Kegan Paul, 1990.

Wilson, Arnold T. *The Persian Gulf, An Historical Sketch from the Earliest Times to the Beginning of the Twentieth Century*. Oxford: Clarendon Press, 1928.

— *South West Persia, A Political Officer's Diary*. London: Oxford University Press, 1942.

Wilson, Samuel Graham. *Modern Movements Among Moslems*. New York: Fleming H. Revell, 1916; repr. 1976.

Wright, Denis. *The Persians Among the English*, London: I.B. Tauris, 1985.

Yared, Nazik Saba. *Arab Travellers and Western Civilization*. London: Saqi, 1996.

Yapp, M.E. *The Making of the Modern Near East 1792-1923*. London: Longman, 1987.

Young, Robert J.C. *Colonial Desire: Hybridity in Theory, Culture and Race*. London: Routledge, 1994.

— *Postcolonialism: An Historical Introduction*. Oxford: Blackwell, 2001.

Zetland, The Marquess. *Lord Cromer*. London: Hodder and Stoughton, 1932.

Index